HOUSE
about it

DREAM / DESIGN / DWELL

HOUSE
about it

Sheri Koones

Gibbs Smith, Publisher
Salt Lake City

For Gene—gone, but not forgotten.

First Edition
08 07 06 05 04   5 4 3 2 1

The information on the systems, products or materials presented herein is provided for informational purposes only. The technical descriptions and details expressed do not constitute an endorsement, approval or acceptance of the subject matter. There are no warranties, either expressed or implied, regarding the accuracy or completeness of this information. Neither the author nor the publisher can be responsible for any product or material that does not perform as indicated in this book.

Published by
Gibbs Smith, Publisher
P.O. Box 667
Layton, Utah 84041

Orders: 1.800.748.5439
www.gibbs-smith.com

Designed by Steve Phillips
Printed and bound in Canada

Library of Congress Cataloging-in-Publication Data

Koones, Sheri, 1949—
    House about it / Sheri Koones ; illustrations by Bruce Sanders.— 1st ed.
        p. cm.
Includes index.
ISBN 1-58685-377-5
    1. Dwellings—Remodeling. I. Title
TH4816.K66 2004
643—dc22
                    2004008159

Contents

Acknowledgments

Writing a book is such a personal experience; however, it cannot be written in isolation, without inspiration and information from so many. This book required so much research into materials and resources, some which have been around for many years and others that are just emerging. I owe a tremendous gratitude to all of the organizations, magazine editors, scientists, professors and manufacturers who took the time to talk with me, explain their new products and review the text for accuracy. Many of them began to feel like old friends, and they made the project so much more interesting and pleasurable. I am so grateful to all of you—a heartfelt thank-you to you all.

I owe a very special thank-you to John McLean, who is not only a talented architect and a good friend, but who has endless knowledge of every aspect of construction and design and meticulously reviewed every chapter of this book.

My love and gratitude to my husband, Rob, for the opportunity to experience construction first-hand and for his encouragement to continue exploring this area. My children are a continuing source of great inspiration, and I thank them from the bottom of my heart for their encouragement. Special thanks to Barbara Corpuel for all of her special contributions to my work and my life. I am very grateful to my terrific friends and family who have been a wonderful support system. My thanks to all my writing friends, Lynn Flaster, Lucy Hedrick, Julie Jenson and Jane Pollack, for setting a high standard for writing and for all of their encouragement through the process. Thanks to Cheryl Barton for keeping the writing process going through her technical skills and support, and to Mariashi and Yossi Deren for their spiritual encouragement.

I am very grateful to Bruce Sanders for his skillful drawings and incredible flexibility on this project, and I would like to give a thank-you to Steve Phillips for the attractive book design.

It was a pleasure to work with the entire crew at Gibbs Smith, Publisher. A special thank-you to Suzanne Taylor, who was a joy to work with and was so supportive of this project. And thank you to Alison Einerson and her crew for their enthusiasm and professionalism. Thank you also to Hollie Keith for her fine editing job.

This project, though very intense at times, was so enlightening and inspiring. Although the world is very turbulent and sometimes feels very unsafe, it is comforting to know there are so many ways to build a comfortable nest and sanctuary for ourselves and our families.

Introduction

People have so many choices to make when they decide to build or remodel their homes. There is an enormous variety of options to select from, more than has ever been available before. There are many new materials and techniques coming out each year; the options are expanding constantly. Many of these options will increase the value, comfort and aesthetics of a house. *House About It* will present these options in the simplest possible format so that you, the homeowner, can make educated preliminary decisions. Some decisions will be determined by the architectural style; a large percentage of them, however, will be determined by personal preference and budget. This book should cut down the time needed to research all of the items to be considered. When I started building my own house, I didn't know the difference between a casement window and a double-hung window. It took several trips to hardware stores and several conversations with salespeople to determine the advantages and disadvantages of each. This is an attempt to save the homeowner hours of footwork and investigation.

While I was working on this book, I was constantly impressed with the scope, beauty and practicality of the available options. With each chapter I found techniques and materials that made me wish I could build a dozen homes. I found building techniques that were new and innovative, such as new concrete construction types, and techniques that have been used for centuries, such as timber-frame and log construction—still beautiful and efficient. In each of these areas, I found builders who were enthusiastic and dedicated to their fields and their customers.

Industries are constantly finding new and better ways to build a house. Many are also finding ways to preserve our natural resources in the process. Flooring options now include products such as bamboo and coconut palm, which are quickly replenished by nature and available in abundance. Homeowners can build beautiful homes while being conscious of preserving our natural resources.

While many choices may be limited by regional restrictions and budget limitations, there are still many to select from. Often people go blindly into making major decisions about home construction without the necessary information needed to do so. Homeowners should be aware of these options, their ramifications, as well as their advantages, so they can be explored with an architect or engineer helping to design the home.

Today more than ever, there is a trend toward making the house energy efficient. Many materials are available to lower the infiltration of air, keep the house warmer in the winter and cooler in the summer. This will not only cut down on our need for fossil fuel but lower heating and cooling expenses.

Along with the aesthetics of the home, there is also a trend toward making our homes safer, more accessible and healthier. Several programs have developed in this country to survey the options and educate the public. The program of Universal Design at the State University of South Carolina has studied the needs of all people and worked with various industries to develop home materials that will make life more comfortable for everyone, for any eventualities in life. The American Lung Association developed their Health House Program to help make the house a healthier place to live, particularly for those with asthma and other breathing disorders. Thousands of people are killed in their homes each year because of house fires. The use of fire and carbon monoxide detectors, along with fire sprinkler systems, have proven to save lives. These are all worthy items to consider for our home. They will not only increase the value of the home but can make the home a healthier and safer place to live.

A workbook is included at the end of the book for keeping notes on preferences for the items reviewed. One of the great challenges that faces homeowners is keeping all of their construction information organized, both during construction and later when the house is complete. The workbook is intended to help meet that challenge. Throughout the pages there are bold-faced words, which are explained in the terms list at the end of the book.

Although there is a description of many of the available options, this book cannot take the place of a talented architect who can use these choices and make them into a cohesive, workable, beautiful plan. Whichever materials and systems are selected is irrelevant unless they are used in a well-designed and executed manner. Both excellent materials and a beautiful plan contribute to a well-constructed, energy-efficient, aesthetically pleasing house. If either the design or the construction is poorly done, there will be future problems such as leaks, warping, air infiltration and so on.

This book should be a handy guide to most of the components you will have to select when you are remodeling parts of the house, the entire house, or building a new house. It is not meant to be comprehensive in any area but an introduction to the many possibilities. Web addresses, telephone numbers and additional readings are included so you can more easily research your areas of interest. This is meant to be merely a starting point.

I'm hoping this book will empower you, the homeowner, to make educated decisions concerning your home. Most people have busy lives and don't always have the time to investigate every possible option in life; this book should help to open up those options and cut down on the time in selecting them.

Top 10 List

1. Be sure to take the time to explore all available options in the design stage. There are many to select from, so take the time to choose those that you prefer, are healthy choices, are energy efficient and environmentally sound.

2. Make sure you get a sample that shows the precise color, texture and thickness for any product you are considering purchasing.

3. Find out about the warranty on products you are considering. Be sure who is offering the warranty (the manufacturer, the dealer or the contractor) and what the limitations are.

4. Find out about the availability of the product and installer before selecting any item. One small item can hold up the construction for days or weeks.

5. When making a product decision, consider how much maintenance you will be required to do. Although some products are more beautiful, they may require more upkeep.

6. Consider how the products will fit into your budget. Prioritize your options wisely.

7. Before making component decisions, consider how long you plan to live in your house. Is it a starter home, or do you plan to live there for many years? Some of your options may change depending on how long you plan to own it.

8. Make sure you have hired a team of people you trust and enjoy working with—an architect, general contractor, landscape consultant and so on.

9. Consider the cost of installation on all options. In some cases the labor may cost more than the product. Also make sure there are skilled professionals to do the type of installation required. Some products are more easily installed in some regions of the country than others. Consider shipping costs that can add greatly to the cost of an item.

10. Always consider your personal needs and those of your family over recommendations. Architects can tell you what is the most architecturally correct, builders can tell you about how to construct it, but only you know what is right and comfortable. Consider the advice and then make the decision—you will live in the house when all the professionals are gone.

Architectural Styles

One of the important initial decisions to be made when deciding to build a house is the basic style. There are numerous styles to choose from and numerous variations of those styles. You may decide you don't want your house to be strictly designed as any particular style. It is a good starting point, however, to have an idea of which styles or aspects of styles you like the best. Certain features of preferred styles can be included, others eliminated. Modern technology and personal preferences will usually alter some characteristics to meet your individual tastes and needs. The style you pick will be somewhat dictated by the following:

Neighborhood—You will probably want your house to fit into the neighborhood, in terms of style and size. In some areas it may also be difficult to find a craftsman to construct a particular style.

Weather—Some styles are more conducive to certain locations because of the weather. French Colonial is more suited for a warmer climate where the **corridors** can be used for outdoor living for longer periods throughout the year.

Size—Some styles are more conducive to smaller-size houses, such as the bungalow, whereas the Châteauesque would be more practical for a larger house.

Size of the lot—This will determine how large the house is and if it is more practical to build out or up.

Budget—This is always an essential consideration. Some styles will cost more than others. Houses in the Georgian style, for example, with its many details, will cost more than a Cape Cod, which generally has a more simple design.

Local covenants—Some areas require that a particular style house be built in that area.

Personal taste—Without question, this is the most important consideration.

The following information is not meant to be an exhaustive study of architectural styles. Some of the most popular ones are listed here. In the appendix is a list of books to review that more extensively show architectural styles. Once you have narrowed your selections to a few, you can check libraries and bookstores for entire books on each style.

There is a great deal of overlapping between the various styles. Many have evolved over the years with several different versions and with labels such as "neo" and "revival." There are styles that have developed in different parts of the world and have different labels. Regional differences are possible in many of the styles as well. This chapter is meant to help those who have not decided what style they like and to offer ideas on aspects that may be incorporated into the building or remodeling of their home. This will also be helpful in discussions with the architect you choose; they prefer to work with clients who can indicate specifically what they like and don't like for their future home.

Adirondack

Architect William West Durant is often credited with developing this style in the 1880s as rustic getaways for wealthy clients and their guests. The first "Great Camp" was built in Raquette Lake in the Adirondack Mountains (in New York State) and was called Camp Pine Knot. Later camps were built in other mountain areas such as the Appalachians in North Carolina.

Typical Characteristics
- Rustic look
- Log construction
- Built with other natural materials
- Shake roof with broad overhangs
- Steep, sloping roof
- Intersecting **gable**
- **Corbel** log ends
- **Shed dormers**
- Native stonework
- Rubble-work foundation
- Exposed log **rafters**
- Decorative **half-timber**
- Large **double-hung windows**— sometimes paired
- Decorative use of twigs, branches and bark
- Recessed porch with rough poles
- Natural colors with the exception of window trim, which is often red or green
- Stone fireplaces
- Furnishings made by local craftsmen

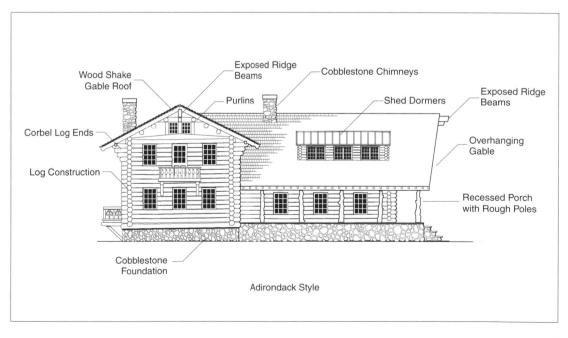

Wood Shake Gable Roof
Exposed Ridge Beams
Cobblestone Chimneys
Purlins
Shed Dormers
Exposed Ridge Beams
Corbel Log Ends
Overhanging Gable
Log Construction
Recessed Porch with Rough Poles
Cobblestone Foundation

Adirondack Style

A-Frame

Rudolph Schindler built the first A-frame in Lake Arrowhead, California, in 1934, it was an attempt to find a creative way around the French Revival style building requirement for all new homes in that planned community. Popular mostly as a vacation house for many since World War II, A-frame houses are built in the mountains, by lakes and near the ocean. They are inexpensive to build and have a rustic "chalet" appearance, but they have a great deal of unusable space and limited access to light.

Typical Characteristics
- Triangular shape
- Built with large timbers
- Two floors
- Steeply pitched roof
- Low-hanging **eaves**
- Rubble-work masonry
- Front and/or rear gables
- Extended beams
- Wood shingles
- Plate glass gable
- Large windows on front and rear facades
- **Hopper windows**
- Large decks with sliding door access

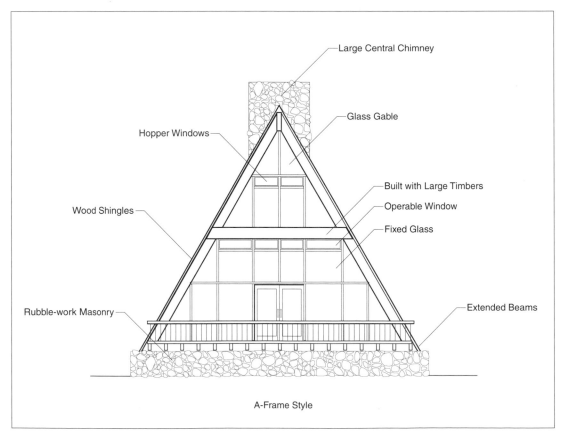

A-Frame Style

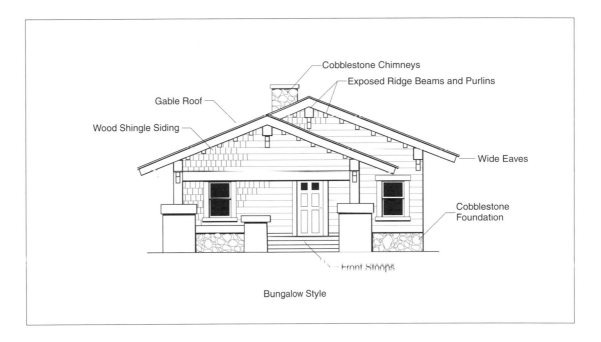

Bungalow Style

Bungalow

In *Craftsman Homes* (1909) Gustav Stickley described the bungalow as "a house reduced to its simplest form, which never fails to harmonize with its surroundings, because its low, broad proportions and absolute lack of ornamentation give it a character so natural and unaffected that it seems to sing into and blend with any landscape." He went on to say, "It is beautiful, because it is planned and built to meet simple needs in the simplest and most direct way . . .," Bungalows became popular when Sears, Roebuck and Company picked up on the concept and offered several models in their mail-order catalog. The bungalows were delivered complete with materials, fixtures and building instructions. The bungalow has many variations that are regionally influenced.

Typical Characteristics

- Simple design
- Usually one story
- Front-facing gable and gently pitched gable roof
- Lower part of the roof covering a large front porch
- Natural materials used
- Exposed rafters, ridge beams and **purlins** extending beyond the wall and roof
- Wood shingle or stucco siding
- Cobblestone foundations
- Chimneys and interior fireplaces—cobblestone or brick
- Wide overhanging eaves
- Sometimes having low shed **dormers**
- Front stoops
- Front doors opening directly into the living room
- Ceilings beamed in major rooms
- Glass doors opening to terraces
- Natural wood finishes in the interior

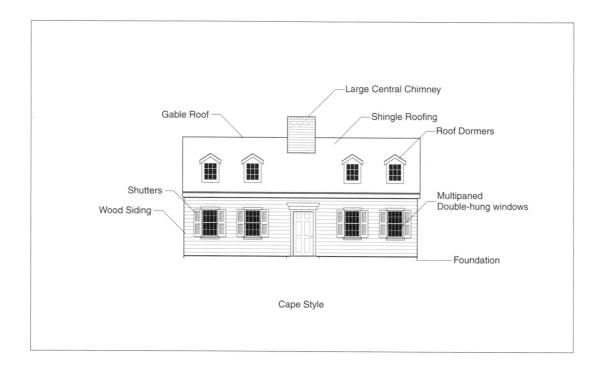

Cape Style

Cape Cod

The Cape Cod design originated in New England in the late seventeenth century when it was brought by the English colonists who first arrived in the United States. It is one of the most popular of the Colonial Revival styles; others are the Saltbox, Dutch Colonial and so on. The term Cape Cod was coined by Reverend Timothy Dwight, the president of Yale University.

Typical Characteristics
- Gable or **gambrel** steep roof
- Post-and-beam frame
- One or one-and-a-half stories
- Wood siding with wide clapboard or shingles
- Large central chimney later moved to the side of the house
- Symmetrical look with a door in the center
- Roof dormers providing light and space
- Multipaned, double-hung windows
- Decorative shutters later added
- Formal center hall floor plan
- Little exterior ornamentation
- No projections

Châteauesque
(Picturesque Eclecticism)

Châteauesque is a combination of French Gothic style with Italian Renaissance details. It was popularized with wealthy society in the United States in the 1880s and 1890s by architect Richard Morris Hunt. From 1843 to 1855 he studied at the Ecole des Beaux-Arts and professionally practiced in Paris. It is one of the grandest and excessive of the Victorian styles.

Typical Characteristics

- Steeply pitched hipped or gabled roofs
- Stone walls
- Elaborate dormers, **towers,** rounded **turrets, spires, finials, pinnacles,** gable **parapets** and decorated chimneys
- Gothic detailing—gargoyles and griffins
- Cast-iron roof **cresting**
- **Cross windows** (a pair of windows divided by a **mullion** and **transom bar**)
- Semicircular arches
- **Hood molds** above windows and doors
- Railings on the balconies
- Basket-handle arch (an arch without a point) over the front door
- Ornamental iron railings

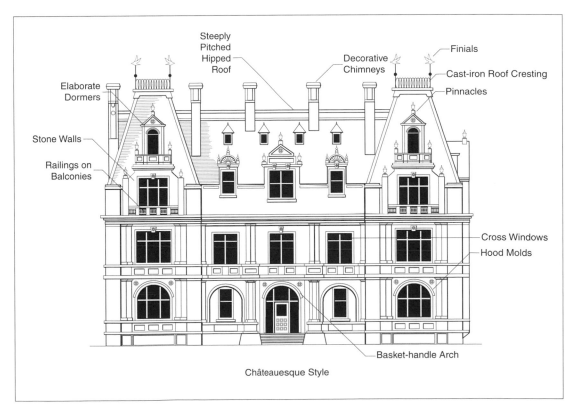

Châteauesque Style

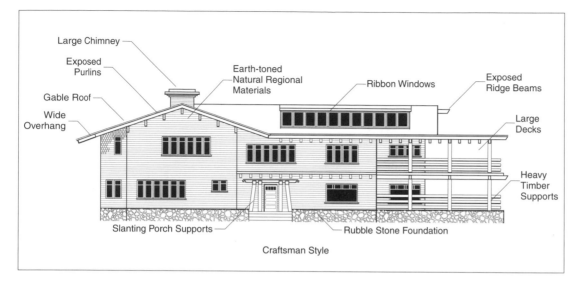

Craftsman Style

Labels on the illustration:
Large Chimney
Exposed Purlins
Gable Roof
Wide Overhang
Earth-toned Natural Regional Materials
Ribbon Windows
Exposed Ridge Beams
Large Decks
Heavy Timber Supports
Slanting Porch Supports
Rubble Stone Foundation

Craftsman

The Craftsman (American), or California, style was influenced by the Arts and Crafts movement in England, which favored simplicity of design, the use of natural materials and quality craftsmanship. It was a rebellious response to the mass-produced goods that came with industrialization. The concept was popularized by Gustav Stickley's magazine, *The Craftsman,* which published plans for Arts and Crafts–style houses and sent them to subscribers who requested them free of charge (1903–1916). The style was expressed best in the more expensive houses designed by California architects Charles and Henry Greene, but less costly kit versions were ordered from catalogs such as Sears, Roebuck and Company and Aladdin Redi-Cut or built by local builders using Stickley's Craftsman home plans.

Typical Characteristics
- Asymmetrical facade
- Low-pitched gable roof with wide projecting eaves
- Decorative beams or braces under the gables
- Natural materials native to the region
- Exposed structural elements
- Rubble (or random) stone foundation—assembled one stone at a time
- One to two stories
- Porches, terraces and **pergolas**
- Squared porch supports, sometimes slanting in
- No break in porch support bases extending to the ground
- Open floor plans
- Exposed rafters at the eaves
- A variety of building materials used—cobblestone, brick, shingles and so on
- Bands of **casement windows—ribbon windows**
- Picture windows
- Earth-toned colors
- Interior hand-polished wood details
- Built-in cabinetry, **inglenooks** and benches
- Emphasis on detail
- Exposed beams
- Large fireplaces

ARCHITECTURAL STYLES

Federal

The Federal style was a rejection of the more ornamental Georgian style and was originally developed by the more elegant and simple style of the Adam Brothers, who had a successful architectural practice in England. Brought to the United States by architect Charles Bulfinch, the Federal style became symbolic of the American aristocracy after the United States gained independence from England after the Revolutionary War. One of the first houses to be built in the Federal style was outside of Philadelphia in the late 1780s by William Hamilton; it was called The Woodlands.

Typical Characteristics

- Moderately to gently pitched **hipped roof**
- Symmetrical square or rectangular shape
- Decorative **balustrade** usually at the top of the roofline
- Redbrick or white-painted clapboard siding
- Split-wood shingles
- Two stories high (not counting the basement and attic levels)
- **Cornice** emphasized with tooth-like **dentils** or other decorative molding
- Double-hung elongated windows, typically with small panes
- Thin **muntins**
- Windows decreasing in size on upper floors
- Some louvered shutters used
- Emphasis on the front door design
- Paneled door with decorative sidelights and elliptical or semicircular fanlights above
- Plain wall surfaces with minimal decoration
- Columns and moldings narrow
- Interior rooms oval, circular or octagonal
- Classical details such as swags, rosettes and garlands used inside and out

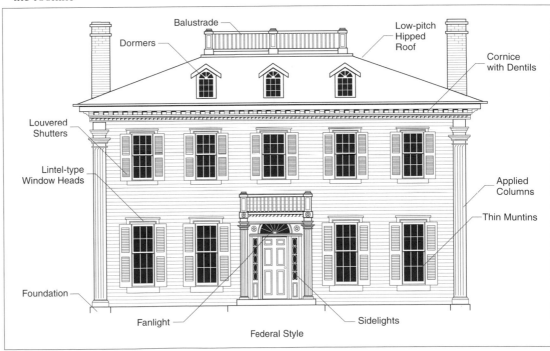

Federal Style

French Colonial

The early French settlers built a *poteaux-en-terre* (posts in earth)–type construction around 1720. The dwellings were built with vertical logs set into the ground to protect the house from flooding and with a sloped roof over an outside *galerie* (gallery) to shade the walls of the house. Later houses were built without galleries around them but with a steeply hipped roof, louvered French doors and a stuccoed half-timber wall construction known as *briquette-entre-poteaux* (small bricks between posts), which took the place of the earlier construction.

Typical Characteristics

- Rectangular shape
- Stucco walls
- Steeply pitched hipped roof
- Four-sided wide porch or gallery covered by a more shallow pitched roof (later houses had flare in roof, although not covering a gallery
- Posts
- Tall, narrow double-casement windows—latch in the center and hinge on the side
- Exterior staircase
- Shake roof
- Second-floor dormers
- Raised basement
- Double louvered doors (French doors)—direct access to the porch from several rooms

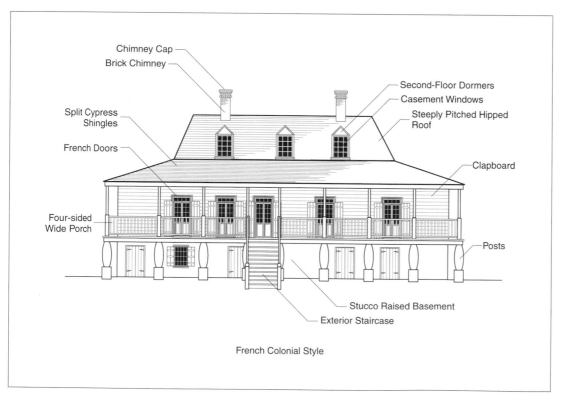

French Colonial Style

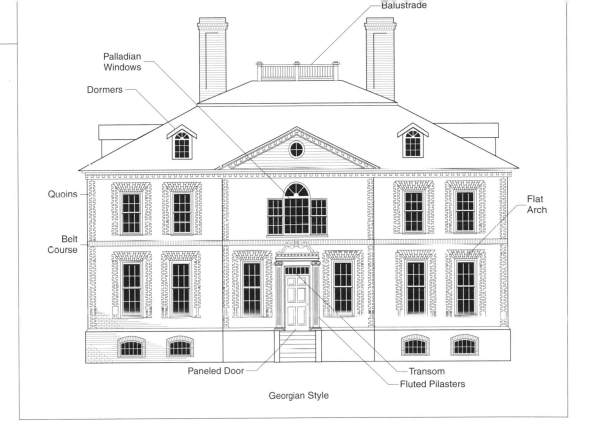

Balustrade

Palladian
Windows

Dormers

Quoins

Belt
Course

Flat
Arch

Paneled Door

Transom

Fluted Pilasters

Georgian Style

Georgian

Georgian houses were built by the affluent society for comfort, convenience and as symbols of wealth in the early 1700s. The styles varied regionally in New England, the Middle Atlantic states and the Southern states.

Typical Characteristics
- Symmetrical design
- Balanced proportion
- Aligned uniform double-hung multipaned windows (capped with classical crown moldings or cornices)
- Ornately decorated entrances (with cornices with decorative moldings and pilasters)
- Siding of wood, brick or stone, depending on location
- Paneled doors
- Shutters seen only on Georgian houses in the Middle Atlantic states
- Steeply pitched roof—gambrel (common in New England), gabled or hipped (common in the South)
- Balustrades on roof
- Multiple dormers
- Classical details
- **Palladian windows** on the second floor
- No porches
- **Quoins** (sometimes)
- Tall brick chimneys
- Specialized rooms designed for all functions—entertaining, dining, cooking, sleeping
- Interior wood-paneled walls

Gothic Revival

Architectural details of Gothic Revival were inspired by medieval castles and gothic churches. This is a romantic and picturesque style. It was first introduced in the United States by architect Alexander Jackson Davis and Andrew Jackson Downing, who designed many of the Gothic Revival houses in the mid-1800s.

Typical Characteristics
- Asymmetrical massing and varying heights of the facade
- Towers and **crenelations**
- Walls extending into the gable with no break
- Steeply pitched roof with cross gables
- Contrasting wall and roofing colors
- Masonry and wood construction
- Windows extending into the gables, which are often with pointed arch and trim
- Paired casement windows
- Stained and leaded glass
- Angled **bay windows**
- Porches
- Gables with decorated **verge boards** (or bargeboards)
- Wall dormers
- Polygonal **chimney pots**
- Curvilinear trim along the eaves and gable edges

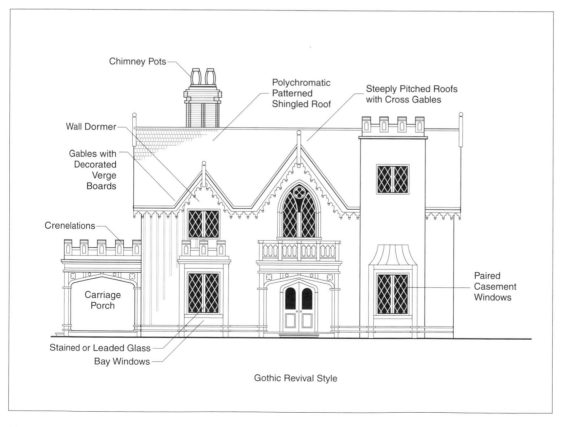

Chimney Pots

Polychromatic Patterned Shingled Roof

Steeply Pitched Roofs with Cross Gables

Wall Dormer

Gables with Decorated Verge Boards

Crenelations

Paired Casement Windows

Carriage Porch

Stained or Leaded Glass

Bay Windows

Gothic Revival Style

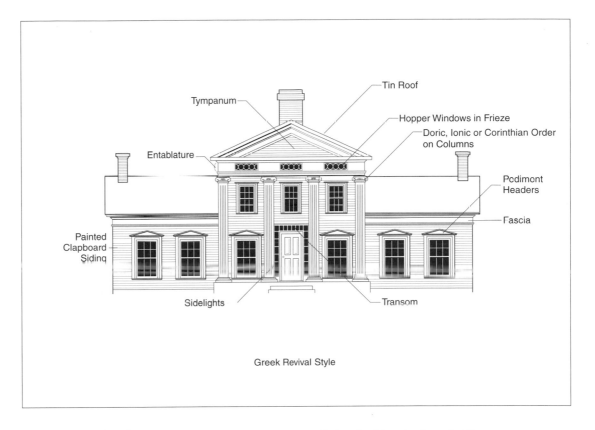

Tympanum

Tin Roof

Hopper Windows in Frieze

Doric, Ionic or Corinthian Order on Columns

Entablature

Pedimont Headers

Fascia

Painted Clapboard Siding

Sidelights

Transom

Greek Revival Style

Greek Revival

Architect and engineer Benjamin Henry Latrobe was born in England but later lived in the United States and was the first to incorporate classical Greek design into American architecture in the mid-1800s. The columned southern plantation house seen in the movie *Gone With the Wind* was an example of Greek Revival style. The decorative elements and proportions of monumental ancient Greece were employed.

Typical Characteristics
- Gabled or hipped low-pitched roof
- Front **pedimented** gables on **entablature**
- Symmetrical facades
- Painted white clapboard siding
- Tin roof
- Decorative pilasters
- Entry porch supported with columns
- Details of Doric, Ionic and Corinthian order on the columns
- Narrow horizontal transom over the front door and narrow sidelights on the side of the door, both with rectangular panes of glass
- Hopper windows fitted into the frieze below the cornice
- Bold, simple interior and exterior moldings
- Tall first-floor double-hung windows
- Pediment-shaped window heads
- Cornice line with wide band of trim

International

The name came from an exhibit at the Museum of Modern Art in New York City in 1932 when architects from fifteen countries exhibited drawings and photographs of their work, which was later compiled in *The International Style: Architecture Since 1922.* These architects rejected nonessential decoration and focused on modern structural principles and materials such as concrete, glass and steel. Le Corbusier's Villa Savoye (1929) near Paris, which was part of the MOMA exhibit, is an excellent example of International style.

Typical Characteristics

- Asymmetrical facade
- Functionality
- Flat roof
- Stucco or plaster with a flat, skin-like finish
- Attached garage
- Steel and concrete used as structural elements
- Closed or boxed eaves
- Large expanses of floor-to-ceiling glass
- Ribbon casement and sliding windows
- Corner windows
- Metal casement windows and unornamented doors flush with the surface of the house
- Glass blocks
- No pattern, texture or ornamentation
- Built-in furniture

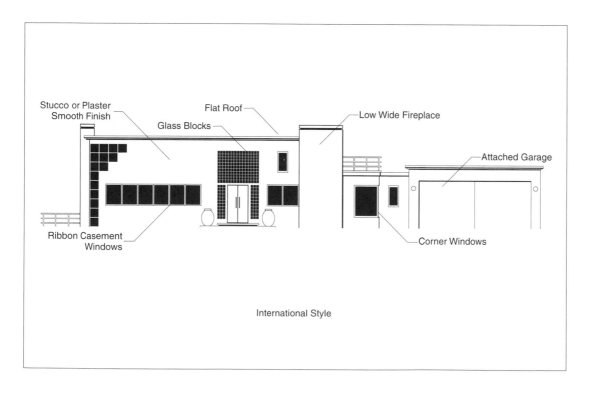

International Style

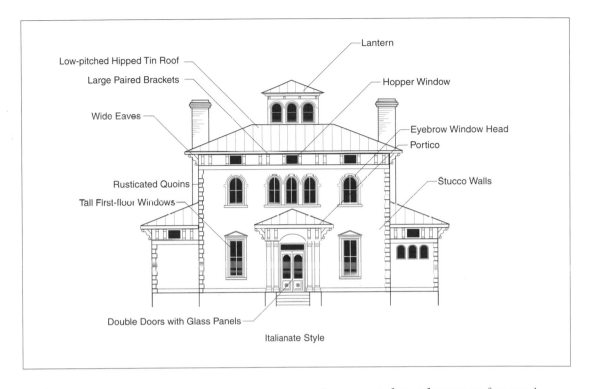

Low-pitched Hipped Tin Roof

Large Paired Brackets

Wide Eaves

Rusticated Quoins

Tall First-floor Windows

Lantern

Hopper Window

Eyebrow Window Head

Portico

Stucco Walls

Double Doors with Glass Panels

Italianate Style

Italianate

This is also known as the Tuscan, Lombard and the American Bracketed style. Although it originated in northern Italy and mimicked the rambling Italian country villas, it was introduced to the United States by the English in the late 1830s.

Typical Characteristics
- Symmetrical and asymmetrical facade
- Stucco walls
- Low-pitched hipped tin roof
- Square- or rectangular-shaped house
- Two or three stories with a vertical emphasis
- Wood frame
- Wide overhanging eaves supported by large decorative brackets, which are often in pairs or evenly spaced

- Square **cupolas** or **lanterns** often used
- Double doors with glass inset panels
- Tall, narrow double-paned windows on the first floor
- Rounded arches above windows and doors
- **Eyebrow windows**
- **Awning windows** often used between the brackets
- Long porches
- Cast-iron balconies, railings and fences
- A central long **veranda** or a small front porch typical
- Corner quoins
- High ceilings
- Interior plaster decorations such as ceiling medallions, cornices and wood corner blocks on door casings

Mission

Built mainly in California and the Southwestern United States, the Mission style developed in the late 1800s and emphasized simplicity, harmony and the tradition of the area. Although it is not considered a formal style by many historians, the influence of this style can be seen today in the prevalence of Spanish- or Mediterranean-style houses.

Typical Characteristics
- Curvilinear roof gable
- Bold, round, arched openings
- Arched entranceway
- Exposed roof rafters
- Whitewashed smooth stucco
- Red-tiled roof
- No ornamentation
- Square bell towers
- Roof parapets
- Round or **quatrefoil (clover-shaped) windows**
- One-story-high porch with large, square pillars

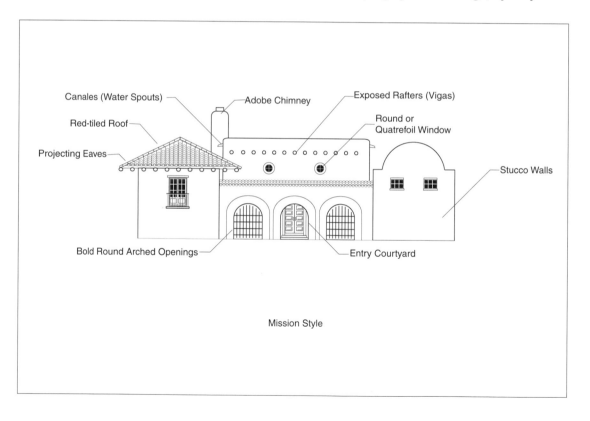

Mission Style

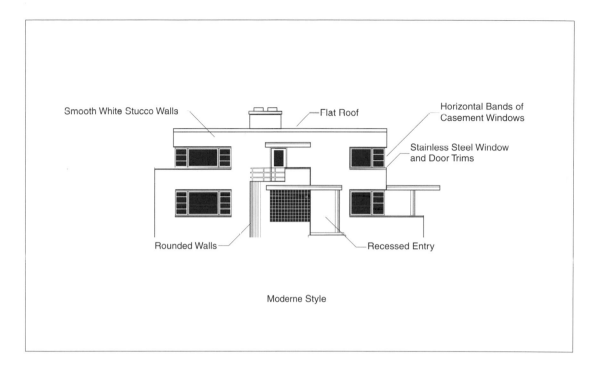

Smooth White Stucco Walls — Flat Roof — Horizontal Bands of Casement Windows

Stainless Steel Window and Door Trims

Rounded Walls — Recessed Entry

Moderne Style

Moderne or Art Moderne

Although Moderne style is considered an American concept, it was inspired by an international group of architects looking for new design concepts in the 1930s. Moderne style was an outgrowth of the machine age and the availability of washing machines, telephones and dishwashers. It rejected traditional design concepts, and the architects who worked in this style were seeking a better way of living.

Typical Characteristics
- Asymmetrical facade
- Smooth surfaces
- White stucco walls
- Flat roof
- Smooth wall finishes
- No ornamentation
- Curved walls
- Steel railings
- Recessed entry
- Horizontal bands of casement or double-hung windows
- Curved window glass wrapped around corners
- Stainless steel window and door trim
- Open floor plan

Prairie

Frank Lloyd Wright personalized this style in the early twentieth century. There were other architects (such as Greene and Greene) who designed in this style, many who worked in Wright's studio. Wright's most famous prairie house is the Robie House in Chicago, Illinois. The movement began in the Midwest in an attempt to have the house relate to or blend in with the prairie terrain. It was later used in many other areas of the country by various architects.

Typical Characteristics

- One or two stories
- Low-pitched hipped or gabled roof
- Wide overhanging eaves
- Horizontal low-to-the-ground look
- Natural materials
- No curves
- Off-white or earth-toned stucco over a brick or wood structure
- Decorative dark wood strips or bands on the exterior and interior of the house
- Extended wings on either side of the house
- Terraces
- Central large and low chimney
- Continuous band of casement windows (ribbon windows)
- Some windows with stained glass patterns
- Raised porches and **porte cocheres** extending from the center of the house with massive, square porch supports
- Open floor plan
- Built-in cabinets
- Furniture often designed by the architect

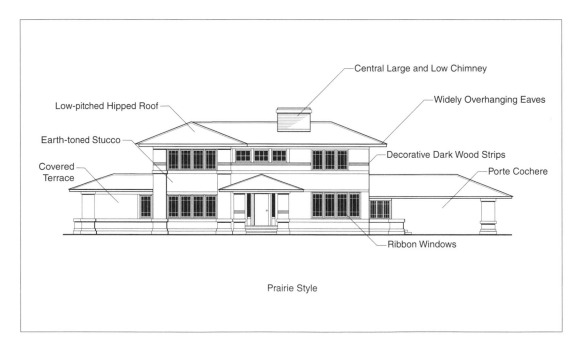

Low-pitched Hipped Roof

Earth-toned Stucco

Covered Terrace

Central Large and Low Chimney

Widely Overhanging Eaves

Decorative Dark Wood Strips

Porte Cochere

Ribbon Windows

Prairie Style

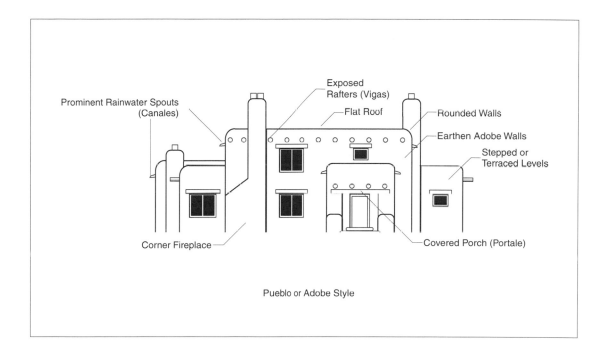

Pueblo or Adobe Style

Pueblo or Adobe

In the 1600s the Indians in the Southwestern United States first built pueblo-style houses as multi-family dwellings. There were no doors on the first level to protect them from attackers; they used wooden ladders to access the second level. The design of the pueblo has evolved and is still very popular today, particularly in the Southwest.

Typical Characteristics
- Projecting, rounded roof beams (vigas)
- Earthen adobe walls (made of mud, water and organic material such as straw)
- Flat roof
- Rounded walls
- Stepped or terraced second- and third-floor levels
- Deep window and door openings
- Covered porches (*portales*)
- Porch roof covered by wood framework
- Prominent rainwater spouts (*canales*)
- Beehive corner fireplace
- Niches carved out of interior walls for displaying various items
- Brick, wood or flagstone flooring

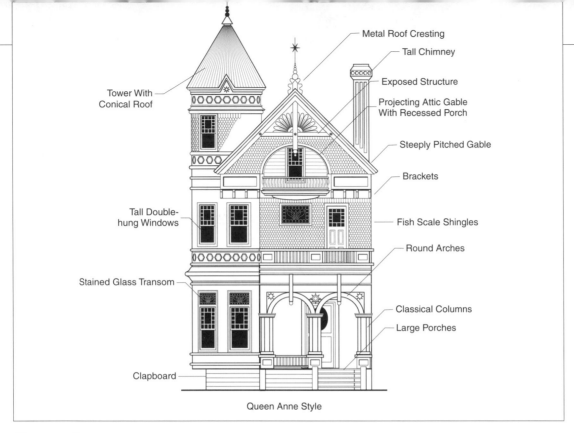

Metal Roof Cresting

Tall Chimney

Exposed Structure

Tower With Conical Roof

Projecting Attic Gable With Recessed Porch

Steeply Pitched Gable

Brackets

Tall Double-hung Windows

Fish Scale Shingles

Round Arches

Stained Glass Transom

Classical Columns

Large Porches

Clapboard

Queen Anne Style

Queen Anne

The English architect Richard Norman Shaw is often associated with the Queen Anne style. It was first seen in America at the Philadelphia Centennial in 1876. The first Queen Anne house to be built by American architect Henry Hobson Richardson is the William Watts Sherman House built in Newport, Rhode Island, in 1874. A Victorian-style, this house was the most elaborate and eccentric of that era. It is distinguished by the use of contrasting forms, textured surfaces and colors.

Typical Characteristics
- Asymmetrical facade
- Variety of siding materials on the house with brick or stone on the first floor, and stucco, clapboard or decorative varied shingles on upper floors
- Decorative brick and cedar shingle pattern
- Steeply pitched gabled (gable ends ornamented with half-timbering or a relief decoration) or hipped roof with odd roof patterns
- Tall chimneys
- Metal roof cresting
- Projecting **oriel windows**
- Tall double-hung windows
- Banks of windows
- Rounded arches over terraces
- Stained glass panels in windows
- Classical columns
- Brackets
- Large encircling porches, verandas and balconies
- Corner turrets, towers and gazebos
- Beamed ceilings
- Open floor plans
- Corner fireplaces
- The upper portion of interior doors with a large glass panel

Ranch

The ranch is not really considered a style but a type of building. It is sometimes called a California Rambler, California Ranch or Texas Ranch. The ranch evolved from the Prairie School, Bungalow, Cottage, Spanish Rancho and Spanish Revival styles. It is a house commonly seen in the suburbs of the United States and often associated with track, or cookie-cutter, houses. The ranch was first designed by architect Cliff May in San Diego, California, in 1932. It became popular in the 1940s across the United States with Levittown and continues to be popular today.

Typical Characteristics

- Single story
- An informal-type house
- Post-and-beam construction
- Low-pitched gable roof
- Projecting eaves
- Horizontal layout and low to the ground (sometimes without a basement)
- Rectangular, L-shaped or U-shaped design
- Asymmetrical
- Large double-hung, sliding or picture windows
- Louvered shutters
- Sliding-glass doors
- Patios and porches
- Attached garage or carport
- Simple floor plan
- Open floor plan with few walls
- Clapboard and/or brick veneer exterior
- Porch roof supports

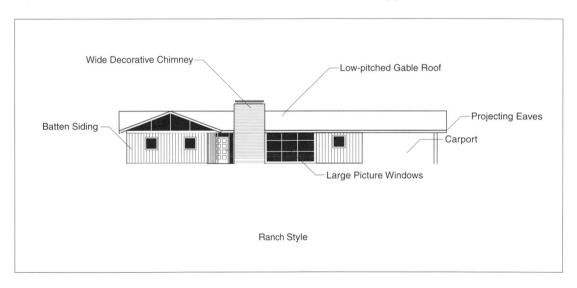

Wide Decorative Chimney — Low-pitched Gable Roof

Batten Siding — Projecting Eaves — Carport

Large Picture Windows

Ranch Style

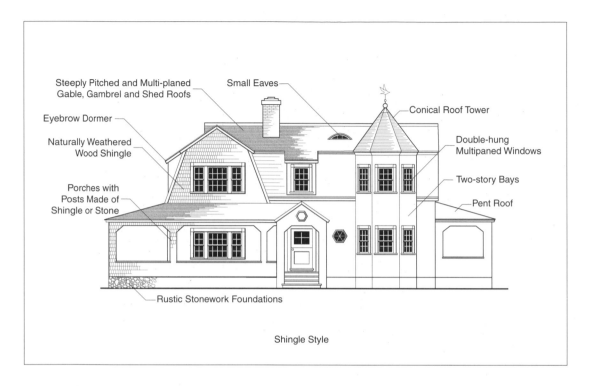

Steeply Pitched and Multi-planed
Gable, Gambrel and Shed Roofs

Small Eaves

Conical Roof Tower

Eyebrow Dormer

Naturally Weathered
Wood Shingle

Double-hung
Multipaned Windows

Porches with
Posts Made of
Shingle or Stone

Two-story Bays

Pent Roof

Rustic Stonework Foundations

Shingle Style

Shingle

This is an American style that evolved from the informality and openness of the Queen Anne style but with a new emphasis on texture, site sensitivity and space. It originated in New England, especially around coastal towns. The term **Shingle style** was coined by Yale professor Vincent J. Scully Jr. whose book *The Shingle Style* was published in 1955 and traced the history of the style. Frank Lloyd Wright built himself a Shingle-style house in 1893 in Oak Park, Illinois.

Typical Characteristics
- Unpainted (naturally weathered) continuous wood-shingle siding and roofing
- Irregular steeply pitched and multi-planed gable, gambrel and **shed roofs**

- Two or three stories
- Decorative wood structural elements with exaggerated proportions
- Hipped or eyebrow dormers
- Porches with posts made of shingles or stone
- Rustic stonework foundations
- **Pent roof**
- Small eaves
- Small casement and **double-hung multi-paned windows** paired in twos or threes
- Two-story-high bay windows
- Conical roof towers
- Window trim painted white or green
- Open floor plan

Spanish Colonial

This style house was influenced by the Spanish missions (established by Spanish and Mexican missionaries to convert the Indians to Catholicism) and presidios (fort-like structures built in the eighteenth century to house the soldiers sent to protect the missions) built in the Southwestern United States.

Typical Characteristics

- One-story building—low to the ground
- Adobe brick with plaster finish
- Red-tile shed or hipped roof
- Heavy wooden doors—sometimes paneled or carved
- Roofed porches—called verandas or corridors—on the interior side of the three U-shaped sides of the house and connected to all the rooms
- Carved wooden posts along the verandas or corridors
- Overhanging roof
- Parapet wall closing fourth side of the enclosed patio
- A few small windows
- Curved gables
- Roof beams or rafters (vigas)
- Rounded or rough square porch posts
- *Canales* (water spouts)—projecting gutters
- *Fogon*—a bell-shaped corner fireplace

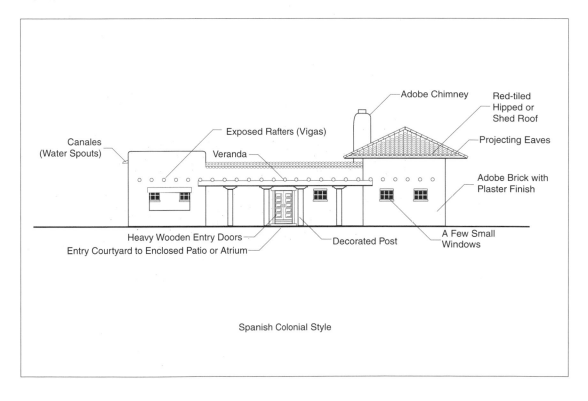

Canales (Water Spouts)

Exposed Rafters (Vigas)

Veranda

Adobe Chimney

Red-tiled Hipped or Shed Roof

Projecting Eaves

Adobe Brick with Plaster Finish

A Few Small Windows

Decorated Post

Heavy Wooden Entry Doors

Entry Courtyard to Enclosed Patio or Atrium

Spanish Colonial Style

Stick

The name Stick style was developed by the architectural historian Vincent Scully a century after the style was developed. An American design, it was influenced by many earlier styles, including Swiss Cottage, Carpenter Gothic, Italianate and so on. The most famous Stick-style house is the Griswold House, designed by Richard Morris Hunt in 1863.

Typical Characteristics
- Asymmetrical design
- Steeply pitched gable roof
- Overhanging eaves with exposed rafter ends
- Shake roof
- Exposed framing members
- Brick foundations
- **Board-and-batten** vertical siding or horizontal clapboard siding
- Pointed dormers
- Cast-iron cresting
- Decorative vertical, horizontal and diagonal boards over the siding (resembling half-timbering) or stick work
- Large roof projections
- Large ornamental brackets
- Diagonal and X bracing
- Wide verandas and porches decorated with vertical braces
- Stick-like porch posts and railings
- Double-hung windows with or without divided lights

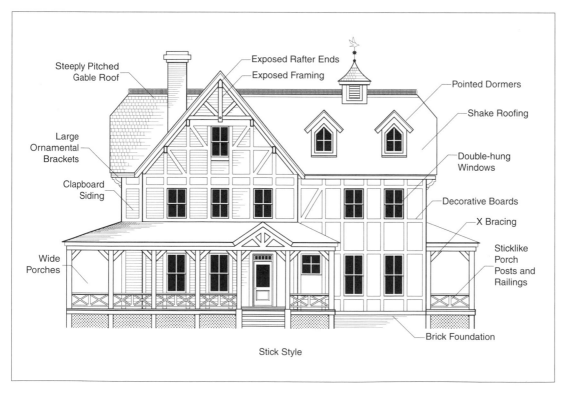

Steeply Pitched Gable Roof · Exposed Rafter Ends · Exposed Framing · Pointed Dormers · Shake Roofing · Large Ornamental Brackets · Clapboard Siding · Double-hung Windows · Decorative Boards · X Bracing · Sticklike Porch Posts and Railings · Wide Porches · Brick Foundation

Stick Style

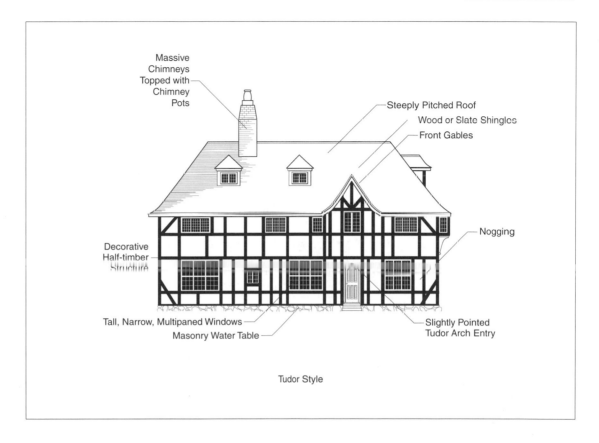

Tudor Style

Tudor

Sometimes called Medieval Revival, based on the English Elizabethan and Jacobean styles, Tudor style was developed in the sixteenth century and is still popular today.

Typical Characteristics
- Decorative half-timber structure
- Nogging (a brick filling covered with cement stucco) between the timbers
- Steeply pitched roof—usually side-gabled
- Front gables
- Long rows of leaded casement windows with small window panes
- Massive chimneys, often topped with chimney pots
- Entry with round arch or slightly pointed Tudor arch
- Wood or slate shingles
- Tall, narrow windows commonly in multiple groups and multipaned

Construction Types

There are many beautiful construction options: timberframe, log construction, panelized, modular, structural insulated panels, steel frame and several types of concrete construction. If you are contemplating building or remodeling your home you may want to consider an alternate method of construction. Even if you decide to build a traditional site- or stick-built home, it is interesting to know that other options exist; you may someday want to consider one of these for a second home or vacation home.

Houses can be built on-site; they can be delivered as an entire house, in varying levels of completeness, or they can be shipped in parts to be assembled. Stick construction built on-site has become the predominate method of construction in this country, a type of construction that most of us are familiar with. There are also methods of construction that haven't been used for many years and are popular again, such as strawbale construction, a very earth-friendly method of building a home.

A manufacturer can be contracted to produce all or part of the house. Components may be factory produced in another location and transported and assembled at the construction site later. These are called building systems, now a common type of construction for residential and commercial structures.

Some systems manufacturers offer a part of a house, such as the frame, and others offer a complete house including appliances and carpets. These components are designed, engineered and possibly assembled in the controlled environment of a factory and then shipped to the construction site. Most systems manufacturers are able to hasten the construction time substantially and decrease the cost of the house, unless the distance the parts will have to travel decreases the advantages of the factory construction. Before selecting any particular systems manufacturer, consider the following questions:

- Does the manufacturer's system comply with local codes?
- Is the company reliable and solvent? Check to see how long they have been in business, that they have a good credit rating and if they have a record with the Better Business Bureau.
- Do they have three references from recent clients whom you can call? Is it possible to see their homes?
- Will they offer a complete and detailed description of what is included in the contract? Also find out what is not included. Find out how much of the production they will do and how much you will have to contract.

- What are the delivery costs?
- What are other additional costs? Find out so you will have a realistic idea of the final cost of the house.
- What is the warranty? Check to see if it is an in-house or third-party guarantee.
- How much customization is possible?
- What brands are used for various included items such as windows, doors and appliances? Find out if alternate options are available.
- How much field assistance is given from the company if they are not building the entire house?
- Will you need to hire a builder to erect the parts or complete the house? Find out if they have a list of recommended builders or contractors in your area and if they can give you references for them.
- Do they offer financing?
- Can the company give you an accurate production schedule?

There are advantages and disadvantages to all of these various methods. If you are aware of your options you can select the type of construction that best fits your needs, building site, budget, schedule and preferences.

Traditional Site, Stud, Balloon or Stick Construction

Most people think about traditional site or stick construction when they are thinking about building a house. The styles are as numerous as the design possibilities. Standard stud construction is the most widely used method for building homes in the United States and Canada. It requires less skill and precision than the older method of post-and-beam construction, a more precise and skillful construction joining large structural framing components that carry the weight of the entire house.

In some areas it is easy to find qualified builders to construct custom homes. In those areas, stick construction may be the most practi-

A stick-constructed house.

cal method. There are also styles that may be difficult to build with a system, and there is a hands-on element to site construction that is not possible on some systems. Changes can more readily be made during the various stages of construction as well. There are areas in the country, however, where it is more difficult to find a builder, skilled carpenter and mason; in those cases manufactured systems should be considered. Labor costs are also very high in some areas. The cost of construction may make building a stick home prohibitive. The weather in some areas of the country can slow down the construction process for extended periods of time; for those areas, other types of construction may be more practical.

Building a stick house, depending on weather conditions, the size of the house and the complexity of the design, may be a very lengthy process. If time is an important issue, other methods such as modular or panelized construction can expedite the process and may be preferable.

With stud construction, after a foundation is built, a floor frame is constructed and walls are built with studs (vertical members of a framed wall) on the subfloor. Where there are windows and doors, a large header is put across the top of the opening to carry the load to either side of the opening. If there is another floor or two they build up in the same way with studs, walls and floor/ceiling joists. The roof is made of rafters that sit on top of the walls and support the roof **sheathing.** The foundation supports the floor frame, which supports the walls, which support the rafters, which support the roof. This is a popular technique because of the ease of purchasing materials, but since the load is spread out over so many areas of the construction, there is a margin for error, which is not as possible with the earlier post-and-beam method of construction. All of the materials used are of a manageable size and don't require special machinery to complete the construction of a house.

Although it can be expensive to alter the plans on a stick house after the construction has begun, it is more difficult with some other types of construction, such as modular and panelized, where the parts are preciously cut to size and arrive at the site in varying degrees of completeness.

Advantages
- Many builders are available to build stick houses.
- Changes can often be easily made during construction.
- Homeowners can watch their home being built.
- Some designs are most easily and efficiently executed with stick construction.
- Special machinery is not generally required.
- Construction can be completed on lots that may be difficult with other types of construction because of the terrain.

Disadvantages
- It can be a very timely process.
- During extremely nasty, cold or hot weather, construction may be delayed.
- Materials are often cut on-site and there is a great deal of waste.
- During construction, materials can be left outside for a lengthy period of time.

- Warranties are shorter than those offered by many systems construction companies.

Steel Construction

Steel has been used commercially for many years, but it is becoming increasingly popular for residential construction. It is used in very much the same way as wood studs, except that the material is steel; this type of steel construction is called "lightweight steel construction." It can also be used in the same way as timberframes are used, as a structural element; this type of steel construction is called "structural steel construction." Both types of steel construction are on the rise. The reasons for the increasing popularity of steel are the scarcity of quality wood, the increasing cost of wood and the growing trend in some municipalities to limit the use of combustible materials. Steel is very reliable and uniform in strength. It can be cut on-site by the contractor or can be ordered as a pre-cut package from the manufacturer. Several companies are listed here that offer a variety of options. Some companies have models to select from in a variety of sizes. Some of the houses can be customized with a variety of levels of adjustment. Each company offers different types of packages (from just a frame to cladding, etc.), so if you have interest in this type of construction, you have to contact companies individually. It may take as little as a week (or more) to get the drawing and then seven to eight weeks for the materials to be delivered, depending on the company. Manufacturers use **red iron** (a structural steel coated with a red oxide coating or paint to resist rust) with lightweight galvanized steel studs and framing members. Any siding can be used on steel-framed homes, and when they are complete, they are indistinguishable from a conventionally built wood-framed house.

37

Advantages

- Ability to withstand up to 150 mph wind loads (traditional stud construction can withstand 80 to 90 mph winds) and can meet the highest earthquake ratings.
- Resistant to termites, carpenter ants and other insects.
- Resistant to rot and deterioration.
- Steel can reduce the spread of fire.
- If the material is precut by the manufacturer there is a savings on labor.
- Steel is one of the most recyclable materials.
- Some woods are impregnated with chemicals that affect some people with hypersensitive allergies. Steel is a good alternative for those people.

- Steel-frame studs are straight and true in form, unlike wood that may be delivered warped, twisted or bowed.
- Most of the steel used is precut by the manufacturer. Wood arrives at the job site in stock lengths, and there is a great deal of waste when it is cut to size.
- With steel frames there is more insulation used because the framing members are at a greater distance apart and the studs are less thick; therefore, there is more space for insulation. Steel headers can also be insulated in their interior space.
- Steel is so strong it can span large areas of the house without requiring load-bearing support walls. It also makes it easier to mod-

ify the interior space for remodeling.
- Screws and bolts are used instead of nails and glue, which may loosen over time and are less permanent.

Disadvantages

- It may be difficult finding contractors who are able to build with steel.
- Assembly requires particular power tools that are commonly used by commercial builders but rarely used in residential construction.
- Cranes may be necessary to hoist the steel members into place.
- Structural steel connections (bolted or welded) require inspection and/or certification to insure the required bearing capacity is achieved.
- Copper plumbing may cause a problem in proximity to the steel. Copper must be insulated from contact with steel to avoid galvanic corrosion of the steel.

Above: A house with a steel frame.

Left: A house under construction with a steel frame.

Some of the companies that offer steel frames:

American Steel Frame Services, Inc.	www.americansteelframeservices.com
Classic Steel Frame Homes	www.metalhomes.com
Excalibur Steel Structures	www.excalibursteel.com
Heritage Building Systems	www.heritagebuildings.com
Northern Steel International	www.nsteel.com
Premium Steel Building Systems	www.premiumsteel.com
SteelMaster	www.steelmasterusa.com
Tri-Steel Homes	www.tri-steel.com

MBCI of Houston, TX

Modular Construction

Typically people have always thought of modular houses as boxy, simple, traditional-style houses. Few people would guess that some of the gracious and unusual houses popping up around the country today are modular built. In 1990 there were 20,000 modular homes built in the United States, and in 2002 that number jumped to almost 36,000 and is still growing (according to an annual survey on modular construction by Hallahan & Associates, a marketing consulting company).

There are three types of modular companies: those that specialize in affordable housing, those that offer a wide range of plans and those that are more custom oriented and build to buyers' specifications.

Modular houses are built in a factory in controlled conditions. The modules are built in size to the maximum that can be transported by large trucks. Houses can consist of anywhere from one module with no limit to the high end. A thirty-three-module house was recently featured in *Building Systems Magazine*. Most companies have a variety of plans that can be selected and in-house design staffs that can alter these layouts to meet individual needs. Most of a modular house will be constructed in a factory, the balance completed on-site by one of the company's recommended network of builders. In some cases, the client will choose a builder, select a design and then bid the design among several modular companies. The prior scenario is the more common method of working with a modular company.

As important as it is to find an architect who will design within the restraints of modular construction, it is also important to find a builder experienced with this type of construction who can install the foundation and handle interior finishes and details. It may also be an option to have exterior trim and siding done on-site by the builder.

A metal barrel-vaulted weekend house.

Modular construction can also be used for remodeling a house, particularly for a second-floor addition. This is also a fast and economical way of constructing a weekend or vacation house. It is especially practical for houses that are being built out of the owners' local area where they may not have the time and opportunity to oversee the project on a regular basis.

Advantages

• The modular company can set the house in a month with finishing touches done by a local builder in two to five months. One of the biggest concerns people have in dealing with building a new house or remodeling their current house is the time it will take to complete the project. In many areas where land is not readily available, it is common to demolish a house that is on the property and build a whole new house either utilizing or eliminating the foundation of the house. In this type of situation, by using traditional site construction, a family might typically be out of their home for a year or two. Realistically this could possibly mean a year or two of rental costs and storage costs or the cost of another mortgage on a current house while the other is being built. Although many people can afford the construction, they may not be able to afford the cost of a rental or second

SteelMaster

mortgage for that length of time. Using modular construction, they may be able to return to their home in three to six months, depending on the square footage and the architectural design of the house. The construction of the house and site preparation can be done simultaneously, saving tremendous time. Because the weather doesn't have any effect on construction productivity, the work can be continued with no lost days because of snow, rain or extremely cold weather.

- An added advantage is that the materials used in a modular house are not subjected to inclement weather since the construction is done in a climate-controlled environment. This puts less wear and tear on the materials, which is not the case in traditional construction where materials are exposed to the elements before the house is closed up.
- A modular house is built heavier than a standard home because it has to travel at high speeds to the site. The construction is stronger since each module has to withstand being transported and lifted by a crane onto a foundation. Most modular homes will exceed all local building codes and are inspected by an independent third-party inspection agency. Check with local building officials on their certification requirements.
- There are also financial advantages; modular houses generally cost 10 to 30 percent less.

Because the construction time is less, the cost of the construction loan will also be less. The time period of a modular construction project is nine to ten months and a frame construction for the same project is twelve to fourteen months. This is a savings of two to three months' interest. The consumer is then able to secure permanent financing quicker, which begins to pay down the principal sooner. Some banks will inspect the delivered modular house to be sure that it is set correctly. Depending on the type or level of inspection, this could give the consumer an added level of protection in assuring them against future problems. It is therefore important to find a bank familiar with this type of construction that will be able to check on the construction.

- Materials are purchased in great quantity by modular companies, bringing down the overall cost of the house. In upscale areas, labor is far less expensive with the modular manufacturer than would be possible in the local area. The modular company also saves money in reduced job-site theft and damage.
- Some modular companies offer a limited selection of designs; some offer as many as 100. One of the advantages of using these plans is that they have been used many times before, and they have been perfected over the years. There are other more custom-oriented companies that build unique homes to the customers' specifications. In those cases an architect's services may be required. The architect can provide a custom design to the owner's requirements. Because the architect does not have to submit the same documentation for modular homes, the design fees will generally be less, depending on the complexity and amount of involvement the architect will have in the project. Whereas the architect's responsibility is more limited in the need for full construction documentation, the

A modular house being set.

A beautiful example of what can be done with modular construction.

Photo by Philip Jensen-Carter, Epoch Homes and the Batkin family

architect still assists you with securing special permits (other than the basic permits), does a shop drawing review of the completed documents and executes interior detail design and lighting plans. Because it is more difficult to make changes after the modular house is complete, the architect's shop drawing review is a particularly important function, which is not necessary or as intense in site-built houses. It is important that the architect communicates the design requirements to the modular company and makes himself familiar with the company's methods and procedures. Most modular companies have an architect on retainer who is responsible for the final design of the house.

- Today it is often difficult to tell modular homes from site-built homes. There are houses popping up in upscale communities that are often indistinguishable as modular homes.
- Modular companies generally offer a ten-year warranty. Most builders of standard construction homes will offer no more than a one-year warranty. Modular companies use maintenance companies around the country that are familiar with their construction and will take care of problems that arise after the house is completed.
- Materials are warehoused in a secure environment, so there is less waste due to weather and job-site theft.

Disadvantages

- The biggest deterrent to modular homes at one time was the limitations in design. There are still modular companies that tend to build very traditional style homes and offer limited choices of materials and design. There are also styles that the modular company may not be able to build, such as contemporary houses with great variations in rooflines.
- Some companies may limit the materials that can be used. A company may use a particular window supplier, for example, and may not be willing to use a different one.
- It is more difficult to make changes on modular homes. Changes can generally not be made after the final plans are approved. This might not work well for people who are very visual and who may not be happy with certain aspects of the layout until it is seen.
- There are fewer checks and balances in the design and construction of modular houses. In frame or stick construction there are more people overlooking the project and the best interests of the owner. In modular construction one company is basically handling all aspects of the work.
- In some areas local labor is competitive with that of the modular company, limiting the financial advantage of using a modular company.
- There are also areas where it would be impossible to bring a crane to set the house. In these areas, modular construction is not an option.

- There is a limit to the distance a modular company will deliver a house. Some manufacturers will ship as far as 1,600 miles. The longer distances will add extra expenses.

Modular construction is on the increase. It is not a perfect method for everyone to use, but it should be considered as an option for homeowners considering building or remodeling their homes.

resources

For further information about modular construction or for a listing of modular manufacturers, contact the Modular Building Systems Council at National Association of Home Builders (NAHB) at www.nahb.org or 800-368-5242 or contact the Modular Building Systems Association at www.modularhousing.com or 717-238-9130.

Log Home Construction

What started as humble beginnings for German and Scandinavian settlers who brought the log construction technique to America around the 1600s became society dwellings in the Adirondacks in the late nineteenth century. Government programs established during the Depression put unemployed people to work building log structures in national parks and spurred interest in log houses. People became more aware of the beauty of this type of construction and began to build more lavish log homes. Today there are simple log houses and spacious log houses, owned generally by homeowners who have a strong interest in this type of lifestyle.

Log construction has surged in the last several years. Currently 90 percent of log homes are manufactured; only 10 percent are handcrafted. Often used as weekend houses in the past, approximately 90 percent of log homes are used as primary residences today.

Log homes are generally energy efficient because of the thermal mass of the wood. In simple terms, wood retains heat that it releases over time. The usual use of R-values can be misleading here because of the thermal mass element of the material. Good design is needed in joining the logs to insure there will be no air and water infiltration. Compression gaskets, caulks and/or chinking are used to provide airtight seals. Systems must be designed with flexibility to allow the logs to settle over time. A well-designed system will be energy efficient and avoid expensive heating costs.

Ask the following questions when selecting a log company:
- What species and grade of wood will be used?
- Has the wood been dried and to what degree? Wood dried to 19 percent moisture content is considered stable and is less likely to shrink and settle.
- What wood profiles and corner designs are offered?
- What type of fasteners will be used? Are they included in a log home package?
- Will the package include galvanized spikes, screws, windows and doors, special frame stock, gasket material, log rafters or joists and hardware? Get a listing of everything that is included and everything that is not.
- Do they supply instruction manuals as well as field support?
- What type of preservatives, sealants and stains do they use?

Longer and wider logs are often used on handcrafted log homes.

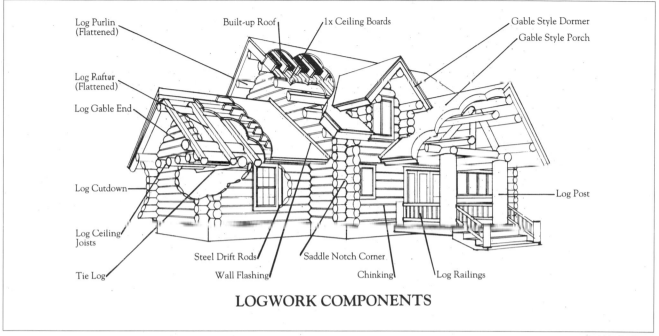

Log Purlin (Flattened) — Built-up Roof — 1x Ceiling Boards — Gable Style Dormer — Gable Style Porch — Log Rafter (Flattened) — Log Gable End — Log Cutdown — Log Ceiling Joists — Tie Log — Steel Drift Rods — Wall Flashing — Saddle Notch Corner — Chinking — Log Railings — Log Post

LOGWORK COMPONENTS

Maple Island Log Homes

Handcrafted

Handcrafters work in a variety of styles with traditional hand tools and chain saws. They will peel the bark off the trees, cut and shape the logs to fit together. The logs will be stacked on a temporary foundation or piers in their own log yard, with each log labeled as to its specific location in the final structure, before being dismantled and moved to the actual site. Openings for windows and doors are cut out of the logs after they are reconstructed at the home site. Because handcrafted logs are not milled to be all the same size, the handcrafter scribes each log to fit with the one below it. There are basically two styles that handcrafters use. In a Swedish cope (also called Scandinavian Scribe) the handcrafter cuts a groove along the length of each log so it will fit the profile of the logs below it. Because this creates a tight fit between logs, Swedish cope homes may not require chinking to seal gaps between the logs. In the other form, chink style, the logs are simply laid on top of the others and only cut to fit at the corners.

Some handcrafters will build just the frame of a house; others will build the entire house. Handcrafters usually use longer logs that will span the entire length of a wall rather than piecing several logs together. Because handcrafters tend to use wider and longer logs and do much of their work by hand, the homes they build tend to be more expensive than manufactured log homes. Some handcrafters will also produce roof framing systems built from logs as part of their shell package. This can add to the cost because of the labor intensity of this part of the house. The process is, in general, slower and more expensive. The house may, however, be unique and authentic; since the logs are generally larger, they have a higher thermal mass and may be more energy efficient. The International Log Builders' Association represents handcrafters and sets standards of quality for workmanship.

resources

For further information about handcrafted construction or to locate a handcrafter, visit www.logassociation.org or call 800-532-2900.

Manufactured or Milled

Machines are used to peel the logs and shape them to a uniform thickness and profile. The corner joints are also cut by machine. The result is a home with a uniform look. Manufactured log homes can be built with shorter logs and logs of smaller diameter that are pieced together. Because this saves money, manufactured log homes tend to cost less than handcrafted homes. A manufac-

Maple Island Log Homes

tured log home will take far less time to build and requires a small crew. There are log home kits that can be purchased with many degrees of completeness from log home companies across the United States and Canada. Find out if the company is a member of the Log Homes Council (LHC). This is a nonprofit organization setting industry standards and a code of ethics for their members. (Only one-quarter of the log companies join, however, because they don't see a benefit in

doing so.) Log home manufacturers may offer a book of standard designs to choose from, may customize their plans, may create a design from your sketch and/or may employ designers or architects to design each house on an individual basis. These companies cut the wood into its final shape and profile in mills with sophisticated machinery. The companies sell different types of kits or packages:

Basic package—The manufacturer designs the house and cuts the logs for the basic shell of the house. The logs are numbered so the house can be assembled by the homeowners or their contractor. In addition to the logs, basic packages usually include the sealants and fasteners and sometimes will include roof trusses and log siding for dormers or gables.

Weathertight package—Manufacturers can design the house, cut the logs and deliver the frame, walls, roofing materials, trim, exterior windows and doors and sometimes interior wood items (such as railings, partitions and floor systems) to make the house weathertight, but the house is completed by the homeowners or their contractor. Some companies will also construct the shell of the house.

Complete package—Manufacturers design the house and provide all the parts in the weathertight package, plus more of the interior finish items such as interior doors, roof insulation and drywall or other interior wall paneling. This is sometimes referred to as a "turnkey" house. What constitutes a turnkey house in the log industry might differ from the popular use of the term. This might not mean you are purchasing a house in move-in condition. Items such as wiring, HVAC system and so on may not be included in the package. Be very clear as to what is included when purchasing a turnkey package.

The interiors of log homes have a rustic charm.

Tomahawk Log & Country Homes

Half-log homes like this one are usually difficult to differentiate on the exterior from a traditional log home.

Half-log manufacturer—This involves a stick-built construction with logs on the outside and/or inside of the house. It gives the appearance of a log house while providing room for insulation, wiring and plumbing between the logs. A half-log package usually includes everything needed for the house other than subcontracted items such as the foundation, plumbing or electricity.

resources

Three of the companies that do manufactured half-log construction are Tomahawk Log & Country Homes, Inc. (www.tomahawklog.com or 800-544-0636), Wilderness Log Homes (www.thewildernesscompany.com or 800-707-0449) and Wisconsin Log Homes (www.wisconsinloghomes or 800-678-9107).

Module-built log home—These houses can arrive at the site approximately 80 to 85 percent complete. Module-built homes can be built more quickly and at a lower cost than site-built log homes.

resources

Fore further information about modular-built log homes, check the Web site of ABC Modular Log Homes at www.abcmodularloghomes.com or call 800-514-4114, Ameri-log White Cedar Homes at www.ameri-loghomes.com or New Horizon Homes at 615-855-0565.

Cost

There are other items to consider before building a manufactured or milled log home. The cost of log houses will vary depending on whether they are handcrafted or manufactured, a stock design or custom designed, small or sprawling and basic or detailed. The packages purchased from a log home manufacturer, which typically include the log walls, roof system, doors, windows and porches, comprise approximately one-third of the total cost of the building of the log home (unless it is a turnkey package). This excludes the cost of the land, land development, mechanical systems, septic system and well system (when necessary), light fixtures, bathroom fixtures, plumbing fixtures, fireplaces, floor coverings, kitchen appliances, hardware, cabinets and countertops. Make sure you know in advance if there will be delivery costs and charges for erection and fastening of the walls as well. Square-footage prices are misleading; it is very difficult to evaluate a figure that must be established after a house is complete. Houses are built with different items of different quality, making it difficult to compare one company's square-foot price with another's. Be careful in selecting a package based on square-foot price. To estimate square footage of a log house, some companies use floor area square footage and others use walkable square footage. Make sure when comparing prices per square foot that you are using the same method of determining the area.

Design

It is best to work with a designer or architect who is experienced with or is willing to

learn the requirements and limitations of log homes. They will have a better idea of how the logs will react and what types of details work best in a log home. Some companies offer set designs and/or the option to customize the design with in-house designers or architects. Before meeting with a log company or architect you should decide what style you like (Adirondack, mountain or ranch), what your personal requirements are in terms of number of rooms, types of rooms, whether you prefer one floor or two, type of room flow you prefer and so on.

Log Home Styles

Adirondack—These houses resemble the Adirondack Great Camps with full round hand-crafted logs and corners and a very natural look. Sometimes the bark is left on the timbers and twigs, and branches are sometimes used in decorative railings. They tend to have porches rimming the perimeter, which are often screened to protect against mosquitoes and other flies. Roofs are often gabled, and windows are divided into smaller panes. The trim on windows and doors is cranberry red or blue-tinted green.

Ranch—Typically ranch houses have round logs with overlapping corners or square logs with dovetail notches. They resemble the houses of the Old West pioneer. Generally they have one

shallow-pitched roofline with a horizontal look and wide wraparound porches. They are best adapted to a level terrain. Windows are smaller than those used with some of the other styles, and today they are often arranged together to bring more light to the interior of the house. Simple single doors are used for entry, and interiors are informal.

Mountain—These are rustic with steeply pitched heavy roofs to match the mountainous terrain. Porches have a shallow-pitched overhang to allow more light to enter. The logs can be round or square, but they are generally large to protect from the cold mountain air. Smaller windows are mixed with larger ones, which can be used to view the scenery and are set higher on the walls.

Early American—Logs are square with dovetail corners, the way they were first built by early settlers. Sometimes old logs are used to build Early American–style houses; however, several of the major log companies that work in this style use new logs. The houses are boxy with either one or two floors. Rooflines are simple with dormers in shed style for added interest. Slate, metal or cedar shakes are all roofing options. Windows are rectangular with divided-light windows and trim in white, green or dark brown. The front door can be in a contrasting

Log Home Styles

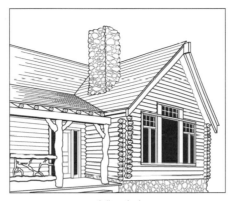

Adirondack

Ranch

Mountain

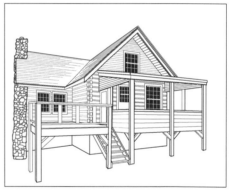

Early American

Pacific Northwest

Storybook Cottage

color and have small-paned sidelights and over-head transoms. Hardware should be heavy and matte or with a brushed finish.

Pacific Northwest—These are handcrafted and have a linear, Asian look. Corners have corner posts or dovetail notches. They have broad roof overhangs and shallow roof pitches. A variety of roofing materials is appropriate for this style. Shingles are sometimes used as details, and windows are rectilinear with grille patterns. Trim around the windows and doors is simple and usually a shade of green or rust. This is not a house that should be used in snow country because the shallow roof does not work well with heavy snow loads.

Storybook Cottage—This is a charming, romantic style with lots of variety of log styles and corners used together. A variety of materials can also be used—mixing stone, shingles and board and batten with the logs for interest. Pitches are varied and there are lots of porches. As with the other elements of this style, the window styles can be varied. The front door should be special and complement the style of the house either with a simple, Victorian, or Arts and Crafts look. Like Victorian-style houses, these houses have many details and variety.

It is helpful to review the myriad of publications (see page 53) and attend some of the log home shows and seminars to become educated in this type of construction. Log homes can be built as A-frames, ranches, two-story and so on. It is best to have some idea of your needs and preferences before working with a professional.

Basic Design Recommendations

- Large overhangs protect the logs from rain and sun and are generally recommended as a design feature to be incorporated into log homes. This is especially important for the corners since the ends of the logs are more susceptible to weather damage.

- Logs should be at least 18 inches off the ground to avoid contact with rain and snow accumulation and to discourage insects. The foundation should be planned accordingly.
- Wide porches help to protect the house from the damaging effects of rain, snow and sun.

Wood for Log Homes

Wood is affected by the elements—snow, rain, moisture and ice. Ideally, the wood that is selected is decay-free, decay resistant, durable and has wide-diameter trunks. (The diameter of the trunks will be a larger issue with handcrafted homes than with milled homes, which generally offer milled wood that is 6, 8 or 10 inches in diameter.)

Species—There are many species that can be used for log homes. Wood that is indigenous to the local area is usually used because it costs less to harvest locally than to transport another species from a distance. Pine is popular because it is readily available, grows quickly and grows tall. Cedar is also popular because of its resistance to the elements and insects. Some of the other common species of wood are hemlock, oak, fir and spruce. For a complete listing of wood species by location, check the Annual Buyer's Guide of *Log Home Living* (see page 53).

Grade—All logs should have a Certificate of Log Grading, showing inspection by a log grader according to standards developed by the American Society for Testing Materials. There are three categories: header grade, wall grade and utility grade. This certification system was put in place in 1984 and helps determine the structural soundness of the logs rather than visual appearance, their ability to withstand the vertical and lateral stresses put on them by log construction.

Degree of dryness—Wood needs to be in equilibrium with the environment, which may be anything from 10 to 24 percent water content. Until it reaches that equilibrium, it will continue to shrink and the log walls will settle. Wood that is moist, above 30 percent, will be prone to fungi, which will cause the wood to rot. Wood preservatives prevent living organisms from penetrating the wood, while also allowing moisture to escape. The most important factor is how the builder accommodates this moisture level in the construction. Logs will not only shrink in diameter but will also settle on top of each other. A house built with green logs may shrink and settle six inches or more in the first three to five years. The builder needs to accommodate for this or else windows and doors may stick and break.

How Can Dry Wood be Purchased?

Green—These are trees with a high moisture content, which have not yet been kiln- or air-dried. When the wood does dry it will shrink substantially. A builder must be able to take the shrinkage into consideration when constructing the house.

Naturally dried—Some companies will stack the wood for six months to a year and a half to allow the wood to dry naturally.

Kiln dried—The wood is put in ovens, which not only dries the wood but also kills insects and larvae that may be present.

Dead-standing trees—These are trees that have been killed by fires or insects but are still standing. They have already dried out and are very stable.

Glue-laminated logs—This is a type of manufactured log constructed by gluing (or laminating) together several pieces of wood that are then milled into the shape of logs with various profiles. Each piece of wood is kiln-dried to a very low moisture point before being laminated, which ultimately produces a very uniform, low-moisture content log. The logs are structural beams and are tested for strength. They eliminate the problems of

Log Types for Log Construction

Round Logs

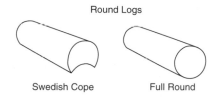

Swedish Cope   Full Round

Rectangular Logs

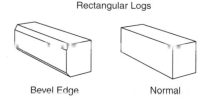

Bevel Edge   Normal

Square Logs

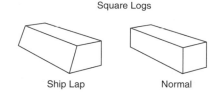

Ship Lap   Normal

D-Logs

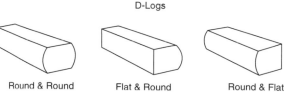

Round & Round   Flat & Round   Round & Flat

warping, cracking and twisting that may occur with other logs. Glue-laminated logs are available in several thicknesses and many profiles. Because of the labor necessary to produce them, they are more expensive than natural logs.

Two of the companies that produce glue-laminated logs are Glu-lam Log, Inc., at www.glulamlog.com or call 406-777-3219 and Anthony Log Homes at www.anthony-loghomes.com or call 800-221-2326.

Wood profile—This is a horizontal design of the wood, which will determine how it will interface with the other logs to form a wall. There are several wood profiles possible. Each manufacturer and handcrafter offers his own style. Look at homes to see which ones you prefer, and then find suppliers that offer the profiles you like.

Wood Fastening

Logs are stacked on top of each other to form a wall that must resist vertical forces, lateral forces and stress coming from wind, snow and seismic activity. One of the elements creating the stability is the fastening of the wood. The variety and placement of these fasteners will vary depending on the local weather conditions, size of the logs, size of the house, wood species, wood profile, corner style, the moisture content of the wood and the location of the windows and doors. Fasteners are usually included in manufacturers' log home packages; handcrafters often do not require fasteners.

Spikes—Very large nails that are driven into pre-drilled holes by sledgehammers.

Lag screws—Pointed bolts of varying diameters that are inserted in pre-drilled holes (at varying intervals) and tightened with an impact wrench.

Through-bolts—Threaded rods inserted in pre-drilled holes that go through an entire wall assembly. They are tightened at the foundation level as the logs settle.

Drift pins—Galvanized pipe or rebar that is

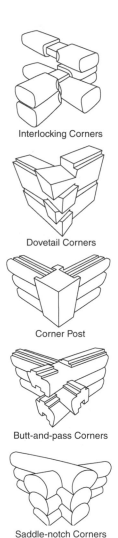

Corner Designs

Interlocking Corners

Dovetail Corners

Corner Post

Butt-and-pass Corners

Saddle-notch Corners

inserted vertically in pre-drilled holes in the wall assembly. This type of fastener may be required in earthquake-prone areas.

Threaded log-home screws—Stronger-than-usual screws that are driven directly into logs, saving the expense and time of first pre-drilling holes.

Corner Design

The type of corner design used will significantly influence the look, cost and speed of on-site construction of the house. There are many types of designs, and some companies have their own names for these styles. Companies may offer one type or many, and the costs may vary depending on the complexity of the design.

Butt and pass—One of the simplest and commonly used corners is formed when the log on one wall butts against the side of the adjacent wall. The log on the adjacent wall "passes" the first log, hence the term butt and pass. The logs alternate from layer to layer, so every other log on one wall is a "butt" and the logs in between are "passes."

Dovetail—This corner is used with square or rectangular logs. The ends of the logs are notched out and lock into the notches of the perpendicular logs. With the natural settling of the logs, the joints will be strengthened with this type of corner configuration. Forming these corners requires a skilled handcrafter or precise cutting machinery.

Saddle-notch (round-notch)—A notch is cut out of the bottom of each log and the perpendicular log below it fits into the notch. The logs both extend past the corner. This is a traditional corner design commonly used by handcrafters.

Corner post—This design has a post at the corner with a mortise along its length that the logs butt into. The logs sometimes have a tenon at the end that fits into the mortise. This is essentially a post-and-beam type design where the corner post stabilizes the logs forming the wall.

Interlocking corners—This is a complex corner and can only be economically produced on a milled log. Recesses on four sides of the log are locked into the intersecting log.

Maintenance

There are several products available to preserve and treat logs. These need to be applied properly (according to manufacturer specifications) and maintained on a timely basis. All of the products are not the same, so find out what products will be used, and check with other customers and professionals in the industry to make sure they are the best available ones. Compatibility between products is essential. Before using a product, check with the manufacturer to make sure the product will be compatible with what may already be on the logs and compatible with other products you might consider using. When purchasing a log home package, find out what products are used and make sure they are the most elastic and durable ones. All houses have different requirements depending on the species, the moisture content of the wood and the environment. Make sure you are aware of proper maintenance procedures before the handcrafter or manufacturer leaves your construction site. Some handcrafters use no chemicals on their houses in an attempt to offer a totally natural environment. Find out what will be used and make sure that is your preference before purchasing the package. Below is a list of some products used on log houses.

Preservatives—Preservative products contain fungicide and mildewcide and are applied to clean, bare wood to protect it from different types of fungi and insects. One of the most effective methods of preventing termites is treating the wood with borate-based solution before the logs are delivered to the house site or applied on-site before the logs are erected. Borate is an environmentally friendly preservative that is odorless and colorless; it stops rot and decay by killing fungus and insects. Fungicides should be applied periodically, depending on the climate and the preservative used.

Stains—Stains are wood finishes that seal the wood surface to prevent water penetration, add pigment to stabilize the color, and protect the wood from mold and spores settling on the surface. Many stains that have been formulated specifically for log home use are breathable and don't trap moisture in the wood. However, if the moisture content in the logs is high when the house is built, the stain should not be applied until the moisture content is 19 to 20 percent. A moisture meter is used to determine the moisture content; this can be purchased or rented from a local lumberyard. The logs should be cleaned before stain is applied. To maintain the natural color of the wood, a matching stain should be used; the pigment in the stain works as a sun-block to protect wood from the damaging effects of UV rays. A clear stain should never be used on the exterior logs. All high-quality finishes contain mildewcides and UV-inhibitors, but in areas where mold and mildew are prevalent, additional mildew additives should be used. The interior walls should also be stained to slow down the fading process, prevent the walls from absorbing household odors and make it easier to remove dust adhering to the logs. Clear stains can be used on the interior walls.

Sealants—Sealants are used to prevent infiltration of air (increasing the R-value of the wall) and moisture between the logs or around doors and windows. Wood will lose moisture and shift even after it has reached the equilibrium moisture content (EMC), or the point at which the internal moisture content is in balance with its environment. Most of the movement occurs in the first three to five years, but there will probably be some movement after that. Sealants are used in the construction of the house as well as to remedy infiltration that may occur later. Chinking is used not only for its sealing properties but also

for its aesthetic appeal. External types of sealants are chinking and caulking. Internal sealing systems may include one or a combination of the following: caulk, adhesives, foam gaskets, expanding foam and splines (thin strips of rigid material used in butt joints and corners to connect two logs). They vary in the method of application, cost, durability and look. Two of the popular types of sealants are chinking and caulking.

Chinking—When the early settlers came to this country they built their log homes and filled the open gaps between logs with chink made of mud, sticks, clay, stone and other materials found in nature. As the house settled, the material would fall out. Today synthetic chink is elastic, pliant and durable, is available in many colors and won't readily fall out with the shifting of the logs. The chink may split, but it can be patched. Chinking is both decorative as well as functional. Sealants such as chink are applied to stop water intrusion, air infiltration and to prevent insects from nesting in small crevices. Chink looks like mortar, although it is not, and helps to eliminate heat loss. In chink-style construction there is often dead airspace between the logs. Backerod is placed between the logs on either side. Chinking is then placed on the backerod to seal and create a visual appearance of traditional mortar.

Caulking—Some companies use caulking for sealing the joints between the logs. Caulking is a type of joint filler often used where the movement is very small to fill the gaps in wood left from shrinkage to accommodate wood movement and avoid air infiltration. Most caulks are rated according to the total amount of movement they will absorb. There are several kinds of caulk: acrylic, butyl, oil-based, urethane and silicone (this should never be used on a log home because it cannot be stained and it is not flexible). Caulking will only span about a $1/4$- to $1/2$-inch thickness, depending on the formulation. (Chinking will span up to a 4-inch area, also

There are several publications that deal with log homes:

Name of magazine	Web site	Telephone #	Issues per year
Country's Best Log Homes	www.countrysbestloghomesmag.com	800-219-1187	6
Log & Timber Style	www.logandtimberstyle.com	888-645-7600	6
Log Home Design Ideas	www.lhdi.com	877-235-2233	9
Log Home Living	www.loghomeliving.com	800-234-8496	11
Log Home Living Annual Buyer's Guide	www.loghomeliving.com	800-234-8496	1
Log Homes Illustrated Magazine	www.loghomeexpo.com	212-262-2247	8
Log Homes Illustrated Magazine Annual Buyer's Directory	www.loghomeexpo.com	212-262-2247	1
Luxury Log & Timber Homes	www.countrysbestloghomesmag.com	800-219-1187	1
Vacation Log Homes	www.countrysbestloghomesmag.com	800-219-1187	1

dependent on the formulation of the product.) Traditionally, high-grade caulking materials are shiny because of the polymers used in the formula. Recently some companies have introduced texture to the caulking materials to make them look less shiny.

Bondbreaker—There are several types of bondbreakers, including backerod, Styrofoam and masonite board cut to fit. Bondbreakers are substances put between two joints in the stacking process (as a prelude to chinking) or in checks (cracks) that develop over time. They prevent the caulking or chinking from adhering to the back of the joint. If the caulking or chinking adheres, it will tear as the logs move with changes in moisture content. The logs need to move as freely as necessary with the shrinkage. Backerod, a commonly used bondbreaker, comes in the form of a rope in different diameters. Ideally, wherever caulking or chinking can come into contact with the two sides of the joint and the back, you should install bondbreaker. Manufacturers who build chink-style walls always use a backerod behind the chink for stability.

resources

Some of the companies specializing in log home products: Perma-Chink Systems, Inc., www.permachink.com or 800-548-1231; Sashco Sealants, www.sashco.com or 800-767-5656; and Weatherall Company, Inc., www.weatherall.com or 800-367-7068.

Heating

If the climate requires air-conditioning, you may want to install a forced-air heating system so you can use the ductwork for an air-conditioning system. If, however, air-conditioning will not be necessary, radiant heat is an excellent method for heating log houses because it avoids the necessity for concealing ductwork. With radiant heat, the house is easily separated into zones that can be independently controlled.

Lighting

The plans for manufactured log homes should incorporate an extensive lighting plan before the walls are up. Handcrafted homes often do not need preplanning because there are spaces between the logs that allow horizontal wiring. Often keyways (anyplace that you can run wires or mechanical equipment) are cut for vertical wires. Wires can be hidden in miscellaneous stud walls, chink lines or even in grooves cut in the logs. It is difficult to hide the wires after the house is complete in some manufactured houses. Holes have to be drilled before the wall is closed to accommodate the wires. It is a good idea to plan for more than is needed, since all wires don't have to be used, but it is difficult to add them later.

Roof Systems

There are several possible roof systems that can be used with log homes. The system selected will depend on budget, personal preference and what the manufacturer or builder offers. Roof framing systems can be built with traditional framing, or they can be built with full-log construction. The latter system will add beauty with exposed logs and value to the house but will also add significantly to the cost.

Roof Coverings

Natural choices for roofing on log homes are wood shingle, slate, asphalt and metal. Other options are cement and terra-cotta. Metal reflects the sun, so it keeps the house cool in the summer; it is excellent for shedding snow in the winter, is lightweight and comes in many styles and colors. Many people opt for asphalt roofing, which is the least expensive and is the area where many decide to cut corners. Roof overhangs are an excellent way to protect the sides of the house from fading, the joints between the wall and roofline from leaking and the logs from rotting. A roof overhang 24 to 36 inches keeps the rain away from the logs.

Landscaping

Keep shrubs and plantings a distance away from the house so air can circulate and dry out the logs after it rains. Aim sprinkler systems away from the house.

All log homes settle from compaction of the joints as well as shrinkage due to drying of the wood; the extent depends on several factors including the moisture content of the wood, the weight of the walls, structural members and the home's environment. A competent producer will take all of these factors under consideration when designing the house.

Advantages
- They have a back-to-nature appeal.
- Log homes are strong.
- They are energy efficient.
- They are very durable.
- Log homes are adaptable to many styles.
- They have an aesthetic appeal to many people.

Disadvantages
- They require maintenance, as does any wood construction.

Because of the interest in log homes today, some architects are incorporating aspects of log construction into the stick homes they design. This includes such items as log stairways, tie beams across interiors and so on, which give the look of logs. This is in addition to the half-log construction that is also becoming more popular.

Before making any decisions, take the time to attend log home shows and seminars and check out the magazines and books available. Tear out pictures of the various types of houses you like, and keep notes on the handcrafters and manufacturers you speak with. Only then will you be a fully informed consumer and ready to take on this type of endeavor.

resources
To locate a log homes company: Log Homes Council of the National Association of Home Builders at www.loghomes.org or call 800-368-5242, extension 8577 or contact the International Log Builders' Association at

The interior of a timberframe house with beautiful joinery.

www.log-association.org or call 800-532-2900. The Log Home Living Institute is a consumer resource organization; contact them at www.lhli.org or 800-826-3893.

Sponsored log home shows and seminars: *Log Home Living* magazine, www.loghomeliving.com or 800-782-1253; *Country's Best Log Homes* magazine, www.countrysbestloghomesmag.com; and *Log Homes Illustrated,* www.logexpo.com.

Post-and-Beam/Timberframe Construction

Post-and-beam is a type of construction involving the use of **posts** (structural vertical members) and **beams** (structural horizontal members) interlocked to form a framework that is self-supporting and laterally stabilized by the use of masonry, diagonal braces and metal connectors and wood-joinery techniques. The vertical posts support the horizontal beams that support the roof. Timberframe is a type of post-and-beam construction dating back to the Middle Ages when master craftsmen built homes for nobility. Timberframe construction was brought from Europe by a group of artisans and was popular in the United States in the eighteenth and nineteenth centuries before stud construction became popular. Stick framing took hold during the industrial revolution when people wanted a faster, cheaper and easier method of construction. Timber framing was not popularized again until the 1960s when people became more interested in environmental issues and a more back-to-nature type home. The beams used for the roof rafters are usually left exposed. The post-and-beam method of construction used today grew out of timber framing and includes the use of additional materials, other than wood, and includes the use of additional joinery. Differences are listed a little further in this section, but in general, the two types of construction are more similar than they are different. Many styles can be built with a timber- or post-and-beam frame; most people using these types of construction appreciate the visibility of interior exposed beams and cathedral ceilings.

Because the frame rather than the walls supports the roof, it is easier to have more windows and doors and large open interior spaces. This is a very sturdy type of construction and has a beautiful, natural feeling. On the other hand, it also requires some skill and several people working together to manage the large timbers. In some areas it may also be difficult to find the large timbers necessary to construct a timber house. For these reasons, systems are often purchased with all or some of the components along with recommendations for skilled professionals to build them. In areas where natural disasters (earthquakes, hurricanes and tornadoes) are common, the posts and beams should be tied together with metal brackets to further support the structure of the house. In timberframe homes these metal brackets are usually hidden. It is becoming increasingly popular to use post-and-beam construction in just a

	Post and Beam	Timberframe
Materials	Wood timbers, laminated wood, steel or concrete	Solid wood timbers
Connectors	Metal fasteners—screws, nails and through-bolts. Can also use wood pegs. Lap-style joints (a notch with a straight cut) are used. In some cases the metal is hidden, although this is not always the case.	Mortise (hole or slot)-and-tenon (wooden peg) and pegs. If metal hardware is used it is hidden with trim applications. The steel can be used as a design element for extra support, usually in heavy snow load areas of the roof.
Stability	The support comes from the shear walls (exterior walls with plywood membranes), which handle the lateral loads.	Most timber houses use timber braces, or knee braces, which are part of the system that helps to resist lateral load, which comes from wind or seismic movement.
Cost	Generally, this type of framing is less expensive than timberframe. Although it is more expensive to use metal than the pegs used on timberframe, it takes more time and craftsmanship to build a timberframe.	Timberframes are usually more expensive than post and beam because of the craftsmanship of the joinery and the time it takes to complete.

section of the house, for a great room or other room where a high ceiling and exposed beams are desired.

Timberframe Versus Post-and-Beam Construction

These two types of construction are very similar, more alike than different. The differences between the two are very hazy. Much of the literature doesn't make a clear distinction; as a result most people think they are one and the same. The joinery is the main difference although they can both have a similar look. The following table shows some of the differences.

These differences, although generally true, are not universally true. Some post-and-beam companies do use knee braces and some timber-frame companies may use plywood for shear walls. The most universal difference is the use of mortise-and-tenon joinery; timberframe companies use it and post-and-beam companies do not. Some companies will produce both types of systems, but generally companies will produce one

or the other. Check in some of the publications mentioned at the end of this section for suppliers.

Advantages
- Many timberframe and post-and-beam houses are built with energy-efficient stress skins. Not all houses use this system and will then depend on the type of wall system, roof system and insulation used for their energy efficiency.
- They can be designed in any style: Cape Cods, Colonials, Arts and Crafts and so on.
- They can be used with any siding.
- Floor plans are flexible because load-bearing walls are not needed in the interior. Interiors can be easily redesigned and additions can be easily added.
- They are ecologically efficient because they use fewer natural resources.
- Instead of the walls supporting the house in stick construction, the frame supports all the weight of the house. This eliminates the need for load-bearing walls and eliminates the need for any particular configuration of

interior walls, allowing for open floor plans.
- The greatest incentive to timberframe or post-and-beam construction is the aesthetics; many people like the warmth and charm of exposed beams.
- There may be a cost incentive to use post and beam, which tends to be less expensive.
- The mortise-and-tenon joint is a beautiful, handcrafted look.

Disadvantages
- Depending on the wood species and type of truss, this type of construction will generally be more costly than stick construction.
- If there is not a company able to do this type of construction, someone may have to be brought in to complete this work. It could be inconvenient to have repairs done later under those circumstances.
- It is more difficult in some areas to find adequate timbers. It can be costly to transport them from a distance.

Wood
There are several types of wood that are used for timberframe/post-and-beam houses. The differences in the type of wood selected, along with the species, will have an effect on the cost of the house.

Green lumber—This wood has not yet aged. It has a high moisture content and will shrink a fraction of an inch in the direction of the cross grain but rarely in the length. It can take about three to five years to dry. The wood will shrink, twist and check while it is drying, but this will not affect the stability of the structure or the joinery, if the potential movement has been accommodated in the design.

Distressed timbers—A planer machine is used to distress green lumber and make it look rougher, more like recycled timbers at a lower cost.

Timber Joinery

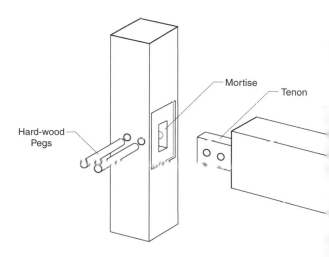

Mortise

Tenon

Hard-wood Pegs

Mortise-and-tenon Joint

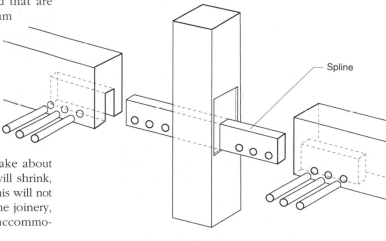

Spline

Splined Joint

Air-dried lumber—Some companies will air-dry the wood for a year or a year-and-a-half to partially dry it either piled up or "stickered," which is a method of stacking with small pieces of wood between the logs so air can circulate around them and hasten the drying process.

Radio Frequency Vacuum (RFV)—Radio frequency waves, similar to those used in a microwave, evenly heat the wood and cause the interior water to move to the surface and evaporate. During the drying process, pressure is applied to the wood to minimize checking, twisting, bowing and warping. While this process adds additional cost to the wood, it shortens the drying time of the wood substantially and helps minimize the need to accommodate normal shrinkage and movement that occurs when constructing with green lumber.

resources

For more information about RFV wood, contact SunDried Wood Technologies at www.sundriedwood.com or 304-965-7700 and Fraserwood Industries at www.fraserwoodindustries.com or 604-892-7562.

Kiln-dried lumber—This wood is dried in a kiln (a type of oven) to speed up the drying process. It is dried over several days, which reduces the necessity to allow for future shrinkage of the wood in the design of the house. Many companies do not have the facilities to dry lumber in this way.

Recycled timbers—These timbers are salvaged from other structures. They are very stable since they have already dried and will not shrink or check. It is often possible to find longer and wider timbers because that was what was used in older structures. Recycled timbers have an aged look, often with holes made from bolts, which is sometimes considered appealing. This lumber is usually more expensive.

2001 North Woods Joinery and Carolyn Bates

Timberframe houses can be in any style, including modern, such as the interior and exterior of this one.

Species

There are many species of wood used for timberframe homes. Framers in different areas of the United States and Canada generally use indigenous species. Oak, hemlock and pine are mainly used in the Eastern and Midwestern parts of the United States and Canada. Douglas Fir and Port Orford cedar are used in the Western areas. Certain species have a larger capacity for load and/or are stiffer than others. Before deciding on a particular species, find out the potential load and availability of several species.

Craftsman-Built or Company-Built?

Some craftsmen build timberframe homes by cutting all the wood with saws and chisels. This can take a long time and be very costly. Other craftsmen use precision machinery. Many timberframe homes today are built by companies that specialize in this type of construction. They build an entire house or just a section of the house. Some companies have architects or designers on staff to customize a design, while others have books of plans for consumers to choose from. Some companies will construct just a section of the house, such as the truss roof or frame, and others will complete the entire house. There are three ways to design a timberframe house:

Timberframe or post-and-beam company—Some companies will offer design assistance with designers or architects on staff. Others may just offer their portfolio of plans to choose from and some may be willing to customize.

Architect—If you choose to hire your own architect, choose one with an understanding of this type of construction, if possible. The architect should begin working early in the design process with the framing manufacturer to organize some of the more difficult aspects of the design such as plumbing and electrical components.

Published plans—People sometimes choose to purchase published plans from a magazine or book. Be aware that they will probably have to be altered for the particular site and personal preferences.

Construction

There are companies that will design, fabricate and construct the entire house. Some companies will design and fabricate the house and you assume responsibility for construction at the site; others will raise the frame and you must be responsible for the balance of the construction.

With most of these scenarios, the homeowner will need some work done by local contractors. Some people choose to be their own general contractors, hiring the plumbers, electricians and so on, while others will hire a general contractor to work with the timberframe company to complete the construction.

Design Considerations

There are many options for the homeowner to select when building a timberframe house. Besides selecting the type of wood, if they want a craftsman- or company-built home and the type of company they will choose, homeowners also have to select the type of roof, enclosures and siding they will use.

Roof

There are several different **truss** options. Talk with an architect or designer (who works with the manufacturer), and select the one you prefer and the one which will be most appropriate for the design of your house.

Enclosures

Post-and-beam/timberframe houses can be enclosed in many ways. The following are some of the most popular systems:

Structural insulated panels (SIPs)—This is a category of factory-produced panels that have a core of rigid insulation and two structural skins bonded to either side, as in a "sandwich." SIPs are commonly used independently to frame the roof, floor and walls of houses. They are also the most commonly used enclosures for timberframe/post-and-beam houses and are the base to which the siding and roofing are attached. In addition they augment the strength of the structure. Timberframe manufacturers often refer to their enclosures as stress skin panels. This term can refer to anything from a plywood and lumber panel with no insulation (which is one of the correct definitions of a stress skin panel), a

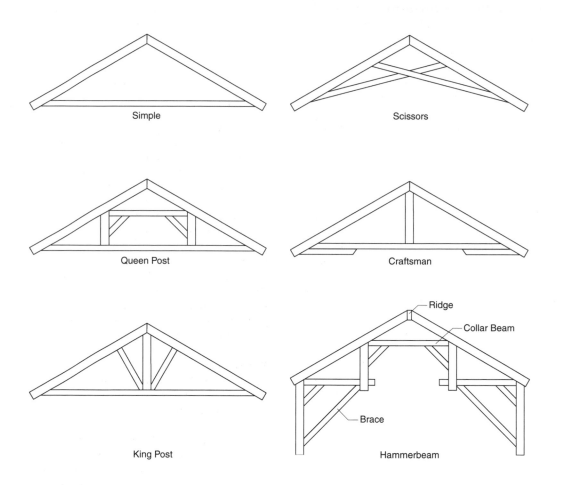

Simple

Scissors

Queen Post

Craftsman

King Post

Ridge

Collar Beam

Brace

Hammerbeam

Roof Trusses

curtain wall panel (a sandwich panel with one structural skin and one nonstructural skin bonded to an insulated core) or a structural insulated panel (with two structural skins bonded to a rigid foam insulation core). A stress skin panel can have either one or two plywood skins. Neither stress skin panels nor curtain wall panels will give the same strength to a timberframe structure as will a true SIP panel with two structural skins.

When SIPS are used as an enclosure for a framed house, an architect or engineer must evaluate the load requirements of the house to see if the proposed element will give enough support.

The interior of a timberframe house.

resources

For further information about SIPs, see Structural Insulated Panels on page 63 or check the Web site of the Structural Insulated Panel Association at www.sips.org or call 253-858-7472. Also check *Automated Builder* magazine at www.automatedbuilder.com or call 800-344-2537.

Concrete—Concrete has been used for home construction in Europe for many years where wood is not as available as it is in the United States and Canada. It is a tried and true method of construction. One of the concrete methods that has been used with timberframe/post-and-beam construction is Insulating Concrete Forms (ICF). This is a concrete form system, originally developed in Europe that creates permanent outer layers of rigid foam insulation over the reinforced concrete. It uses forms and spacers into which concrete is poured and cured. ICF systems have a high R-value, create consistent insulation because there are no studs, eliminate air infiltration and can reduce energy costs. ICF systems are resistant to rust, rot, fire and mold and can withstand harsh weather conditions such as hurricanes and tornadoes. Forms are lightweight and most can be set in place without the use of lifting devices. Forms are made of different components and are constructed differently depending on the

manufacturer; most are made of expanded polystyrene (EPS) or some other form of plastic, but Rastra is made of EPS and cement. Any siding can be attached to the concrete over the rigid insulation, but the easiest and most practical is a stucco finish. On the interior of the wall, drywall can be applied over the inner layer of rigid insulation. All companies' forms have different properties for density, R-value, compressive strength, cost and so on. Find an installer who is experienced with ICF systems and can help to select the proper one.

Thistlewood

resources

For further information about ICF and concrete construction, see page 70 or contact the Insulating Concrete Form Association at www.forms.org or call 888-864-4232.

Stick or stud-in construction—In traditional stick construction the studs are resting on the foundation wall, which generally carries the weight of the house. However, in post-and-beam or timber construction the posts and beams are carrying the weight of the house to the foundation. The external wall (which includes the interior finish wall, insulation, sheathing, siding, windows and doors) only has to support its own weight. A method of constructing the nonbearing walls is with studs. There are two methods used: (1) An exterior method where the walls are built around the timbers. This first system is very labor intensive, and (2) an infill method where studs are built between the timbers. If this second method is used, dried or standing-dead timbers should be used to avoid the settlement problems that can occur if the timbers dry and there is movement in the frame. With this method the timbers, which are the beauty of the frame and joinery, are mostly hidden.

Hanging wall construction—The studs are hanging from the rafter extensions of the roof assembly rather than sitting on a foundation. The timbers are on the interior of the house; going outside of the timbers is the interior wall finish (Sheetrock, plaster and so on), vapor barrier, studs, insulation (between the studs), sheathing and siding.

resources

Hanging wall construction information: *Fine Homebuilding* magazine (April 1982), "Hung Walls: An Effective Way to Insulate Post-and-Beam Buildings," by Pat Hennin.

Siding

Any siding can be used with timberframe construction: stucco, brick, stone and so on.

How the House Is Built

A foundation is laid in the same way it would be for a stick-built house, generally by a local contractor. The timberframe or post-and-beam company will factory-cut or fabricate the timbers, assemble them on-site and then raise the structure. The frame is usually raised with the help of a crane. The wall panels, stud walls or other selected enclosures are installed along with the windows and doors. Unless the timberframe/post-and-beam company will complete the house, the local contractor is called back to install the interior walls and siding.

In recent years there have been many companies popping up that build timberframe and post-and-beam houses. To find companies, check with the various publications and trade associations listed below.

resources

Information about timber framing or to locate a timberframe company: Timber-Frame Business Council, www.timberframe.org or 888-560-9251 or the Timber-Framers Guild, www.tfguild.org.

There are several publications that deal with timberframe homes:

Name of magazine	Web site	Telephone #	Issues per year
Timber-Frame Homes	www.timberframehomes.com	800-294-7006	4
Timber-Frame Homes Annual Buyer's Guide	www.timberframehomes.com	703-222-9411	1
Timber Framing Guild	www.tfguild.org		4
Timber Homes Illustrated	www.timberhomeexpo.com	212-262-2247	6
Timber Homes Illustrated Annual Buyer's Directory	www.timberhomeexpo.com	212-262-2247	1
Log & Timber Style	www.logandtimberstyle.com	800-266-5360	6

Timber Homes Illustrated runs the Log Home & Timber-Frame Expo in several cities each year. For further information on the locations and times, visit www.logexpo.com. Log Home Living Home Shows feature timberframe and log homes or visit www.timberframe-homes.com or call 800-782-1253.

Structural Insulated Panels (SIPs)

The first true SIPs were developed by Alden P. Dow when he built SIP Styrofoam houses in Midland, Michigan, in 1952. SIPs have become more popular in the last twenty years with the costs of lumber, labor and energy going up and the quality of the lumber going down. In the last five years there has been an increased demand for SIPs construction because of an interest in reducing construction time and an increased interest in energy efficiency.

SIPs are panels used structurally for walls, floors and roofs or used with other structural elements, such as timberframes and log homes. The panels are connected to each other in a variety of ways to form the shell of a house. All panels are not the same; the materials, the method of attachment and thicknesses vary by manufacturer. SIPs can support lateral loads, such as wind and impact, and axial loads, which are the loads coming down on a vertical panel that would otherwise be dealt with by studs, posts and rafters. SIPs are strong structural panels that are used in the place of stick construction.

Panels have a rigid foam core interior sandwiched between two exterior skins that are bonded to the core with resin and can be used for walls, floors or roofs. The core of rigid foam insulation is commonly EPS but polyisocyanurate or urethane are also used. On an equal R-value basis, EPS and the other foam materials are comparable in price. Polyisocyanurate has more insulating value per inch and is less flammable. Some municipalities, such as White Plains, New York,

will not allow the use of EPS because of its flammability; builders will then have to use panels with one of the other cores. The outer structural skins can be plywood, oriented strand board (OSB), waferboard (waferlike wood particles or flakes of wood bonded together with resin) or other engineered wood. Fiberglass and metals can be used on the exterior of SIPs instead of engineered wood for different architectural applications or various environmental conditions, such as in areas of high insect infestation or high moisture conditions. Panels come in a variety of size and thickness, depending on the structural requirements.

Major advantages to these systems are the reduction in construction time and their energy efficiency. The panels have an R-rating ranging from R-19 to R-45 (depending on the thickness of the foam) and form an uninterrupted insulating blanket around the house except for the areas of the doors, windows and corners. According to a test conducted by the government's Oak Ridge National Laboratories (ORNL), a properly sealed SIP room had fifteen times less air leakage than one that was stick-built and used 9 percent less heating energy. The panels are particularly useful for cathedral ceilings; they are a quick and efficient method of producing these structures. Most panels are light and can be lifted into place with a small crane. Although the materials are more expensive than those used in stick construction, labor is reduced because of the time saved in constructing with them. With cathedral ceilings there is about a 10 percent reduction in the cost of using a SIPs system over a stick-framing system.

It is helpful if architects and designers anticipate all design requirements as well as future electrical and plumbing needs to avoid additional work on-site. Wire chases can be installed in SIP products if necessary or required. Manufacturers may put plans into a computer-aided design (CAD) program and convert them to a SIPs system. The pieces are then precisely cut according to the computer specifications, and numbers are put on them so they can later be put together by the installer. Window and door openings are also cut to the specifications of the plan. Most companies include chase-ways (routed holes in the foam) in the interior of the panels to carry wiring. A technical representative can go to the construction site to train the crew on installing the units. Most manufacturers can recommend installers who specialize in SIPs production. Some companies have classes for homeowners, so they can learn to put together their own homes. People may buy the panels and even cut them out themselves. Then openings for windows and doors are cut on-site. Some contractors also choose to cut the panels themselves on-site, substantially increasing the construction time. Whenever possible, SIPs systems should be purchased in the local area to avoid expensive trucking costs.

Questions to ask:

- Will you need a crane to off-load or assemble the panels?
- Is borate-treated foam (prevents termites and other insects) offered?
- What kind of panel-joining system is used?
- What plastic is used? Some municipalities will not allow expanded polystyrene in SIPs because the EPS can melt in the case of a fire and render the panel nonstructural.
- What is the R-rating of the panels? Consider what your future plans will be.
- What is the composite nature of the panels, and what is the quality consistency of the particular manufacturer?

Advantages

- The composite action of the wood panels and the core in the panels helps them retain their shape and not shrink, decompose or disintegrate with age or weathering. They are very strong and durable.
- They reduce construction time substantially since the panels are pre-made in a factory.
- They help create maximum interior living space without the need for bearing walls.
- SIPs structures are airtight and are therefore resistant to mold and mildew growth behind walls.
- Structures may be enclosed in a short time, from a few hours to a few weeks, shortening the time necessary for a construction loan.
- They are less flammable than conventional stick structures.
- SIPs are made with polystyrene or polyisocyanurate, which is a by-product of the petroleum industry and OSB, an engineered wood made from the wood chips created during the milling of lumber, which is often considered waste.
- Because SIPs systems are a continuous solid

A house built with structural insulated panels.

Structural Insulated Panel Association

envelope around a structure, without studs, sills and headers, they are more energy efficient. In stick-built houses approximately 20 to 30 percent of the walls are studs, sills and headers, which are noninsulated. In panelized structures there are no breaks except for windows and doors, cutting down on heating and cooling costs. According to a study by the government's Oak Ridge National Laboratories (ORNL), SIPs outperform stick construction because there are no breaks in the insulation. They perform at 97 percent of their stated R-value, only losing 3 percent to nails, seams, splines and so on. There are three issues to consider when evaluating the energy efficiency of a house: system efficiency or system R-value, insulation material and how many windows and doors there are and what type—this will significantly add or detract from a house's energy efficiency.

Disadvantages

- Once the design is complete it is more difficult to make changes.
- It is difficult to foresee unknown site conditions that affect the design.
- It is important to work with an architect and general contractor who are experienced in working with panelized systems because plans must be precise. Some design elements, such as floor-to-ceiling glass walls, are difficult to include without other structural components.
- It is more difficult to change wiring or to add wiring that is not included in the initial plan.
- It may be expensive to ship the panels if the manufacturer is at a distance.
- In a fire, the EPS core of the SIP can melt. When this happens the panel is no longer structural.

resources

Information about SIPs: Structural Insulated Panel Association, www.sips.org or call 253-858-7472;
or *Automated Builder* magazine, www.automated-builder.com or call 800-344-2537.

Strawbale Construction

Strawbale construction has been used for homes in this country since the early 1900s by early settlers in the Nebraska sand hills, when they used their horse-powered baling machines to create blocks that were inexpensive and easily available. For many years strawbale construction fell out of favor as the railroad came through Nebraska and other areas, transporting timber and bricks; the settlers began to use other materials to build their homes. There has been a recent revival of the use of strawbale because of our concern for energy efficiency and the effective use of natural resources; it reduces the demand for timber in half. Straw is an excellent insulator and is a resource that has been generally considered waste, burned in the fields after the grain (from such crops as wheat, oats, rice, barley, rye and flax) has been extracted. When people think about strawbale they often consider it an alternate, boxy-type of construction; today, however, there are many examples of sophisticated, beautiful homes built in a variety of styles. Some of the concerns people have about strawbale construction are the fear of its flammability and the possibility that it will be damaged by insects and rodents. In fact, with proper construction neither of these are hazards. The greatest challenge is keeping the bales dry, which can also be overcome with proper care and construction. The interior and exterior walls can be covered with stucco or plaster.

Strawbale can be used as a load-bearing system (the strawbales act as structural members and distribute the load, supporting the weight of the roof) or as infill (straw bales are used to fill in between the structural members) as in a post-and-beam structure. The straw bales are built on a foundation, end to end and with overlapping joints on consecutive rows. The bales are secured with wire or rope to provide stability. Openings for windows and doors are incorporated into the structure where they are required with lintels to distribute the loads imposed by the roof. The straw will compress when the full weight of the roof is applied. The walls are then sometimes covered with wire mesh and stucco to provide a weather-tight finish. Straw can also be transformed into a wood-like product by compressing it under high temperatures that bond the straw fibers together, sometimes without adhesives. To create a stronger panel, the straw board can be sandwiched between two pieces of OSB. Some of these panels, if very large and dense, can be heavy, requiring the use of a crane for installation. There are several recent books with beautiful examples of the variation in strawbale construction. Check the books in the reference section and the Web sites listed below.

Advantages

- Straw is an inexpensive commodity although contractor construction can be expensive.
- It is an excellent insulator, reducing the cost of heating and cooling.
- Less timber is required, reducing the demand for natural resources.
- With bales weighing between 50 to 90 pounds, straw is easy to work with.
- It has sound-absorbing qualities.
- Strawbale construction, when properly completed, is fire resistant. A plastered strawbale wall has a two-hour fire resistance.
- Strawbale walls provide excellent thermal insulation.
- Straw has little nutritional value to support a pest population.
- Strawbale homes require minimum maintenance.
- Strawbale construction allows for a great deal of flexibility and creativity in design.
- Straw is an annually renewable product.

Catherine Wanek

An Adirondack-style strawbale home.

Disadvantages

- Once the straw is baled it must be kept dry until it has a final protective finish applied.
- Finding professionals to build with straw bales may be difficult in some areas of the country.
- Appropriate bales can be difficult to locate.
- Walls must be thicker than for most other types of construction.
- Straw should not be used in flood zones.
- Some states have not granted approval for strawbale construction but have approved infill-type construction more so than for the load-bearing type.

resources

Information about strawbale construction: California Straw Building Association (CASBA), www.strawbuilding.org; MidAmerica Straw Building Association (MASBA), www.thelast-straw.org/sban; or the Straw Bale Association of Texas, www.greenbuilder.com/sbat; or *The Last Straw* journal at www.thelaststraw.org.

Panelized Systems

According to the Building Systems Council of the National Association of Home Builders, home panelization is one of the fastest growing segments of residential new construction. It is a type of construction with sections or components of a house manufactured in a factory and then assembled on-site. The manufacturer ships the panels or materials cut to size with several possible levels of completeness from factory-cut parts to entire sections with the siding, and sometimes the drywall, attached. Packages are available in different levels of completeness. Some come with just the shell while others include all components, including appliances. Systems usually include everything except the foundation, wall panels, floor decks, roof and floor trusses or with just some of these components included.

Panels are often produced in an automated factory, transferring panel-cutting instructions from CAD drawings. Parts are produced according to exact specifications. Pieces are then coded to indicate step-by-step instructions for assembling the parts. In some cases components can be constructed in a few weeks and the house completed in two to three months. Some companies offer a selection of floor plans; they may or may not alter plans to meet personal preferences. Some companies will produce custom homes designed by an in-house designer or an independent architect. A manufacturer's involvement can include delivering all parts to be installed by a general contractor, a crane and a small crew to work with the general contractor in completing the frame, providing and supplying all the materials and labor to complete the house.

There are a variety of materials used for panelized construction. Some companies use steel framing instead of wood, and they use a variety of skins, including OSB, plywood, light-gauge steel and fiberglass. A variety of companies use different materials and methods of construction.

Some components can be very large, requiring a crane to set them in place; other companies ship components that are smaller in scale and may not require a crane for installation. Components may come "closed," which includes windows,

wiring, plumbing, insulation and drywall completed at the factory—but these are not commonly used today. More often components are "open," without the insulation, wiring, plumbing and drywall. These items are installed on the job site to comply with local building codes that require inspection before walls are closed.

Usually the site work (utilities, sanitary and storm drainage, grading and landscaping), foundation and finishing work are done by an outside contractor and the home package constructed by the manufacturer. Panelized systems are widely used today because they reduce construction time, reduce the cost of labor and

A panelized house under construction.

This completed panelized house was made water-tight in a few days.

Wausau Homes

Wausau Homes

A circular house, another type of panelized home.

Deltec Homes

materials, increase design flexibility and have many practical applications.

Questions to ask concerning panelized systems manufacturers:

- What level of detail will the company include in the design?
- How much can the plans be altered to meet personal needs?
- How knowledgeable is the sales representative?

There was a study done in 1996 called Framing the American Dream by the Wood Truss Council of America in cooperation with the Building Systems Council of the NAHB, wherein two homes were constructed, one by stick construction and the other with a panelized system. Some of the results of that study are included in the following section.

Advantages

- There is less on-site labor required for panelized houses than for traditional stick construction. According to the above-mentioned study, on-site man-hours were less than half.

- After the materials are delivered to the site, a house may be watertight in a few days to a week and complete in sixty to ninety days. Time is not wasted because of poor weather conditions. According to the above study there was approximately a 75 percent reduction in man-hours to frame the panelized system.
- Fewer materials are wasted since they are systematically cut in a secure environment with less waste removal as well. Panelized manufacturers predetermine the best use of the materials to limit waste. According to the above study there was a 25 percent reduction in the amount of lumber used in the panelized construction and about a 75 percent reduction in scrap generated. Virtually all the material and all of the individual components have a specific location to be used in the construction of the building. Very little waste product is generated on-site and therefore scrap cleanup and collection time are substantially reduced.
- Because the house is completed faster, there is a savings on the financing.

- Many companies offer longer warranties than those given on traditional stick houses.
- It is easier to stay on budget because costs are known up front. On-site changes are possible but should always be made through the change order process so cost effects will be known and agreed upon before construction changes are made. Change orders can be one of the biggest expenses people can have on custom homes. Complete and thorough Building Construction Design Documents (plans and specifications) will generally reduce the number of site changes required and allow for more accurate initial bidding of the contract.
- Components are produced in a factory with a professional crew in a controlled environment. Quality control and material usage is more easily monitored and established standards are met.
- A panel company (or any manufacturer of homes) buys lumber by either the tractor trailer or train car load. This is cost savings and gives the manufacturer the ability to be very selective about the wood they receive. Because the components are built in the factory, the materials are kept dry and then built to very square and close tolerances because they are built in manufacturing jigs.
- Walls are almost always fully sheathed with plywood or OSB. This adds rigidity to the panels and keeps them from racking (getting out of square during transportation and erection). Many of today's stick-built homes only have (from out to in) siding, foam board, insulation and drywall.

Disadvantages
- Some people like to have the opportunity to make changes as they see the house going up. It is more difficult to do this since all parts may have been precut and preassembled.
- It can be costly to ship components out of

the regional area. However, this is rarely an issue.
- Some local architectural review boards may restrict the use of manufactured homes in their area. But factory-built components see very little of the prejudice that may be inflicted upon modular and mobile home construction. Most component manufacturers offer manufacturing plant tours to consumers, builders, code officials and administrators, and the specifying community (architects and engineers) to showcase the strengths and benefits of factory-built components. The efficient use of natural resources to control quality to control cost speaks well for factory-built components.

resources

The Building Systems Council of the National Association of Home Builders, www.nahb.-org/buildingsystems and *Building Systems Magazine*—subscriptions can be ordered by contacting the circulation manager at tsaylor@nb.net.

Concrete Homes

The use of concrete for residential housing is on the rise. According to the Portland Cement Association, approximately 14 percent of all houses today are built out of concrete. It has been used in Europe for many years because of the shortage of available trees for timber but is a relatively new trend for residential use in this country. Any exterior siding can be used with concrete on any style house. Many of the houses built today are made of concrete, and it would be difficult to differentiate them from stick-constructed houses. In the United States in 1844 the first recorded house with above-ground concrete walls belonged to an innkeeper, William Goodrich, who built his house out of concrete to protect himself from fire and Indian attacks. Today

Rastra

Rastra

A house under construction with ICF.

A completed house built with ICF.

ness and intrinsic insulation, reducing the energy needed by 30 to 40 percent—lowering heating and cooling costs.

- Concrete can reduce sound transmission.
- The upkeep on concrete is minimal.
- Most concrete systems can be completed with a variety of interior and exterior finishes, as well as a variety of shapes.
- The savings on energy and reduced insurance premium costs given on concrete homes will reduce monthly carrying costs.
- There is a significant reduction in wood products.

Disadvantages

- An experienced carpenter with some concrete experience is required on the job to make sure that the concrete is properly mixed, poured and **vibrated.**
- Most concrete construction will be more expensive than stick construction. (It may, however, be cost efficient in the long run because of its durability and energy savings.)
- Some local code officials may need to be educated about the particular type of concrete system you propose to use before giving their approval. Check with your local building office before selecting such a system.

It is best to work with an architect who is experienced in working with concrete to make the construction go more smoothly and effectively. Note: There are six types of concrete construction that can be used. This decision should be made with the architect and be dependent on location, availability of able contractors and the style of the house.

Insulated Concrete Form (ICF)

This technology began in Europe in the 1940s but did not become popular in North America until the 1990s. This is a growing segment of the residential market for wall systems and foundations. ICFs are pre-formed, insulated

this structure is still standing and is a museum in Milton, Wisconsin. Frank Lloyd Wright used concrete slabs for his Fallingwaters house in Bear Run, Pennsylvania, completed in 1937. Wright was an advocate for the use of concrete for home construction because of its support and design possibilities.

Advantages

- Some insurance companies are offering a discount on insurance rates for concrete homes.
- Rot, rust and termites will not develop.
- Concrete can survive high-force winds from hurricanes and tornadoes. With reinforcement it can survive earthquakes as well.
- Concrete construction is energy efficient because of its thermal mass, overall airtight-

expanded polystyrene (EPS) or extruded poly-styrene (Styrofoam) forms, either interlocking blocks or separate panels connected with plastic or metal ties. Most forms provide 2 inches of insulation on both faces of the concrete wall, providing excellent insulation. These forms are stacked by hand to form walls, and reinforcing steel (or rebar) is inserted horizontally and verti-cally inside the forms, then clamped or glued for temporary support. Ready-mixed concrete is pumped in the hollow cavities. Windows and doors are cut on-site before the forms are filled. The forms are left in place as a permanent part of the wall assembly. The polystyrene functions as the insulation, and the concrete functions as the structure. In addition to providing insulation, ICFs provide a sound barrier and a backing for siding on the outside and drywall on the inside. Wall assemblies can have an R-40 or R-50 for thermal performance and can accept any material on the interior and exterior walls. These systems can be flat systems (a continuous thickness of concrete), grid systems (a waffle pattern where the concrete is thick in some areas) or post-and-beam systems (beams and columns of concrete encapsulated in foam insulation). ICF systems can also be available as prefabricated wall segments that may already include part of the reinforce-ment and window frames. These systems are fast to erect if builders are experienced with this type of system. A skilled mason or carpenter is required on-site to supervise. Because the forms have a minimum of 2 inches of insulation on both sides, concrete can be poured even in sub-freezing conditions. Once the walls are complete, channels are cut in the insulation with electric hot knives for cables, wires, and hot and cold water lines. There are several types of ICF systems:

Panel systems—Panels usually measure 1 to 4 inches high and 8 to 12 inches long.

Plank systems—These are similar to panel systems but the planks are 1 to 2 feet high and 4 to 8 feet long with a slightly different assembly. There are many companies that produce this type of system.

Interlocking block system—These usually run 8 to 16 inches high and 16 inches to 4 feet long.

EPS and concrete system—This system uses recycled plastic material (such as extended polystyrene pulverized into beads or pellets) that is mixed with concrete in the factory and then cast into a panelized form. On-site it will receive the required reinforcing rods and Ready mix cement in the panel's voids. The use of re-cycled plastic makes this system environmentally friendly. The precast individually long modules are available in thicknesses from 8 1/2 to 14 inches, depending on the amount of insulation.

resources

EPS and concrete system: Rastra, www.ras-tra.com or call 877-935-3545.

ICF information: Insulating Concrete Form Association, www.forms.org or call 888-864-4232. Or contact the Concrete Homes Helpline at 888-333-4840.

Concrete Masonry

This is one of the oldest concrete systems. The blocks today are lighter, have improved insulation and are more energy efficient. They can have a variety of colors and textures (fluted, ribbed, scored, ground face, polished, sand-blasted, striated and glazed finishes). Concrete blocks have three types of insulation:

Interior insulation—These are the most popular and generally least expensive blocks. They provide better moisture protection and an attractive appearance. Water-repellent material is incorporated into the blocks during produc-tion, and additional sealer and flashing can be applied on-site.

Tierra Concrete Homes, Inc.

A beautiful example of a tilt-up constructed house.

Exterior insulation— Finishes on the block can simulate stucco or stone and are placed over rigid foam insulation mounted on the outside of the blocks. The thickness of the insulation can be adjusted by the builder to construct a more insulated house.

In-block insulation—The insulation is between the interior and exterior surfaces. There are three types of in-block insulation:

Cavity-insulated block—The insulation is installed as a piece of rigid foam inserted into block cavities at the factory; a material is poured into the cavities after installation or an expanding foam is sprayed into the cavities during construction. This system has a moderate R-value and is most suited to climates in the South.

Pre-insulated block—Insulation is mixed into the block while it is being manufactured. These blocks are lightweight, easier to cut and have a moderate R-rating, making them suitable for use in the North.

Mortarless insulated block—Foam inserts are inserted in the cavities and a coat of bonding cement is applied inside and outside. The blocks have a flat, finished look and are resistant to moisture.

resources

For further information, contact the National Concrete Masonry Association (NCMA) at www.ncma.org or 703-713-1900.

Removable Forms

This type of form is more likely to be used for condominiums or home developments because the forms can be reused up to 3,000 times. Removable forms are being used for single-family homes but are more apt to be used for home developments.

resources

Removable forms information: Concrete Homes Council (CHC), www.concretehomes-council.org or call 319-895-0761, and the Concrete Foundations Association (CFA), www.cfawalls.org or call 319-895-6940.

Precast Concrete Houses

This is a method of precasting and curing the concrete parts of a house in a manufacturing facility and then shipping the modules to the site for installation. The facility is a controlled environment where all variables such as mix design, weather conditions and so on can be monitored to create a quality product. Time is saved by producing the parts when they are needed, with great flexibility for any size and shape. These

E-Crete, LLC

An adobe-style house built with Autoclaved Aerated Concrete (AAC) blocks.

parts can be used for floors, roof deck systems and also wall panels. They can be cast 300 to 600 feet long and then cut to custom size and shape, with windows and doors already framed. Electrical conduits and plumbing can also be precast into the panels.

resources

Precast concrete information: National Precast Concrete Association (NPCA), www.pre-cast.org or 800-366-7731 and the Precast/Prestressed Concrete Institute (PCI), www.pci.org or 312-786-0300.

Tilt up

This method of production has been used for industrial building production for about 100 years but has only recently been used for some home construction. Like precast-type slabs, these are load-bearing reinforced concrete wall panels that are poured on-site in a horizontal form. They are then tilted up to a vertical position and moved into place with mobile cranes. Colors can be added to the mix and textures produced in a variety of patterns (stone, brick, wood grains and so on). This is a fast method of construction but one that is rarely used for custom homes.

resources

For further information on tilt-up concrete, contact the Tilt-Up Concrete Association (TCA) at www.tilt-up.org or 319-895-6911.

Autoclaved Aerated Concrete (AAC)

AAC was first developed in Sweden by the Ytong Company in 1929 as a material for building homes and commercial buildings. In the United States this is a fairly new building material with new products currently under development. Aluminum powder is added to the concrete mixture, molded into shapes (blocks or panels) and baked in a special oven that steam cures the concrete under pressure. A cellular block is produced that weighs a fifth of conventional concrete of the same size. The end result is a building material that is very lightweight and easily fabricated with conventional woodworking tools, making construction less strenuous. The block is assembled using thin-set mortar, forming walls that are very strong, have excellent thermal insulation and greatly reduced noise transfer. Mortar joints are one-sixteenth of an inch, which is less than for masonry blocks. AAC is resistant to mold, rot and infestation, and because heat transfers slowly through this material, it is energy efficient, having an **Underwriters Laboratories** (UL) classification of four-hour fire rating. AAC construction is free of volatile organic compounds **(VOCs)** and fiberglass fibers, making it an option for the severely allergic. These precast units are used for interior and exterior walls.

resources

Autoclaved Aerated Concrete information: Aerated Concrete Corporation of America, www.acco-aac.com or Autoclaved Aerated Concrete Products Association, www.aacpa.org.

Concrete construction: Portland Cement Association (PCA), www.concretehomes.com or call 888-333-4840; the Cement Association of Canada, www.cpca.ca or call 613-236-9471; the Environmental Council of Concrete Organizations, www.ecco.org; and the American Concrete Institute (ACI), www.aci-int.net or 248-848-3700.

Geodesic Dome

Geodesic domes were invented in 1947 by R. Buckminster Fuller, an inventor and engineer, as a means of providing low-cost shelter that was in cooperation with nature. He developed this spherical, geometric, prefabricated design with the idea of improving housing options. These are usually factory-produced triangular networks that provide a self-supporting structure requiring no internal structural supports. This type of structure allows for maximum flexible use of internal space. It is like the timberframe structure because there are no

interior bearing walls, and the designer is free to use any interior configuration.

Design—Most of the companies that sell geodesic domes will offer standard floor plans that they will adapt to personal needs and preferences, or an architect can be employed to aid in the design.

Cost—The cost will be dependent on the site, size of the dome, finishing materials used and local labor costs. The cost of a contracted geodesic dome with comparable materials will generally run about 10 to 15 percent below that of a conventional house.

Construction—Some companies will design the home and also construct the entire project, while others will design the home and supply the materials for the shell of the dome (structural framework, "skin" or panels, skylights, extension kits and special hardware) to be constructed by the homeowner or local contractor. Some companies can offer a list of qualified contractors in the local area. Most domes are built with panelized materials that are precut in a factory. Any foundations that are used for conventional homes can be used for domes, with basements an option. The windows and doors used for domes are also the same as those used for conventional houses. Some companies will provide special triangular windows made specifically for dome construction.

Advantages
• They can withstand tornadoes, hurricanes and earthquakes better than conventional rectangular homes.

Geodesic domes can be very simple or more elaborate, such as this one.

Some of the manufacturers of geodesic domes:

Albata Geodesics	http://domebuilder.wecre8.com/index.htm	
Composite Geodesic Domes	www.compgeodome.com	413-222-6235
Natural Spaces Domes	www.naturalspacesdomes.com	800 733 7107
Oregon Dome, Inc.	www.domes.com	800-572-8943
Timberline Geodesics	www.domehome.com	800-366-3466

- They are energy efficient with less roof and wall area for air to penetrate, reducing heating and cooling costs. According to a study in 1986 by the National Dome Council of the NAHB, typical dome houses require less insulation than rectilinear homes to achieve energy efficiency, thereby enabling the builder to use insulation with a lower R-value than would be needed with typical rectilinear houses. If the same insulation was used, the house would have reduced energy costs.
- Fewer building materials are used than with a rectangular structure of the same floor space and volume. This is both good for the environment and cost reducing in terms of materials.
- Some of the construction can be done by unskilled people. The foundations and roofing, however, require qualified professionals.
- The construction of the dome shell takes far less time than a conventional frame, which saves on labor costs.
- Floor plans can be open and flexible, without concerns for bearing walls.
- Most of the companies that sell geodesic domes will offer standard floor plans that they will adapt to personal needs and preferences, or an architect can be employed to aid in the design. It is easy to add extensions to the dome when the need arises, if the dome is designed with this option in mind. This also allows the house to be built in stages.
- The cost will be dependent on the site, size of the dome, finishing materials used and local labor costs. The cost of a contracted geodesic dome will generally run about 10 to 15 percent below that of a conventional house.

Disadvantages
- Kits often have to be shipped long distances, which adds to the expense of the project.
- It may be more difficult to get a mortgage on geodesic domes because getting comparables is more challenging.
- Some room proportions can be awkward because of the round shape.

resources

For information about many of these systems, check with the Building Systems Councils of the National Association of Home Builders at www.buildingsystems.org.

Umicore Building Products USA/makers of VM Zinc

Roofing

Roofing is one of those construction items that does not have a lot of conversational appeal. It is not easy to investigate, and so many people will go with the roofing recommendation of their architect or builder without learning anything about it. There are, however, many options worth considering. You may want to stay with the asphalt-type roofing that you are familiar with, but consider the alternatives before making a decision. The roofing industry has developed a host of innovations and materials that are worth consideration.

Getting a good roof is more dependent on getting a qualified contractor than even selecting the right materials. Although the difference in materials may make some difference in aesthetics and durability, the contractor influences the outcome throughout the roof's life. A good contractor is usually a member of state and sometimes national roofing contractors' organizations and has been in business for five or more years. A contractor should have liability and workers' compensation insurance and be licensed where required. Most good roofers are authorized or certified by the roofing materials manufacturer; they will have that authorization prominently displayed in their offices and often in their advertising. They will be knowledgeable in the products they install and will be able to give good reasons as to why they install the products they are recommending.

If possible, get references on any contractor you are considering hiring.

Types of Roofs

A listing of the types of roofs and parts of the roof are included, so when you have a roofing discussion with a professional you will have a better idea of the terminology. There are six basic styles of roofs. Several of these are often combined on the same house.

Gable roof—This slopes on two sides and forms a triangular wall at each end. The two slopes meet on the horizontal upper edge of the roof called the **"ridge."** The **eaves** are the horizontal lower edges of the slopes, and the **rakes** are the sloping cdgcs that frame the gable.

Hip roof—This has slopes and eaves on four sides.

Low-slope roof—A roof that has a slope from 0 to 14 degrees.

Shed roof (lean-to)—This has a single slope.

Gambrel roof—A gable roof with a steep lower slope and a flatter upper slope on each side of the ridge.

Mansard roof—This has two steep slopes on the bottom and two gentle slopes on each of its four sides with an almost flat top—a gambrel roof with hips.

Roof Parts

Flashing—These are metal accessories used for water shedding where there are intersections and projections in a roof. It is used on joints around a projection, seams where roof slopes meet and where a roof meets a wall. It can be in the form of a collar that fits around vent pipes, a wide strip that runs the length of a valley, a double-layer pattern (called counter and base flashing) or at the seams where roof slopes meet walls or chimneys. Flashing is perhaps the most important component in a roofing system. Poorly fabricated or installed flashing voids the manufacturer's warranty on the roofing material. In addition, there are issues of chemical compatibility of various flashing materials and specific roofing materials. Flashing is often metal but can be made from rubber-like and composite materials.

Roof decking—This is the wood **substrate,** connected to rafters, to which the roofing materials are applied. It is also referred to as **"sheathing."** Plywood is the most commonly used material, but other materials can be used including boards and **OSB.** The deck can be any number of structural materials such as concrete or steel.

Roof insulation—The thermal-resistant materials used to reduce heat gain and cooled air-flow out of the house.

Soffit—The horizontal trim applied to the underside of the eave overhang.

Fascia—A flat board enclosing the exterior ends of the rafters and providing a finished trim for the eaves of the roof.

Rake—The extension of a gable beyond the end of the house.

Ridge—The horizontal upper edge of the roof where the two sides meet.

Eaves—The horizontal edge of a roof that overhangs the outside wall.

Underlayment, or felt—A thin layer of material made of glass fibers (glass-fiber felts), vegetable fibers (organic felts) and asphalt coating placed over the substrate to provide a separator

Roof Styles

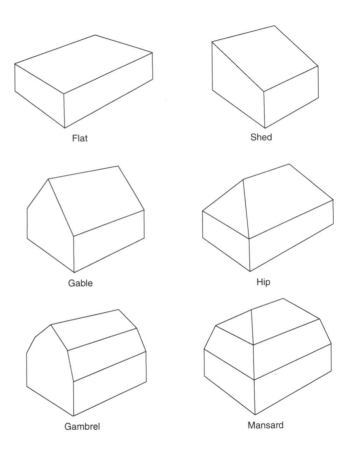

Flat

Shed

Gable

Hip

Gambrel

Mansard

for the finish roofing. The underlayment serves to keep the building dry while the building shingles are installed, and it separates the roofing from the decking to accommodate the difference in expansion and contraction of the two materials.

Vapor retarder—A material controlling water vapor transmission through walls or other construction elements.

Roof membrane, or covering—The waterproofing material chosen to cover the roof.

Surfacing—Used on **low-pitched** roofs to

protect the roofing material from sunlight and weather exposure and, depending on the surfacing used, may offer protection against fire and impact resistance and aesthetic appeal.

Overhang—The part of the roof that projects beyond the house to carry rainwater away from the siding and foundation.

Rain gutters—These usually hang from the eaves and fascia and carry water away from the house.

Snow guards—Used in colder climates and mounted above the eaves, preventing frozen snow from sliding off the roof in sheets.

Roof Accessories

Dormers—Roof projections designed to house vertical windows.

Ridge vents—Provide a continuous opening along the ridgeline for the flow of air in and out of the attic space. Ridge vents require eave and soffit vents.

Gable vents—These are mounted high in end walls and also provide a means for venting air into and from the attic. They need to be in pairs.

Soffit vents—Positioned at the eave of the roof and allow outside air to move into and out of the attic, helping to equalize the attic with the outside air. (See ridge vents.)

Turbine vents—When wind is driven from any direction the turbine spins and the reduced air pressure in the unit draws the hot, humid air from the attic. Another vent opening is needed in order to allow air movement.

Cupolas—A small structure on top of a roof that usually incorporates a weather vane; this can be decorative and a ventilation source.

Skylight—A window in a roof.

Roof vents—A static vent that is set into the slope of the roof.

Stack vent—Usually called a "plumbing vent," it is a three- or four-inch pipe that releases gases from the plumbing system. Usually the vent rises from one of the main slopes near the ridge. ("Stack" is an older term associated with clay pipes.)

Chimneys—May be set into the roof slope or built into a gable wall.

When selecting roofing material, consider the slope and drainage of the roof. Certain materials require minimum roof **pitch.** Pitch is the angle of inclination that a roof makes with the horizon, measured in inches of rise per foot of run. A low-slope roof is defined by the National Roofing Contractors Association **(NRCA)** as any roof at or less than 3/12 pitch (14 degrees); a steep-slope roof is any roof greater than 3/12 pitch (14 degrees). A gentle-sloped roof may get more ponding of water and slower runoff. A steep-pitched roof

Anatomy of a Roof

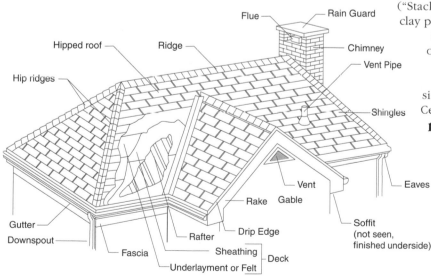

Flue — Rain Guard

Hipped roof — Ridge — Chimney

Hip ridges — Vent Pipe

Shingles

Gutter — Vent — Eaves

Downspout — Rake — Gable

Fascia — Rafter — Drip Edge — Soffit (not seen, finished underside)

Sheathing — Deck

Underlayment or Felt

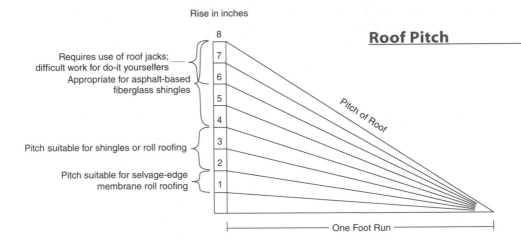

Rise in inches

Roof Pitch

Requires use of roof jacks; difficult work for do-it yourselfers

Appropriate for asphalt-based fiberglass shingles

Pitch of Roof

Pitch suitable for shingles or roll roofing

Pitch suitable for selvage-edge membrane roll roofing

8
7
6
5
4
3
2
1

One Foot Run

should have no ponding, less direct sunlight than a gentle-sloped roof and less drag by the runoff of water, allowing less granule loss. What works with one pitch may not work for another. Adequate drainage will also be necessary. The NRCA specifies that a good roof design is one where there is no ponding water forty-eight hours after rainfall under conditions that are conducive to drying.

Other Roofing Considerations

Your budget—Consider how much you would like to spend on roofing. Is a beautiful roof a priority in the overall design of the house? Would you prefer an extra bathroom or fireplace to a more expensive roofing material? You can check the cost of various roofing materials in the *R. S. Means Estimating Guides,* which are standard guides used by professionals with schedules for labor and materials, adjusted by location. You can find the most up-to-date books at libraries or at www.rsmeans.com.

Aesthetics—Choose a roof that you will enjoy looking at. In some cases the roof is totally

out of view so it's less important, but in most cases the roof will be seen. Getting the look that not only fits the style of the house but one you will like to look at is important. It is now possible to get a particular look from the multitude of available materials.

Location of the house—This will have an effect on the cost of various materials. In the Southwest, for example, where terra-cotta is more prevalent, a terra-cotta roof may cost substantially less than it would in the Northeast, where the material is less prevalent.

Local code requirements—All urban and many suburban areas of the country have fire districts and classification requirements for roofing. Areas in California, for example, do not allow wood roofing even if it is treated because of the vulnerability to fire. Check with the local building office before making a decision about roofing materials, and only use products approved by the local building code jurisdiction.

Style of the house—Certain house styles look best with particular style roofs and roofing materials. Mediterranean-style homes, for example, look particularly attractive with a tile roof.

Styles in adjoining homes—You may want to consider what types of styles are on neighboring roofs, if you don't want your home to stick out unnecessarily.

Climate of the house's location—Consider the climate, wind, proximity to the sea and humidity of the location of the house. Wet climates can cause wood to rot if it's untreated. In windy places three-tab shingles may suffer wind uplift damage. Salt air can damage certain types of metal roofing.

Earthquake locations—Consider whether the roof may have to endure earthquake conditions. Certain materials, such as **stone-coated steel**, are more apt to endure the movement caused by an earthquake.

How long you plan to own your home—Certain materials such as tile or slate will last for a lifetime. If you plan to live in your house for a very long time you may want to consider a material that is long lasting and comes with a long warranty. If you plan to live in your house for a short time you may want to consider an inexpensive material with a shorter warranty.

Warranty—Find out how long the roofing is warranted. Warranties differ among the various materials and manufacturers, as well as by quality within each category. Find out what is covered under the warranty. Some are dependent on the quality of the installation. Ask about the limitations and exceptions on the warranty. Roofing manufacturers require, as a condition of the warranty, that their roofing material be installed by roofing contractors who are trained and certified by the manufacturer.

Special requirements—Make sure that the roof you select will meet all of your special requirements. If, for example, you need something special such as a roof that serves as a walking deck, contact the manufacturer to make sure the product being considered will serve the application.

Fire classification of roofing material—As with many other materials used in the home, roofing materials are tested by Underwriters Laboratories (UL) for their properties when exposed to fire. Some municipalities require a particular fire rating for houses built in their area. Class A labeling means the material is effective against severe fire exposure; class B is effective against moderate exposure; class C will resist only slight exposure. Often roofs are installed over one or more existing roofs. The rating of the resulting roof will then be determined not only by the new roof but by the one or two underneath. The type of decking installed beneath the roofing material will also affect the rating of the roof. Before installing a secondary roof you should consult with a professional to determine what its effect will be on the fire rating, the chemical compatibility, and structural and building code issues.

Color—Certain materials are better at absorbing or repelling the heat of the sun. A dark roof will attract heat and should generally be used in areas where keeping the house warm is a concern. A lighter roof will reflect heat. In a location where keeping the house cool is a bigger concern, a light-colored roof should be considered.

Available installers—The durability of the roof will be dependent on the materials used and the quality of the installation. Before selecting a particular material, make sure the available installer is certified by the manufacturer to install their roofing material. Only accept for review original certificates of fitness; otherwise call the manufacturer to verify.

Maintenance—Consider how much maintenance you are willing to do or have done on the roof. Wood roofs, for example, require periodic cleaning and refinishing. Roofing manufacturers publish maintenance manuals.

Noise generated by material—Some types of metal may be noisy unless they are properly insulated and laid solidly to the deck.

Ecology—There are some new eco-friendly products on the market that, although more expensive, may be a reflection of the homeowner's values. There are several roofing types now available that are made from recycled materials. Other options are wood, which is a replaceable commodity that breaks down easily and goes back into the soil. Some metals are recyclable—it is said that most **copper** used today is 75 percent recycled. Asphalt takes many years to break down in the landfill.

Hints for Upgrading Roofs

Roofs for new buildings are generally designed, detailed and specified by the architect. When it is time to replace or upgrade a roof, besides consulting with an architect, consider the following:

Make sure that proper ventilation will be incorporated, upgraded or maintained in the construction of the roof—this will prolong the life of the roofing material and lower energy costs. It will help to make sure that the roofing material will dry properly. Insufficient ventilation will cause damage to the sheathing, rafters and insulation. Roof venting must be continuous at all times, regardless of the season.

Gravity ventilation is a system of vents in the roof which continuously equalizes the relative humidity of the air in the attic with the outside air. This is achieved with the proper use of turbine vents, **power ventilators, roofline louvers,** cupolas, ridge vents, gable vents, and vent inserts for flat roofs.

Power ventilators are another method that can continuously vent the air spaces in a roof structure. A **whole-house ventilating fan** installed in an attic floor, for example, draws cool air from open windows and vents in lower floors, pulls the air to the attic and forces it out through attic vents. **Power attic exhaust fans** are placed in ceiling vents and help to reduce the load on air-conditioning. These fans are primarily intended for summer conditions and do not necessarily do the required venting during the winter.

Most roofs today utilize a gravity or **cold-roof system** in which a ventilating air channel is created with intake and outlet vents at the soffit

GAF Materials Corporation

A home with fiberglass asphalt shingles that replicate a slate look.

and ridge of the roof. The space created by this construction is called "dead airspace." The purpose of venting the dead airspace of the roof structure is to prevent condensation of water vapor. As stated above, the venting equalizes the relative humidity (the water vapor content at a specific temperature) of the dead air to the outside air and thereby prevents condensation. The condensation can saturate insulation and rot the insulation or leak through the ceiling and walls. In Southern climates the almost continuous use of air-conditioning can be a source of condensation, which must be designed for in a way that is different in the northern states. An architect should be consulted in working out a proper system.

Vapor barriers or retarders, in addition to roof venting, are required in order to prevent water vapor transmitting into the insulation and therefore lowering the **R-value** and causing other damage. Vapor barriers are applied to the warm side of the insulation. In the case of saunas or indoor swimming pools, special design, equipment and construction are required to handle the added humidity.

All of these systems can be used with any material. Some shingle manufacturers, however, specify the use of their own ventilation system to get the full warranty on their materials.

Before purchasing any roofing material, look at a sample of the roofing, check out the brochure from the manufacturer and try to visit a house with that roofing already installed.

When selecting a roofing material, make sure there will be proper insulation in the roof's construction, a building code requirement. This insulation is usually the thick batt fiberglass insulation placed between the ceiling **joists.** This is mainly to prevent the escape of interior heat or heat gain in the summer. It will reduce heating and cooling costs. For low-slope roofs it is common to use an additional layer of rigid insulation on the top of the deck to provide a smooth base or substrate for applying the roofing material. If the wood-roof deck is not pitched, the roofer can install tapered insulation to create the pitch, to augment the interior insulation and to create a separation between the deck and the exterior membrane, to accommodate possible differences in their movement. On metal roofing it will thermally isolate the metal decking and protect it.

Secure a copy of the manufacturer's maintenance manual for the roof before the roofer leaves your project.

Are you trying to decide whether to tear off the existing roof or install one over it? You should check with a roofing contractor to find out if the existing roof is salvageable or if you will need a complete replacement. The roof may just have loose flashing or a few damaged tiles. Have the contractor check to see that the roof deck is not damaged. This is hard to do without removing sections of the roofing, which must be patched afterward. Make sure the structure of the house can support an additional roof. This can be done with an architect or structural engineer. Check with your local building office to find out what the local codes permit. Most areas will allow one roof to be put over an existing roof; some areas may permit two. Find out if the warranty on the new roofing material has any restrictions if the material is placed over another roof.

Consider using a solar system for your roof, which will reduce energy dependence. Many states are offering incentives to people using these systems by giving tax rebates and reductions. Grants and low- or no-interest loans for the purchase of solar systems are offered because of the high initial setup cost. You must check with the local building and zoning regulation office to make sure there are no restrictions on this type of system in your area. Photovoltaic (PV) systems are a way of generating electricity by using the energy of the sun. This is particularly advantageous in areas where bringing electric lines would be costly. A general rule of thumb is to seriously consider using this type of system when you have to go 500 meters (1,640 feet) or more to connect to electrical service. PV systems require little maintenance and produce energy without polluting the air. PV roofing is available in several types of systems that transfer the solar light into energy. One requires the use of flat panels or modules placed on a supporting rack or array support located on the top of the roof. Also available are PV roofing products, which substitute for conventional roofing materials such as shingles, tiles or a product similar to standing-metal seam roofing that must be installed by an experienced roofer and electrician. These are considered by many to be more aesthetically pleasing than a rack/array of PV panels. There are two forms of PV material deposited on the tiles—one uses a very thin flexible layer of steel; the other uses crystalline silicon cells to be incorporated into tiles. Both are used to supply the house with some or all electrical needs. Any grid-connected PV array or roofing is connected to an **inverter** (a device for converting direct current into alternating current), which is installed at the house side of the electric meter or just before the house circuit breaker/fuse box. This solar technology is more acceptable to many people than the obtrusive panels that were used in the past. The cost of setting up such a system has also come down substantially in the last several years.

In January 2003 a PV unit was installed (in a maintenance building) at the White House to supplement its energy needs. Some states may

allow the purchase of surplus energy generated by the system—in a program called "net metering." To find out whether your state offers incentives for setting up this type of solar energy system, check your local government Web site using the words "solar" or "solar energy" as keywords.

resources

Information for roofing systems: Energy Efficiency and Renewable Energy Clearinghouse (EREC), www.eere.energy.gov/consumerinfo.html or call (800)-363-3732 and The Solar Energy Industries Association (SEIA), www.seia.org. To find out about incentives by state, go to the site for the Database of State Incentives for Renewable Energy at www.dsireusa.org.

Common Types of Roofing

Roofing materials can generally be divided into those that are appropriate for steep-sloped roofs and those for roofs with only low slopes or flat roofs. **Steep roofs** require water-shedding types of waterproofing systems; low-pitch roofs require weatherproof systems. Slope is the first criterion for selecting the material to be used on the roof. All of the other criteria listed above should be considered along with the conditions that prevail in the particular location in terms of climate, wind, proximity to the sea, humidity and pitch of the roof. All roofing materials are sold by the **square,** which is 100 square feet of coverage.

Steep Roofing

Steep roofs are covered with materials that are water-shedding; they carry the snow and rain away from the roof substrate. They are not designed to hold standing water for any length of time. The steeper the roof, the more quickly the water should run off it. A steep roof is defined by its pitch—any roof 3/12 pitch (which means the roof rises 3 inches for every horizontal foot) and steeper. The pitch of the roof will dictate the type of material you can use. Manufacturers usually specify the minimum slope for their materials. The following are those materials that are appropriate for steep roofs.

Organic (Paper Mat) -Reinforced or Fiberglass (Fiber Glass Mat) -Reinforced Asphalt Shingles

Sometimes called **composition shingles,** these are the most commonly used steep roofing material. Shingles used to be made of asphalt and asphalt paper and were called asphalt shingles. Today the shingles consist of a thin mat of asphalt-soaked felt or fiberglass with a coating of asphalt and mineral-based granules, which serve as protection from fire, UV rays and as decoration. Most fiberglass shingles today have a class A fire label; most organic mat shingles are a C label. This is generally the most economical roofing available. These shingles come in a wide range of colors, weights, textures and styles. Some are made to look like wood shakes, slate or tile. Most come in three-tab strip shingles that have two cutouts dividing the three sections of the shingle. These make the roof stripes look like individual shingles. They come in a variety of other styles as well—one-tab, two-tab and interlocking (these were developed for wind resistance, but are not as popular as the heavier **architectural shingles** that are even more wind resistant). Different textures and lighting

A home with fiberglass asphalt architectural shingles.

effects can be created with strip shingles. The heavier a shingle is, the longer the anticipated life of the shingle. The quality rating and price go up with the length of warranty. Inexpensive shingles may have a twenty-year warranty; better shingles may have a lifetime warranty. Most shingles today are self-sealing; they have strips of asphalt that seal each shingle to the one above it. The sun then heats the strip and bonds the two shingles together. Shingles have a higher wind resistance once they are sealed. Architectural, laminated or three-dimensional shingles are a type of asphalt fiberglass shingles that are thicker than other asphalt shingles. They are contoured to look like shakes or slate and have a more textured appearance. They are heavier, more expensive and have longer warranties.

Shingles have to be laid over solid sheathing or decking. Underlayment, dry sheet or saturated felt paper should be put over the decking. This felt comes in fifteen- and thirty-pound material, the heavier being more efficient. The shingles are self-sealing, but they need to be attached to the decking with nails. The purpose of the underlayment is to keep the building dry while the building shingles are installed and to separate the roofing from the decking. The movement of the decking and shingles are different; the shingles, having low elasticity and being more brittle than the wood, will swell and then dry out. The underlayment keeps them apart because the movement is different. If the shingles were stuck to the decking, they would crack or split.

The American Society for Testing and Materials (ASTM) has standards for measuring the composition and physical properties of asphalt shingles (ASTM D 225 for organic shingles and ASTM D 3462 for fiberglass shingles). Not all shingles comply with these standards. The NRCA recommends the use of ASTM-approved shingles. Check the literature on the selected product and on the packaging to see that it meets these standards.

Advantages
- Shingles are widely available.
- They are lightweight.
- They are easy to maintain.
- They are available in most fire classifications.
- They come in a large selection of colors and textures.
- Shingles are inexpensive to purchase and install.
- Shingles are water-shedding.
- They are also easy to repair.
- They can be long lasting, depending on the particular material used.

Disadvantages
- When the surface coating of granulated minerals (which are pressed into the exposed portion of the shingle to add color and protect it from sunlight) wear off, the shingle will degrade quickly.
- Shingles are not as fire resistant as some other materials.

resources
Information about asphalt roofing: Asphalt Roofing Manufacturers Association (ARMA), www.asphaltroofing.org or 202-207-0917.

Wood Shingles and Shakes
Wood roofing comes in the following forms:

Shingles—These come in 16-, 18- and 24-inch lengths. Shingles are usually applied three layers thick. Shingles are thinner and lighter than shakes, machine sawn on both sides and have a smooth surface. The cost of the shingles will depend on the wood species and grade selected.

Shakes—These come in 18- and 24-inch lengths as shingles. They are split (rough edged), sawn or split and sawn (the face would be split and the back would be sawn) from logs or wood blocks, are thicker at the bottom than shingles and less uniform than shingles. They have a more rustic, textured look because they are split along the length of the grain.

The most popular varieties of wood for roofing are:

Red cedar—Its heartwood has a natural durability.

White cedar—It has some natural durability, but generally it should not be used on a roof because it may include flat-grain wood, which would give it a short life, and UV rays will cause it to turn black. It can be used as a siding in salt air, which will cause it to weather silver gray.

Redwood and cypress—They also have some resistance to rot but should be treated with preservatives.

Southern yellow pine—It is not commonly used and application may be more difficult to adequately place this wood.

The above woods are insect resistant and rot resistant except Southern yellow pine. Other wood species are available but are not as durable as these mentioned. Decay develops when the wood is wet for long periods of time. Mildew, lichen, algae and moss will grow on the wood due to extended moisture or if the roof is heavily shaded. A lack of ventilation and/or poor installation will cause dry rot, which is another way that the wood will deteriorate. Dry rot results from the repeated wetting and drying of the wood.

Other considerations for wood shingles and shakes:

Preservatives—The preservatives used on wood to protect it from rot have copper. This can turn the wood a green color, which should disappear after about three months; with preservatives the wood should last thirty years or more. Preservatives with tin are also used; it will not turn the wood green, but it won't last as long (about five years). Pigments painted on the wood will also protect it from turning green. Finishes with pigment can be used to reduce the effects of weathering and to prevent the change in the wood color to silver, dark gray or dark brown. It is recommended that you do not use finishes such as paint, solid-color stains or varnish since they do not allow the wood to shrink and swell and may cause the roof to crack and deteriorate quickly. The most effective finish is a semi-transparent penetrating oil-based stain with a wood preservative and water repellent. This is most effective if it is applied before the wood is installed. Some manufacturers offer pretreated wood with a preservative that will last for the life of the wood. This type of wood should be used in humid or coastal areas. This wood is not necessary in dry areas where preservatives are not needed. In dry areas the wood should be treated with roofing oil. Preservatives can be put on by the roofing professional but don't have to be put on until it is necessary—five or six years after installation. A cedar or shake roof should hold up well for many years if it is installed properly by an experienced roofer. It is important that the nails are hammered in at the appropriate areas and that they are the appropriate size and type (hot-dipped **galvanized** or stainless steel) to avoid future problems.

Fire retardants—Some areas of the country require the wood to be impregnated or treated with a fire retardant to meet code in that area. ("Fire retardant" means that the wood will stop burning if the source of ignition is extinguished or removed.) Some areas of the country require wood to have a higher degree of fire retardancy than others. If a fire-resistant product is required, there are different classes of fire resistance. One method of treatment is pressure-impregnating the wood with fire retardant. Chemicals are forced into the cells of the wood under pressure and the wood is thermally cured at high temperatures. These cedar shingles and shakes or the treatment of cedar and shakes are available from Chemco (the only product currently approved by the California State Fire Marshal's Office for cedar shingle and shake roofing in high-risk wildfire areas). Check with your local building official to find out what class is required. Note that wood must be pretreated for fire retardancy by the manufacturer; this treatment should then last for the life of the roof.

For further information about Chemco, call 866-624-3620 or visit www.chemco.us.

Grade—It is preferable to use shingles or shakes with grade 1. Each bundle of shingles or shakes is labeled with a grade label. Grades 2 and 3 can be used with reduced face exposure, which increases the amount of labor and materials needed.

Interlayment—Wood shakes require a layer of interlayment, (a thirty-pound asphalt saturated felt) between each layer of shakes for water-shedding. Wood interlayment should never be used with shingles.

Ventilation—It is important that wood shingles have proper ventilation on all sides of the wood to prevent rot, mildew and bacterial growth on the wood, which accelerates its deterioration. They should be placed over spaced **battens,** open planks, skip or space sheathing or breather felt. They may allow preservative-treated wood to be applied to a solid deck. All building codes specify installation requirements for wood roofing in their areas.

Maintenance—Wood needs to be properly maintained: kept clean with power washing (by an experienced professional), swept with a broom or washed with a hose. Overhanging tree limbs and vines, which provide shade, keep the roof wet and encourage moss growth; they should be cut back periodically. If moss or lichen grows on the roof, it can be removed by using a sprayed application of a herbicide that contains **zinc** sulfate or a solution of one-quart bleach, one-ounce detergent and three-quarts warm water. After the moss dies it must be hosed or brushed off the roof. Zinc, galvanized flashings and copper flashings will prevent moss and algae from growing on the wood. Only products that are designated for wood roofing should be used to treat the shingles and shakes. When a treatment is put on the roof, the Cedar Bureau recommends looking for a water repellent, UV-inhibitor and/or U.S.

EPA-registered wood preservative. Whatever product is used should not contain unfortified linseed oil or diesel fuel. Make sure you know what product the contractor will be using before treatment is started on the roof.

Advantages
- Wood has a beautiful, natural look and is a natural insulator.
- Shingles and shakes can be easily replaced when they are damaged.
- Wood is highly heat resistant, insulative and wind resistant.
- Wood is ecologically sound because it can naturally reproduce itself.
- Wood adds structural stability to the house because each piece has been nailed in at least two places.

Disadvantages
- Wood is expensive to purchase and install.
- It needs maintenance.
- It is more flammable than some other roofing materials, regardless of whether it is treated.
- Wood requires qualified professional installation.

Information about wood roofs: The Cedar Shake and Shingle Bureau, 604-820-7700 or www.cedarbureau.org.

Recycled Synthetic Roofing Shingles
There are several recycled synthetic materials available in a range of colors resembling wood shingles and slate. In general, these products have a longer life expectancy and are lighter and easier to install than the materials they resemble. Most are resistant to hail, UV rays, wind, mold, mildew, fungus, freeze-thaw cycling and rot. Most require no maintenance. Some of the synthetic shakes have a class A fire label and may possibly be used in areas where wood is banned, but this

Some suppliers of recycled synthetic roofing shingles:

Crowe Building Products Ltd. (C)	905-529-6818	www.authentic-roof.com
EcoStar, Inc.	800-211-7170	www.ecostarinc.com
Enviroshake	866-423-3302	www.enviroshake.com
TeelGRT	800-322-8335	www.teel-grt.com
Re-New Wood, Inc.	800-420-7576	www.ecoshake.com
SlateDirect	210-826-8504	www.slatedirect.com

(C) = Canadian

would depend on local approval. The synthetic slate is substantially lighter in weight than real slate and therefore does not require the same structural support. Some insurance companies offer incentives for using synthetic materials because of their resistance to wind and hail. Several companies offer up to fifty-year limited warranties on their products. Besides all of the other benefits, recycled roofing is good for the ecology. The prices for these products are similar to the cost for natural products.

Metal Roofing

Metal roofing can be difficult to select because of the variety of styles, patterns and metals and alloys. It is available in standard-size sheets, panels and shingles and can often be cut to custom size. Metal is sometimes textured or colored to resemble other forms of roofing, such as slate, tile or shakes. Metal requires good flashing, ventilation (to prevent condensation below the roofing) and good drainage to make it function efficiently. All metal roofing needs a solid, flat base, but some metal roofing can be laid over another roof. Because water vapor condenses easily on chilled metal, the moisture can saturate insulation and leak through ceilings and walls. Most metal roofing therefore uses a cold-roof system in which a ventilating air channel is created under the metal roofing with intake and outlet vents at the soffit and ridge of the roof. Metal reflects the UV rays back into the atmosphere and

quickly cools down, unlike asphalt and concrete roofing, which will remain hot for a long time after the sun has set. Some materials are surface mounted with nails, which is an inexpensive method, or there are many types of locking systems created for metal roofing, which span various price ranges.

Naturally Weathering Metals

Roofing metals can be divided in two categories: naturally weathering metals and coated metals. Naturally weathering metals include aluminum, copper, lead, stainless steel, zinc, terne-coated stainless steel and lead-coated copper. These form their own protective layer through

Re-New Wood, Inc.

An example of recycled synthetic roofing shingles.

oxidation and are able to withstand weather exposure common to roofs. Some of these metals outperform others, depending on location and environmental conditions. Select a metal that is suitable to the specific location where it will be used. Sometimes the oxidation changes the look of the metal substantially, as is the case with copper. Some of the naturally weathering metals currently used are as follows:

Aluminum—Aluminum is durable, corrosion resistant and is the lightest of all roofing materials. It also will not stain adjoining materials. Aluminum dents easily and is therefore difficult and expensive to install. Aluminum panels will dent in a hailstorm, and aluminum requires a solid decking and good insulation. Some aluminum roofs can be very noisy. They reflect radiant heat and can reduce energy costs. Aluminum roofing can be made to emulate shake, shingle and slate. It is long lasting, comes in a wide range of colors and textures and requires little maintenance. Aluminum will tolerate salt air if it gets a paint finish (PVDF is most often used), which is generally factory installed. Untreated or uncoated, it will weather and pit, especially in salt air. Aluminum expands and contracts more than other metals, so the roof must be designed to accommodate the movement. It cannot be soldered and therefore the durability of the roof will be dependent on the quality of the installation and the sealant to keep it watertight.

Some sources for aluminum roofing:

Alcoa	800-962-6973	www.alcoahomes.com
ATAS	800-468-1441	www.atas.com
Berridge	800-231-8127	www.berridge.com
Peterson Aluminum Corp.	800-323-1960	www.pac-clad.com
Classic Products	800-543-8938	www.classicroof.com

Stainless steel—Stainless steel is made with chromium, which creates a protective skin on the surface of the steel that resists oxidation and makes it corrosion resistant. There are several grades of stainless steel. Regardless of the grade, stainless steel roofing requires careful design and detailing to ensure that its surfaces are exposed to air and kept dry. Some grades (type 304) should not be used near the ocean, because although stainless steel resists corrosion and rust better than most other metals, over time salt air will cause **pitting** and the roof will begin to leak. There are grades of stainless steel (type 316) that can stand the exposure and not cause the metal to pit. It is impervious to rust and corrosion, very strong and has a low coefficient of expansion (lower potential for thermal movement), but it is expensive, in line with the cost of slate, tile and copper. Stainless steel is up to 75 percent recycled and 100 percent recyclable, so it is also good for the environment. It is available in a shiny finish, a matte finish and other textures as well. Stainless steel is very lightweight and is good for reroofing; it can go over an existing asphalt or wood roof. It is used for some roofs coated with terne (an alloy of zinc and tin). The terne coating enhances its resistance to corrosion and weathers to a warm gray patina. The runoff from a roof with a terne coating with lead, will, however, be toxic if it gets into the water or into homegrown produce. It should not be used if these conditions exist. Stainless steel does not require paint, but terne creates a very paintable surface that can receive a large spectrum of colors. The zinc and tin terne alloy produced by Follansbee is a permanent roofing material and does not contain lead. They now have a line of twenty factory baked-on colors that are solar reflective and do not require maintenance, other than a touch-up for nicks and scrapes. Another stainless steel product available is from Millennium Tiles, which uses a process to bring out one of several colors (pewter, bronze, slate or gray) from within the metal. They are also introducing copper finishes that will not patina. Their color is permanent and will not fade, peel or chip. It is currently the only stainless steel available in shingle-style tiles. This system has a class A fire label and is maintenance-free, designed to withstand strong winds and carries a transferable fifty-plus-year limited warranty.

Copper—Copper is beautiful and timeless. It can last for a lifetime and requires little or no maintenance, but it is expensive. It weathers first to a bronze color and then to an antique green patina at different rates, in various locations, depending on heat, humidity, moisture and pollution. It does not need a protective finish, but coatings are sometimes added to preserve the original color or to give the copper a more gray color. The water runoff from a copper roof can stain concrete, brick or stone walls. If the copper is lead-coated it will cause a light or dark gray stain. Care should be taken to keep the runoff away from a water supply and vegetation. Copper is also available with a zinc and tin coating that weathers to a gray color. It is also available pre-patinated, so there is no wait to get to the natural green patina color. This copper may be used to repair areas of copper on existing roofs that have already become patinated. Copper is highly susceptible to acids that leach out of other products such as cedar shingles, slate and tile—the copper will turn an orange color. This orange color is the result of tannic acid washing off the patina. As this continues, the metal erodes and becomes thinner over time until failure. Copper should therefore not be used in combination with other materials that might create a leaching problem. Copper is lightweight, so it doesn't require additional structural support and has a class A fire label. It comes in panels, shingles and sheets. Copper roofing requires professional installation.

resources

Copper roofing information: Copper Development Association, 212-251-7200 or www.copper.org.

Zinc—Zinc is more popular in Europe than in the United States and Canada but is a beautiful though expensive roofing option. It doesn't require any coating or paint and takes a much longer time to corrode than most other metals. The life expectancy of zinc is over 100 years. Weathering turns the metal a natural gray (depending on local environmental conditions), which, unlike copper, will not stain adjacent surfaces. Zinc, like copper, should be attached to a solid substrate (rather than purlins); otherwise it will stretch and sag. Zinc is easily soldered to itself. The natural acids in some plywood, which is often used as a roofing substrate, can have an adverse effect on zinc. As a result, one zinc supplier has developed zinc with a protective backside coating that allows installation over potentially

2001 Millennium Tiles, LLC

Permanently colored stainless steel roofing tiles display subtle variations in color under changing light and angles.

Conklin

noncompatible substrate (VM Zinc Plus). Another option is to include a plastic matting between the zinc and substrate that allows air to circulate and will prevent the acid from affecting the zinc. Pine can be used as the substrate instead of plywood since pine is compatible with zinc. Zinc is available in three formulations:

- Natural zinc is shiny and will weather naturally as a result of exposure to water and carbon dioxide.
- Factory-weathered zinc comes in a middle gray color and looks like it has weathered for about five years.
- Slate-colored zinc is almost black, darker than it would weather naturally.

Zinc inhibits the growth of moss and algae, so it is well suited for damp climates or areas prone to mold and mildew. Care must be taken if zinc is installed in cold climates because if the metal is folded it can develop small cracks. Once the zinc is installed the cold weather is said not to be a problem. Zinc has a high rate of expansion, so proper installation is a necessity.

Titanium—The use of titanium for construction is relatively new in the United States and Canada; however, it has been used in Japan for many years. It is still relatively unfamiliar to many

A house with a copper roof.

and is considered to be expensive. It will cost approximately 5 to 10 percent more than copper, zinc or stainless steel, but it will last for an extremely long time, so it can be considered cost effective over many years. It is highly corrosion resistant, lightweight, environmentally friendly, maintenance-free, has a low coefficient of thermal expansion and is very strong. It is available in several natural finishes. Residential use of titanium was inspired by the architect Frank Gehry when he used it on the Guggenheim Museum in Bilboa, Spain.

Some suppliers of copper:

ATAS	800-468-1441	www.atas.com
Canadian Brass & Copper (C)	800-845-1134	www.canadianbrass.ca
Classic Products	800-543-8938	www.classicroof.com
Conklin Metal Industries	800-282-7386	www.metalshingle.com
Copper Craft	800-486-2723	www.coppercraft.com
Gregg Steel Shakes Bremet Systems Ltd. (C)	800-565-5703	www.unaclad.com
Ettel & Franz Company	612-646-4811	
Metalworks	877-ROOF-INFO	www.metalworksroof.com
W. F. Norman	800-641-4038	www.wfnorman.com
Revere Copper Products, Inc.	800-490-1776	www.reverecopper.com
Stillwater Products, LLC	800-326-5355	www.decoroof.com
Zappone Manufacturing	800-285-2677	www.zappone.com

(C) = Canadian

Information about zinc roofing:

ATAS	800-468-1441	www.atas.com
Canadian Brass & Copper (C)	800-845-1134	www.canadianbrass.ca
Rheinzinc	269-353-0726	www.oldworlddistributors.com
VM Zinc	919-874-7173	www.vmzinc-us.com

(C) = Canadian

Umicore Building Products USA

resources

For further information about titanium, contact the International Titanium Association at 303-404-2221 or www.titanium.org, or contact Timet at 303-296-5600 or www.timet.com.

Coated Metals

The other category of roofing metals consists of coated metals. Metals with a base layer of steel require a coating of paint or other metallic coating for protection against rust and corrosion. The metals that are used for roofing are made of aluminized steel (steel coated with aluminum), galvanized steel (steel coated with zinc), **Galvalume** (steel coated with aluminum and zinc) and terne metal (steel coated with a lead and tin or zinc and tin alloy). Steel is one of the most commonly used metals for roofing. It is sturdy, inexpensive and comes in a variety of factory-painted colors, patterns and styles that can be warranted for twenty years or more. Steel often has a multilayered finish, which is a zinc-galvanized

base coating, a sealer, an epoxy primer and a baked-on coat. All steel must be coated with zinc-galvanized coating to prevent it from rusting. Proper finishes on both sides of galvanized steel make it very resistant to corrosion. It shouldn't be used near the ocean because the salt may cause the metal to rust even with a coating.

Metal roofing must be cut in the field during installation. Therefore, it is important that the installer always coat the exposed edges before installing, especially the metals that do not corrode.

Sheet metal is the basis of metal roofing. The thickness of the differing metals is measured by a schedule unique to each metal type called "gauge." Roughly, 16 gauge is about $1/16$-inch thick. The higher the gauge number, the thinner the material.

Stone- or granular-coated steel—This is a 26-gauge precoated Galvalume metal (see page 94 for more information). It is coated with a layer of fired ceramic stone granules on top. Made to look like terra-cotta tile, copper, wood shake, slate and shingles, it is available in tiles or panels. It is resistant to hail, wind, corrosion, snow and fire. It is also resistant to mildew, fungus, UV radiation and airborne pollutants. It can be installed over other roofing and is maintenance-free. The

arofalo Architects, Inc.

Left: Double-lock standing-seam metal roofs, like this zinc one, allow much greater water tightness in low-slope applications than other roofing materials.

This home has diamond-shaped titanium skin over the curvilinear geometry of a new addition.

Right: A terne roof.

Follansbee Terne Metal

Far right: A stone-coated steel tile roof suits this Tudor home in Texas.

panels are interlocking, which make them sturdy in hurricanes and tornadoes. This is currently a popular roof covering in southern California because it is made to hold up in earthquakes. There are several manufacturers that produce these types of roofs in a wide variety of colors and styles. If a stone-coated roof is installed properly it should never have to be replaced. Stone-coated steel products generally have a limited lifetime warranty that is dependent on the quality of the installation. The tile and shake products are expensive. Stone-coated steel can be used with insulation but is very energy efficient when used with a cold roof system, which uses the space created between the batten boards for insulation. It is also much lighter in weight than most other roofing materials.

Terne metal—Terne metal is a time-tested metal that has been used on American roofs since the early eighteenth century. President Thomas Jefferson used terne roofing on his mansion at Monticello. President Andrew Jackson also specified a terne roof on the 1836 reconstruction of the

still-standing Fourth Hermitage, the historic home to which he retired when he left the White House. Terne has a steel base with a thin coat of zinc and tin. The coating is put on to offer resistance to weathering, to provide a paintable surface, to make it easily soldered, to protect it from salt air and to form a gray patina. Its malleability makes it adaptable to any type of roof, including rounded surfaces such as geodesic structures or free-form structures. Terne is less expensive than most other metals, it is very durable and strong, and it is fireproof and waterproof when properly installed. Terne has the lowest coefficient of expansion of any metal roof although it is still more than nonmetallic roofing materials, such as wood and slate. Terne can be used near the ocean as long as it is properly maintained. The underneath part of the terne should be painted before it is installed in case there is internal humidity, so the interior

Gerard Roofing Technologies

surfaces won't rust. The exterior part of the roof should receive two coats of paint as soon as the roof is finished to avoid rust. Specific paints are required for terne metal. To maintain the terne metal it should be painted every seven to eight years. Acrylic paint or acrylic emulsion-based paint may be used with the zinc and tin coating.

resources

For more information on terne metal, contact Follansbee at 800-624-6906 or www.follansbeeroofing.com.

Some suppliers of stone-coated steel:

ATAS	800-468-1441	www.atas.com
Decra	877-463-3272	www.decraroofing.com
Dura-loc	800-265-9357	www.duraloc.com
Gerard	800-237-6637	www.gerardusa.com
Metro	866-638-7648	www.metroroofproducts.com

Galvanized and Galvalume metal—These are the most commonly used metals for roofing. Galvanized steel has a coating of zinc while Galvalume has a coating of zinc and aluminum. The zinc coating provides a layer that galvanically protects the underlying steel from corrosion. The aluminum in Galvalume provides an added barrier protection. Galvalume steel comes with a warranty against corrosion for up to twenty years, with a seacoast exception; galvanized steel doesn't carry a warranty. If a roof will be unpainted, Galvalume is the preferred material. For painted roofs, either metal will work well for strength and durability. The preferred weight for galvanized roofing is G90; G60 will work adequately for siding.

Both metals are available in formed products such as tiles, shingles and shakes, as well as in long panels with vertical ribs or seams. Panels are either through-fastened—attached with screws that penetrate the metal—or secured to the roof deck with fasteners concealed under the seams. Such standing-seam roofs are preferable but more expensive to install.

Paints applied on steel coils in the factory come in many colors and even have colors to replicate other natural metals. Silicon-modified polyester paints offer good durability but are subject to fading in richer colors, such as red. The introduction of Kynar 500, a fluoropolymer resin that protects the color from fading and chalking, greatly expanded interest in upscale commercial and residential metal roofing. Fluoropolymer resins make the colors strong, crack- and UV-resistant, and carry a warranty against chalk and fade resistance. In order for a paint to carry the Kynar 500 name it must be licensed and contain 70 percent of the additive.

A properly installed standing-seam metal roof is often warranted for thirty years and can generally last much longer. The cost of a steel roof will be comparable to a tile roof and meets or exceeds tile's resistance to high winds, hail, fire and snow damage.

Whenever metal roofing is used, all of the metal used for flashing, fasteners and the roofing material must be the same metal or compatible. When dissimilar metals meet in the presence of moisture, galvanic action can cause corrosion of the metal and, eventually, leaking. When nails are used that are dissimilar to the roofing material, washers (made of neoprene or EPDM rubber) are sometimes used to prevent the two metals from touching. Often, however, the washers wear out, and the roof will eventually leak through the nail holes. The roofer should check on the compatibility of the different metals he may want to use before proceeding with any type of metal installation.

Standing-seam metal-panel roof systems are classified as either architectural or structural. Structural metal roof systems are used as water barriers on roofs with a $1/2$/12 pitch or greater. They are mid-span reinforced and structurally strong. Panels are overlapped and surface fastened with exposed screws. They come in manufacturer's stock colors and are warranted for up to twenty years. Standing-seam metal roofing is the most inexpensive metal roofing on the market. Architectural metal roof systems are water-shedding with seams that are not necessarily watertight. These are meant for roofs with a 3/12 pitch or greater.

Thomas Jefferson's home in Monticello was built with a terne roof. Terne is still successfully used as a roofing material today.

There are several ways of attaching and seaming metal to make it watertight. Two of the most common are standing seams and batten seams.

Seam Types or Configurations for Metal Panels

Standing seam—This can be self-sealing; a raised vertical seam is crimped after it's in place.

Pan and batten—Has a wide seam that is covered by a cap.

Flat seam—A seam that is formed flat against the surface of the roof and secured with **clips** or **cleats** and then usually soldered.

Closing the Seams

Mechanically seamed—Can be completed by hand tongs or automated seaming devices. This produces a weatherproof seam with inseam sealant.

Snapped-together seam—A snap-cap, or batten-cap, is used to complete the seam. Some now have a gasket installed in the field to make the seam more watertight. It is not waterproof and must be used on a steep-slope roof.

Tongue-and-groove seam—One edge is inserted into the edge of the next folded edge. This is not waterproof and should be used on steep roof applications and walls.

Hooked seam—This is a flat-locking seam used in horizontal panels or metal shingles. These should be used for water-shedding.

Panels come in 22- to 28-gauge metal. These can be rolled to custom length at the job site or pre-purchased in the correct sizes. Locking roof systems are usually adequate for all roofs 3/12 pitch or steeper. For low-slope/flat-roof applications, mechanically seamed panels may be recommended where there is an inseam-installed sealant to make the seam watertight.

Advantages

- Most metal roofs are long lasting and durable.
- They are lightweight.
- They do not burn (most have a class A fire labeling).
- Metal resists insects, mildew, rot and adverse weather conditions.
- Metal is easy to maintain.
- Metal roofs have warranties from twenty years to a lifetime, depending on the particular product.
- Most metal can be installed over other roofing.
- There is a wide variety of colors and styles available.
- Much of the metal used has been recycled, which is good for the environment.

Disadvantages

- Metal expands and contracts with weather changes, so roofing must be designed to accommodate this movement.
- Metals corrode, so if they don't come with a protective covering, they have to be protected.
- Metal can transmit noise if it is not installed properly.
- Imitations of other materials are sometimes unconvincing.
- Some metals, such as aluminum, can dent in a hailstorm and some scratch or dent when walked on.
- Metal has a very low R-value. However, this is compensated for with the use of the proper insulation material. Some aluminum products, for example, are now available with an optional polystyrene backing, which adds strength for high-traffic areas and also increases the R-value of the overall roofing. The insulated shingles or roofing can be installed in a particular path leading to a satellite dish or chimney, for

A painted Galvalume roof.

MBCI of Houston, TX

95

example, to prevent damage from foot traffic or hail, or installed on the entire roof.

- Installation and materials may be costly.

resources

To get additional information about metal roofing or to locate a roofing contractor, check with the Metal Roofing Alliance at www.metal-roofing.com.

Slate

Slate comes in a variety of colors, depending on the location it is found. It is very durable and will last for a long time. Its durability will depend on the other elements used on the construction of the roof—the flashing should be a high grade of copper (16 to 20 ounces minimum), copper nails should be used and thirty-pound felt or roll roofing should be used under the slate. It is one of the most expensive roofing materials because there is a limited supply; it is also one of the most attractive. Slate comes in several hardness grades; make sure to purchase a good grade for roofing. The color of all slate changes due to exposure to weather. Slate that changes minimally is called "unfading"; slate that changes more obviously is called "weathering." When selecting slate for roofing, check the stability of the color by asking which of the above describes the particular slate. Always check to see that there are counter-sunk or punched holes in the slate you are selecting; some of the domestic and imported slates do not have holes and have caused problems for homeowners.

Advantages
- Slate won't corrode or burn.
- It won't wear out or need replacement for a very long time.
- It is beautiful and fire resistant.

Disadvantages
- Slate is expensive to purchase and install.

- It sometimes requires a long lead time to get the particular color.
- It is heavy and requires a stronger-than-average construction to secure it; the engineer or architect should be able to tell you if the house can structurally carry a slate roof.
- It may be difficult to get replacement slate if some are later damaged; it would be a good idea to purchase extra slate with the original order.

resources

Slate roofing information: NRCA, www.nrca.net.
Slate resources by region: PreservationWeb, www.preservationweb.com.

Tile

Tile roofing is comprised of clay or concrete, and both types come in high profile, low profile (mostly concrete) and flat. Because a tile roof will last for a very long time, the other materials used on the construction of the roof should also be top quality to last as long as the tile. These other materials include copper flashings, heavy felt and copper nails. Stainless steel nails are also commonly used. Tile roofs are very heavy, so the roof structure is designed to carry the weight of the tile. Concrete tiles are less expensive, easier to install and lighter in weight than clay tiles. They are available in many of the same styles. Both of these tiles come in a variety of colors and shapes, such as barrel-shaped like mission tiles (sometimes referred to as pan and cover tiles), plain (also referred to as flat-slab or shingle tiles), ribbed or S-curved. Clay tiles are available in glazed and unglazed. **Underlayment** is also recommended with tile roofs to protect the roof during installation and for added weatherproofing.

Antique tiles are available from several suppliers. These are salvaged from buildings that have been demolished or reroofed to replace or reinforce a building's structure. The tiles are generally durable as they have already withstood years of use. However, they usually do not come with warranties.

Advantages

- Some tile is very durable and can withstand repeated freezing and thawing.
- Concrete and clay tile has to be produced to resist freeze-thaw. Concrete used only in the South is different than concrete used in the North.
- Tile won't rot, bugs don't like it and animals can't chomp on it.
- It is unaffected by salt spray and pollution.
- It won't split or crack.
- It has a good fire rating.
- Tiles are available in a variety of colors and styles.

Disadvantages

- It is expensive to purchase and install.
- It requires a strong roof structure to handle the weight of the tile roofing.
- It is not as readily available in certain areas of the country as in other areas.
- It may be difficult to get replacement tiles to repair damaged tiles. (Make sure to purchase additional spare tiles for this purpose.)

resources

Roof Tile Institute: www.ntrma.org.

Fiber-Cement Shingles

Fiber-cement shingles were developed as lightweight, less expensive tile roofing. Natural and synthetic lightweight fibers are used to strengthen the concrete. This reduces the weight and cost of concrete tiles. They are currently marketed only in the southwestern United States. They come in many colors and are molded to look like wood shingles, clay Mission tiles and slate roofing. When tested they were found to deteriorate with the freezing and thawing in cold climates and so should only be used in warm climates.

Advantages

- They are lighter in weight than traditional concrete tiles.

Some manufacturers of fiber-cement shingles:

CertainTeed Corp.	800-233-8990	www.certainteed.com
James Hardie	949-348-4441	www.jameshardie.com
Re-Con Building Products	877-276-7663	www.re-con.com

- They resist insects, rot, fire and fungus.
- They cost less than concrete tiles.

Disadvantages

- They cannot be used in cold climates.
- Because of their uniformity, they may not look as charming as many of the tiles they try to emulate.
- The long-term performance, although stated as thirty to fifty years, has been questioned by the NRCA as being less.

Low-Pitch Roofing

Low-pitch roofs are those roofs with a pitch of 0/12 to 3/12. On low-pitch or flat roofs water is likely to pond; therefore low-slope roofs should have a minimum of $1/4$-inch-per-foot pitch (which most codes require) and proper drainage. When the roof slope is less than 2/12 pitch the system must prevent water penetration by the use of waterproof roofing materials designed to seal off the water. The NRCA recommends that drainage be installed that drains water quickly and can adequately drain all water within forty-eight hours after the source has stopped. If not, the ponding must be addressed by a roofer to eliminate the pond. Low-pitched roofs are comprised of a deck (the structural surface that supports the roof), a vapor retarder or a vapor barrier (which prevents moisture from accumulating within the insulation), when needed. Not all systems or climates require a vapor barrier; sometimes thermal insulation (which slows the passage of heat into and out of the house and stabilizes the surface the roofing is on top of), and a membrane, which is a sheet of waterproofing material that keeps water out of the house, are all that is needed. The

97

insulating material used with low-pitch roofs should have a high R-value and enough strength to resist denting, gouging, moisture, decay and fire spread. In some flat-roof assemblies, the insulation is inverted or placed on top of the membrane; this is called an inverted roofing membrane assembly (IRMA). The choice of materials will depend on budget, the site condition (areas with potential movement, such as earthquake-prone areas, require materials that are very flexible), the length of time you plan to live in your house, the materials which are available locally and the ability of local roofers to install the roof.

Built-Up Roofing

Built-up roofing (BUR) is also known as tar and gravel or hot-mopped roofing. It requires specialized equipment and trained labor and may not be as available for residential applications as some of the other products. BUR is composed of layers of hot bitumen (asphalt or coal tar) or cold-applied adhesive between layers of asphaltic plies and reinforced felt material (organic fibers, fiberglass or synthetic fibers), resulting in a multiple-ply configuration. These are constructed on the roof by the contractor. Asphalt melts during application and becomes a solid when it cools. The cost and durability of the roof will depend on the number of layers or plies installed. At a minimum these roofs should have three plies: a base ply (mopped or nailed to the deck), a reinforcing ply and a top or weathering ply. An additional reinforcing ply is sometimes added. Professional installation is necessary in order to have the manufacturer's warranty enforceable and because of the use of hot asphalt, which can be dangerous without experienced installers. After several layers are installed, they are topped off with crushed rock or gravel, granulated cap sheets (also called 90 pound) or aluminum-based coating, which minimizes the damaging effects of the sun. The top coating has several purposes—it gives impact resistance against hail and foot traffic, **ballast** against wind uplift, and the roof a class A fire labeling. Eave vents coupled with metal vent hoods inserted in the surface of the membrane can provide venting, but this requires skillful design and detailing by the architect to be effective.

Advantages

- BUR roofing is inexpensive.
- It is easy to maintain.
- It has good impact resistance. Some roofers feel it is an advantage to use a multi-ply system as opposed to a **single-ply** one.
- BUR roofs are waterproof and can meet fire class labeling.
- They can have colored stone on a granulated cap sheet as the top surface. With adequate building structure they can serve as the base for paving stones or other walking surfaces.

Disadvantages

- In plain black it is not as attractive as other forms of roofing.
- Each layer of roofing must cool before the next layer can be put on, so this type of roofing can take time and be expensive to install.
- Installation can be dangerous because of the hot bitumen used between layers.
- Moisture due to leaks in the membrane can be trapped, causing the roofing to blister and rot.
- BUR roofing does not lend itself to installation on three dimensionally curved roofs, such as domes.
- BUR is subject to worker error and material inconsistencies. It is also very brittle below 30 degrees.
- It may need surface recoating (from granule loss) to protect it against UV rays.

Single-Ply

Single-ply membranes are flexible sheets of compounded synthetic materials made in a factory to assure strict quality control. They are applied to the roof in one layer for waterproofing. They are composed of a variety of synthetic membranes that vary in their individual properties and in the installation methods they require. They are less labor intensive than other low-pitch installations, usually more elastic and less prone to cracking and tearing. The membranes are attached to the roof in several ways: with adhesives, with the weight of some type of ballast, with fasteners concealed in the seams between sheets or with some other mechanical fastener. There are materials with similar performance properties; they fall into two groups:

Thermoplastics—These are flexible plastic sheet materials that are used in one-ply configurations and are based on plastic polymers (chemical compounds). Once the sheets are laid, the seams are bonded together with heat. There are two main types of thermoplastics that are used: polyvinyl chloride (PVC), which is the most commonly used thermoplastic, and thermoplastic polyolefin (TPO). There are many products available in this category, each with its own unique formula. Their seams are sealed using either type heat, which produce permanent bonds and are very strong. Most thermoplastic membranes are made with a reinforcement layer, usually polyester or fiberglass, to increase the stability and strength of the roofing. They are resistant to bacteria, fire, UV light, tears and extreme weather conditions. They must be applied on a dry surface when no precipitation is expected. The material also must be perfectly flat before being seamed. This requires professional installation. These are easy to maintain and repair and may last more than fifteen years. Many of the products used are white or light colored and reflective. This reduces the heat that enters the house and helps reduce air-conditioning costs. PVC roofing membrane material should be carefully researched in order to make certain that the material has been tested and formulated to prevent the plasticizers from migrating out of the membrane over time. The result is that the membrane will become brittle and crack.

Thermosetting—These are also single-ply materials that are "set," or cured, by heating during the manufacturing process and must be seamed with liquid-applied adhesives or pressure-sensitive tapes rather than by heat. Ethylene propylene diene monomers (EPDMs) are compounded from rubber polymers and are the most commonly used polymer materials used for single-ply roofing. Sometimes referred to as "rubber roofing," it is not commonly available in colors (it is normally black) or in a variety of thicknesses. It has excellent resistance to UV light, ozone, oxidants, severe weather and extremes of high and low temperatures. It is highly flexible, pliable and able to accommodate structural movement. This material requires no maintenance but is easy to repair if a portion is damaged. It is heat resistant and is easy to install. The seams are formed into a waterproof seal at the overlaps with a liquid or tape. Ballast can be used for certain situations. The companies that produce EPDMs offer contractor training and architectural specification guidance.

Advantages

- Single-ply materials are more elastic and can be used on curved roofs.
- They have a smooth surface and are easy to maintain.
- They are strong, flexible, durable and long-lasting.
- There is a consistency to the quality of the material.
- Custom-colored products or coatings may make the product fit the aesthetics of the house.
- Single-ply systems can be installed during cold weather, allowing a building to be roofed in winter.

Disadvantages

- Different products have different drawbacks. EPDMs, for example, are not readily available in colors but can be coated with a Hypalon or acrylic coating that does come in colors.
- A professional is needed for repairs for all single-ply membrane roofs.

- Only heavy-thickness products should be used where rooftop traffic may exist, such as a balcony or roof patio.
- It is inexpensive-looking.

Modified Bitumen

Modified bitumen are factory-made layers of asphalt that are modified using a plastic or rubber ingredient to increase flexibility; therefore the term "elastomeric" is often used. A prefabricated reinforcement sheet is imbedded between layers of the bitumen for strength and flexibility. These have the advantage of incorporating the high-tech prefabricated formulation of single-ply with the traditional installation of BUR. These are durable, flexible and light. They are installed in layers with the top layer either a granulated surface similar to a shingle surface, or smooth surfaced and then post-coated with a colored acrylic or aluminized coating. Modified bitumen are resistant to UV rays and harsh weather conditions. These sheets are sometimes incorporated into a BUR system for their strength and durability. There are two main types of modified bitumen systems:

Atactic Polypropylene (APP) is a plastic-type material that is applied with an open flame. It is therefore used only on new construction where flame protection measures are not as exacting or detailed. The recommended installation is two plies with the upper ply given a silver coating for an extended warranty period. Another approach is to install a granule-coated top ply for the second ply. It is inexpensive and easy to install but has a fifteen-year or longer life span, depending on whether the surface is plain or granulated.

Styrene Butadiene Styrene (SBS) is an elastic-type material that is applied with hot or cold asphalt adhesive. It is more expensive but will last longer.

Advantages
- They are inexpensive.
- They are easy to maintain and have good impact resistance.
- Some roofers feel it is an advantage to use a multi-ply system as opposed to a single-ply one.

Disadvantages
- Installation can be a fire hazard if torch-applied.
- APP-modified bitumen are also brittle below 30 degrees, which limits cold weather installation.
- Granular-surfaced products may need some limited surface recoating (from granule loss) to protect them against UV rays.
- These materials are not compatible with many petroleum, solvent-based materials and other chemicals.
- A professional is needed for repairs.

resources
Single-ply roofing: www.spri.org.

Sprayed Polyurethane Foam-Based Roof Systems (SPF)

SPF roof coverings can be used on structures that are too weak or complex in structure to carry a conventional membrane. Two components (part A and part B) are mixed together and are then sprayed onto the roof. The installer must balance the mixture to get the optimum durability and R-factor (how much heat transmission the insulation will resist). The mixture then expands twenty to thirty times and does provide some water resistance alone. A protective coating or membrane is then needed for UV protection, aesthetics or waterproofing. This type of roofing is very light and can last a long time. It does require a great deal of maintenance. It is subject to environmental damage—birds peck through it, ants can get into it and raccoons and other animals can cause foot damage. This is one of the most difficult installations and requires a lot of experience and skill. It can be sculptured to look very attractive. It can also be used over an existing, deteriorating BUR roof.

Advantages
- It is a lightweight roofing that is used in areas that cannot support heavier roofing.
- Coating maintenance is relatively easy.

Disadvantages
- It is difficult to install and repair.

Flat-Seamed Metal Panels

Flat-seamed metal panels are structural roofing, rather than architectural, usually used on steep roofs. Flat panels have open hems on two sides that lock together, are crimped down with a mallet and soldered together. These are primarily used for restoration work over another roof or for replacing a roof. Mechanically seamed panels are similar to the ones used on steep slopes; a machine comes down and folds the seam twice. These panels are usually steel. Mechanically seamed panels are expensive and are rarely used for residential purposes.

Advantages
- Flat-seamed metal panels have structural strength.
- They are long lasting.
- They are easy to maintain.

Disadvantages
- They are expensive.
- Lead coating can pose some environmental and health concerns.

resources

For more information about roofing or to find a professional roofer in your area, visit the National Roofing Contractors Association (NRCA) at www.nrca.net.

There are some terrific new materials and new applications of old materials. Consider some of these options before making a roofing decision. Check with manufacturers and trade associations about the material before deciding. The choices you make will have an aesthetic and possibly monetary consequence in the future.

Siding

Siding is needed for eye appeal and protection from the elements, including moisture penetration. In some areas it can also serve as protection against biological contaminants (such as mold, dust mites and bacteria) and pests (carpenter ants and termites). There are many siding options to consider. The style of the house may dictate the type of siding you will use. Stucco, for example, is an obvious choice for a Mediterranean-style house. If budget is a major factor, there are many alternatives in all material categories. If you would like to have a brick house, for example, traditional bricks might be the preferred option, but bricks are expensive to purchase and install. You then have the option of a less-expensive alternative, such as a thin-brick system or a mortarless brick. Another major consideration is location. Wood siding should not, for example, be used in areas prone to fires. Consider your personal circumstances, location and preferences before deciding on any siding.

Siding is the finish of the exterior wall. The parts of the interior construction of siding from the inside going out (for a typical stick-constructed house) are as follows:

- A finished surface, such as painted gypsum wall board
- The stud framing
- Within the airspaces between the studs, insulation is applied, with the vapor barrier (foil or paper-like facing) facing the warm side or interior
- The sheathing, usually exterior-grade plywood
- A moisture/wind barrier, such as tar paper or the house-wrap product such as Tyvek, a form of plasticized paper. The moisture/wind barrier is a permeable building paper used between the sheathing and the siding to prevent rain and snow from penetrating to the sheathing and then through to the walls but allowing the escape of water vapor (permeability).
- Finished siding

Ask the contractor, supplier or builder for samples of the various siding products you are considering. Request literature, with information on durability, warranty information and so on, for the products you are most interested. Make sure a qualified person installs the particular siding you select. Many manufacturers offer information and support to installers. Some manufacturers will offer a list of qualified installers in your area. The durability and beauty of the siding will depend a great deal on the material you choose and on the quality of the installation.

Criteria for Selecting Siding

Cost of the material and installation—both of these are important issues. The material may be inexpensive but the installation expensive. Find out about the cost for each of these factors before making a decision.

Resistance to the elements—Consider what conditions—wind, rain, snow, pollution, moisture, earthquakes—your siding will have to endure.

Resistance to damage by impact—Particularly if you have children, consider the damage that may be caused by a ball tossed into the siding or a bicycle slamming into the siding.

The style of the house—Certain styles look particularly well with certain sidings. A Mission house, for example, looks good with a stucco siding.

Color and design preferences—There are many options available to suit everyone's preferences.

Fire resistance—Particularly if the house is in an area prone to fires, this is a major consideration.

Resistance to bugs and animals—The location will dictate how much of a consideration this will be.

How much maintenance you are willing to do—Some sidings, such as shingles, require treatment every so often. If you are looking for a maintenance-free siding you should consider another option.

Siding on other houses in the neighborhood—Consider what the resale value may be in the future if yours is the odd house on the block.

Future additions or renovations—Some materials, such as brick, may be expensive to remove and to match.

Available contractors to do the installation—Although you may prefer a particular material, if there is not a qualified installer available locally, this cannot be an option, unless you want to go through the expense of hiring a contractor from out of town for the installation.

Hints

Find out if your installation will include a vapor barrier between the interior space and outside walls. This prevents interior moisture from getting into the insulation and outer wall covering. The condensed water vapor can cause the deterioration of the exterior walls and loss of functionality of the insulation.

Insulation is necessary with all exterior wall construction. Most codes in the northern part of the United States require a minimum of R19 overall rating for the exterior wall. Insulation board panels can be put between the sheathing and siding for added insulation over and above the required bats or blankets used between the studs. There are many forms of insulation; make sure that you will have adequate insulation for your needs.

If you are planning to re-side the house because of an expansion or because some areas

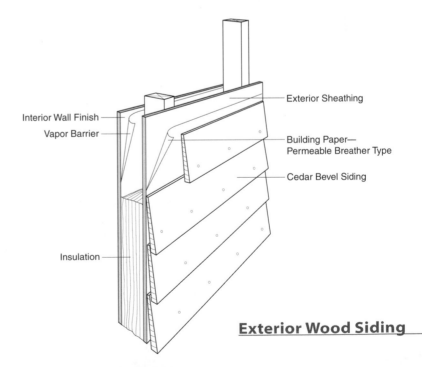

Interior Wall Finish

Vapor Barrier

Insulation

Exterior Sheathing

Building Paper—Permeable Breather Type

Cedar Bevel Siding

Exterior Wood Siding

Finish	Expected life (years)
Natural finishes such as water-repellents and water-repellent preservatives and oils	1–2 on horizontal surfaces 2–4 on vertical surfaces
Semi-transparent stains	2–4 on horizontal surfaces 3–5 on vertical surfaces
Paint	Up to 10
Solid color stains: oil water-base	Approximately 3–5 10

of the current siding are damaged, first consider keeping the current siding by matching the material you already have.

resources

SidingMatch.com will try to match your current siding for material (vinyl, steel or aluminum), color and texture. They have a large database of siding in the United States and Canada dating back to 1960. It is worth the limited expense to try and match the current siding before redoing the entire house. Contact them at www.siding-match.com or 888-936-8424.

Wood Siding

Wood siding is made of solid lumber or composite lumber, such as plywood or hardboard. It comes in various shapes and sizes.

Solid Wood

Solid wood comes in the form of **boards** and shingles and **shakes.** Boards can be used horizontally, vertically or diagonally and are often manufactured with special edges and profiles. Boards are milled to be used in one direction. The boards are available rough sawn and also smooth on three or four sides. As with most other sidings, a moisture/wind barrier is needed behind the siding, as well as venting, to prevent condensation from soaking the wood and causing the outside paint to peel and the wood to rot.

There are many available species of wood that can be used for wood siding—cedar, redwood, Douglas fir, cypress, white pine, ponderosa pine, spruce, hemlock and yellow poplar. All wood that will be used for siding, even if it has a natural preservative (to protect it from decay, weather and insects), such as red cedar, should be treated with a protective coating on all sides (front, back and both ends) before it is installed. The coating will protect the wood from water penetration, help prevent staining and increase the life of the top coat. There are four types of coatings to use on wood, all with varying life expectancies.

The type of coating used should be determined by the appearance desired and on the recommendation of the manufacturer and dealer. The primer coat should be applied by the finisher or installer prior to installation; the final coat can be applied after the wood is installed. Wood can be purchased unfinished, or it can be sent by the mill to one of the many finishers available around the country to put on a preservative or water repellent. Often the finisher will offer a fifteen- to thirty-year warranty on the wood, provided it is installed properly. The wood can also be finished on the job site, but no warranty will then be available. The maintenance required depends to a great degree on the type of finish used and the type of exposure. If the wood is painted, it needs to be repainted every six to eight years, or if it is stained, it should be repainted every six to eight years or finished with water repellent every two years. Some paints and stains are water repellent themselves and don't need to be treated for water repellency. Unpainted, some woods will darken to a deep grayish brown.

The heartwood (near the tree's center) of the wood will be stronger, darker and in some cases more resistant to rot than the sapwood, which is the outer part of the trunk. A tight-grained, older, knot-free wood is the most desirable, most rare and the most expensive. The wood from younger trees will be less expensive, but will warp, split and will not take a finish as well.

Some of the considerations when selecting wood are:

Kiln dried or seasoned—Wood is available kiln dried or seasoned. If it is purchased unseasoned it has to be air dried for several weeks until it reaches the recommended moisture content of 9 to 14 percent, depending on the region. The time it takes will depend on the local climate and the particular species.

Grade—Wood is available in several grades, which varies with the species. Check with the Web sites of various wood species to find out the categories and grading system before purchasing wood. Western red cedar, for example, is available in clear and knotty categories with several grades available from A Clear, B Clear, C Clear and D Clear (which has the largest and most natural characteristics). A grade description is only meaningful if you know the system for the particular wood. Knotty grades are sometimes preferred for their rustic appearance. More natural characteristics may be more desirable for a casual look; fewer for a more formal look. Check on the grading system for the wood that you select so you will know exactly what you are getting.

Siding pattern—There are many available designs for wood siding. Some can only be used horizontally, vertically or diagonally, and some can be used in all three ways. They must be milled for the way they will be used.

- Bevel siding or clapboard—**Bevel siding** or **clapboard** is installed horizontally and gives a shadow line that varies with the thickness of the siding selected. The wood surface is milled at an angle in a wedge-shape cross section. Both sides may be saw textured or one side may be smooth, depending on personal preference. This siding is installed starting at the bottom of the wall and going up.
- Pattern Siding—There are many types of **pattern siding** where interlocking or overlapping joints have been machine cut into the boards. Two of the popular patterns that can be installed horizontally, vertically or diagonally are tongue-and-groove and **lap siding.**
- Tongue-and-groove siding—**Tongue-and-groove siding** has joints that are usually V-shaped, but they can be flush, reveal or radius jointed as well. They provide interesting shadow effects.
- Lap siding—This comes in several patterns, channel siding being one of the most popular. It has a rustic look with the profiles of each board partially overlapping that of the board next to it. Channel siding usually comes in unseasoned knotty grades.
- Board-and-batten siding—Board-and-batten siding is always used vertically. Boards are spaced apart with narrower boards or battens covering the joints. Often 1x10 boards are used with 1x3 battens, but any combination is possible.

The grade of the wood and the application, which includes installation, moisture/wind barriers, flashing and ventilation, are the most important factors in preventing **cupping** and shrinking of the wood.

Advantages
- Wood siding comes in a large variety of species, grades, patterns and sizes.
- The boards can have many different finishes.
- Wood siding has a natural look.
- It can go over existing siding.
- If well maintained it can last fifty years or more.
- For those ecology-minded people, wood is a renewable resource.

Disadvantages
- It can split, warp or burn. (A pressurized, impregnated cedar is available that is fire retardant. For further information about this product, contact Chemco at 866-624-3620 or visit www.chemso.us.)
- It is expensive in premium grades and species.
- Wood siding requires maintenance every few years.

Siding

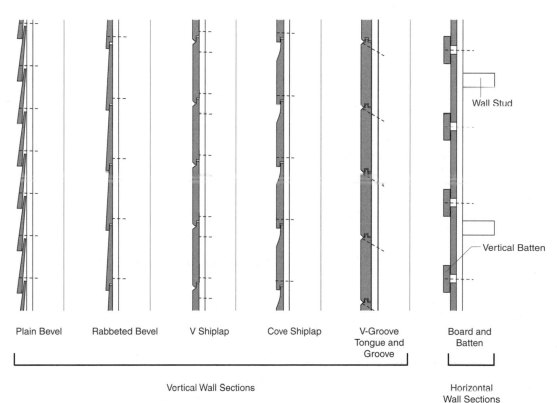

Plain Bevel Rabbeted Bevel V Shiplap Cove Shiplap V-Groove Tongue and Groove Board and Batten

Wall Stud

Vertical Batten

Vertical Wall Sections

Horizontal Wall Sections

- It is attractive to animals and birds, such as woodpeckers, which may cause holes in the siding.

resources

For more information on wood siding, contact the Western Wood Products Association at www.wwpa.org, Northeastern Lumber Manufacturers Association (NeLMA) at www.nelma.org, the California Redwood Association at www.calredwood.org, and the Forest Products Laboratory established by the U.S. Department of Agriculture Forest Service at www.fpl.fs.fed.us.

For information on environmental sources regarding trees, check www.greenspirit.com and www.forestinfo.org.

Wood Shingles and Shakes

Wood shingles and shakes for siding often come from cedar as do those used for roofing materials. Most cedar starts out a reddish color and weathers with time to a gray or brown color, which may vary with the amount of sunlight and humidity. Shingles are smoother and more uniform; shakes are more rustic and rough in texture. Some red cedar heartwood has a natural preservative, while other types of wood need to be treated with preservative every five or six years. Make sure to purchase a high grade of wood that does not have a great many knots and is relatively free of defects. Shingles are graded #1, which are the best, and #2, which some people find acceptable but have more natural defects. Shingles and shakes are especially appropriate on Cape Cod–, Victorian-, Shingle- and Craftsman-style homes. Shakes are thicker than shingles and come in a variety of shapes and textures; they can be scored, sawed, split or machine grooved (called sidewall shingles).

Also available are shingles and shakes that are stapled and/or glued in the factory to 8-foot plywood panels. These expedite installation and reduce installation costs. They are available factory stained, painted or pressure treated with fire retardant and/or preservative. They should be factory treated with flame retardants.

Shingles and shakes should last twenty to forty years or more, depending on the local conditions and how well they are maintained. In dry climates the shingles and shakes should be oiled periodically; in humid, hot climates, they may need to be treated with a fungicide/mildew retardant.

resources

In high-risk wildfire areas, cedar shingles and shakes from Chemco that have attained a class A fire rating are available. For further information about this product, contact Chemco at 866-624-3620 or check their Web site at www.chemco.us.

Advantages
- They have a rustic look.
- They provide good insulation.
- They are easy to repair.
- Wood shingles and shakes are adaptable to rounded walls.
- They may be installed over existing siding.

- Shingles and shakes are available in a variety of species, grades, sizes and patterns.
- Damaged pieces are easily replaced.

Disadvantages
- They are expensive to purchase and install.
- Wood is susceptible to fire and should not be used in areas particularly prone to fire unless they are treated for fire resistance.
- Shingles and shakes may exhibit **checking** and cupping if defective wood is used or poor application is applied.
- Depending on location, they may need to be stained periodically.

resources

For further information about shakes and shingles, check the Web site of the Cedar Bureau at www.cedarbureau.org.

Composite and Engineered Wood

Also available are wood by-products, which include plywood, hardboard and oriented strand board (OSB) siding manufactured as sheets or panels. These are made of wood chips and shavings and/or sawdust bonded together under pressure with special resins and glues.

Plywood

Plywood siding is composed of an odd number of layers of wood veneer bonded together under pressure. Lap siding (panels) is available with a brushed, rough-sawn, or texture-embossed surface. The panels sometimes have grooves, such as from V-grooves or deep channels that imitate the look of board siding. The face veneers are from Douglas fir, redwood, cedar and Southern pine. Though most plywood siding is sold unfinished, redwood plywood is usually mill-treated with water repellent. Plywood comes in a variety of thicknesses and grades, the better grades having fewer patches of wood, synthetic resin blotches or both. Panels come in 4-foot widths and 8- to 12-foot lengths. All plywood should be painted or stained, even that with a natural resistance, because it will help to withstand weather erosion and will camouflage the patches that are particularly visible on the lower grades. If the wood will be stained, a higher grade of plywood is needed to avoid the appearance of all the patches. If the wood will be painted, an economical lower grade of plywood can be used. Although the lower grades have patches, they are still flat and smooth, and the patches will not show under a coat of paint. Plywood is easily installed and can provide added structural strength to the exterior wall of the house. Only plywood that has been bonded together with tough waterproof glue and intended for the exterior should be used. The grade labeling on the panel will indicate its approved application.

Advantages
- It is inexpensive.

Disadvantages
- Plywood requires maintenance, restaining or painting periodically.

Oriented Strand Board (OSB)
This is a fiberboard composed of layers of mostly wood strands of fiber, with each layer consisting of compressed wood particles in one direction and with layers oriented at right angles to each other, all compressed together under extreme heat and pressure with resin. OSB comes in a variety of textures and can be made to look like cedar shingles or stucco but is rarely used for siding. It is less expensive than lumber or plywood but looks like lumber siding when painted. To prevent moisture from seeping in, OSB must be painted and the edges sealed with water repellent, stain sealer or exterior wall paint primer before they are installed. This is often done in the factory. Unprimed and factory-primed OSB should be painted or stained within sixty days of installation, then repeated every five years. If well cared for, OSB

can have a twenty- to thirty-year warranty but can last much longer.

Advantages
- OSB is available in a variety of textures and patterns.
- It has a uniform appearance without the flaws found in lumber.
- It can be put over existing siding.
- It is moderately expensive.

Disadvantages
- Transparent finishes cannot be used.

Medium Density Fiberboard (MDF)
MDF is a hardboard that is the finished face of a plywood panel, specifically manufactured for exterior siding. The veneer is hardboard, which is a material made from bonding wood by-products, fibers, shavings, dust and strands with an adhesive under hot pressure and high temperature and bonding to plywood panel. Various manufacturers offer different materials and use various processes for producing hardboard. Masonite is one of the trade names for hardboard. Priming is for water protection, and most of the hardboard produced is factory primed. In addition, it can be factory finished with paint or opaque stain. Paint is the preferred finishing because it makes the hardboard more durable. Hardboard is available in a variety of textures, patterns and colors and can be made to look like other materials, such as cedar. Most hardboard comes with approximately a thirty-year warranty.

Advantages
- Hardboard is lighter and easier to install than other wood siding materials.
- It is more uniform in texture and color than other wood products and offers an excellent painting surface; it has no knots and splits and other natural defects.
- It is easier to paint than other products.
- There are more patterns and textures available

For more information on Medium Density Fiberboard (MDF):

The Collins Companies	800-329-1219	www.collinswood.com
Georgia-Pacific Building Products	800-284-5347	www.gp.com
Louisiana-Pacific Corporation	800-648-6893	www.lpcorp.com
Stimson Lumber Co.	800-445-9748	www.stimsonlumber.com
Temple	800-231-6060	www.temple.com

because these can be pressed into the material when it is being produced.

- It is generally less expensive than other wood products.

Disadvantages

- It cannot be used unfinished.
- Hardboard may be more sensitive to moisture than other wood products.
- Vapor can be trapped inside the wall because it is not permeable, causing rot and mildew.
- All wood is susceptible to termite damage when in direct contact with soil. Care should be taken with the installation of wood siding to prevent this situation.

Exterior Wood Composite Paneling

This is a relatively new product in this country but has been used in Europe for about ten years. It is a laminated wood composite panel. The veneers are treated with phenolic resins on both the front and back faces. They are laminated with an inner core of Bakelite, which is kraft paper treated with thermo-hardened resins, compressed under extreme pressure at high temperature. Installation is with a ventilated curtain facade, leaving an approximately one-inch airspace behind the panels and a ¼ -inch expansion gap between panels. It comes in a variety of wood species and colors with panels that are 48 inches (1,220 millimeters) x 96 inches (2,440 millimeters) approximately ³/₈ inches (10 millimeters).

Advantages

- This product is dimensionally stable and durable.
- It is resistant to stains, mold, mildew, fungus and impervious to termites.
- It has the warmth and beauty of wood.
- It is resistant to varying climatic conditions, including freeze-thaw, salt spray, dry climate and UV rays.
- It is non-toxic and maintenance-free.
- It comes with a ten-year warranty.

Disadvantages

- The lead time for delivery of the material may be twelve weeks.
- It requires professional installation.

resources

For further information about exterior wood composite paneling, contact Finland Color Plywood Corporation at www.fcpcusa.com or call 310-396-9991.

Vinyl

Vinyl is the most commonly used siding in America today. In fact, according to the 2002 Sabre Report, it is the siding of choice on 44 percent of all homes. Constructed of polyvinyl chloride (PVC), its most popular feature is the minimal maintenance it requires. And, while once available only in a limited pallet of light colors, today it is available in a vast array of shades, including deep, rich tones.

Vinyl siding is available in various profiles (contour of the board), including traditional clapboard and dutch lap, as well as regional architectural favorites such as beaded, board and batten and decorative styles such as shakes and scallops. Vinyl siding is available in various grades and as a general rule of thumb, the greater the thickness or

Finland Color Plywood Corp., architect and photographer: Dane Twichell, designer: Ken Mori

Wood-composite paneling is used on the exterior of this house.

gauge, the more resistant to damage. However, some manufacturers incorporate structural design elements (rolled over nail hem, special locking system, etc.) that add increased strength and rigidity. While the typical length of vinyl siding is just over 12 feet, some manufacturers also offer extended length panels, reducing the number of laps (where two siding panels meet) on the home.

During installation, vinyl siding is not nailed tight to the wall, but rather hung to allow proper expansion and contraction. With the exception of rotting wood, vinyl may be installed over a home's existing siding. There are a number of new products available that offer increased **R-value** to a home's exterior walls. One such product is a contoured foam underlayment. Available laminated or as a drop-in, it provides additional support to the siding and increases its impact resistance. Fullback Thermal Support System with PerformGuard is a backing added to the siding that also resists carpenter ants and termite infestation.

resources

Check to find out if the vinyl siding you select is approved under a Vinyl Siding Institute (VSI)–sponsored program at www.vinylsiding.org. Certified vinyl siding is siding that is verified by an independent process to meet or exceed ASTM D3679, the long-standing accepted industry standard for quality vinyl siding.

Advantages

- Vinyl is low maintenance.
- It is reasonably priced.
- The color is molded through the entire thickness, so scratches won't be as apparent.
- Vinyl siding is available in a vast array of colors and is fade resistant.
- It can convincingly look like wood siding, yet it does not require the upkeep that wood demands.
- It will not rust, rot, peel, blister or be eaten by termites.
- It resists fire (many have a class A fire classification) but will burn if ignited.
- It is relatively easy and inexpensive to install; however, hire a professionally trained installer to ensure it is hung correctly.
- Premium vinyl siding will stand up in harsh weather conditions and high winds.
- It is easy to repair if damaged.
- Vinyl siding warranties are typically excellent; many have warranties from fifty years to limited lifetime and some transferable to the next homeowner.

Disadvantages

- If not installed correctly, it can buckle or ripple.
- While now available in more colors than ever before, vinyl still does not have the range of hues that painted wood can offer.
- Some vinyl can become brittle in extremely cold weather and can shatter on impact.
- Dark colors can fade with time if not made with special compounds for increased weatherability.

Alside

Fiber Cement

Fiber cement is a product consisting of 90 percent cement/sand and 10 percent wood fiber. It is a mixture of Portland cement, ground sand, cellulose fiber and select additives mixed with water. It is formed into lap siding, panels, shingles and shingle panels with a variety of textures that are smooth or textured to look like wood, stucco, **stone** or brick. It is available primed, stained, painted or as raw siding and comes in horizontal as well as vertical boards. Fiber-cement siding is more durable than wood and will work particularly well in hot, humid climates where siding is prone to rot and fungus. It will hold paint longer than wood and requires less maintenance than wood. It does not have the knots and other natural inconsistencies, which sometimes make wood less durable. Moisture can be a problem if the boards are not installed and treated correctly in accordance with the manufacturer's recommendations. Prime coat and paint coat are needed on all exposed areas of the board. The cost is less or equal to the cost of hardboard siding. Labor is a bit more intensive than for wood siding. It must be installed on a flat surface or imperfections beneath will show through. Flashing and house wrap (or tar paper), as with any siding, are required before the installation of the siding and trim. The boards are generally warranted for about fifty years; shingles for about thirty years. GAF Materials Corp. has the only fiber-cement siding that is the same thickness and size as the previously produced

This home's exterior is outfitted with vinyl siding.

Some companies offering vinyl siding:

Alcoa	800-962-6973	www.alcoahomes.com
Alside	800-922-6009	www.alside.com
CertainTeed Corp.	800-233-8990	www.certainteed.com
Crane Performance Siding	800-366-8472	www.cranesiding.com
Gentek Building Products	216-514-3534	www.gentekinc.com
Heartland Building Products	800-432-7801	www.heartlandsiding.com
Kaycam Ltd.	802-865-0114	www.kaycam.ca
Louisiana-Pacific Corporation	800-566-2282	www.lpcorp.com
Mitten Vinyl Siding (C)	800-265-0774	www.mittenvinyl.com
Owens Corning	800-438-7465	www.owenscorning.com
Resource Materials Corp.	800-846-9599	www.rmcsiding.com
Rollex Corp.	847-437-3000	www.rollex.com
Royal Building Products (C)	800-387-2789	www.royplas.com
Variform, Inc.	800-786-2726	www.variform.com

(C) = Canadian

asbestos-cement siding (which has been taken off the market for the associated health risks). This is a good choice for anyone who wants to easily replace current asbestos-cement siding. This material has a non-transferable twenty-five-year warranty.

Advantages
- Fiber-cement siding is more durable than wood.
- It is resistant to rot, fungus, termites and fire.
- It will not buckle or warp.
- It is impact resistant, making it a good choice in hurricane-prone areas where siding may have to endure windblown debris, wind and hail.
- The cost is less or equal to the cost of hardboard siding.

Disadvantages
- It requires professional installation.
- It requires maintenance with a new coat of paint after several years.

This house has fiber-cement panels.

James Hardie Siding Products

Some suppliers of fiber-cement siding:

Cement Board Fabricators	502-774-5757	
Cemplank, Inc.	877-236-7526	www.cemplank.com
CertainTeed Corp.	800-233-8990	www.certainteed.com/pro/siding/ctsiding/index.html
GAF Materials Corp.	973-628-3000	www.gaf.com
Georgia-Pacific	404-652-4000	www.gp.com/siding/cem_index.html
James Hardie Siding Products	888-542-7343	www.jameshardie.com
MaxiTile, Inc.	800-338-8453	www.maxibuildingproducts.com/newfiles/siding.html
Nichiha USA, Inc.	866-424-4421	www.nichiha.com

Sheet Metal

Although **sheet metal** is used for siding, it is not as popular as some of the other siding materials. It has been used for roofing for many years and is more commonly used today for that purpose, as well as for commercial construction. Sheet metal has had a stigma attached to it because of the old rusty barns and tin shacks many people associate with metal siding; however, there are currently several creative architects around the country designing very beautiful homes with sheet metal siding. It is a very natural type of material and can be incorporated into many design styles. Metal is sometimes profiled (corrugated, box-shaped) for house siding because these formats give the metal strength. Some metals are attached directly to plywood sheathing to give it added strength. It is expensive to custom form metal; it is economical to select metals that are sheets, commercially available.

It is sometimes difficult to find residential construction companies that have the expertise to install metal siding. If metal siding will be used on your home, make sure the contractor has experience with this type of material before signing a contract. For more information about the various metals and suppliers, check the metal roofing section on page 88.

The following are metals that can be used as siding:

Painted steel, galvanized steel, Galvalume— All of these types of steel can be purchased in profiled sheets. That means the metal has already been formed into one of the many available profiles, such as corrugated or standing seam. The sheets can also be custom fabricated, but this will add greatly to the cost of the metal. Galvalume has a coating of zinc and aluminum and will be the most durable of the three types of steel. Galvanized steel has a coating of zinc that will give it some protection from corrosion. Steel can be painted with Kynar 500, a fluoropolymer resin that makes the colors strong and crack- and UV-resistant and carries a thirty-year warranty. If the paint should chip or scratch, that area of the metal will rust. Painted steel will work fine in very dry areas where there is little rain, but one of the other steel products should be considered in other areas with more moisture.

James Hardie Siding Products

MBCI

Zinc, copper, stainless steel, titanium, terne-coated stainless steel—These metals can all be used for cladding, but will most likely have to be custom fabricated and are all expensive. Some of the metals may be purchased in a limited number of profiles—corrugated and standing seams, but most other profiles will have to be custom made. For more information about these metals and resources for them, check the chapter on "Roofing" on page 88.

Advantages

- Most metals are long lasting and durable.
- Sheet metal will not burn (most have a class A finish for flame spread).
- Metal resists insects, mildew, rot and adverse weather conditions.
- It is easy to maintain.
- It is impervious to termites and resists fire, rot and insects.
- There is a wide variety of colors and styles available.
- Much of the metal used has been recycled, which is good for the environment.

Disadvantages

- Steel will corrode, so it has to be secured with a protective covering.
- Metal can transmit noise if it is not installed properly.
- Metal does not, in general, add to the overall R-value; however, this can be improved with insulation backing.
- Installation and materials may be costly.

Above: Fiber-cement shingles cover the exterior of this house.

Left: A house with unpainted or bare Galvalume wall panel siding.

- It is sometimes difficult to find a qualified installer.

Aluminum Panels

Aluminum has been a popular siding material for many years. It comes in many colors and usually comes with fifty-year (or more) warranties. Aluminum is available in a variety of horizontal and vertical panel sizes and styles. There are vertical panels that look like bevel-edge siding, and vertical siding that has the look of board-and-batten strips; other styles are available as well. Enamel is baked on to give the aluminum a smooth or textured finish. It can be made to look like wood siding, but it is easily dented and scratched; there are many other more durable metals available.

Advantages
- Aluminum requires little maintenance.
- It is durable, depending on the grade.
- It will not rust, blister, split, warp or crack.
- It is available in a large variety of colors, textures and finishes.
- Thicker aluminum (0.12524 inch) should be used for durability.
- It will not burn and resists rot and insects.
- It is easy to install and goes over most existing siding.
- It is waterproof.

Disadvantages
- Unless it is installed over a stiff backing material, it will dent.
- The surface color can be scratched off.
- It can be eroded by sea air or industrial pollutants.
- It may clatter without proper insulation.
- After several years, the aluminum will have to be repainted.
- Patterns used for siding may be discontinued, creating a problem if there is a damaged panel. Additional panels should be purchased to use as replacement panels.

Stucco or Cement Plaster

Stucco is a versatile material that can be used on wood and masonry construction—each of which is dealt with differently. This section focuses on wood construction, since it is the substrate of most houses. The choice of systems will depend on budget, environmental conditions, the desired appearance and the type of construction. Stucco is commonly used on Pueblo-, Mediterranean-, Craftsman-, Tudor- and ranch-style houses. There are three wall systems that give the look of stucco:

1. Traditional three-coat system—This stucco is a mixture of Portland cement or air-entrained (where freezing conditions occur year round) Portland cement, sand, lime and water. This mixture is troweled on, and, in the case of wood construction, a layer of vapor-permeable, water-resistant building paper is attached to the sheathing. As with any siding application, this layer is the moisture/wind barrier and usually has tar paper that protects the interior of the wall from outside elements. Then a layer of metal **lathing** or mesh is attached about $1/4$-inch out from the tar paper with a **furring** attachment to leave a space for the mixture to penetrate the lath. Then galvanized steel, zinc or stainless steel control joints are applied. Request stainless steel or zinc because they are more durable than galvanized steel. The control joints will render the stucco into panels in order to minimize the effect of curing and movement in the future. The joints also minimize the effect of the differing rates of expansion and contraction of the stucco and the sheathing due to humidity and temperature changes. The material is applied in three coats. A scratch coat is the first, or base, coat, which is forcefully pushed through the lathing. It creates a layer of metal in the middle of the base coat for strength and rigidity. The first coat is then scored, usually in horizontal scratches, so the second coat can mechanically interlock with the first. The second, or brown coat, is thinner than the first coat. The third, or finish coat, which is the thinnest, is applied before the second coat fully cures, or sets. The finish coat may be textured or smooth and is usually colored or tinted. There are two ways for the second coat to be applied. For the double-back method, the brown coat can be put on immediately following the base coat, before it fully cures.

For the traditional method, the base coat must be cured first. This requires wet curing; the base coat should be wet down for the first forty-eight hours after the installation. In areas with high humidity, such as Florida, the base coat may only have to be wet down three times a day; in drier areas it may require five or six times to keep the coat wet. This will help the cement to reach a strong and durable base coat. Although the former method has been approved by the Uniform Building Code (UBC), it is still controversial as to whether the faster method is as effective as the more traditional method. Since the base coat must be cured properly before the brown coat is installed in the traditional method, this system can be a time-consuming process and fairly expensive. It is the responsibility of the contractor to assure that the carpentry work beneath the stucco is rigid and does not move before the base coat of plaster is applied. Therefore control or expansion joints should be installed about every ten to twelve feet to allow for the natural expansion and contraction of the stucco material. A **weep screed** and weather-resistant barrier should also be applied to allow for proper drainage. The finish coat can be made of acrylic or cement. Acrylic stucco finish is a method introduced in the 1970s that is popular because it can be tinted in an unlimited spectrum of colors. These finishes are uniform in color, stain resistant and water repellent. Different grades of acrylic stucco finish will provide varied crack resistance; however, acrylic finishes will typically lose elasticity over time, becoming more brittle. A variety of pigments can be added to the cement finish coat and, although there aren't as many colors available as in the acrylics, it is available in up to thirty colors, which should satisfy most tastes. Since the color goes throughout the coating, if there is a scratch on the surface, the color will not be scratched away; the same color will show under the abrasion. The cement finish has more permeability and is less likely to trap water and vapors below the surface. Cement has a modeling, or shading, effect that is unique to Portland cement finishes. The cement finish has been used since the 1800s and is a tried-and-true method. The three-coat system is $7/8$-inch thick, consisting of a $3/8$-inch scratch coat, 3-inch brown coat and $1/8$-inch finish and has good impact resistance due to the thickness of the material. If you select stucco as a siding, be sure you are aware of all the options available.

The application of stucco is a matter of craftsmanship. There is no substitute for an experienced applicator who knows how to deal with the day's temperature, sun exposures, relative humidity and wind conditions, as well as the workability of the batch of cement plaster to apply. Master plasterers are becoming less available, particularly in some areas of the country. Make sure that you will be able to find a capable craftsman before selecting stucco as a siding.

Advantages
- Stucco is very durable.
- It is highly resistant to fire.
- It needs little maintenance.
- Stucco can be used on almost any architectural detail.
- A variety of color and texture options are available using integrally colored stucco finishes.
- It is also crack and impact resistant.
- It is impervious to rot, mildew and termites.
- Stucco can correct deviations in the substrate.
- This system works well on rounded structures, such as adobe-style houses.

Disadvantages
- Depending on the method selected, it may

take a long time to apply, so installation can be expensive.

- Stucco may crack from a slight movement or settling of the house; however, cracking is a common occurrence in stucco and does not automatically constitute a failure of the stucco system. The siding will most likely continue to function fine, and the crack does not have to be addressed unless it is more than $1/8$ inch, where water may be able to get in.
- Acrylic stucco finishes may have a tendency to fade and will lose their elasticity over time.
- Traditional three-coat stucco is not as commonly used as in the past; there are therefore fewer qualified installers, particularly in some areas of the country. It may be difficult to find an experienced installer; this is a necessity for a successful stucco installation.

2. Thincoat, fiber-reinforced stucco (FRS) or synthetic stucco—Only one brown basecoat is applied (the scratch coat is eliminated) with a colored cement stucco or acrylic-based finish coat applied on top. A lower-gauge wire mesh is used because the weight is less due to there being one less coat. Thin coat is $1/2$- to $3/8$-inch in thickness. The cost of this material may be as expensive as the three-coat method because the mixture must be factory mixed instead of mixed on-site by the contractor. There is, however, a savings in installation cost because there are fewer steps and less time involved. The weep screed, weather-resistant barrier and top coat are the same for this system as for the three-coat system.

Advantages

- The installation is less labor intensive and there are fewer materials needed, so it is less expensive than the three-coat system.
- It can be used on almost any architectural detail.
- It is more crack resistant and is impervious to rot, mildew and termites, as is the three-coat system.

Disadvantages

- This system is only moderately impact resistant because of the fewer layers.

3. Exterior Insulation and Finish Systems (EIFS)—There are multi-layered exterior wall systems commonly used instead of stucco. They are sometimes referred to as synthetic stucco or insulated stucco. They are also applied in layers, as is stucco, but include an insulating layer. The insulating layer is applied over house wrap (moisture/weather barrier) or other chemically compatible products and is secured to the outer wall with either adhesive and/or mechanical fasteners. The water-resistant base coat is applied, reinforced with a layer of fiberglass mesh and then a thin finish coat, which is colorfast and crack resistant, and is either troweled or sprayed on, depending on the finish. This system also requires a weather-resistant barrier and a weep screed to allow for drainage. It is now recognized that the insulation board should be furred out with an airspace to allow any condensation to drip down and out behind the insulation. This type of top coat is available for use with the other two stucco systems.

Advantages

- It is less time consuming to install.
- The material is more flexible, so it is less likely to crack.
- Insulation is included in the system, which increases the overall R-value of the exterior wall of the house.
- It can be easily cleaned and hosed down if it gets dirty.
- It is resistant to dirt, mildew and mold, and it won't fade.
- It is water resistant if properly installed.

Disadvantages

- There have been many reports of problems with EIFS in the past. The problems were found to be related to poor resistance to hurricane pressures, leakage and mold due to improper use or lack of sealants in window installations, improper underlayment and a lack of an airspace for drainage (weepage), and with faulty or no installation of flashing.

- Maintenance requirements are critical and include inspecting sealants annually at all terminations to ensure they are still performing.
- To have these systems work efficiently requires good quality windows and flashing in vulnerable areas of the installation, as well as a stable base, such as concrete or masonry.
- It does require professional installation by a knowledgeable, experienced applicator who should have current approval or certification by the manufacturer.
- EIFS are considered a liability by insurance companies, making it difficult for homeowners to maintain insurance.
- EIFS have a low-impact resistance and can be easily damaged. This also means special provisions must be made for installing sconces or any other household attachment, such as a hose rack, to the EIFS surface.

resources

For further information about EIFS, contact the EIFS Industry Members Association (EIMA) at www.eima.com.

Brick

People in the real estate business often say that brick houses appreciate more than identical houses with vinyl, wood or aluminum siding. This is unverifiable, but brick does give people a sense of stability, timelessness and the feeling that it will never be out of style. And as it is portrayed in the famous nursery rhyme about the three little pigs—it will never fall down. It is time tested and one of the few materials that can create the illusion of antiquity. Although brick has been around for hundreds of years, the brick industry has gotten into the fashion business with many more colors,

styles, mortar colors, shapes and textures. The trend in residential homes is toward more textured brick and those that have the look of old colonial times. The items to consider when selecting brick are budget, type of brick, availability of the brick and the availability of an experienced mason. There are several ways to get the look of brick. There are standard brick, thin-brick systems, fiber-cement brick and a mortarless brick system.

True or full-face brick—The most beautiful is true, or full-face, brick; it has a timeless look and will last a lifetime. Once you have chosen brick, there are three types of manufactured-face brick you should know about:

- Extruded-face brick—This includes the majority of brick available. These are extruded (forced out through a die) in columns and then cut into evenly shaped, rectangular brick. Various textures can be added to the brick as it is extruded, and hundreds of colors are available. This is the least expensive brick available.
- Machine-molded-face brick—This brick is produced by mechanically dumping the clay material into brick-shaped mold boxes. The boxes are then turned over, releasing the brick, which are less uniform in shape and are reminiscent of colonial brick. Coatings can also be fired onto this brick to add various textures and effects.
- Handmade-face brick—This brick is made by craftsmen who "throw" the material into wooden molds, one brick at a time, the way they were made 100 years ago. This unique brick is slightly larger than the previous two types of brick, requiring fewer bricks to complete a project. They are often used for interior walls and fireplaces (not to be confused with the refractory brick used for the fire box) as well as for exteriors of houses.

There are other types of brick, such as paving brick (pavers) used for landscaping and flooring, and shaped brick, which is used for detailing curved archways, **water tables** and other architectural details. Besides selecting the type of brick there are several other factors to consider when selecting brick.

Cost: Along with the initial cost of the brick, buyers should consider the cost of labor, maintenance, future value and the life expectancy of the brick. The cost of the brick seems to be lower in areas of the country where the material is plentiful. However, that may not be consistent with regional labor costs. Another consideration is future maintenance. If a homeowner plans to keep the house for a number of years, there may be a substantial savings in maintenance expenses over the long run. There is a difference in the various types of brick as well, the most expensive being the handmade-face brick, then the machine-molded-face brick and the most reasonably priced, the extruded-face brick.

Colors: Many colors are available from the traditional red color to white, tans, creams, roses, reds, burgundies, earth tones and so on.

Mortar: Mortar comes premixed in many colors, with other colors available custom mixed. Because mortar takes up about 20 percent of the brick wall's surface, it is an important element in the overall visual effect, and it is the product that holds the brick together.

Sizes: Brick is available in a variety of sizes. Generally, the larger the brick, the fewer that will be needed and the lower the labor cost. When brick dimensions are given they are stated as: thickness x height x length. Different-sized brick are sometimes combined to give various appearances and patterns. Oversized brick is becoming popular. King- and queen-size brick are available, which give the same look as the smaller brick but cut down on the cost of brick, mortar and installation. King-size brick requires five bricks per square foot; queen sizes require six bricks per square foot and standard bricks require seven bricks per square foot. They are available in over 100 colors. There are many companies that offer this product. Check with your builder or local brick distributor to find a queen- or king-size brick available locally.

Textures: Texture is one of the hot new factors homeowners are currently considering. There are many textures available: smooth, wire cut (velour), bark, brushed, soft sand coated, dusted and so on. Various textures interact with light, creating differing shadow effects. The ease of cleaning will also depend on the texture selected; get this information from the dealer before making a final decision.

This exterior features specially textured brick with an applied coating, which gives a mono-chromatic Mediterranean look.

Boral Bricks, Inc.

Grades: Because of the variety of climatic conditions possible, brick is available in three grades: those needed for severe (SW), moderate (MW) and negligible weathering (NW) conditions.

Shapes: Brick is available in shapes other than rectangular that can be used to create architectural details over windows, in corners, arches and so on. Some of these are sloped, ogee, cove, bullnose and lipped brick. Water tables are horizontal, linear projections in the wall that add dimension and can reduce water penetration by diverting water away from the structure's foundation. Water tables as well as other special-shaped brick details should be designed by the architect in the planning stage of the exterior of the house.

Bonds: There are many patterns, or bonds, that can be used to stack brick—running bond, stack bond, common bond, English bond, Flemish Bond, English Cross or Dutch bond. These are laid in patterns of **stretchers, soldiers** and **headers.**

Current Trends

There is a variety of innovations in brick available. There are new ones continually coming out, but these are a few of the current styles:

Mediterranean brick—There is a brick finishing system available that gives the look of a Mediterranean, monochromatic exterior and is a low-maintenance alternative to stucco and painted brick. For further information about this system or to find a local PastelCote distributor by

Boral Bricks, Inc., check www.boralbricks.com or 800-526-7255.

Machine-molded antiques—There are many companies producing machine-molded-face brick that offer the look of handmade-face brick with its uneven texture and soft edges. Extruded-face brick is also available that has been tumbled or otherwise distressed to give it an old-world look.

Installation

There are three ways that brick can be installed.

Veneered wall—This is the most commonly used method for construction today. A brick veneer is attached to the frame of the house as follows: After a house is wood framed and sheathed and a moisture/weather barrier is installed, a brick veneer is built around the exterior walls and is connected to the building with metal or **brick ties.** The frame, rather than the bricks, supports the weight of the house. There is a space (generally about 1 inch) left between the sheathing and the brick to allow water to escape. At the bottom of the wall are flashing and **weep holes,** which are required to enable water trapped behind the brick to escape (this is also required by code). A lack of weep holes may cause damage to the framing of the house.

Structural or load-bearing wall—In this type of installation the brick wall supports the weight of the house. There is no frame behind the brick, but a masonry unit or brick provides direct backup support for the brick veneer, which

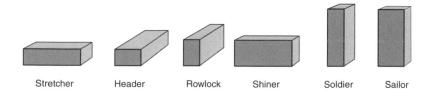

| Stretcher | Header | Rowlock | Shiner | Soldier | Sailor |

Types of Brick Orientations

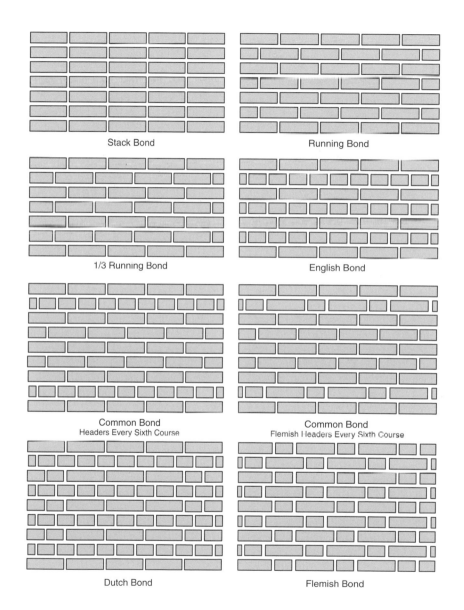

Stack Bond

Running Bond

1/3 Running Bond

English Bond

Common Bond
Headers Every Sixth Course

Common Bond
Flemish Headers Every Sixth Course

Dutch Bond

Flemish Bond

Types of Brick Bonds

becomes structural. There is no space within the wall. This type of wall construction is most often used for freestanding walls, such as in landscaping design, and is sometimes used in residential construction.

Cavity wall—This type of system may also serve as a bearing wall but has a cavity between the brick and backup masonry that may be filled with rigid insulation that provides vertical grooves for moisture to fall and weep out. This may often be used if the interior wall will be exposed brick.

Before making a final selection of any brick, take a look at the brick itself and check out the options available. Some distributors offer computer or Web-based programs where you can see the look of the brick in various colors in combination with different mortar colors. Some of these programs will also allow you to see how the brick and mortar will look with various options in shutters and roofing. Ask if you can look at houses built with some of the various brick they are showing. Discuss your options and costs with the architect and builder on your project.

Brick is generally priced in quantities of 1,000, which can easily be converted to square foot coverage based on the brick size. Labor costs vary substantially by region; other influencing factors are the number of stories, brick size, number of openings and offsets and the time of year.

For those who want to remodel a house with a brick siding they don't like, painting it is one solution. However, the paint will have to be redone every five years or less. Check with a professional paint store or a painting contractor to find out what the implications will be in terms of future maintenance and the best way to complete such a project. If the right type of paint isn't chosen, it could result in some moisture-related problems. Latex paints are generally okay, but their water vapor permeability decreases with each coat. It is important that the surface be properly prepared, removing the efflorescence (the deposit of water-soluble salts on the surface), mildew and old paint, primed with an alkaline-resistant primer and painted with a latex paint. There are other solutions for changing the look of the brick. Plaster (stucco) or cement-based paint are the most compatible with brick. They have a very good water resistance and adhesion but allow the masonry to breathe. Stains are used to create bands, blends and colored bond patterns, as well as individually coloring brick and mortar. This means the look of a brick wall can be maintained, if desired, while changing the brick and mortar to a more desirable color or blend of colors. The stains also have excellent water vapor permeability and do not require the maintenance of paint, as guarantees range from twenty-five years to a lifetime.

Advantages
- Brick has a classic, beautiful look and is long lasting.
- There are many colors and textures available.
- Brick is fireproof and durable and requires minimal maintenance.
- Brick will not warp, crack, rot, corrode, split, dent and is impervious to heat, wind, hail and insect damage.
- It is said that brick offers a better resale value than other sidings.
- Many companies offer 100-year warranties on their brick.

Disadvantages
- Brick is one of the most expensive sidings and requires a skilled mason for installation.
- The mason must know the properties of his materials.
- The airspace in the cavity wall construction cannot be clogged with excess mortar because that may cause water to accumulate and efflorescence to occur.
- Brick should not be allowed to freeze before it is cured. Special precautions must be taken if installation will be done in cold climates.
- For additions or changes in the structure of the house, it is expensive to remove the bricks and difficult to match them with new brick.

For further information about brick or to find a local distributor, visit The Brick Industry Association (BIA) at www.gobrick.org.

Thin-Brick Systems

These are systems that are used to attach thin brick to a wall. They can be used on the entire home or can be used to accent a portion of the home while using other sidings, such as vinyl, on the rest of the home. At seven pounds a square foot, these lightweight systems do not require the structural support (brick ledges and steel lintels over doors and windows) that are needed for 4-inch brick (at about forty-five pounds a square foot). Both thin and full brick are made from the same materials and in the same way; they are kiln-fired clay brick. Thin-brick systems are used on new homes for the cost savings they offer over full-brick construction. It is not necessary to have a skilled mason to install thin brick, which is a cost savings. This type of system is particularly advantageous in areas where it is difficult to find a qualified mason. Thin brick can be installed by carpenters or siding people, as well as handy do-it-yourselfers.

A house built with a thin-brick system.

Universal Brick Systems, Inc.

In the past, brick was never used for remodeling because the structural support needed for full brick was not available and would have to be added before the home could be bricked. This is costly and also damages yards and landscape as heavy equipment is brought across the yard and the landscape is dug up around the foundation. Now the existing chimney on the roof can also support the thin-brick system.

The most important aspect of installation for these systems is that the brick is mortar locked to the panel rather than relying on adhesive to hold the brick, as eventually all adhesive will dry out. There are also miniature brick ties called "brick locks" that surround each brick and become encapsulated in the mortar, holding each individual brick to the panel. This system makes the brick assembly very strong and durable.

Advantages

- The installation cost of thin-brick systems is generally less expensive than laid-in-place full brick ones.
- Thin brick is fireproof and durable.
- It is available in many colors and textures.
- It requires minimal maintenance.
- Thin brick can be used for remodeling.

Disadvantages

- They do not offer the same variety of textures, colors and shapes available as with full brick.
- The antique-looking or tumbled brick that is popular in full bricks is not as readily available in thin bricks.
- While most common brick patterns can be used with the panel systems, complex brick patterns cannot be done.

For further information on thin-brick systems, contact the American Brick Company at www.ambrico.com or Universal Thin Brick Systems at www.bricksystems.com. One of these panel manufacturers can recommend a local distributor and assist you in finding the thin brick you want for your home.

Novabrik

Novabrik is a mortarless brick siding system that is made of concrete, hangs on the wall and is patented in Canada. This product is particularly advantageous in areas where it may be difficult to find an available mason; Novabrik can be installed by a contractor or carpenter.

Advantages

- Novabriks are warranted for fifty years.
- They are easy to install and do not require a skilled mason for installation.
- Whereas brick should be installed in dry, warm weather so the mortar will dry, there are no necessary conditions for installation of Novabrik.
- The cost of the material is a bit less than the cost of brick, but installation is substantially quicker and less expensive.

Disadvantages

- This brick cannot be used for fireproof construction. It has not been tested and classified as of yet.

resources

For further information about Novabrik or to find a dealer or installer, see www.novabrik.com or call 1-800-265-2522.

Simulated Brick

Simulated brick is made from Portland cement and closely replicates natural brick. It is installed over sheathing, a weather barrier and metal lath and then set in mortar or masonry adhe-

sive. It is a practical siding to use for remodeling because it doesn't need additional structural support and doesn't require a skilled mason. Many of the simulated or concrete bricks are made from molds of old bricks to give them a more weathered appearance.

Advantages

- This product does not require a skilled mason, so it cuts down on the cost of installation.
- Unlike true brick, concrete brick does not require structural support and can be used for remodeling without building out the foundation.

Disadvantages

- There is far less variety in colors, shapes and styles than in full brick.

Fiber-Cement Brick

There are also brick panels made from fiber cement. For more information about this type of product, see Fiber Cement on page 112.

Stone

Stone has a beautiful and natural look. It has been used for hundreds of years and has held up to the test of time. It can be used for the entire house or as a trim or accent. Natural stones and the currently more popular manufactured stone veneers are available in a large range of colors and textures.

Some suppliers of stone siding:

Boulder Creek Stone Products	800-762-5902	www.bouldercreekstone.com
Coronado Stone Products	909-357-8295	www.coronado.com
Mountain Stone, Inc.	866-947-8663	www.mountainstone.biz
Owens Corning	800-255-1727	www.culturedstone.com
Tejas Textured Stone	866-578-5616	www.tejasstone.com

Natural Stones

There is a large variety of stones available in different parts of the country. They are available in full thickness stone and split stone.

Full-thickness stone—Full-thickness stone, or natural stone, is usually used on new constructions rather than on renovations because of the need to have the proper foundation to support the stone. It can be installed on a renovation if the foundation is revamped and the structure can support it. Installation requires an additional ledge in the foundation of about 4 inches all around and requires brick ties to attach the stones and weep holes to allow the water to escape.

Split stone—Natural stones can be split very thin and installed into a lath and mortar. This gives a very natural look without the expense of an additional foundation and a time-consuming, expensive installation.

Advantages
- Natural and split stone is beautiful.
- Stone is non-combustible, maintenance-free and has proven to be durable.

Disadvantages
- For full-thickness stone, not all stones are available everywhere in the country.
- If a stone is chosen that is not from the local area, shipping expenses may be significant.
- Installation can be time consuming and expensive.
- Full-thickness stones require footings to support the stone and mechanical fasteners to attach the stone to the wall.
- Installation is expensive and requires a skilled mason.
- Natural stone does not have the design flexibility of the lighter synthetic stones.
- For renovations and additions it may be difficult to match the stones and removal is difficult work.

- Certain stones are more sensitive to weather conditions than others.
- There is no warranty on natural stone.

Manufactured Stone Veneer (MSV)

MSV is made from Portland cement and closely replicates natural stone. Stone veneers are very popular, assuming the largest part of the stone market share, and are available from many suppliers. They come in a variety of styles (from antique-looking to rustic), colors and sizes, and it is often difficult to differentiate the real from the synthetic.

Advantages
- Installation does not require a skilled mason and can occur in a relatively short time.
- It is installed directly on the wall and does not require additional footings or mechanical ties.
- It is lightweight and can be flexibly used in a variety of designs.
- Many varieties of stone can be found in most locations in the United States and Canada and do not have regional restrictions or require the added expense of shipping it in from another location.
- For later additions, the stones are usually easily matched.
- MSVs are non-combustible.
- Some insurance companies will offer a reduction for using them.
- It is easy to replace broken stones—they are chiseled out and replaced. For stress fractures, a repair kit is available to fill in the crack and color to match. MSVs require minimal maintenance.
- Most companies offer a fifty-year warranty.

Disadvantages
- Stone veneers are more expensive than most other sidings.
- Some varieties may not look as authentic as real stone.

Manufactured stone veneer is used on this house.

Additional Innovations for Siding

Liquid Vinyl Coating

An interesting product to be aware of is liquid vinyl coating. It can be used on any of the above products to add protection and durability. It can also be used on siding that is in need of remodeling to prevent additional deterioration from weathering and the damage caused by UV rays. It is available through distributors in twenty-two states who apply this coating with a 3200 psi sprayer (a high-pressure sprayer that sprays at a pressure of 3,200 pounds per square inch). A special primer is applied followed by a liquid vinyl, which together leave a solid film that is fifteen times thicker than standard paint. Because it is highly elastic, it will stretch to cover cracks that may occur in the substrate (such as stucco) beneath, and will prevent water from getting into the cracks to cause deterioration. Since it can act as a sealant, it is important that areas that allow water to get through should not be covered or closed by this coating. It is also vapor permeable and will prevent vapor from being trapped behind. Textures will show through the coating, maintaining the original look of the material, such as cedar or stucco. It is available in 1,488 colors and has a lifetime warranty for the original owner and a fifty-year transferable warranty; it can, however, only be expected to last for the duration of the material beneath.

resources

Liquid vinyl siding information: www.liquid-vinylsiding.net or 800-430-3225,

Some manufactured stone veneer suppliers:

Boulder Creek	800-762-5902	www.bouldercreekstone.com
Coronado Stone Products	909-357-8295	www.coronado.com
Eldorado Stone	800-925-1491	www.eldoradostone.com
Mountain Stone, Inc.	866-947-8663	www.mountainstone.biz
Owens Corning	800-255-1727	www.culturedstone.com
Performax Building Materials	866-230-4655	www.performaxstone.com
Tejas Textured Stone	866-578-5616	www.tejasstone.com
Telluride Stone Company	970-728-6201	www.telluridestone.com
Texas Stone Designs, Inc.	800-336-1131	www.texasstonedesigns.com

Wedge Vent System

The wedge vent system is a siding accessory. It is a patented wedge that is installed between the siding to prevent moisture buildup behind red cedar shingles and clapboard. It prevents paint from blistering, cedar from bleeding and nails from rusting due to trapped water. Water vapor can condense behind the siding material, like shingles, under the right weather conditions. If it cannot get out through the siding, it will be trapped, rotting the substrate and the siding. The wedges can be installed with new siding but are generally retrofitted in older siding. The vents are easy to install and cost approximately $97 for an entire house.

resources

For further information on wedge vent systems, go to www.wedgevent.com or call 800-933-4366.

There are so many options that could appropriately be used with the large variety of architectural styles. Review all of these materials, take a closer look at those which are of interest and select a siding that will look attractive, be durable and be one that you will be able to maintain over the long run.

Windows

Opposite Page: A casement window with awnings stacked above with simulated divided lites.

This California house overlooking the mountains has several different types of windows, including stationary out-swing windows.

There is an incredible variety of windows and doors available for the home; it can be overwhelming to the homeowner in making a selection. Today more than ever there are many choices in manufacturers, styles, materials, colors and extra features. Some windows can be bought from stock, and many companies offer the opportunity to customize their windows. The following will give you an idea of what your options are before venturing out to the marketplace. The initial factors to consider when selecting windows are as follows:

Kolbe & Kolbe Millwork Co., Inc.

Energy efficiency/insulating value of the window—The insulating value of the window will be with you for the life of the window, twenty years or more. This will also have a direct influence on heating and cooling costs initially and throughout the years.

Budget—Windows are available in a variety of price ranges.

Location—Different locations will pose special needs. In some areas, such as shore areas, safety glass will be required. In very cold or hot areas, ventilation will be a consideration. In some locations there may be a desire to keep the windows open for most of the year to let in breezes; in these areas screens may be desirable. Other locations such as near busy streets or airports may demand sound reduction.

Style of the house—Be sure that the window style you choose is consistent with the style of the house. A sliding glass window should never be used, for example, in a Federal-style house.

Personal preference—Find windows that are available in the colors, styles and designs you like.

Bells and whistles—Some companies offer more special features than others. Decide your priorities before selecting windows.

Stock windows or custom-made windows—Budget and design will determine which of these you will select.

Egression—Windows can serve as a second means of emergency egress when installed as required by the local building code.

To avoid a long investigation, here is a basic list of the types of windows available. Consider all the options and alternatives before making a decision. Once you have an idea of what you want, you can find the manufacturer that makes the window that meets your needs and desires. Often, more than one type of window may be used on a house, depending on exposure and style.

Fixed Windows

These are windows that cannot be opened. They are available in a wide range of standard and custom (to be ordered) sizes, shapes and colors. Some are to be used alone or in combination with other windows. Some of the shapes available are octagons, triangles, circles, half-rounds, ellipticals, quarter circles, ovals and more. Fixed windows are also available with a large variety of novelty glazing and grille patterns. There are many locations in a house where it is

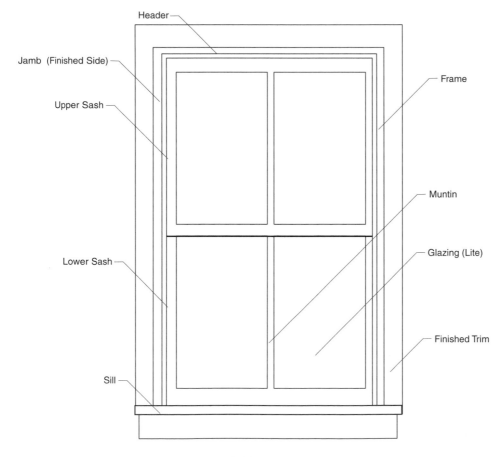

Parts of a Double-hung Window
(exterior view)

Although casement windows usually swing out, those that are in-swing are a bit more unusual and give the house a European look.

Kolbe & Kolbe Millwork Co., Inc.

advantageous to have glass, to view beautiful scenery or just to enjoy the additional light, but where ventilation is not necessary; fixed windows should be used in these areas.

Windows That Open

Casement

These are windows that swing open on hinges like a door. Often they are opened with a cranking knob. They usually open from the side, but some casements open from the top as well, for easy cleaning and ventilation. Even if they don't open at the top, most casements are made with "arm" room between the sash and the frame to make it is easier to clean the windows from the inside. Cranks can stick out quite a bit, getting in the way of shutters or other window treatments. Smaller cranks that are less obtrusive are available. Casement windows are usually used on more contemporary-style houses, but they can be made to look more traditional with grilles. Casements are particularly practical in areas that are hard to reach, such as over sinks. There are casement windows available that open in, as well as the more common out-swinging ones.

There is a variety of different types of windows in this house, bringing a great deal of natural light into the interior.

Double- or Single-Hung

These have upper and lower sashes that open and close the window. In single-hung windows, only the bottom sash moves. In double-hung windows, both sashes move. The movement of the windows is controlled by springs, weights or friction devices. They have a traditional look and were used on many of the early house styles. There is less ventilation than with casement windows. Some double-hung windows are difficult to clean, but there are many companies today that offer tilting windows for easier access.

Awning

These are windows with a single panel of glass that are hinged at the top and open out. They are sometimes available in pairs, offer good ventilation and are easy to clean. They are often used above or below a window or above a door.

Sliding

Sashes slide on a metal or plastic track. As with the similar double-hung windows, in some windows both sashes move; in others the sashes are stationary. They are sometimes difficult to clean and do not offer as much ventilation as casement windows. The advantage of sliding windows is the low cost. They do offer limited ventilation.

Kolbe & Kolbe Millwork Co., Inc.

Hopper

These are hinged at the bottom and open in from the top. They are typically used in the basement where the window openings may be at or slightly below grade. They provide good ventilation and are easy to clean, but they can allow rain to come in.

Tilt-Turn

These can be operated as an in-swing casement window and a tilt-in-from-the-top (hopper-type) window. Specialized hardware used on

these windows helps to adequately operate the windows in several configurations. They are easy to clean, energy efficient, allow for ventilation in rainy weather and meet most egress codes. They are, however, very expensive and have a modern or European look.

Rotating

They pivot on a central axis to open partially. They are good for ventilation and can be purchased in very large sizes for unobstructed views.

Jalousie

They have many small, pivoting panes. They are good for ventilation and are easy to reach for cleaning.

Clerestory

A window located in the upper part of a lofty room, where light shines down into the center of the room.

Transom

A small opening above a door or window separated by a horizontal member that usually contains a sash or a louver panel hinged to the transom bar.

Radius, or Arched

These are windows with arched or semicircular tops. These are becoming very popular.

Glass Block

Glass blocks allow for the entrance of light and privacy, without a traditional window. They come in several colors, patterns and sizes and are usually installed by a mason.

Projecting Windows

These are windows that project out (cantilevered) from the room and can be stationary, moveable or a combination of both. They

Tilt-turn windows.

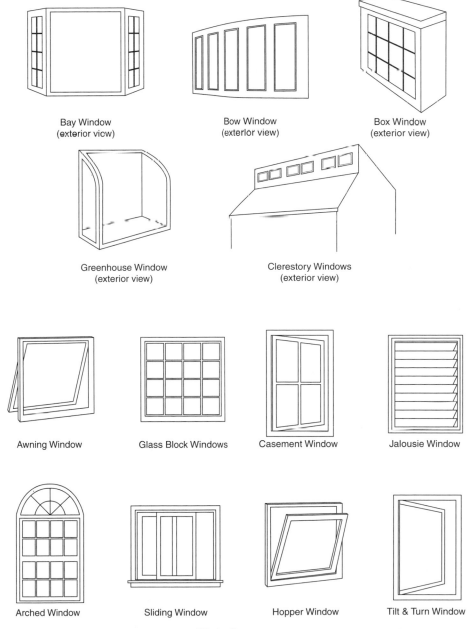

Bay Window
(exterior view)

Bow Window
(exterior view)

Box Window
(exterior view)

Greenhouse Window
(exterior view)

Clerestory Windows
(exterior view)

Awning Window

Glass Block Windows

Casement Window

Jalousie Window

Arched Window

Sliding Window

Hopper Window

Tilt & Turn Window

Window Types

sometimes give the room added floor space and offer additional light.

Bay

Usually a combination of two angled side windows with one straight window in the center.

Box

Two-sided windows that are perpendicular to the center window.

Bow

A bow window has all curved panels projecting out from the wall.

Greenhouse, or Garden

Designed for growing plants, they are generally prefabricated and come with shelves and some panels that open for ventilation. They come in standard window sizes but can also be custom made.

Skylights and Roof Windows

These are excellent windows for areas of the house that cannot be otherwise lit, where there is no other convenient place for a window for added ventilation or where it is a preferred design feature. Skylights come in a variety of sizes, materials (glass and plastic), shapes (circular, square, rectangular) and installation methods (self-flashing or curb-mounted—they must be mounted and flashed by the installer). Skylights can be fixed or ventilating, which can be opened with long poles or mechanically operated. They can be flat or arched or can be in square pyramid, octagonal pyramid, extended pyramid or spherical configurations. Roof windows differ from ventilating skylights because they have sashes that pivot on each side of the frame and are usually installed on sloping walls or sloped ceilings of attics. They are

often available with shades and blinds that can manually or electronically be opened and closed. One company (Andersen Windows) has roof windows that automatically close when it rains.

Some resources for skylights and roof windows:

Andersen Windows	800-426-4261	www.andersenwindows.com
Fakro America, LLC	630-543-1010	www.fakro.info
Skywin-Fakro (C)	519-352-6587	www.fakro.ca
Velux America, Inc.	800-888-3589	www.veluxusa.com
Wasco Sky Windows	800-988-0293	www.wascoskywindows.com

(C) = Canadian

Tubular Skylights

These are used to transmit indirect, diffused sunlight, evenly dispersed throughout a room, reducing the potential damage to carpets and furniture caused by UV rays and providing natural light to illuminate the home. Some tubular skylights have integrated electrical lights, so they can be used day or night; some have mechanisms for controlling the light coming into the room and some have ventilation fans available. Tubular skylights should be used on areas of the roof that receive direct light for the largest portion of the day. These skylights can only be used to light rooms directly under the roof; they usually don't provide ventilation and never provide a view. They are energy efficient, using a renewable energy source and cutting down on power usage. They provide the full spectrum of light, making it a more comfortable light; it helps plants grow and it is said to make people feel good. Tubular skylights are substantially less expensive than traditional skylights. They are available in several sizes from 10 to about 21 inches.

Structural Skylights

These are design features that can be incorporated into many types of designs and bring a lot of natural light into the house. They are usually larger than skylights and can be purchased in standard sizes or custom fabricated

Some tubular skylight suppliers:

Creative Energy Technologies	518-287-1428	www.cetsolar.com
Daylite Corporation	888-329-5483	www.dayliteco.com
Innovative Tubular Lighting	713-880-9898	www.texassolartubes.com
Sky-Tech Industries, Inc. (C)	800-447-0644	www.sunscope.com
Solar Bright Corporation	800-780-1759	www.solarbright.com
Solartube International	800-966-7652	www.solartube.com
Sun Beamer Skylights	916-339-0152	www.sunbeamer.com
Sun-Dome	800-596-8414	www.sun-dome.com
The Sun Pipe Company, Inc.	800-844-4786	www.sunpipe.com
Sun Tunnel Systems	512-323-6696	www.suntunnel.com
Tru-Lite Tubular Skylights	800-873-3309	www.tru-lite.com
Tubular Skylight, Inc.	800-315-8823	www.tubular-skylight.com

(C) = Canadian

to site specifications. They are available in a variety of shapes (polygons, radius domes, hip ridges, pyramid and so on) and can even be motorized to open up the house to fresh air. Skylights are generally made of extruded aluminum, which is available in a variety of colors through the process of anodizing or painting them with Kynar. The glass should be tinted for climate control and to prevent furnishings from fading. A wide variety of colors (bronze, green, blue and so on) and effects (such as using white to make the glass translucent) can be achieved. Codes in some areas require that tempered glass be used on the outside and laminated on the inside for safety. There is a wide variety of glass configurations available, from double glazing to triple glazing, low-E glass and so on. In addition, a system must be incorporated into the mechanism for channeling rain, water seepage and snow away from the glass.

resources

For additional information about skylights, check the Office of Energy Efficiency and Renewable Energy's article on "Skylights for Residences" at www.eere.energy.gov/consumer-info/refbriefs/ba7.html.

Glazing Options

Historically glass was available in only small dimensions. Many older houses have windows with many small panes because that was what was available at the time of construction. People

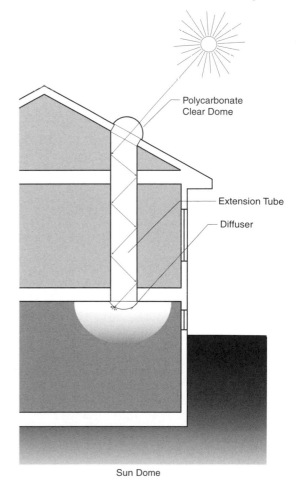

Sun Dome

Some Configurations for Structural Skylights

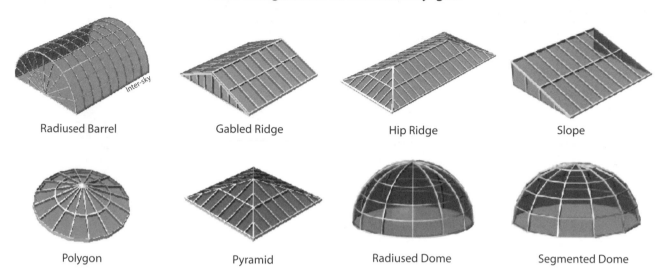

Radiused Barrel Gabled Ridge Hip Ridge Slope

Polygon Pyramid Radiused Dome Segmented Dome

still use divided-light panels of varying sizes because they like the appearance or to keep in step with the particular style of the house. With today's technology there are many decisions to be made in windows but specifically with the glass itself.

Single, Double or Triple Glazing

Whereas all windows were once single-paned, today double- and triple-glazed windows are available from most manufacturers. Single panes have a small amount of insulating value (approximately R-1); increasing the number of panes increases the window's ability to resist heat flow because of the air layers created. (These are not the same as insulated glass, which is described below. The air layers on single-, double- and triple-glazed windows are not hermetically sealed.)

Novelty Glass

Stained—This is colored glass assembled into designs. Metallic oxides, which add color to

Some resources for structural skylights:

Bristolite Skylights	www.bristolite.com
Distinctive Skylights	www.distinctiveskylights.com
Dome'l	www.domelinc.com
Gammans Architectural Products	www.gammans.com
Inter-sky Skylight Specialists	www.inter-sky.com
Starlight Skylights	www.starlightskylights.com
Super Sky Products, Inc.	www.supersky.com

the glass, are added to the mixture during the melting process.

Art—This defines a category of glass designed for its artistic appeal rather than functional need. It includes stained glass, etched glass and so on, with combinations of colors and special effects.

Leaded—Leaded glass is a type of art glass that is made by connecting pieces of glass with a lead channel and soldering the intersections of the lead channel. This is the way most large stained glass works are made, coupled with stiffening bars. Lead is very strong and offers good support

Frame Material

Materials	Advantages	Disadvantages	R-value of the material*
Wood—Interior wood is most often yellow pine. Other options can be Douglas fir, maple, cherry, oak or mahogany (pre-painted or primed only).	• Traditional and natural • High R-value • Doesn't promote condensation • Can be ordered raw, primed or painted	• Requires periodic painting or staining; otherwise the frames will swell and eventually rot, warp and stick.	√√
Aluminum—Also available with a thermal break to interrupt heat loss	• Very strong, durable—can support large glazing • Lightweight • Low maintenance • Less expensive than wood	• Conducts and loses heat faster than other materials (most suitable for mild climates). • Prone to condensation, which can cause mold, fungus and rot. • Anodizing or a coating is required to prevent corrosive deterioration. • Subject to nicks and scratches.	√
Steel	• Has a modern, clean look • Frame is narrow, allowing maximum visibility • Durable • Maintenance-free	• Expensive. Not as energy efficient as other materials (is available with thermal breaks as an option). Not as many styles are available.	√
Vinyl (made of polyvinyl chloride—PVC)—Available with and without insulation	• Wide range of styles, colors and shapes • Because the color goes all the way through, nicks and scratches will not be apparent • Moderate to high R-value • Less expensive than wood • Easily customized • Low maintenance • Durable and resists moisture—won't rot or warp • Excellent in areas of high humidity where wood is likely to rot	• Not as strong as metal or wood (large windows can be reinforced with aluminum or steel-reinforcing bars). • They cannot be painted and are not generally available in dark colors, which absorb too much heat.	√√

*Dependent on the thickness of the material and the thermal breaks that are used in the particular frame. The entire window assembly is used to evaluate the overall R-value by an independent testing laboratory.

Frame Material (continued)

Materials	Advantages	Disadvantages	R-value of the material*
Fiberglass pultrusion— With wood interior	• Highest R-value of the available materials • Will not warp, shrink, swell, rot or corrode • Impervious to heat, moisture and cold conditions • Less bulky • Very strong, durable • Can hold a large pane of glass • Many colors available • Maintenance-free • Most come with a resilient paint finish, but they can be painted on-site for a custom color	• They are expensive and may not be available in many styles.	√√
Fiberglass composite — With wood interior	• Very strong, durable, not bulky • Impervious to heat, moisture and cold conditions • Will not warp, sag, stretch, or dent • Impact resistant • Can be painted on-site with custom colors	• Available in limited colors from the factory.	√√√
Composite— A combination of organic material, plastic or other additives for strength, flexibility or fire retardance	• Low maintenance • Durable • Resistant to fading and rot • Good insulation • Paintable • Environmentally friendly, using sawdust and wood scrap that would otherwise be discarded	• Some composites cannot be painted and not all of them come in a lot of colors. Most companies do not offer as many styles.	√√√

for the glass while being flexible enough to withstand the thermal expansion of the glass and window encasement.

Beveled—It has the edge of the glass cut off at an angle that bends the light and produces a prismatic effect. The width of the bevel may vary but $1/2$ inch is the most common width. It is typically available only on entry doors or interior doors.

Etched—Etched glass has some or all of the polished surface removed by either a chemical or sandblast process. The glass is then slightly thinner in the etched region and has a diffused reflective surface, which appears whiter in color.

Obscure—This is clear glass through which images cannot be seen because the light waves are bent by the texture on the glass surfaces. This type of glass is used where light is desired but visibility is not, such as on a bathroom door.

Tempered—This is glass that is treated with heat in its processing, creating a product that can withstand higher force or pressure on its surface. When it breaks, it breaks into small, dull pieces rather than sharp-edged pieces for safety.

Insulation and Safety Options

Glass is durable and allows a high percentage of sun to enter a home, but it has poor resistance to heat flow. Over the last few years there have been many innovations to improve the performance and efficiency of windows, with several new ones just beyond the horizon. The energy efficiency of windows is described by manufacturers in terms of the windows' U-values (conductance of heat range is from 1.1 to 0.3) and R-values (resistance to heat flow range is from 0.9 to 3.0). The higher the R-value, the less heat the window will lose. The lower the U-value, the less heat the window will lose. When buying a window, check for the R-value and U-value and make sure that the manufacturer has calculated these numbers for the entire window, not just the glass. Then check that the number is for the same size

window you are selecting and that the figures are based on the current standards of the American Society of Heating, Refrigerating and Air-Conditioning Engineers (ASHRAE). The following are some of the glazing options that are currently available to control heat loss or gain:

Insulating—This term is used to describe two or more panes of glass separated by a hermetically sealed airspace. An additional option is to have a premium gas (other than air) filler in the interior of the insulated glass. Argon and krypton gas are available between some multipaned windows. The gas cuts down the air currents and serves as an insulator, resisting airflow. The space should not be greater than $5/8$ inch or less than $1/2$ inch between panes for optimum resistance for air and argon. With krypton, the optimum spacing is $5/16$ inch. (Triple panes of insulated glass, two surfaces of low-E and two gas-filled airspaces will offer the most energy-efficient glazing system for areas of daily or seasonal temperature swings or constant exposure to sunlight.)

Low-E (low emissivity) coating or film—This is a coating that helps reduce heat loss, glare and UV rays that fade furnishings. There are two types of coatings available—soft or hard coats. The soft coating is installed on multipaned assemblies in the airspace between the panes; it selectively reduces the transmission of certain wavelengths of light. Both types will reduce the flow of radiant heat out of the interior of the house and prevent the radiant heat from entering during the hotter times of the year. The soft coatings will easily degrade if exposed to air and moisture and damage easily; the films are therefore factory installed between panes, where there is less chance of damage. Hard-coat low-E coatings are more durable and are used where handling of the glass is more of an issue and where higher light transmission is desirable, but they are not as efficient as the soft-coat films. (Note: Low-E II is a soft-coat low-E and is still easily scratched.) All soft-coat low-E is on the inside of an insulated glass package. Hard-coat

139

low-E is also primarily used on the inside of insulated glass. Its coating does not scratch as easily as the soft-coat glass. The surface of the hard-coat glass is rough and is only used occasionally as a storm window due to cleaning issues. A third option is a thin plastic film coated on one or both sides with a low-E or spectrally selective coating that is suspended between two panes of glass called a "heat mirror." This film is manufactured by Southwall Technologies and installed during the insulated glass manufacturing process.

Spectrally selective coatings—These coatings are applied to tinted windows and clear glass. They filter out 40 to 70 percent of the heat that would normally be transmitted through clear glass. This kind of coating allows natural light transmittance into a home but controls radiated heat. This provides maximum energy efficiency and reduces the size of the air-conditioning units needed.

Heat-absorbing—These have special tinted coatings to prevent heat gain. Tints can be used with clear glass or glass coated with spectrally selective coatings to further prevent heat transfer. Gray and bronze are the most common colors for tinted glass; they reduce the penetration of light and heat. This glass is very effective when used for skylights.

Reflective coatings—When this coating is applied to clear or tinted glass, it will slow the transmission of heat but will also reduce the transmission of daylight as well. In the evening the coating creates a mirror effect, making it difficult to see outside the house. This may be used in very hot climates to control the heat from the sun, but the energy savings may be small when considering the need for added electrical lighting.

Tinted—This is a tint treatment in the glass, usually bronze, gray or blue, to block solar heat and lower air-conditioning costs. The thicker the glass, the darker it will be. It is sometimes used in warmer climates or unprotected southern or western exposures. Tinted glass is not commonly used in homes because it darkens views and limits the available natural light coming in during the day. Tinted glass, to be effective, requires a low-E coating or a separate piece of low-E in insulated glass to keep the heat from entering the home.

Impact-resistant—This type of glass is required in the building codes of some areas prone to hurricanes and tornadoes. There are two forms of impact-resistant glass: laminated glass and shatter-resistant film. Shatter-resistant film is a less-expensive method, often used for retrofitting existing windows. Not all window styles are available with impact-resistant glazing. If you are in need of this type of window, check on availability before proceeding with your window selection.

• Laminated—This is a safety glass consisting of two or more panes of glass bonded together with a plastic interlayer that holds the glass together in case of impact. An upgraded silicone sealant should be used on the windows purchased for high-risk areas. A stronger frame is required to handle the increased weight of laminated glass. Manufacturers claim that laminated glass reduces outdoor noise, adds a degree of safety from intruders and blocks UV light.

• Shatter-resistant film—This is a less expensive alternative, is placed (usually by a manufacturer's trained installer) on the interior side of a window glass to hold the shards of broken glass after impact. Although impact-resistant glass windows will be more expensive, they are permanently in place and eliminate the need for special preparation for impending severe weather. They have no effect on the appearance of a home but serve as a protection against flying glass and other airborne objects.

Not all window styles are available with impact-resistant glazing. If you are in need of this type of window, because of your location, check on the availability from various companies before proceeding with your window selection.

Tempered—This is also a safety glass that is treated with heat in its processing, creating a product that can withstand abnormal force or pressure on its surface. When it breaks, it breaks into small pieces rather than large sharp-edged ones. This type of glass is used in bathrooms, on patio doors and areas with large windows for safety.

Spacers

Metal (often aluminum) is used to separate the multiple panes of insulating glass. The metal, however, will conduct heat. In cold weather thermal resistance is less around the edges than in the center of a pane of glass, causing heat loss and condensation around the edges. To lessen the heat loss and condensation there are several warm-edge spacers now on the market. Examples of warm-edge spacers are Swiggle, Super Spacer, Intercept, Hy-Therm and Warm-light.

Divided Lights

True divided-light windows are not considered as energy efficient as some other windows because of the multi-glazed edges. Many of the windows today are simulated divided light, and this is not a problem. The different options available are no divided light (windows with no dividers) and divided light.

True divided light—This is the most traditional type of divided light, the way windows were made hundreds of years ago when the panes were not available as large as they are today.

Simulated divided light—The appearance of a divided-light system is achieved with plastic or wood grilles that are either permanently attached to the glazing or can be snapped on.

Grilles in the airspace—These grilles are inserted between the panes of multi-glazed windows and can be removed. In sealed insulating units they are permanent.

Grilles on the exterior—These snap on and off or can be glued to the glass.

Hardware

Each company offers a variety of colors and styles in hardware. If the windows will be installed in a coastal area, check for corrosion-resistant hardware made of stainless steel, which will be more durable. Usually companies offer several handle configurations: a traditional handle, which is easy to grip; a compact grip; a fold-away handle and/or a T-handle, which is difficult for little fingers to operate. Some companies offer fold-away handles and some offer electric operators for hard-to-reach windows. Currently available is a self-locking system on some windows that locks automatically when the window is closed. Adapters are available to limit the ventilation on casement and awning windows. These will prevent accidents with small children but can create a hazard if the window is needed for escape in an emergency. Check egress requirements in local building codes before such an adapter is installed. If you will be installing shutters, shades or blinds, check to see that the window handle will not be in the way. Some of the typical metals available are antique brass, oil-rubbed bronze, brushed chrome, bright chrome, pewter, gold tone and white. Metals come standard with additional options usually available.

Additional Options

Integrated blinds and shades in multi-glazed windows reduce heat gain in the summer. They also eliminate the need for further window treatment for privacy or light blockage and eliminate the need for dusting and cleaning the window treatment. They are available with and without cords. The cordless types have the advantage of being safer for children and animals (without the cord to get tangled in). The cordless models have knobs, buttons and remote control devices (depending on the manufacturer) for operating the mini-blinds and shades.

Retractable insect screen—This self-storing screen rolls away, out of sight when not in use. Many of the screens are after-market products; they are added after the windows are purchased. There are retractable screens that are an added option on some windows. These screens can be removed when they are not needed or for repair. Preferred Engineering Products has a patent on a self-storing Slide'N'Hide screen sold with some windows.

resources

For more information on the Slide'N'Hide screen, check www.preferred-eng.com.

Standard insect screens—These can be installed in most windows.

Warranty—Windows have different warranties. Find out what each company is offering.

Energy efficiency—When considering energy efficiency, different combinations of window options should be considered for each home, depending on budget, direction of the window and weather conditions in the area. Some homes may require more than one type of window option because of the exposure.

Type of window—Some types of windows are more energy efficient than others. Double-hung windows and horizontal sliding windows are not as energy efficient as most other types of windows, such as casement and awning windows, which have compression seals and allow less air leakage.

Frame resistance—Different frame materials have varying degrees of thermal resistance. (See page 141 for more information.)

Glazing—There are several types of glass that have high energy efficiency, such as low-E glass, reflective glass and so on. The climate, location and the exposure of particular windows will determine which glass system will be most appropriate.

Layers of glass—Single panes have little thermal resistance; two and three panes have more.

Argon and krypton gas—These gases insulate better than air and increase the R-value of the window.

Size of the airspace between the layers—A proper airspace between panes adds to the thermal resistance.

Energy Star—This is a government-backed program of the Environmental Protection Agency (EPA) and was developed to protect the environment through energy efficiency. This program qualifies new homes as well as various products for the home, such as windows. When purchasing windows, ask if they have earned the Energy Star, which must meet strict energy efficiency guidelines.

resources

For additional information about the Energy Star program, visit www.energystar.gov.

NFRC label—The National Fenestration Rating Council is a nonprofit organization created by the window, door and skylight industry. NFRC provides fair, accurate and credible national energy performance ratings for windows, doors and skylights. These ratings help consumers, architects, builders, contractors and others to compare the energy performance of different products on an apples-to-apples basis, and they help consumers to make informed decisions about the products they buy. To learn more about the NFRC, please visit www.nfrc.org.

Caulking and weatherstripping—These can be installed on older windows to make them more efficient. They can be purchased at hardware stores and professionally installed or by a do-it-yourselfer. Newer windows have the weatherstripping included in the window construction.

Storm windows and panels—These can be used to increase the efficiency of single-pane windows. They come in several formats and can be installed on the interior or the exterior of the windows. One option is in the form of a plastic film taped to the inside of the window frame, which can easily be installed and removed but can also be easily damaged and may lessen visibility. Interior storm windows can also be mounted on brackets on the interior of the window and can have glass, acrylic or polycarbonate panes. The types of glazing and installation vary by manufacturer. Rigid and semi-rigid plastic sheets are available in the form of Plexiglas, polycarbonate or fiber-reinforced polyester, which are attached to the outside of the window frame or mounted in channels around the frame. Storm windows can increase energy efficiency, improve sound resistance and decrease condensation, and some may reduce UV-ray transmission. Storm windows can be particularly useful in order to preserve the historic integrity of old windows, while also making them energy efficient.

resources

For further information about energy efficiency with windows and doors, check the Web site of the National Fenestration Rating Council at www.nfrc.org, the alliance to save energy at www.efficientwindows.org, the Office of Energy Efficiency and Renewable energy at www.eere.energy.gov/consumerinfo/refbriefs/eb2.html, and the Eagle Institute at www.eagle-institute.com.

Some of the many window suppliers:

Andersen Windows, Inc.	800-426-4261	www.andersenwindows.com
Caradco	800-238-1866	www.caradco.com
Certain Teed	800-782-8777	www.certainteed.com
Crestline	800-552-4111	www.crestlinewindows.com
Eagle Windows and Doors	800-453-3633	www.eaglewindow.com
Eurotech Windows	800-282-9044	www.eurotecwindows.com
Fibertec (C)	888-232-4956	www.fibertec.com
HH Windows & Doors	206-763-3438	www.hhwindows.com
Hurd Millwork Company	800-223-4873	www.hurd.com
H Window	800-843-4929	www.hwindow.com
Kolbe & Kolbe Millwork Co., Inc.	888-831-5589	www.kolbe-kolbe.com
Lincoln Windows	800-967-2461	www.lincolnwindows.com
Loewen (C)	800-563-9367	www.loewen.com
Marvin Windows and Doors	800-346-5128	www.marvin.com
Milgard Windows	800-645-4273	www.milgard.com
Norco	888-476-6726	www.norcowindows.com
Norwood Windows (C)	506-532-0908	www.norwoodwindows.com
Peachtree Doors and Windows	800-732-2499	www.peachtreedoor.com
Pella	800-524-3700	www.pella.com
Pozzi Window Co.	800-821-1016	www.pozzi.com
REPLA Ltd. (replacement only)(C)	800-387-7914	www.replawindows.com
Semco Windows & Doors	800-333-2206	www.semcowindows.com
Simonton Windows	800-542-9118	www.simonton.com
Thermal Line Windows	800-662-1832	www.tlwindows.com
Vetter Windows and Doors	800-838-8372	www.vetterwindows.com
Weather Shield	800-477-6808	www.weathershield.com
Windsor Windows & Doors	800-218-6186	www.windsorwindows.com

(C) = Canadian

Replacement windows—Many manufacturers offer windows to replace defective or worn-out windows. Some windows can be replaced by the original company that produced them, but if they are very old, custom replacement windows may have to be purchased. These windows can be installed without ripping apart the entire frame and siding. Double-hung windows can often be replaced by handy do-it-yourselfers; casement windows are more difficult to replace and should be installed by a professional. If the original window manufacturer cannot replace the windows, there are several companies that only make replacement windows as well as national chains that offer custom-made windows.

The national chains usually only offer vinyl replacements, whereas wood frames can be purchased from window replacement manufacturers.

resources

For information on locating appropriate replacement windows, contact the National Fenestration Rating Council at www.nfrc.org.

New Innovations

There are several very exciting glass innovations in the works; some of them are already available, and some are still in development.

Switchable glazing—This is a new technology in which the glass will adapt to changes in lighting and heating—either in a passive or active way. Both types of innovations will potentially lower cooling costs and/or add to the comfort of the home.

Passive technologies—The three passive technologies are thermotropic, thermochromic and thermoscattering glass treatments. They use no electricity and will automatically work when the sun shines. Thermotropic glass will work anytime the sun is shining to control the heat entering the house, obstructing the view. Thermochromic glass will work anytime the sun is shining to control the glare and heat entering the house but will preserve the view to the outside. These technologies will work even if you are not at home or forget to pull the shades, blinds or curtains. Some of these technologies will help block UV rays and will reduce the harmful effects of the sun's energy in the fading of furniture, carpets and artwork. Because passive technologies do not use electricity, there is no wiring or electrical hookup involved. This makes operable windows possible, as well as shaped windows, such as circles and other designs. Passive glazing will be used to alter the light transmission according to temperature variations and the directness of the sun. Thermoscattering glass, which is already available, changes according to temperature but is used for privacy rather than for controlling the heat in the house.

- Thermotropic glass—This is a type of glass that goes from clear at room temperature to opaque when the sun warms the glass. In the opaque state it is white and reflects some of the sun's energy. When thermotropic glass changes to an opaque state, the view is obscured. This will potentially limit the heat of the sun in the house. At this time, thermotropic glass is not available. It is in the development stage but is like all of these technologies that are not yet available; they are emerging soon and will change the way we think about windows.
- Thermochromic glass—This glass is treated with a thermochromic film. The film is laminated between two pieces of glass or plastic, which will variably change from clear to a darker color as the temperature rises, while preserving the view. When available, thermochromic glass will automatically change and not be controlled by the homeowner. It will be useful in cutting down on sunlight glare and heat gain in the house.
- Thermoscattering—This glass is already available and is used for privacy rather than blocking the sun. As the temperature rises on the glass the opaque surface changes to a clear one. The glass will obscure the view when cold. On a skylight, when the sun is shining and the glass is still cool, it looks like a fluorescent light; when heated, it becomes clear, like ordinary glass. This glass could also be used for privacy on windows and sunrooms. At night the glass would be opaque for privacy, yet when the sun is shining it would be clear. Another practical application, though unrelated here, is the use of thermoscattering glass on a fireplace. It hides the ash when the fireplace is not in use and becomes clear when the fire is raging. It can also be used on oven doors to obscure the window when the oven isn't on and to make it visible when the heat is on. This glass is available in blue, green and gray tints as well as with reflective and anti-reflective coatings. The threshold

point at which the glass becomes clear can be altered from 40 to 65 degrees Celsius, depending on the application and/or geographic location of use. By adding an electrically conductive coating to thermochromic or thermoscattering glass the threshold point can be actively changed.

resources

For further information on either of the latter two passive types of glazings, check with the Pleotint, LLC at www.pleotint.com or The U.S. Department of Energy at www.eere.energy.gov.

Active technologies—The active technologies allow consumers to either control the glare/heat entering the house or to obscure the view with a small amount of electrical current. One of the scientists interviewed for this book said he is sure someday children will comment to their parents, "I can't believe you weren't able to turn off your windows when you were a kid." This reflects the optimism of several companies that are actively developing this glass for residential and commercial use. These switchable glazings, or "smart" windows, are being developed to electrically control the amount of sunlight and solar heat that enters the home through windows, skylights and glass doors. Electrochromic and suspended particle devices (SPDs) have practical applications in controlling the sun's glare for use of the computer, television and home theater without the need for curtains, shades and blinds. This will also reduce the cost of heating and air-conditioning by controlling the amount of heat entering the house, while consuming a minimum of electricity itself. In addition, it will reduce the harmful effects of the sun's energy in fading furniture, carpets and artwork by reducing the sun's UV rays. By controlling the effects of the sun coming into sliding glass doors, the need for shades or blinds, which can be cumbersome in these applications, will be reduced. An additional benefit is blocking out

street lights and other light that may be a nuisance at night. Liquid crystal, a third active-type system, can only create a clear or milky white opaque state, with no variations in between. This is a technology used for privacy rather than the reduction of glare. All of these technologies are already available in a limited way from a small number of suppliers. The following is a thumbnail sketch of these new technologies.

- Electrochromatic windows—Electrochromatic technology consists of a glass substrate that has been coated with electro-optical thin films that can control visual light and completely shut down the transmission of solar heat. The glare of the sun is blocked with the flip of a switch. The windows change from transparent to shaded by an electrical signal. Although this technology works a little slower (it may take three to four minutes) than the SPD system, it will block out more of the heat, has a wider dynamic range, uses DC voltage and is clear in its nonenergized state. This technology has passed U.S. government approval (by the National Renewable Energy Laboratory) for all durability tests. Electrochromatic windows are currently available from VELUX America.

resources

For information about electrochromatic technology, contact SAGE Electrochromics at www.sage.ec.com or 507-333-0078 or VELUX America at www.veluxamerica.com.

- Suspended Particle Devices (SPDs)—This is another method of controlling the level of light (SPDs do not block heat; heat is only active in the visible part of the light spectrum) coming in through the glass with a thin film that is sandwiched between two pieces of glass. It is a laminated glass that switches instantly, uses AC voltage and is dark in its nonenergized state. It is the only system that can currently be used on plastic and glass and can also be used on curved surfaces. SPDs are available from several window manufacturers in a very limited way.

resources

For further information about SPDs or to find a local manufacturer, contact Research Frontiers Incorporated (which holds the patent on this technology) at www.smartglass.com or call 888-773-7337.

- Liquid crystal (LC)—With this technology, a flick of a switch will transform a milky-white opaque glass panel to a clear one. This system does not control glare, heat or light; it is used for privacy only. When an AC voltage is applied, this glass permits parallel light to pass through and the glass is clear. In the nonenergized state the liquid crystal molecules are arranged so light is dispersed and the glass is opaque. These liquid crystals are bonded between two layers of glass. LC glass does not have the durability for exterior applications but is used for privacy in bathroom doors and for windows in conference rooms.

resources

Information on liquid crystal: Polytronix, Inc., at www.polytronix.com and Switch Lite Privacy Glass at www.switchlite.com.

For further information about new technologies, contact the National Association of Home Builders (NAHB) Research Center at www.toolbase.org or the U.S. Department of Energy at www.eere.energy.gov.

Other New Technologies

Self-cleaning glass—This glass is already available by several window manufacturers in the United States and Canada. It significantly reduces the need to clean the glass; titanium dioxide is the active ingredient. Organic material on the glass is broken down by the sun's UV rays (by a process called "photocatalytic

technology"), and the remaining dirt is washed away when it rains or when water is sprayed on. Water spreads evenly on the surface rather than in droplets (this process is called "hydrophilic") and then dries more quickly than conventional glass, without leaving drying spots. The coating is environmentally friendly, contains no harmful chemical substances and reduces the need for cleaning agents used on other glass. This glass can be purchased as standard or tempered glass.

PPG Industries, Inc.

Typical clear versus self-cleaning glass.

resources

For further information about this self-cleaning glass, contact Pilkington North America, Inc., at www.activglass.com or call 866-882-2848, PPG Sun Clean at www.ppg.sunclean.com or AFG Glass at www.afgglass.com.

Super-insulating windows—These are also being developed to further increase the energy efficiency of homes. Two new technologies that are still in the development stage are Aerogel and vacuum windows.

- Aerogel is a foamlike material comprising 90 percent air. The microscopic cell size and entrapped air work to highly insulate the windows. Aspen Aerogel is a company that is working on the material. At present, Aspen

Aerogel is being funded by the Department of Energy for feasibility of use in a window. There are significant problems to overcome, the greatest being a high haze level due to the cell structure of the foam. The Aerogel foam would be sealed between two pieces of glass. It could be used for windows, skylights or transparent wall panels. Currently there are no commercial window products made with Aerogel.

resources

For further information about Aerogel technology, check with Aspen Aerogel, Inc., at www.aerogel.com.

All of the windows in this Michigan lodge are casement units.

- Vacuum windows are two panes of glass separated with very small spacers, and then the windows are evacuated and sealed. The vacuum glass has a very high level of insulation due to the lack of air or gases in between the glass panes. This minimizes the convection currents that can be set up in traditional IG window units. Vacuum windows have spacers that must be there to keep the glass panes separated and not collapsing onto each other.

Kolbe & Kolbe Millwork Co., Inc.

Vacuum windows are becoming available on a limited basis in Japan by Nippon Sheet Glass (NSG). For further information about this technology, check with Nippon Sheet Glass at www.nsg.co.jp.

- Solar panels spaced within the window are another unique window product. The panels absorb the sunlight, turning it into electricity; the panels are spaced apart enough so some light and views are possible. These produce small amounts of power. By spacing the solar panels in the glass, you can create interesting designs while still getting some view and some power. These products have to be oriented in the correct manner to be effective at capturing the sun's energy. For high-end homes they may be desirable as eco-friendly products. These panels are available on the market today.

resources

For further information on solar panels for the window, check the Web site of Pleotint, LLC at www.pleotint.com.

Note: Window-covering safety glass is receiving attention. Each year infants and toddlers are strangled in window cords because they are within reach of cribs or because children climb on furniture or beds to reach cords.

For information on childproofing corded window blinds, shades and draperies, check with the Window Covering Safety Council at www.windowcoverings.org.

It is essential that a qualified professional install any window you select. The finest window can malfunction if it is installed incorrectly. As with all construction professionals, check references and make sure the installer has experience with the particular products you are selecting. You can ask manufacturers or local distributors for recommendations for contractors who consistently install their brand of windows and doors.

Nana Wall

Exterior Doors

There are more patio and entrance door options available today than ever before. A variety of sizes and shapes can be found in several materials. Exterior doors will be important selections because they are used often and they have the potential for energy efficiency. In the case of the front entrance door, it is the first impression visitors will get of the house. Building codes also treat the exterior doors as the first means of egress in the case of a fire or an emergency.

Patio Doors

At one time having a patio door meant having one single sliding metal door to the outside. The window and door industry has come a long way in providing many more options for consumers. In addition to sliding glass doors, there are doors that swing either in or out. Security has been vastly improved with multi-point locking systems becoming standard on patio doors. They not only provide more safety but also prevent doors from warping. Other options include divided lights, transoms, side lights and corresponding fixed windows. Patio doors are now available in a variety of sizes—8, 9 and 10 feet high. There are multi-door units that can open up an entire wall to the outside. Some people still prefer steel doors, but there are many more choices available: wood, vinyl, aluminum and fiberglass. Doors come **factory-hung** (including jambs, hardware, locks and weatherstripping) or **separate.** There are two main types of patio doors: swinging and sliding glass.

Swinging Door (Hinged Door)

Doors that swing in or out are available. They require more space than a sliding door. If they are weatherstripped in a factory then they are effective; however, if weatherstripping is done in the field it is labor intensive and not as effective. There can be a variety of configurations of glass panes. A French door (which refers to its divided lights) can be a swinging door or a sliding glass door. Traditional patio doors are hinged in the middle and one panel is fixed. French doors are hinged on the outside, and both doors operate from the middle. The doors can swing in or out.

Sliding Glass Door

Sliding glass doors require less space for door swing, seal tightly and are easy to incorporate into the system. On sliding doors, one panel is stationary; the other moves.

Materials

Patio doors are usually made out of the same material as the windows in the house, although this is not the rule. Most often the doors are purchased from the same manufacturer as that of the windows, in keeping the style consistent.

Size

The standard height for patio doors is 80 inches. Widths can vary from a standard 6 feet; smaller and larger sizes are available. Patio doors are now available in 8, 9 and 10 feet heights.

Glazing

Doors are available with a variety of different types of glass, including low-E glass, laminated glass and so on; in the future this list may include switchable glass. Most doors come with tempered or impact-resistant glass; these are required by code in some coastal states. Doors are available with low-E glass and warm-edge spacers. Some doors are available with decorative glass. These types of options are the same as for windows (stained, leaded, beveled and so on), and descriptions can be found in the window section.

Complementary Items

Patio doors can be purchased with transoms, fixed side lights, fixed doors and casement or awning windows above or to the sides; all must be safety glazed.

Divided Light

As with windows, patio doors are available with true divided lights, simulated divided lights, removable grilles and grilles between the panes. Grilles inside the panes are often available in a range of colors and may be contoured or flat. Sometimes these grilles are available in two colors, with one color showing on the inside and one on the outside. Removable grilles are also available.

Argon and Krypton Gas

These gases help to improve the overall insulation value of the door and are available on some models.

Hardware

Along with the traditional shiny brass handles, there are now many brushed chrome and nickel options available as well. Multi-point locks, which are relatively new, have two or three locking points and add security while protecting wood doors from warping.

Warranty

Check to see what type of warranty is available.

Accessories

There are many bells and whistles now available with patio doors.

Door with an internal blind—A French door and sash door are available with a horizontal Venetian blind sealed between two pieces of tempered glass for use as a patio door (or even as an interior door for added privacy). It magnetically opens and shuts the blinds with a small finger-touch slide but does not lift them. These help block out some of the light without the need for curtains or added blinds, which often get in the way of the door.

resources

Doors with internal blinds can be found at the Simpson Door Company under the name Invisions at www.simpsondoor.com or Pela at www.pela.com. Other internal shades and blinds may also be available.

This door features blinds enclosed between two panels of glass, providing a dust-proof and maintenance-free door while also blocking out the sun.

Trinity

Storm doors—There are aluminum storm panels available for single and double in-swing doors. These attach to screen doors, which in turn attach to the interior of the door and swing in. Weatherstripping is attached to the perimeter for energy efficiency. Other companies also offer a storm door to be used with their doors.

Screens—There are different types of screens available. Retractable screens are self-storing and retract out of sight when not in use. They are available for patio doors in three ways. Some are built into the door system and can be removed and others are permanent. There are also retractable systems that can be purchased separately (after market) to be installed on already-owned doors. Self-closing screens are available from one manufacturer. The screen gently closes and latches after the door has been opened wide enough to let someone pass through.

Foot locks—These are used on sliding patio doors and prevent the panel from being lifted out.

This system is a beautiful way of opening up a room to the outside.

Nana Wall

Innovations

Vanishing sliding glass door (wall)—This is a system that, when closed, has the appearance of a row of floor-to-ceiling windows and offers protection from the elements. It has a hidden track-and-roller system that allows the entire wall to be opened, so it disappears, bringing the outdoors in and giving an unobstructed view. Overhead tracks support the system; flush-floor track designs are possible. The rugged components provide acoustic barriers as well. A nearly unlimited number of configurations are available for interior or exterior use, including straight track, right angles and curves. Design options are limitless because the company engineers each wall to fit most custom needs. This wall is available from NanaWall and may be available from other resources.

resources

For further information, check www.nanawallsystems.com or call 800-873-5673. There may be other manufacturers who make a similar type of system.

Lift slide doors—This is another method of opening up a small area or the entire wall up to 40 feet. These doors lift up about $1/2$ inch and slide easily on an upper track. The threshold is low, which makes it wheelchair accessible. These are available with a variety of types of glass and multi-point locks for security.

151

For further information about lift slide doors, visit www.hhwindows.com. Most window manufacturers also offer patio doors. Contact Dayton Technologies at www.daytontech.com or call 513-539-5460, or Therma-Tru Doors at www.therma-tru.com or call 800-537-8827.

Pressure-treated wood doors—A new pressure treatment process has recently been introduced (using an environmentally safe process) that protects the wood from decay and termite infestation.

Entrance Doors

Basic Parts

Frame—Includes the head frame, or header, at the top of the frame; the strike frame, or jamb, which is the side of the door where the lock is installed; and the hinge frame, or jamb, the side where the hinges are set in.

Stiles—The vertical edges of the door.

Rails—The top and bottom edges of the door. There can also be a lock or intermediate rail in the center of the door running horizontally.

Core—The interior section of the door in flush doors.

Panels—The interior section of the door in the case of paneled doors.

The entrance door is the first part of a house's decor that a visitor sees. It should be attractive and be consistent with the style of the house. Doors also need to protect the house from the elements. Today there are many beautiful stock and custom doors available. Doors can be purchased at lumberyards, home centers and salvage yards and through home design centers. There are many options to consider when purchasing an exterior door. The first consideration other than aesthetics is durability and function. Be sure that the door you select will open and close easily and will not have to be replaced quickly.

Loose or Prehung

Most doors are purchased prehung, which includes the frame, hinges, lockset, threshold and/or sill and weatherstripping. Doors are sometimes purchased separately for retrofits, where the frame is still in good condition. Steel doors are generally sold as prehung since it would be very difficult to build a steel frame. Wood doors are sometimes purchased separately, but they are much more difficult to install than the prehung assemblies.

Finished or natural—Doors that have been sold unfinished can be stained or painted.

Weatherstripping—The weatherstripping around a door helps to keep out the elements. Foam-filled weatherstripping is usually added to seal tight and be flexible.

Style of the house—There are doors that are consistent with every type of design. Select a door that goes with the style of your house.

Door style—Numerous door shapes and styles are available.

Flush or Panel

Most doors have panels (floating or fixed) or are flush (flat and smooth).

The panels on wood doors can be raised or recessed. On fiberglass, the panels are molded recessed or elevated, never floating, as they are in wood. Wood-paneled doors are usually constructed with stiles (vertical elements) and rails (horizontal elements) with inset panels of wood or glass. Doors can have single or multiple glass insets with clear glass or one of the many novelty glasses available.

Flush doors have a smooth surface with a wood veneer on the exterior. The core is covered by two or three layers of ply on either side, with the outermost ply being the **veneer.** A door with three layers on either side is called a seven-ply door (six layers and a core). The quality of the door is determined by the strength of the frame and the nature of the veneer material.

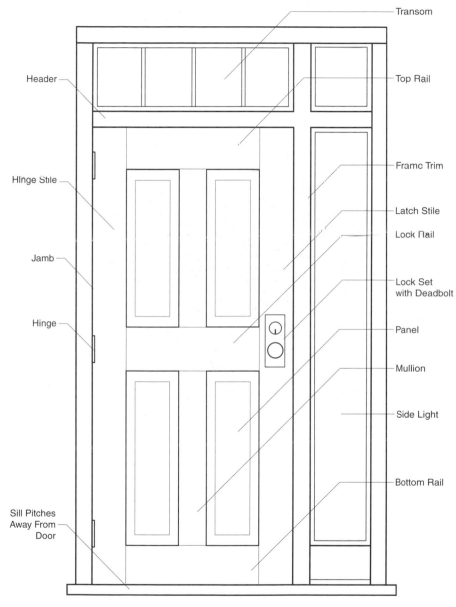

Transom

Header

Hinge Stile

Jamb

Hinge

Sill Pitches Away From Door

Top Rail

Frame Trim

Latch Stile

Lock Rail

Lock Set with Deadbolt

Panel

Mullion

Side Light

Bottom Rail

Exterior View

Shapes

Radiused-head top—The top is a half-circle.

Gothic top—Has an arch that comes to a point.

Eyebrow top—The two doors have a shallow S-curve on top and meet at a high point.

Segment top—Has a slight arch.

Raked top—The two doors meet on top at a point in the middle.

Jeld-Wen IWP Custom Doors

Glass Insets (Door Lites)

Glass can be installed in the door with one lite or several lites in numerous configurations. The types of glass are equally as numerous. Many decorative glasses are sandwiched between clear glass on the inside and tempered glass on the outside to increase insulation and safety. Doors can have true divided light, simulated divided light, lights between the panes and removable grilles. Glass can also be low-E for added insulation. Be sure to consult the local building codes on the requirements for safety glass in doors, side lights and transoms.

Novelty Glass Types

Plain glass—Still a popular choice.

Beveled glass—It has an edge of the glass cut off at an angle, which bends the light and produces a prismatic effect.

Leaded glass—A type of art glass that is made by connecting pieces of glass with a lead channel and soldering the intersections of the lead channel.

Art glass—A category of glass designed for its artistic appeal rather than functional need. It includes stained glass, etched glass and so on, with combinations of colors and special effects.

Stained glass—Colored glass is assembled into designs.

Frosted glass—Glass that has been washed with hydrofluoric acid, sandblasted, and a film installed on-site or is laminated glass that has a vinyl interlayer.

Etched glass—It has some of the glass surface removed by either a chemical or sandblast process.

Obscure glass—This is clear glass through which images cannot be seen because the light waves are bent by the texture on the glass surfaces.

Wood Textures

Smooth—It has been run through a planer, or sanding has been applied.

Wire brushed—A wire brush has been applied to the wood to get a wavy texture.

Distressed—The wood looks like it has been exposed to fire, chemicals or some type of wear.

Hand-hewn—Wood has been planed by hand rather than by a saw.

Speakeasies with Doors or Grilles

We all remember the massive door in *The Wizard of Oz* with the innkeeper opening the little door to see Dorothy and her group hoping to see the wizard. These openings can have a real purpose—in checking to see who is outside before opening the door. But with today's intercom systems and side lites, these speakeasies are more decorative than utilitarian.

Internal mini-blinds—Some steel and

Jeld-Wen IWP Custom Doors

fiberglass doors and side lites are available with aluminum alloy mini-blinds sandwiched between two panels of glass for added privacy and for light control.

A front entrance door with a speakeasy.

resources

For further information about internal mini-blinds, contact Trinity Glass at 800-803-8182.

Door setups—These come in many combinations: separate, double or with matching side lights, overhead transoms and decorative or plain glass. Dutch doors have two sections that can open independently or together. These are sometimes used in kitchen entrances to take advantage of a special view.

Thickness—Doors come in varying thicknesses. The typical door thickness is 1¾ inches, but they may be thicker as their size increases.

Size—Doors are becoming larger than the typical 6 feet, 8 inches. Heights are available 7, 8 and up to 10 feet tall, but most companies do not offer all of these sizes. Widths are 2 feet, 4 inches; 2 feet, 6 inches; 2 feet, 8 inches; and up to 3 and 4 feet wide.

Material

Wood

Some of the species available are oak, mahogany, alder, cedar, cherry and walnut. The textured wood has been inspired by the Southwest. Knotty and distressed wood is a trend that has been popular in the Southwest region for a long time. There are several textured looks available: wire-blasted, sandblasted, hand-sewn, rough-planed and chiseled finishes. Alder works well for these textures.

Steel

Most steel doors are **galvanized steel** over a steel or wood frame. Galvanized steel is strong, long lasting, durable and doesn't require painting, although plain steel doors are available that do require painting. It is resistant to warping, cracking or peeling. Steel doors must be prehung, however, because they cannot be altered after they come from the manufacturer. Most often doors are embossed with wood grain patterns, but some high-end models are laminated with a wood veneer. Although they are available in wood grain-like finishes, they do not look as authentic as fiberglass or carbon-fiber doors. Steel doors generally cost less than wood, but they can dent and may rust in harsh conditions and require regular maintenance or touch-up painting.

Fiberglass and Fiberglass Composites

There is increased acceptance of fiberglass for doors because of its durability, ease of maintenance, excellent insulation and its close resemblance to wood. It is impermeable to moisture and dimensionally stable. Fiberglass doors will not oxidize or rust and are well suited for ocean areas. They are available in paint colors and various wood grains, which can be stained and repainted. Fiberglass is also environmentally friendly—it is produced from natural products from the earth and is painted with products that have low volatile organic compound (VOC) content, releasing no harmful gases during production or in its formed state.

Carbon

Carbon is similar to fiberglass except that carbon fibers are used instead of glass fibers in the plastic resin. The prices of these materials are similar. Carbon is strong, dent resistant, structurally stable and cold and heat resistant. A carbon door can be painted or stained to give it a wood appearance. It is excellent for insulation.

Stainless Steel

Not commonly used and modern in styling, stainless steel is impervious to weathering, rot, decay, chipping and fading and requires minimal maintenance. Stainless steel doors come complete with frame, hardware and locks for a simple installation.

Right-Hand or Left-Hand Doors

This is determined from the outside

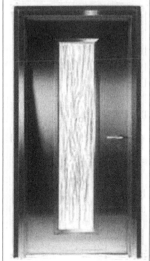

Stainless steel doors can give a special new look to a home.

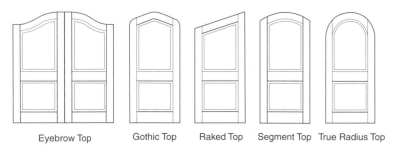

Eyebrow Top   Gothic Top   Raked Top   Segment Top   True Radius Top

Custom Door Frames

of the house—a left-hand door is hinged on the left, a right-hand door on the right.

Hardware

Doors are typically not sold with handles. Many companies offer handles as an option but generally leave the doors without bored holes, so the homeowner can select the hardware later. Hinges come with a standard metal, with other options available. Hardware is evolving with more Southwestern styles and many more metals, such as brushed chrome, brushed nickel, oil-rubbed bronze, bronze and pewter.

Locks

Before selecting a lock, you need to have the following information about the door: style, whether it is right-hand or left-hand, thickness, height (for multi-point locks) and width of the stile and the backset. There are several different types of locks to consider:

Cylindrical Lock Sets

These are operated by a key inserted into the exterior knob; the interior knob is operated either by a key inserted into it or a push or turn button. They are the most commonly used locks and are available in a wide array of colors and finishes. They are easily installed on-site and are available in many price ranges.

Tubular Lock Sets

The locking mechanism consists of tubes that fit in through the edge of the door, with the lower latch always separate from the deadbolt. They use standard conventional spring or deadbolt latches.

Mortise Lock Sets

This is an older-style lock that fits into a large, rectangular recess in the edge of a door. It has one or two lock buttons in the face plate and usually has a deadbolt that double locks the door and a spring-loaded thumb latch on the exterior handle. Mortise lock sets are more secure than cylindrical lock sets but are labor intensive to install and very expensive. They are usually used in high-end wood doors.

Deadbolt

These are usually used as a supplementary lock for added security. They are rarely used as the main lock. There are also double-key deadlocks that have a key on both sides to open the bolt. They are sometimes suggested on doors that are next to glass doors where an intruder could possibly reach in and open the lock. They can, however, present a hazard during a fire or other emergency and are illegal in some areas.

Multi-Point Locks

They are one of the newest types of locks available. They are not commonly used on front doors but are gaining in popularity. They are more expensive than other types of locks and must be factory-installed by the manufacturer. Currently, not all lock manufacturers offer multi-point locks. They are, however, the only locks presently capable of passing the stringent Dade County Hurricane Building Code requirements. While increasing security, they also help to seal off the effects of weather. A new innovation not yet available in this country is electronic key/multi-point lock systems that have combinations that can be easily changed. The key is rubbed against a receiver that is mounted in the frame.

Rim Locks

These are surface-mounted locks using iron keys. They are not commonly used today.

Digital Locks

This is a push-button digital door lock used without keys. These locks have hacksaw-proof dead bolts and easy-to-change combinations. There is no electric connection, and they use no wires or batteries. Installation is easy, and the locks fit any door. They are available in several metal finishes.

Some of the many manufacturers of exterior doors:

Coaba Doors	800-417-3667	www.caobadoors.com
Feather River Door Company	866-689-1234	www.featherdoor.com
Fibertec (C)	888-232-4956	www.fibertec.com
Harvest Creek Millwork (C)	800-903-6786	www.harvestcreek.com
International Door & Latch	541-686-5647	www.internationaldoor.com
International Wood Products	800-468-3667	www.iwpdoor.com
Jeld-Wen IWP	800-468-3667	www.iwpdoor.com
Masonite International Corp. (C)	800-663-3667	www.masonite.com
Neoporte Modern Door	310-450-2100	www.neoporte.com
New Tech Doors	800-622-0688	www.newtechdoors.com
Pease Entry Systems	800-883-6677	www.peasedoors.com
Pella	888-847-3552	www.pella.com
Pinecrest, Inc.	612-871-7071	www.pinecrestinc.com
Simpson	800-952-4057	www.simpsondoor.com
Therma-Tru Doors	800-843-7628	www.thermatru.com
The Stanley Works	800-521-2752	www.stanleyworks.com
Upstate Door Co.	800-570-8283	www.upstatedoor.com

(C) = Canadian

Security

Lock blocks should be solid wood—not foam—and should have a security strike plate, so there is more resistance to an intruder wedging a crowbar between the jamb and strike plate to force open the lock. Use 2 $1/2$-inch screws on the hinges instead of the short screws that usually come with the hinge. Side lites and transoms can be made in semi-obscure and obscure glass for privacy. Transparent glass can also be textured to make it more obscure. Doors are available with several fire ratings; if your home is located in a fire-prone area, consider a door with a ninety-minute fire rating.

Warranty

Some doors are sold with a warranty, from one year to a lifetime. Find out how long the warranty is and if it has limitations.

Fire-Rated Doors

Local codes specify the need for fire rating on doors; they dictate which doors must be fire rated and specify whether the door must be self-closing. Typically, fire-rated doors are required on the entry to the garage from the house and on closets containing a gas-fired water heater or a gas- or oil-fired furnace. They are generally built to resist fire and not for aesthetics. Doors are available with a variety of ratings: twenty, thirty, forty-five, sixty and ninety minutes. This is the amount of time the door should be able to resist fire. Fire-rated doors should have a label identifying the testing agency. Make sure that you, the architect or builder are familiar with local codes when ordering doors.

resources

For further information about windows and doors, check with the Window & Door Manufacturers Association at www.nwwda.org.

Garage Doors

Over the years garages have taken on a much larger role in everyday life. They are used for storage, as work areas and sometimes as the primary entrance to the house. Years ago, the garage was a separate entity with no other purpose but for storing the car. There have never been as many choices in garage doors as there are today; styles to go with every house, a large variety of sizes, numerous colors and many special options—designer windows, automatic openers and many other useful accessories. Doors can be chosen from stock or can be custom made. Some companies offer matching entrance or walk-through doors to go with the garage design. Select a door that aesthetically complements the color and style of the house and, more importantly, fits into your budget.

This custom-made wood door appears to fold open but actually lifts overhead with an automatic opener.

Configuration of the Doors

When building a house, you must decide how many garage doors you will have; some people still have one, while others have been known to have eight. If there will be more than one, you will have to decide what configurations they will be—one big door for two or three cars or one door for each. If there are more than two cars, there can be multiple single or double doors. A possible reason for using double doors is that each single door will need a separate electric opener, increasing the cost. Many years ago, one-piece doors were popular, but today sectional doors dominate the market. They have many advantages, such as they are easier to open when there is snow on the ground. Sectional doors also offer better insulation options. Most doors come in four sections for 7-foot-high doors and five sections or more in higher sizes. Some carriage house doors are three sections high, but these doors are cumbersome and very awkward to operate.

Insulated or Standard?

Some people believe that all garage doors should be insulated to maintain the temperature inside the garage and to muffle outdoor noise. The insulation may protect homeowners from burning themselves when touching the interior of the door in very hot climates. Some doors may require more insulation than others, depending on the uses the garage will serve and proximity to other space in the house. When you are shopping for a door, consider which of these two types of doors you may need. Some environmentalists argue that it is poor practice to insulate and tightly seal a garage because you are also sealing heat and fumes from your vehicles into your garage, which can cause indoor air pollution in your home. Many garages are used to store toxic chemicals (such as gasoline, fertilizers, solvents, etc.), and many of these are known to emit toxic fumes. Several cities across the nation (San Francisco, for example) require as code, fresh-air ventilation in garages, defeating the purpose of insulating the garage and the garage door. In many areas, garage walls are not insulated, so insulated garage doors may not be practical.

If the garage is heated/cooled, a well-insulated garage door will lower heating and cooling costs by reducing the heat flow (R-value—the amount of heat that escapes) through the garage door. The insulation will also offer thermal protection and soundproofing to rooms over or adjacent to the garage. They are also more structurally sound because of additional backing and a double-wall construction. A well-insulated garage will be more comfortable if it will be used as a workshop, and getting to and from the car on very cold and hot days. If sealing against air infiltration is desired, check for a bottom-door seal and perimeter seal offered to reduce air infiltration. The two most commonly used insulation materials for garage doors are polystyrene and polyurethane. Most companies offer one or the other; some offer both. Polystyrene is more commonly used; it comes in a solid state and is molded as needed. Polyurethane comes as a foam and is injected into the door. Most companies claim to have perfected the use of polyurethane, resulting in a door with a more energy-efficient R-value. Polyurethane doors cannot have the insulation removed, so dents cannot be repaired, and the door sections cannot be recycled at the end of their life. Higher R-value garage doors sometimes offer a thermal break separating the outer face of the door from the inner face of the door on each section. You can also add weatherstripping between each section to reduce air infiltration. Doors that will be installed on a heated garage that is attached to the house with either adjoining living space or space that will be used as a

workshop are good uses for an insulated door. Common insulated doors offer R-values of 5 or higher. At an increased cost, you can purchase garage doors with a higher R-value of 12 and up.

All manufacturers offer standard, non-insulated doors. These doors cost less. If the garage is detached, or if the walls between the garage and the home are adequately insulated, this type of door is sufficient for most uses, especially in moderate climates. But non-insulated doors are not as quiet as insulated doors.

When comparing several doors it is not adequate to ask for the "best" door, but find out what type of insulation each door is offering. The best may differ among companies and personal needs.

Size

Doors come in standard sizes and can also be custom made to fit. The most popular heights are 7 and 8 feet, but taller doors are also becoming popular for storage of boats, RVs and other recreation vehicles. The thicknesses vary from 1 to $2\frac{7}{8}$ inches. Popular widths include 8, 9 or 10 feet for single doors and 16 or 18 feet for double doors. Some companies offer triple doors that are 24 feet wide. The width can often be modified in a variety of increments, depending on the company and style. Several companies will customize doors in unusual shapes.

Springs

All doors have one or two springs that move the door up and down. There are two types of springs: torsion and extension. A torsion spring is wrapped around a metal bar that goes above the door. The most commonly used spring, it can be used on most garage doors and is considered to be superior and safer than extension springs. Extension springs go above the track on either side of the door. This is an older system that is commonly used on lighter doors and sometimes costs less.

Cycle Life

Because garage doors are now commonly used as a primary entrance for the home, they get more use than in the past. Industry standards require 10,000-cycle hardware, but many manufacturers produce doors below these standards. You can order garage doors in higher ranges up to 100,000 cycles for doors that are used heavily. The springs are the most expensive cycle-rated part and may cost $150 to $350 or more to replace.

Use this formula to calculate the cycle life you need:

N = Number of times you open and close your door each day
C = Rated cycle life of the door you are purchasing
Y = Number of years the door will function before major repairs are needed

$$C / (N \times 365) = Y$$

For example, if you purchase a 10,000-cycle garage door and you use your door six times a day, your door will probably break down in about 4.5 years.

$$10,000 / (6 \times 365) = 4.57$$

Color

Most companies offer a range of standard colors, and many doors can also be painted to match the color of the house. Most metal garage doors are made from metal received from the supplier with a coil-coating paint, a thin layer of color added to the metal and then baked on in a hot oven. The choice of colors is usually limited. Powder coatings are applied by only a few garage manufacturers. A thick, glossy, high-quality, UV-rated paint is applied to the door sections and hardware (powder coating is optional). This gives the door added protection over the coil-coating process and is available in a wide range of colors, which can be stocked by the garage manufacturer.

Design

Doors are available flush or with raised panels, recessed panels, grooves, glass insets and decorative trim. A new popular design is the carriage or barn door style, which appears to swing open but actually lifts up. Some doors are available that swing out, as they did 100 years ago, but the building codes in some areas prevent installing swing-open doors for safety reasons. They are also impractical because of the issue of snow removal and because they take up a lot of space when opened.

GADCO

Accessories

Windows and door lites—A variety of glass and acrylic options are available from each garage door manufacturer. Plastic or acrylic windows can be made to look like beveled glass, stained glass, leaded glass or opaque glass, which lets the light in but obscures the view from the exterior. There are a number of glass options: single pane, double-pane insulated, divided lites (simulated and true), translucent, tinted, frosted, novelty and more. Check each company to find out what they offer. When ordering windows, acrylic or safety glass is preferred to reduce the risk of injury in the event of a broken window.

Functional hardware—This includes the operating hardware—hinges, rollers, tracks and cables. Hardware is available in different grades: residential, light commercial and heavy-duty commercial. The grade is determined by the gauge of the metal on the hardware and whether or not the rollers contain ball bearings. High-quality rollers contain more ball bearings (seven to ten or more). Hardware is selected by the manufacturer to fit the weight and width of the door. Doors with better warranties will usually include heavier hardware and ball-bearing rollers. Find out which hardware will be put on the particular door you select.

Decorative hardware—Each company offers different hardware. Some companies offer hand-forged reproductions of hinges, pulls, grilles and latches, while other companies offer traditional garage door hardware. Check to see what your options are.

Material

Factory-painted galvanized steel—These comprise the majority of garage doors sold. They are available in several gauges (thicknesses) of steel. The lower the number, the thicker the steel. The thicker steel (26 to 24 gauge) will be more durable and less likely to dent. Steel that is higher than 30 gauge offers little security because it can be easily cut with a pocket knife or scissors. Minimal maintenance is required and steel doors can be painted to match the house. Hot-dipped galvanizing is superior and offers better rust protection than electroplating, which is sometimes available. Metal doors must be protected from de-icing salts.

Aluminum—These doors come in a large variety of colors, are lightweight and require less maintenance than a wood garage door. They cannot rust, and they stand up to the weather better than a steel door. Installation is easier, putting less

A copper garage door can create a unique look.

Martin

These swing-type doors reflect the English cottage architecture of the home.

Designer Doors, Inc.

stress on the hardware and making a double door less heavy. Aluminum requires less maintenance than wood. Aluminum is, however, less popular because it costs much more than galvanized steel doors. Metal doors must be protected from de-icing salts.

Fiberglass—These doors are long lasting, maintenance-free and never require painting. However, since fiberglass is made in a mold, it cannot be customized for individual jobs. The doors also tend to fade or discolor over the years and do not offer good security—they can be cut with a pocket knife. Fiberglass is also more expensive than many of the other materials.

Wood—Wood doors are attractive and many people prefer wood for its architectural quality. It is easier to customize a wood door than a metal door. Wood is self-insulating and will not dent like metal. Sometimes sections of a wood door can be repaired instead of replacing the entire door. However, wood doors are generally more expensive and the higher expense continues as the years pass because they must be maintained with paint or stain to protect the wood from warping and rotting. Hemlock, fir and cedar are commonly used wood species, but manufacturers offer a variety of others as well.

A stainless steel door.

Copper doors—These doors are a new product in the marketplace and cost more than some other metal doors. They have a special look for the right architecture. Copper never deteriorates, so these doors are an excellent type to hold up against the rigors of seacoast conditions and other humid or corrosive environments. Minimal maintenance, such as cleaning away de-icing salts will assure a long life to the door.

Stainless steel—This has an elegant look but, like copper, is more expensive than many other garage door materials. It does have a maintenance-free finish, is very durable and will last for the life of the house. Stainless steel garage doors must be custom fabricated, with minor exceptions.

Warranty

Garage doors come with a variety of warranties from one year to limited lifetime, usually with limitations. The most common items that break on a garage door are the springs. Thousands of service companies make a business of replacing torsion springs on garage doors. Rollers and other

Neoporte

163

moving parts are also prone to wear. Try to find a garage door that covers the springs and other moving parts for at least ten years. Read warranties carefully because it is common for manufacturers to advertise an extended warranty period that only covers door sections against rust-through, while covering moving parts for a very short period of time. Find out exactly what is offered in the warranty before purchasing the door.

Safety

In recent years, the U.S. Consumer Product Safety Commission revealed that garage doors are a leading cause of finger injuries in the United States. The Door & Access Systems Manufacturers Association (DASMA) has passed standards that address this problem. Better doors meet these standards and offer pinch-resistant sections that push fingers out of the way when they come near the section joints and other dangerous hardware. Check www.dasma.com for more information. A professional should be called for service before trying to fix the door yourself.

Matching Entrance or Walk-Through Doors

Some companies offer access house doors to go with the garage door. If the door will be in close proximity to the garage door, this may influence your decision on the choice of doors.

Garage Door Openers

The garage doors of long ago are frequently described as being heavy. Today this is ancient history; most houses have automatic door openers that are generally sold with the garage door.

Considerations

Motor Type

For many years, the industry has used standard electric motors that run on AC current (alternating current). Newer DC (direct current) motors are now available and are quieter and smoother. Find out which motor comes with the opener you are selecting.

Noise—Chain drives are the noisiest; belt drives are the quietest. DC motors are also much quieter than traditional AC motors.

Speed—For safety reasons they should not move too quickly; it could be dangerous if somebody was leaning on the other side of the door. Slower garage openers are quieter and will extend the life of the garage door hardware. Some DC motors offer a variable speed system giving slow start and slow stop features, which will also extend the life of the door hardware.

Horsepower—AC systems come with $1/2$ - and $3/4$-horsepower motors. DC systems come in 500 to 1,000 horsepower Newton motors. Since the springs actually do the lifting, any motor can operate a well-balanced garage door, but some manufacturers will tell you that bigger motors are needed to lift the heaviest doors. Larger motors may last longer because less stress is put on them.

Installation—Most openers require similar installation time. Professional installation is recommended and will ensure proper implementation.

Lighting—Usually there is a light on the opener, some offer two or more.

Safety

There are several safety features available with garage door openers. With rolling code technology the code changes each time the door is opened. Even hackers will have a tough time getting these doors open. But these systems limit the number of transmitters you can use with the door. Other security systems are available. Check with each manufacturer to compare features.

Intruder-proof—Most openers, when properly installed, will prevent an electric door from being opened by an intruder. On other systems, a locking system, which locks as soon as the door goes down, is available.

Self-monitoring systems—These alert the homeowner to malfunctions.

Side light beams—Federal law now requires beams of light on the sides of the garage or safety edges on the bottom of the door to prevent the door from going down on children and objects. If anything interrupts the beam or touches the safety edge while it is going down, the door automatically reverses itself before contact.

Vacation locks—Some systems offer vacation locks that prevent the door from being opened with any code. An interior switch or keypad activates these locks.

Monitors—There are monitors available on some models to let people inside the house know when the garage door opens.

Warranty

Openers come with a variety of warranties from three years to a lifetime. Find out what a lifetime warranty means—some are prorated over the years.

Security

Rolling codes make the door safer from intruders. Lights that come on when a garage

These are just a few of the many garage door manufacturers:

Amarr Garage Doors	800-503-3667	www.amarr.com
Cedomatec (C)	800-363-2336	www.cedomatec.com
Clopay	800-225-6729	www.clopaydoor.com
Designer Doors	800-241-0525	www.designerdoors.com
General American Door Co. (GADCO)	800-323-0813	www.gadco.com
Garaga, Inc.	800-464-2724	www.garaga.com
Martin Door Manufacturing	800-388-9310	www.martindoor.com
Montana Rustics	800-491-9636	www.montanrustics.com
Neoporte Modern Door (stainless steel)	310-450-2100	www.neoporte.com
Overhead Door Corp.	800-929-3667	www.overheaddoor.com
Raynor	800-472-9667	www.raynor.com
Sections, Inc.	877-707-8810	www.sections.com
Summit Door, Inc.	800-768-3667	www.summit-door.com
Wayne Dalton Corp.	800-827-3667	www.wayne-dalton.com
Windsor Door	800-946-3767	www.windsordoor.com

(C) = Canadian

door is opened or closed make it safer to move around in the garage in the evening hours. Most garage door openers raise or lower the door using a trolley that slides along a rail with the trolley moved along by a chain, belt or screw. There are rails installed above the door opening that lift and lower the door.

Chain-Drive Openers

These are the least expensive openers and the noisiest because of the metal chains running along the trolley. They are also durable and long lasting.

Belt-Drive Openers

These use a rubber-like composite material instead of a chain drive. They are quieter than chain-drive models and typically more expensive.

Screw-Drive Openers

These use a threaded steel rod to lift the door. They are more expensive to repair and require special lubricants to prevent them from gumming up in cold weather, which can be avoided if using certain lubricants.

Direct-Drive Openers

These are mounted on the wall above the garage door. They remove the overhead clutter, produce less noise and vibration than other openers and have fewer moving parts that can break. Some models do not require photo-eye sensors. Some models also include a lock arm that comes down to prevent the door from being opened from the outside.

Special Features

Some openers have a programmable pet-opening feature that allows you to leave the door partially open while limiting any other access. This is a patent of Wayne Dalton and is called the "idrive." It can only be purchased with a Wayne Dalton supplier.

Another new optional accessory available on limited models is a battery back-up system that assures access to your garage even if the power is out in your home.

resources

For information on this system, check the Web site of LiftMaster of The Chamberlain Group at www.liftmaster.com. A similar system is available from Re-Source Industries, Inc. To find out which companies offer this feature, visit www.re-sourceind.com.

For further information about selecting a garage door dealer, contact the International Door Association (IDA) at 800-355-4432 or www.doors.org.

Some resources for garage door openers:

Allstar Corp.	www.allstarcorp.com
Genie	www.geniecompany.com
Linear Corp.	www.linearcorp.com
Marantec America Corp.	www.marantecamerica.com
Martin Door Manufacturing	www.martindoor.com
The Chamberlain Group, Inc.	www.chamberlaingroup.com
Wayne Dalton Corp.	www.wayne-dalton.com

This barn-style door has become increasingly popular.

Ann Sacks

Flooring

Not that many years ago, flooring alternatives for homes were not nearly what they are today. Carpeting, wood, stone and inexpensive linoleum were commonly used. Ceramic tile was available, although with far fewer options than are available today. With the interest in high-tech design, the residential market began borrowing from industrial flooring materials, such as concrete, terrazzo, engineered stone, metal, vinyl and rubber. Even the carpeting industry began to develop higher-performing carpets, such as berbers and other level-loop piles not typically used before in residential applications. Other materials, such as linoleum, were vastly expanded and improved, developing a whole new panache. Laminates and vinyls have also evolved into more varied and stronger materials. Out of an interest in preserving our natural resources, the residential flooring market sought out materials that were abundant and replenishable, such as bamboo, palm and cork. Reclaimed materials such as wood, stone, terra-cotta and tile also grew in popularity as interest grew in reusing what we already have, rather than manufacturing anew. Materials that were used for other applications have also been developed for flooring, such as leather and glass. Out of incredible imagination and technology we can now have photographic images of everything from manhole covers to water on flooring tile.

Hexagon terra-cotta with all the natural variations in color.

Today there is an amazing number of wonderful flooring materials to select from for every style home, for every situation and for every budget. The options in this area are immense and exciting.

Considerations

Cost of Material and Installation

Most people realize the immense variation in cost of materials. Many people do not, however, realize the expense of installing some materials or preparing the subfloor. Another possible expense is lowering or raising the level of the subfloor, particularly in a renovation. Find out about the cost of installation and any additional construction costs you may incur before choosing any material.

Location of the Flooring

Consider the area of the house where the flooring will be installed. If it will be installed below grade for example, a **floating floor** may be the best option because of the possibility of moisture leaching up from the foundation. Bathrooms and kitchens generally are moister than other areas of the house and require flooring that will be durable and comfortable in those areas.

Maintenance

Consider the cost and effort needed for upkeep on the flooring. Upkeep can be costly and/or difficult, so find out about the maintenance procedures before purchasing a particular material.

Climate

Climate should be an important consideration in selecting flooring. In colder climates consider floorings such as carpet, which adds warmth to the floor. In humid areas avoid floorings that will trap water and become moldy. In hot climates use floorings with cooler surfaces such as stone, clay, concrete and brick. Where there will be a great deal of moisture, when selecting wood, choose teak flooring, which is more rot resistant than pine, for example.

Comfort

In areas such as the bedroom, where you will be walking with bare feet, it will be more comfortable to walk on materials such as carpeting or rugs. The resilience of the material is another factor to consider. Materials such as stone or hard tile may be more bothersome for legs and feet than wood, especially if you will be standing for long periods of time in areas such as the kitchen.

Durability

Consider the traffic an area will get. In an entranceway, for example, there may be a great deal of traffic and dirty shoes frequenting that area. Certain materials, like wood and terra-cotta, weather well with wear, whereas a white carpet would look like a mess quickly. Also consider whether the flooring will hold up if a heavy object is dropped on it. Glass tiles, although beautiful, may crack with hard pounding. Consider the durability of the material and the amount of time you expect the material to last. If you are not thinking about living in a house for a long time, durability may not be an issue. But if you would

like the flooring to last over a long period of time, look for one with a longer life expectancy. Wood can be re-sanded and restored to last for a very long time. Other materials such as synthetics cannot be restored and may have to be replaced after several years. Purchasing durable, more expensive flooring may work out to be less expensive in the long run.

Sound Insulation

Areas in the house, such as media rooms, with loud, mechanically produced sounds will benefit from flooring that will absorb some of the sound. Soft floorings, such as carpeting, reduce sound; hard floors will amplify sound. Heavily trafficked areas on a second floor can be noisy for those below if the material is not sound absorbing.

Size of the Area

A large pattern may be overwhelming in a small space. The size of the tile, for example, should suit the scale of the room.

Safety

To avoid accidents, bathrooms, kitchens and steps should not have slippery surfaces, such as glazed ceramic tile. Where there is a transition from one level of the house to another, the step should easily be seen by a change in flooring material or some other way of indicating a step. Worn carpet is a hazard; catching heels and loose floorboards can be dangerous. Rugs that are not securely placed on the floor can also be a danger.

Questions to Consider Regarding Style

- What look do you want to achieve?
- What is the style of the house?
- Does each room's flooring coordinate with that of other rooms in the house?
- What is the architectural character of the house?
- What effect are you trying to achieve? A light color will give a room a more open, lighter feeling and a dark floor more warmth and enclosure.

- What are your design preferences? Do you like natural earth tones, bright colors and shiny surfaces or matte or textured finishes? For pattern, do you prefer solid or patterned (floral, geometric and so on)?
- Do you prefer to define certain areas or make the entire space consistent?
- Do you like to use rugs to define areas instead of varying the flooring itself?
- Should the flooring be a focal point of the room or fade into the background?
- Do you want insets, borders and the mix of several materials (slate and metal tiles, for example) used together?

Allergies

Consider the allergies of the people living in the house. Woven materials such as carpeting trap more dirt than hard floors such as wood, linoleum and ceramic tile. Also consider whether there is a dog or cat in the house. Certain floorings will trap fleas more readily.

Children and Pets

With both you may want to consider more durable floorings that can be easily cleaned.

Outlets, Grilles and Registers

Consider the need for outlets, grilles and registers and their options. Some materials are available with cutout patterns; it is best to plan for these in advance.

Heating System

Certain flooring materials work better over radiant heating than others. Check with the heating contractor to see if certain materials, glues (used for glue-down floors), and/or padding (used for carpeting), will work with the radiant heating being installed.

Subfloor

Find out if the subfloor is strong enough to handle the material you select. If you are renovat-

ing an older house, make sure that the floor is not sagging or structurally unsound. Tiles are likely to crack and flooring may buckle if the subfloor is imperfect.

Existing Flooring

It is sometimes possible to put another flooring over an existing one. This can be a problem, however, if the flooring will significantly raise the height of the floor or if it will block appliances that may eventually need to be removed. If the floor will be torn out and you think it may have been a resilient material manufactured before 1986, it should be tested for asbestos before being removed. If it is found to contain asbestos, special care must be taken to remove it.

Remodeling Existing Flooring

Some materials are difficult to refinish but can be given a face-lift, such as tile, which can be re-grouted or patched to give it a new look. Wood can be sanded and/or re-stained or painted to update the look.

Installation

As is true with all areas of home construction, the quality of installation will significantly affect the success of any material. Be sure that you will be able to find a qualified installer for whatever flooring material you select. Also make sure that the installer you select is willing to follow the manufacturer's installation guidelines, which are given with most products, coupled with the "dos" and "don'ts" for each substrate type.

Material Options

Hard Floors

The many varieties of hard floorings give a house a feeling of permanence. They create a healthy environment because there are no fibers for dust mites to get into and no fibers to breathe in. Cold surfaces, usually created by hard floors, can be warmed up with the use of rugs or by

171

installing an under-floor heating system. In some areas of the world, it may be an advantage to have cold floors. Hard floors are durable even in heavily trafficked areas. They do tend to be more costly than other floorings and are not resilient, meaning that they may be tiring on the feet and items dropped on them are likely to break. They usually amplify sounds and should not be used in areas where this may be a problem. Hard floors tend to be heavy and require solid subfloors to bear the load.

Brick

For an interior floor, a strong subfloor is needed to bear the significant load of this heavy material. Various looks can be achieved by installing the brick in a number of different patterns—herringbone, straight rows, staggered rows and basketweave patterns. There are several types of brick to choose from on the market.

Pavers are the most common type of bricks used for flooring. They are thinner than construction bricks, ranging from ³/₄ to 2 inches thick. They are fired at extremely high temperatures, making them waterproof and durable. Engineering brick is thicker than pavers and also very durable. Standard brick is not as durable as pavers and engineering brick. These will erode and eventually become uneven. Handmade brick is the most expensive brick available.

Advantages

- Brick is slow to warm but retains heat for a long time.
- Brick is easier to cut and shape than slabs of stone.
- Brick is resistant to chemicals, hard impact and abrasion. It is also waterproof and nonslip if it is not sealed or polished.
- Brick comes in a wide range of colors and surface textures.
- Brick is less expensive and more readily available than many other hard types of flooring.
- It requires little maintenance.

Disadvantages

- Brick requires professional installation.
- A solid subfloor is required to support brick.
- Joints between brick, as well as special movement joints, must be wide enough to accommodate shrinkage and expansion of the brick due to changes in humidity and temperature.

Natural Stone

Stone is often identified by the location where it is found, such as Portland limestone, which comes from Maine, and York stone, a sandstone from Yorkshire, England. Stone can be worked in several ways: with a diamond-cutter machine, referred to as **"sawn,"** and with more primitive tools, referred to as "handworked." Finishes or textures range from **honed** to highly polished. **Tumbling** or **bushmilling** of the stone produces surface variations associated with wear and tear. Flaming the stone can create a slip-resistant surface that is best used outside. The most expensive stone is antique stone, recovered from old houses, farms and other structures. Although stone tends to be expensive, tiles are usually less expensive than slabs.

Pebbles and cobblestones are sometimes used in a resin backing to form tiles. Stones are available in a variety of colors and veining patterns and can be cut into several sizes and shapes. They can be used in their natural state (flagstone) or can be cut into rectangular slabs or tiles. Straight-edge stones can be butt-jointed, which allows for a minimal grout joint and a seamless finish. Tumbled, antiqued or more rustic-edged stones require a larger grout joint to allow for variation in facial dimension and edge detail. Most stones require sealer. Protective sealers, such as penetrating sealers, absorb into the pores of the stone and help protect the stone and prevent staining. Most penetrating sealers do not change the appearance of the stone. Decorative sealers do not protect the stone; however, they can change the appearance by adding a shiny or matte surface or intensifying the color.

Stone comes from several types of rock:

Igneous rock is formed when molten rock cools in the earth's crust. These rocks are created from magma, usually a mixture of liquid rock, gases and mineral crystals. The rocks are dense, hard, durable, impervious to water and can take a high polish.

- Granite is an example of an igneous rock. It is coarse grained and contains feldspar, quartz and mica, giving it a crystalline appearance. Granite is available in a variety of colors and finishes, from honed to highly polished and is one of the most expensive stones.

Sedimentary rock is softer rock than igneous rock and is formed from deposits of sediment and organic matter, which forms in layers.

- Limestone is an example of a sedimentary rock. It is made chiefly of mineral calcite, sandstone and a conglomerate of sand or gravel particles held together by a mineral cement. It doesn't show much graining and is available in creamy white, tones of yellow, black, gray and brown. Limestone is more likely to stain than marble. It does absorb stains and dirt easily and requires careful sealing.
- Travertine, another kind of sedimentary rock, is a type of limestone that is formed near underground springs. It is a very hard, crystalline rock made mostly of calcite carbonate, with a small amount of iron oxide. Sealing the stone will protect it against stains, and filling in the crevices will prevent water from collecting in these naturally formed areas.

Metamorphic rock is a very hard rock formed when heat and pressure cause a chemical change in the rock.

- Marble is a metamorphic rock that forms from the sedimentary rock, limestone. It is available in slabs, tiles and conglomerate marble tiles and is composed of chippings bonded with hard polyester resin. Marble is available in a wide range of colors and may have a great deal of veining. It does absorb stains and dirt easily and requires careful sealing.

- Slate is another metamorphic rock that comes from shale and is very hard. The slate tiles used on floors are thinner than those used for roofing. Slate is less expensive than granite or marble, is wear resistant and needs little care. It tends to be thin and often splits along natural grains. Slate is available in many varieties of color, but the darker colors may show more dirt and scratches. In addition to slabs and tiles, slate is also available in randomly cut pieces that can be used for a rugged, rustic look. Slate can also be mixed on the floor with metal or other types of tiles to give a more interesting look.
- Soapstone or steatite is composed of several minerals: talc, chloride, dolomite and magnetite and

Biblical mosaic with limestone.

Ann Sacks

is available in 12- and 18-inch squares, honed or tumbled. When soapstone is cut it turns from a light gray to a dark charcoal color, and with mineral oil applied, the color is deepened further. It can have light and dark veins running through it and some patterning. Soapstone takes in heat quickly and will radiate it for hours afterward; it is often used on hearths because it can handle extreme temperatures without cracking. Soapstone is very durable and nonporous, won't burn or stain and requires little maintenance. Acids and alkalis will not etch marks on the stone as they will on other stones, and scratches can be removed with sandpaper. Stone sealer should be used on flooring to protect the stone. One of the products recommended for soapstone flooring is Porosol, a product manufactured in Scandinavia by Wetrok.

- Stone can be slippery, particularly when it is polished.
- It is noisy when walked on.
- Most stone is heavy, requiring a concrete substrate.
- Professional installation is usually necessary.
- Stone is generally expensive because of the cost of finishing and transporting the material.
- Some stone is very porous and will stain easily. It may be treated to prevent staining, but the sealants and polishes used can sometimes make the stone slippery and change the color of the stone.

There are numerous resources for stone of all types. It is sometimes difficult to compare prices because the same stones are often called by different names. If you find a stone that you like and want to compare it to others, it is best to get a sample of the stone, even if you have to pay a small fee to be able to do so.

Some manufacturers of soapstone:

Tulikivi Finnish Soapstone	888-544-5442	www.finnishsoapstone.com
Green Mountain Soapstone Corp.	802-468-5636	www.greenmountainsoapstone.com
M. Teixeira Soapstone	877-478-8170	www.soapstone.com
Stonetrade	401-885-6608	www.stonetrade.com

Advantages
- Stone has a natural beauty.
- There are many varieties and variations of color, texture and pattern to choose from.
- It is available in many different shapes, sizes and thicknesses.
- It can look formal (as with marble) or rustic (as with irregular slate).
- Stone is durable and will last for a long time.

Disadvantages
- It is a cool material underfoot. This, however, can be alleviated by installing under-floor heating. In warm climates the coolness may be an advantage.

Reclaimed Terra-Cotta and Stone
Antique materials have become increasingly popular over the last several years. Because they are not in great abundance, they can also be expensive.

Terra-cotta—Tiles are available in various shapes and sizes and are reclaimed from period buildings, many of which are more than 100 years old. They were molded by hand and fired in wood-burning kilns, giving them varied colors and interesting textures. The tiles reflect the native colors of their origin with yellows, warm pinks and ochres. Generally, within each purchase is a wide variation in color, which adds interest to the overall look of the flooring. The

Above: Antique terra-cotta.

Right: Antique marble is reclaimed from European manor houses and country estates and provides a beautiful floor.

able in many sizes as small as mosaics, and in larger slabs that may be 24-inch squares or larger.

Advantages
- They have a warm, antique appearance.
- They require minimal maintenance.

Disadvantages
- They are expensive.
- They require professional installation.
- Delivery may take a long time.

pieces are available in thicknesses from ³/₄ inch to 1 ¹/₄ inches. Installation is expensive because the tiles often must be washed, laid in a mud base and set in a pattern that takes advantage of the variety of colors.

Stone—There is a large variety of stones that have been captured from many areas and transported to the United States. These stones have been found in country houses, châteaux and farmlands all over the world. There are black Belgian limestones from Java and biblical limestones from Jerusalem. Many of the stones are unique and may be in short supply. Other stones are more abundant and simpler to locate. They come with a rich patina and interesting textures and are often inconsistent in color and size. Stones are avail-

Some suppliers of reclaimed bricks and stones:

Ann Sacks	800-278-8453	www.annsacks.com
Paris Ceramics	888-845-3487	www.parisceramics.com

Terrazzo

This is a man-made composite material that consists of an aggregate of marble, granite, quartz, onyx, glass chips or other chips mixed with concrete or nonporous resin. It is available in a large variety of colors and can be precast (as tiles or slabs) or poured in place. It can be polished to a smooth surface or finished with a textured surface. Terrazzo produced with Portland cement will take time to cure. Depending on the temperature and humidity in the environment, it may take several months or longer to cure and develop the anticipated luster that terrazzo usually has. Make sure that any sealers or dressings used are listed by Underwriters Laboratories for slip resistance (with a minimum friction rating of 0.5).

There are three types of binders used to anchor the aggregate of chips:

Portland cement—This is the most crack-resistant system. It requires penetrating sealers to protect the surface. Spills must be wiped up to prevent staining.

Polyacrylic-modified Portland cement—With this system, the water is replaced with an acrylic (polyacrylic) emulsion. Like the earlier method, this also requires a penetrating sealer to maintain the look of the floor.

Resinous thin-set system of epoxy or polyester—This system is chemical and stain resistant and also more crack resistant than the cementitious systems. It produces a nonporous surface that only requires a surface sealer. Any color can be used to create a variety of surface effects.

resources

For information about terrazzo with recycled glass, contact EnviroGLAS Products, Inc., at www.americanterrazzo.com or call 888-523-7894.

Advantages
- Terrazzo is waterproof.
- It is very durable.
- Water-based sealants will protect against staining.
- Maintenance is simple.
- It may be renewed by polishing and resealing.
- Post-consumer and industrial recycled glass are used for some terrazzo.

Disadvantages
- Hard tiles are cold to the feet.
- Terrazzo is expensive. It is more expensive than most types of hard tile and only slightly less than the best-quality stone.

- It can be noisy in heavily trafficked areas.
- Terrazzo is not resilient; anything dropped on it will break. Other tiles can also be tiring to stand on for long periods.
- Professional installation is usually necessary.

resources

For further information about terrazzo or to locate a contractor in the United States, contact The National Terrazzo and Mosaic Association at 800-323-9736 or check www.ntma.com; in Canada, check with the Terrazzo Tile and Marble Association of Canada (TTMAC) at 800-201-8599 or visit www.ttmac.com.

Engineered Stone (Natural Quartz)

This material is about 93 percent quartz, 7 percent binders, pigments (to add vibrant color) and other aggregates (such as mirror specks) to add interest. It is similar in look to terrazzo but

Terrazzo is a man-made composite material that consists of an aggregate of stone and glass or other chips mixed with concrete or non-porous resin.

Bisazza

contains a higher ratio of stone to binder. Unlike terrazzo, instead of being poured, it is vibro-vacuum compacted, resulting in a product without voids or porosity. On the Mohs scale of hardness, it is seven on a scale of ten (which is diamond). The stone is consistently hard throughout, without the soft spots that are sometimes inherent in other stones, and is sold in slabs of varying sizes, similar to the way other stones are sold. Engineered stone is available in slabs that are 12 x 12, 16 x 16 and 24 x 24. Thicknesses range from about ³/₈ to ¹/₂ inch. The smaller slabs can be set in a rapid thin set, but the larger slabs should be set in an epoxy, which is a bit more expensive. Failures have occurred with engineered stones when they have been set with inappropriate materials.

There are many colors available, and the colors are consistent with little variation from piece to piece. Engineered stone has been popular in the United States as a counter surfacing material for several years, but it has recently become popular as a flooring material as well.

Engineered stone or natural quartz is compacted to create a hard, nonporous surface.

Advantages
- Natural quartz is very hard.
- It is available in a large variety of colors, styles and designs.
- It is not porous, so it doesn't have to be sealed.
- Maintenance is easy.
- It has a high color consistency.

Disadvantages
- Engineered stone must be professionally installed by a knowledgeable professional.
- The tiles may be expensive.
- Like other tiles, engineered stone can be noisy and cold.
- It is not resilient; items dropped on it will break, and it can be tiring on feet.

- It may be sensitive to wear and chemical attack, like other natural stones.
- It is not as readily available as some other flooring materials.

Ceramic Tile

Ceramic tiles are made of clay, mineral components that include clay and special types of clay (kaolin and ball clay), feldspar, shale, talc and so on. Tiles can be handmade or machine-made, glazed or unglazed, inlaid or relief textured. They come in high-gloss, matte and slip-resistant finishes. They can be laid in an endless

Silestone by Cosentino

variety of patterns, textures and colors, mixed with similar or very different types of tiles. They come in a large variety of sizes, shapes and designs. Ceramic tiles are available with printed or hand-painted designs. Many manufacturers offer accessory tiles (bullnoses, borders, trim tiles) that match or coordinate with **field tiles.**

There is a wide variation in the cost of tiles; handmade or antique tiles are expensive and machine-made tiles can be inexpensive. One manufacturer offers a concrete tile with the look of wood pickets that can be paired with a more traditional-looking square terra-cotta tile to give a rustic country look. Solid ceramic tiles can be mixed with patterned tiles, metal tiles and so on. An inexpensive field tile can be used with a more expensive trim tile without costing a great deal. The possibilities are only limited by one's imagination. About 10 to 15 percent more tiles should be ordered than needed in case there are broken or imperfect tiles in the shipment and to have extra tiles for repairs. Grout is used between the tiles and can be another floor design element or can be very limited, almost not showing. When selecting tile, choose grout that is close to the color of the tile or decide if a contrasting color will be used. There are several types of ceramic tiles:

Terra-cotta—These tiles are available as reclaimed antique tiles, handmade or machine-made. Differences in the look of the tiles are derived from the nature of the clay and the variations in firing techniques. Colors are usually earth tones and differ according to region: Provençal tiles are warm pink and yellow shades, tiles from Tuscany are typically ochre and Mexican terra-cotta (Saltillo) has a rough and rustic look with flame marks in the warm orange color. Tiles are available in a variety of shapes and sizes. Often the tiles are unglazed and need to be sealed, so they won't be as porous.

Quarry—These tiles are made from unrefined high-silica clay that is extruded through a die or pressed into a mold and then fired. They are mass-produced and are an excellent alternative to terra-cotta tile. Originally quarry tiles were all unglazed; today they are available glazed, unglazed and in a variety of sizes (including mosaic) and thicknesses. Typically they come in earthy tones—red, brown and buff, as well as in darker colors such as blue. They are dense and durable, but they can become abraded and pocked over time. They are reasonably nonslip, and some varieties contain carborundum, which provides a fully nonslip surface. They are colder than terra-cotta and less expensive. Fully vitrified (they absorb little water) quarries can be used outdoors.

Glazed—These floor tiles are made from a mixture of minerals that are ground into a certain maximum particle size in a device called a "ball mill." The material is milled in a slurry with about 50 percent water. Then the slurry is spray dried to about 5 percent water content. This is now a damp powder that is pressed in a high-pressure mold. The tile body is dried to about 2 percent moisture content, then either glazed or left unglazed and baked in the kiln. The same process is used for porcelain tiles, which are ceramic but with a lower water absorption in the tile body than other types. This is called the "pressed-duct method" and 90 percent of tile made in the world today is made this way.

There are many kinds of glazed floor tiles ranging in water absorption from 0 to 7 percent. They are durable, regular in dimension and color, and impervious to water and most stains.

Glazed ceramic tiles show chips since the interior of the tile is usually cream colored, which is a different color than the exterior. They are available in numerous colors, shapes, sizes, textures, patterns and designs. The color is stable and will not change over time as terra-cotta. Tile is cold on bare feet and hard and ungiving. In areas where you will be standing for long periods, such as the kitchen, glazed tile may be tiring on the feet. Fully vitrified versions are frost resistant and slightly slippery. Nonslip versions containing silicone carbide and tiles with ribbed, ridged or studded textures offer a better grip, but they can be expensive and are heavy. Glazed tiles are available in glossy, matte and textured finishes.

Glazed tiles are also popular wall coverings. They are lighter and stick to walls better than floor tile. They are also easier to cut and shape. These tiles cannot be used in freezing areas and are not recommended for the floor because they have a lower break-strength.

Porcelain tiles—These are the same color throughout so when they chip, it is less obvious, unlike glazed tiles. They are also very hard and impervious to moisture. Porcelain tile can be left either unglazed or glazed; most tiles made today are glazed porcelain. Unglazed porcelain can be ground and polished just like stone. The glaze used on porcelain is sometimes matched to the porcelain material, so if there is a nick or chip on the tile, it will not be obvious.

Encaustic tiles—These tiles, first invented by monks in the twelfth century, were commonly used in this country until about the 1890s, when other types of tiles were developed. Encaustic tiles are decorative unglazed tiles produced with inlaid patterns rather than surface decorated. Early on, different-colored clays were hand-pressed into a mold, dried and then fired. More recently, dry clay in the form of dust was substituted, which allowed for the use of more colors and a more consistent product. These tiles are fired at high temperatures and

are highly durable; they do not fade, and if they chip it is not noticeable because the colors go throughout the tile. Some encaustic tiles are not fired; these discolor easily and stain before they are sealed.

Photographic tiles—This is a new method of transferring images from photographs, slides, transparencies or digital images onto a ceramic tile. The images are burned onto the tile with ground minerals and ores. Tiles can depict any graphic image, including scenes, fruits, vegetables, coffee beans, a manhole cover, grass and so on. Some tiles are stock items; others can be custom made.

resources

For more information about photographic tile, contact Imagine Tile at www.imaginetile.com or call 800-680-8453.

Tile Source

Encaustic tiles are decorative, unglazed tiles produced with inlaid patterns rather than surface decoration.

Advantages

- Ceramic tiles are easy to work with.
- Most of them are very durable.
- Some ceramic tiles are waterproof.
- They are generally easy to clean.

Disadvantages

- Hard tiles are cold to the feet.
- They can be noisy in heavily trafficked areas.
- Some ceramic tiles can be slippery when wet.
- Porous tiles can get stained and harbor bacteria unless they are properly sealed.

- Ceramic tiles are not resilient; anything dropped on them will break. They can also be tiring to stand on for long periods.
- Professional installation is usually necessary.

resources

For further information about tile, check with the Tile Council at www.tileusa.com or call 864-646-8453.

Mosaic Tile

Small cubes of stone, marble, glass, metallic or ceramic tiles are embedded in grouting in decorative or geometric designs. They can vary in size from $3/8$ inch square to a maximum of $2\ 1/4$ inches square. Because the tiles are small, they are generally sheet mounted at the factory. They can be used as trim, as an inset design or for an entire floor. Most mosaic tiles are glazed, but they can be unglazed as well; unglazed tiles must be sealed to prevent water penetration. Patterns and designs can be selected from a large variety of suppliers, or custom designs can be ordered. All of the tiles on a floor can be the same or varied in material and color. Grouting can be varied for different effects as well. Extra tiles should be purchased, if possible, in case of damage.

Advantages

- Mosaic tiles are very durable.
- They are available in a large variety of colors, styles and designs.
- They can be contoured to use on shower floors and other surfaces that are not perfectly flat.
- Mosaic tiles are less slippery than other tiles because of the large amount of grouting.
- Maintenance is easy.

A manhole cover is a whimsical look for this bathroom.

Imagine Tile, Inc.

This bathroom has a multi-colored glass tile floor.

Disadvantages
- Installation can be expensive because it so labor intensive.
- The tiles may be expensive.
- Like other tiles, they can be noisy and cold.

resources
For further information about mosaics or to locate a contractor in the United States, contact The National Terrazzo and Mosaic Association at 800-323-9736 or visit www.ntma.com.

Glass Tile
Glass tile is most commonly used in the bathroom but can be used in the kitchen or other parts of the house as well. It is more often used on walls and countertops but is a beautiful flooring alternative in the right application. Glass tile comes in a large variety of sizes (from 1 x 1-inch to 24-inch squares, with many sizes in between), shapes (squares, rectangles, octagons and so on), colors, designs (fish, flowers, stripes

A two-color limestone floor.

Bisazza

and so on) and textures. It is often available in custom colors and designs as well. Several finishes are available: clear, opaque, sanded or glossy. Some glass tiles have texture so as not to be slippery. Glass tiles can be used alone as field tile or combined with ceramic, porcelain or stone as accent tiles.

Glass tile is available in a variety of thicknesses. If the tile will be used as field tile, the thicker tiles are generally recommended; if it will be used as decorative accent tile, then the flatter tiles can also be used. Wall tiles are usually $1/4$-inch thick. The thicker tiles ($1/2$-inch thick) are always used on the floor but can also be used on walls. The thicker tiles tend to be more expensive than the flatter ones from the same manufacturer, but prices can vary depending on style, finish and design.

Ann Sacks

Careful installation is required for glass tile. It is considered to be durable if it is installed properly. Professional installation of glass tile is essential; the installer should be experienced and should follow the manufacturer's directions carefully, or warranties may be void. Because glass can expand and contract, the adhesive used to install glass tile must be flexible. If the tiles are too close together there will be no room for expansion and contraction, and the tiles may crack. Most manufacturers recommend that a crack-suppression membrane be installed above the substrate to prevent cracking. White adhesive must be used when the tiles are transparent; tiles that are back-painted can be used with other adhesives because the backing will not show through. On transparent tiles, care must be taken even when the adhesive is applied to the wall, since use of a notched trowel could leave wavy lines that will show through the tile. The substrate below the tile must be clean, smooth and even so the tile won't crack. Some applications require adhesive to set the tiles and a special grout to be used around the tiles. Many tiles have special requirements for installation and the manufacturer should provide instructions for their particular product.

Bisazza

Glass tiles are used to line this bath as well as all surrounding walls and surfaces.

Advantages
- Glass tiles have a beautiful look.
- Many color and design options are available.
- Glass tiles are impervious to stains and easy to clean.

Disadvantages
- Hard objects dropped on the tiles may break them.
- Some glass tiles can be easily scratched.
- They require professional installation.

Some manufacturers of glass tiles:

Ann Sacks	800-278-8453	www.annsacks.com
Architectural Glass	845-733-4720	www.architecturalglassinc.com
Bisazza		www.bisazza.com
Bedrock Industries	877-283-7625	www.bedrockindustries.com
Crossville Porcelain Stone	931-484-2110	www.crossville-ceramics.com
Euro-Tile	866-387-6845	www.euro-tile.com
GlasTile, Inc.	336-292-3756	www.glastile.com
Interstyle Ceramic & Glass (C)	604-421-7229	www.interstyle.ca
Maestro Mosaics	312-670-4400	www.maestromosaics.com
Marin Designworks	415-884-2605	www.marindesignworks.com
M2 Innovative Concepts	253-383-5659	www.kaleidoscopetile.com
Oceanside Glasstile		www.glasstile.com
Sandhill Industries	208-345-6508	www.sandhillind.com
Stone Source	212-979-6400	www.stonesource.com
UltraGlas, Inc.	800-777-2332	www.ultraglas.com
Walker Zanger	877-611-0199	www.walkerzanger.com
Waterworks	800-998-2284	www.waterworks.com

(C) = Canadian

- It is necessary to find an experienced or very careful installer.
- The tiles and the installation can be expensive.

For more information on concrete or to find local contractors, contact the following companies:

Bomanite	559-673-2411	www.bomanite.com
Increte	800-752-4646	www.increte.com
Perma Crete	800-607-3762	www.permacrete.com
The Stamp Store	888-848-0059	www.thestampstore.com

Concrete

Concrete is a blend of Portland cement, coarse aggregate, water and sand. It was originally used in more commercial settings but has become increasingly popular in residential applications because of its versatility, durability, aesthetic appeal and ease of maintenance. It is available in precast slabs or tiles, or it can be mixed and laid directly on-site. Concrete has often been used in the past for basements and garages in homes, but today it is being used for the main living areas of the house as well. There are many treatments that can be used on concrete to make it look like a multitude of other materials. Aggregates and color can be added; it can be textured in a variety of ways. Concrete should be sealed to protect the surface. Several coats of acrylic, epoxy resin or water-based sealant should be used to give the concrete a hard finish that is very tough and chemical resistant. There are products to treat concrete that are ready made by several companies. One of these is Bomanite, which is used indoors and out. It is a cast-in-place concrete product available in many colors and patterns and can be made to look like many different stones, bricks, wood and so on. The stamping and coloring process is done on-site. This company has contractors all over the country that install concrete floors. There are several companies that license and train installers and supply materials for concrete flooring.

Some of the treatments for concrete are:

Polishing—Concrete can be ground to a high-gloss finish.

Stamping—Freshly poured concrete imprinted with a pattern.

Stamping overlays—Decorative overlays can be used over worn concrete with polymer-modified cement, which is fast setting and self-leveling. It can be imprinted as thin as $1/8$ of an inch.

Adding or seeding aggregates—Colored aggregates of pebbles, marble, granite chips or glass can be added to the concrete mix or seeded into the top layer of the mix to give it the look of terrazzo.

Brooming—The concrete is poured and leveled. A broom is then run across it in one or more directions to give the concrete traction.

Scoring—Marked with lines, grooves or notches.

Rolling—The concrete can be rolled to give it a variety of patterns. An imprint is put on with a special tool that gives the concrete a repetitive pattern.

Sawcutting—A grinder is used to put shallow cuts in the concrete to make designs or to make transitions for the color.

Painting—Concrete can be painted to look like marble, slate or any other material with epoxy resin. A non-yellowing urethane is then put on top to protect the surface.

Acid staining—This is one of the most popular methods of adding color to concrete. Acid itself doesn't color the concrete, but the salts in the acid water-based solution react with hydrated lime in hardened concrete to give an insoluble color that becomes a permanent part of the concrete.

Pigments—Colors can be added to the mixture (at the ready-mix plant—called integral color) or added later (dusted on the job site while the concrete is wet) to change the look of the concrete. Dusted-on colors are typically more vibrant since they are concentrated on the top.

Advantages

- Concrete requires minimal maintenance.
- Many different types of looks can be achieved with concrete.
- Concrete hardens over several years and gets stronger over time.
- It is durable and long lasting.
- It is a healthy flooring; it will not hold on to dust mites, mold and so on.
- Concrete is impervious to decay.
- It has a look of permanence.
- Concrete is environmentally friendly; it uses fewer natural resources—the ingredients in concrete are virtually inexhaustible and some of the ingredients are recycled.

Disadvantages

- It requires professional installation.
- It can be costly to install as the design becomes more sophisticated, although the materials are not expensive.
- Concrete is not resilient; items dropped on it

Ann Sacks

will break, and it can be uncomfortable on feet for an extended period of time.

- It is cold on feet, unless it is used with radiant heat.

resources

For further information about concrete flooring or to find a concrete contractor, check with The Concrete Network at www.concretenetwork.com.

Hardwood

Wood floors have always been a favorite choice because wood has a natural warm appearance. It works with most styles of homes from traditional to contemporary, and if it is well cared for, can last for the duration of the life of a house.

All wood that will be used in the house must be seasoned. This is the process by which

Above: This is another way of getting the look of terra-cotta and wood pickets, all made of concrete.

Left: A concrete floor given the look of terra-cotta.

Bomanite

green wood, which is newly cut, loses its moisture until it reaches equilibrium with the atmosphere. As the wood seasons, it also shrinks as it loses the moisture. Wood can dry naturally, or it can be kiln dried to a moisture content of approximately 6 to 9 percent. Wood is sometimes left in the environment where it will stay for a period of ten days to two months so it can acclimate fully. If the wood is too moist, it can shrink substantially, leaving large gaps between the wood planks later. If the wood is too dry, it will absorb water from the atmosphere and swell after being laid. It is important to purchase wood that is seasoned correctly for the environment in which it will be installed. Discuss the type of heating you have, particularly if it is radiant heating (which requires a lower moisture content in the wood), with the agent when purchasing wood.

There are twelve items to consider when selecting wood for flooring:

1. Species of wood

There are many species available, domestic and imported. The heartwood and sapwood from the same species often vary significantly in durability and color. When selecting wood, be sure what species and grade you are getting. Before selecting any species, consider the dimensional stability, ease in finishing, availability and appearance (color, texture and grain) of each species.

Softwoods are less durable but are warm, resilient, widely available and inexpensive. Some of the popular softwood species are white pine, yellow pine, Douglas fir and spruce.

Hardwoods are more expensive and are available in a variety of colors, patterns and textures. Some of those available are ash, beech, birch, cherry, chestnut, maple, red oak, white oak, walnut, bamboo, hickory, pecan and birch.

Decay-resistant wood is naturally resistant to rot and decay; these are redwood and western red cedar.

Imported woods are available from around the world. Some of the more commonly imported wood species are teak and mahogany.

resources

For information about wood species, check the Web site of the National Wood Flooring Association at www.woodfloors.org/consumer/whyTypesSpecies.aspx and the Canadian Wood Council at www.cwc.ca.

2. Grading

The grading system for each species is different; some do not have any grading system at all. The terms used are different for each species: the highest classification for unfinished oak and ash is "clear", for unfinished oak, "prime", and for maple, beech, birch and pecan, "first." All of these classifications mean essentially that the wood is free of defects with only minor imperfections. Check on the rating system for the wood you are selecting to know what the grade describes.

resources

For information on grading, contact The Wood Flooring Manufacturers Association at www.nofma.org/gradingrules.htm and Installing Wood Floors at www.installingwoodfloors.com.

3. Unfinished or Pre-Finished?

Unfinished wood was the standard for many years. Prefinished woods are becoming more popular because they are easier to install and eliminate the dust of sanding and the odors from the sealants. Prefinished wood can be installed over concrete. It is less affected by moisture and will not expand and contract as much as unfinished wood. Prefinished wood is available in engineered wood at about $5/16$ inch thick and in solid wood up to $3/4$ inch thick and $2 1/4$ to 8 inches wide. There are many choices of color available. Prefinished wood comes with a three- to fifteen-year warranty.

4. Cut

There are three standard angles that wood can be cut in, in relation to the grain:

Plain sawn—This is the most common cut. It has more patterning than the other two cuts because growth rings are more noticeable. For most applications, plain sawn works well.

Quarter sawn—The pores are tighter, making it less vulnerable to moisture. It cups and twists less than the other types of cuts, but because there is less yield with this type of cut, it is also more expensive. The angle of the lumber is from 45 to 90 degrees of the ring to the face of the piece. Under radiant heating, it is recommended to use quarter sawn or rift sawn because they are more stable.

Rift sawn—The angle is slightly different than for quarter sawn but otherwise is similar. The angle of the lumber is about 30 to 60 degrees of the ring to the face of the piece. This is the most expensive of the cuts because there is more waste due to the angle at which it must be cut. There isn't as much figured grain in the rift sawn, which some people find preferable.

5. Pattern

Wood varies in thickness, length and width. It can be laid in a variety of patterns to change the look of the floor. Wood is usually more expensive as the dimensions of the wood get larger. Wide, long boards are generally more desirable. Some manufacturers glue together several strips to resemble larger boards. Boards are supplied with tongue-and-groove configurations, so they fit together without leaving any gaps, but some come with square edges. All of the wood listed below is available both prefinished and unfinished.

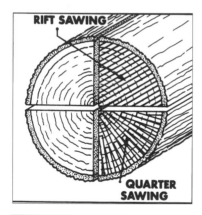

National Wood Flooring Assoc.

Kaswell & Co, Inc.

Top and Bottom Left: Examples of how wood is cut from a tree trunk.

Right: A room with end-grain birch installed.

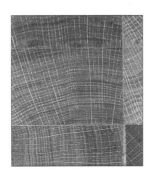

Kaswell & Co., Inc.

variety of different hardwoods. Solid wood parquet can be refinished, depending on the sandable surface above the groove. Other forms of parquet or block consist of solid elements glued together or a hardwood veneer over a softwood base. For a rustic look, there are suppliers specializing in reclaimed parquet.

End-grain parquets—These are made from the short pieces left from the milling of wood for other purposes, such as windows and doors. It is available in many species. There are no tongue-and-groove configurations, but they are glued down, butted up against each other, sanded and then finished with urethane, penetrating oil and/or stain. This wood is susceptible to moisture and must be installed in a stable environment. It is strong, durable and insulative.

resources

Suppliers of end-grain parquet floors: Kaswell Flooring Systems at www.kaswell.com and Oregon Lumber at www.oregonlumber.com.

Tarkett Wood Floors

Above: Samples of end grain.

Right: Engineered hand-scraped hickory burnt umber wood.

Strip—This is solid wood that is available in thicknesses of $^5/_{16}$ inch or $^3/_4$ inch and the face widths of 1 $^1/_2$, 2 and 2 $^1/_4$ inches (and 3 $^1/_4$ inches on $^3/_4$-inch thickness).

Plank—This solid wood is similar to strip wood in all ways, but it is wider. The thickness is $^3/_4$ inch, but the face widths are 3 to 10 or 12 inches. Some are available wider.

Parquet or block flooring—This solid wood is composed of small strips or blocks of hardwood in geometric patterns or designs and held together by adhesive or mechanical fasteners. It can be laid in patterns that range from herringbone to more intricate designs such as basketweave. Modern parquet is supplied tongued and grooved or doweled and is made from a

National Wood Flooring Assoc.

Engineered wood (manufactured wood)— This is a multi-plied wood with four or five layers cross stacked (each layer is 90 degrees from the one above) and bonded together with a water-based bonding material. The cross-stacking construction controls the floor's natural tendency to expand and contract. The top layer is a veneer of any type wood, which can be sanded two or three times to refinish the flooring. Many colors and species are available. Engineered wood is becoming increasingly popular because of its dimensional stability. Because of the cross stacking of the wood, it is not as susceptible to moisture as solid wood. Moisture typically migrates from the concrete substrate, and a moisture barrier is necessary to protect wood flooring. With engineered wood, it can be glued directly to the concrete. The higher yield of the engineered wood also makes this an environmentally friendly product. The two categories of widths are "longstrip," which runs 6 to 8 inches wide, and "strip," which runs 2 $1/4$ or 3 inches wide. Engineered wood is generally available with tongue and groove and is prefinished.

Wood has a natural beauty that adds warmth to any room.

Some suppliers of reclaimed wood:

Aged Woods, Inc.	800-233-9307	www.agedwoods.com
Antique & Specialty Flooring Co.	888-728-3966	
AntiQuus Wood Products	800-852-9224	www.antiquuswood.com
A Reclaimed Lumber Company	617-354-5785	www.reclaimedlumberco.com
Carlisle Wide Plank Floors	800-595-9663	www.wideplankflooring.com
Conklin's Authentic Antique Barnwood & Hand Hewn Beams	570-465-3832	www.conklinsbarnwood.com
Goodwin Heart Pine Company	800-336-3118	www.heartpine.com
Heartwood Pine Floors	800-524-7463	www.heartwoodpine.com
Olde Wood Ltd.	866-208-9663	www.oldewoodltd.com
Pioneer Millworks	800-951-9663	www.pioneermillworks.com
Trestlewood	877-375-2779	www.trestlewood.com
The Woods Co.	888-548-7609	www.thewoodscompany.com
Vintage Beams and Timbers, Inc.	800-790-1837	www.vintagebeamsandtimbers.com

National Wood Flooring Assoc.

Wood flooring can be installed with many types of border and pattern styles.

resources

For additional information about engineered wood, contact the Engineered Wood Association at www.apawood.org or call 253-620-7400.

Acrylic impregnated—This is a prefinished wood product that is treated with acrylic and has color forced through the wood under pressure. This finish goes throughout the wood, creating a very hard surface. Acrylic impregnated wood is rarely used for residential applications but is a consideration in areas of the house prone to abrasion and moisture. It is available in strips, planks and parquet designs.

6. Color

There is a wide variation in color among species. The sealant will also alter the color of the wood. Select wood that suits your design and taste, and then ask to see a sample of the color that you will be purchasing, unfinished as well as finished.

7. Reclaimed Wood

Over the last several years, reclaimed wood has become more in demand not only for its beauty and stability but also because of the concern for the ecology and preserving our natural resources. Wood is often rescued from old buildings and structures, such as factories, mills, barns and piers. Wood is also used from old wine casks, and cider vats, and several companies recover logs that have been sitting at the bottoms of rivers

Reclaimed wood creates a nice touch in this bedroom.

for over a century, lost by loggers taking them to sawmills downstream. Wood can be salvaged from old ships, obsolete bridges and dead and standing timbers. Reclaimed wood has a unique charm, is large in dimension and durable and stable, but it is generally more expensive than new wood would be.

resources

For a complete list of suppliers of reclaimed wood in the United States, check http://www.forestethics.org/purchasing/reclaimed_USA.html; for Canada, check http://www.forestethics.org/purchasing/reclaimed_Can.html.

8. Sealants

Some wood is pretreated or painted in the factory and needs no further treatment. All other wood should be sealed to prevent water penetration and to make it resistant to dirt and chemical attack. Some sealants alter the color of wood. Different finishes are available from satin or matte to high-gloss sheens. The number of coats of finish used will vary by the manufacturer; find out

Vintage Beams and Timbers, Inc.

how many coats are recommended. Some sealants are hard wearing and long lasting; others may become scratched or stained and require more frequent renewal. More natural products that are environmentally friendly include resin, oil or wax, but these are less durable. If possible, use finishes that are non-toxic, such as wax and oil. If a more toxic sealant will be used, be sure to ventilate the room for as long as possible after installation.

Types of sealants include:

Acrylic—This is a quick-drying, nontoxic, water-based varnish. It is easy to apply but must be used two to four times a year for added protection.

Alkyd resin—This is a nonyellowing, non-toxic, quick-drying sealant. It needs to be waxed two to four times a year for added protection.

Epoxy resin—This is yellowish in tone, slow to dry but very durable.

Oleoresinous—It is a mixture of tung oil and resin. It is clear but with a yellowish tint, simple to apply and slow drying. It is less durable than some of the other sealants but easy to patch.

Oil-modified urethane—This is the most commonly used sealant. It brings out the yellow tones in wood and may itself yellow with age. It is durable, but care should be taken to adequately ventilate the area when it is applied because it can cause eye and respiratory irritation.

Water-borne urethane—This is also a commonly used finish. It dries clear and quickly. It is durable and has a mild odor. It is also easy to patch.

Urea formaldehyde—This is a transparent lacquer, ideal for light-colored or bleached woods. It is durable but difficult to patch later on.

Wax—It consists of bees and plant waxes which are durable, water resistant and have a pleasant scent. Wax needs to be renewed every couple of months. It is a more natural and less toxic choice. A penetrating stain should be used under the wax.

Penetrating oil—This is sometimes available

with wax included. It is water resistant and can be tinted with natural stains or colors. This is also a more natural, less toxic alternative.

Aluminum oxide finishes—This finish is durable and will last for a long period of time.

9. Installing the wood

The way the flooring will be laid is dependent on the type of subfloor in the house. Some manufacturers specify the type of installation.

There are three ways to install wood flooring:

Nail down—The wood is attached to the substrate with nails.

• Face nailing—The nails go through the face of the wood and can be filled, or pegs can be used in the same or contrasting species.

• Blind nailing or toe nailing—Nails are inserted into the top of the tongue at an angle. They then go through to the subfloor.

Floated—The planks are connected to each other but not to the substrate. This is done with a tongue-and-groove configuration.

Glued—The flooring is attached directly to the substrate with a factory-recommended adhesive.

10. Decorative treatments

There are many ways to give wood a different look.

Bleaching and tinting—Wood can be given a different look by lightening or darkening the natural color. It can be bleached to take the color out, or it can be treated with a water-based white-pigmented varnish, which gives a similar effect but is very expensive. It can also be lightened by **pickling** the wood, which involves rubbing white paint, pickling wax or gesso into the grain of the wood. This process also gives the wood a weathered appearance. Tinting deepens the natural tone of the wood. Tinted varnishes, wood dyes and stains in a choice of colors can be used.

Color—Wood stains and paints can be used to give the wood a variety of colors.

Stain—Stains change the color of the wood

Some contacts for heat vents:

All American Wood Register Co.	815-728-8888	www.allamericanwood.com
Cape Cod Air Grilles	800-547-2705	www.ccairgrilles.com
Grate Vents	815-459-4306	www.gratevents.com
Launstein Floors	888-339-4639	www.launstein.com
The Reggio Register Co.	978-772-3493	www.reggioregister.com

while maintaining the natural grain. They are available in several formats: oil-, water- or solvent-based. A sealant must be used after the stain is applied.

Paint—This gives a solid, opaque look. There are floor paints available that contain epoxy resin or polyurethane, which gives an extra hard finish, but there are fewer color choices available than for gloss or eggshell paints.

Pattern—Various techniques can be used to achieve patterns. Spattering one or more colors of paints or mineral spirits from a stiff brush will produce a random speckled effect, or combing the paint on with a wide-toothed comb either following the grain of the boards, in squares or at random is another effect.

Accents—Small medallions or other designs can be inlaid on steps, room transitions or in the entrance hall.

Borders—A painted border can add interest to the floor or define a particular area. Contrasting wood strips can be inlaid as simple lines or intricate designs around the border of a particular area.

Stenciling—This can be used for borders, edging for stairs or as an overall pattern.

Trompe l'oeil—This is a French word for "trick the eye." It involves simulating another material, such as marble. This is done with layers of paint and requires artistic painting techniques.

11. Radiant heating with wood

For radiant heating to work well with wood floors, the concrete or plywood subfloor must be dry. If the subfloor is moist, the water will enter the wood flooring and cause it to expand and contract, shrink, crack, cup and bow. Radiant heat should be turned on for a period of at least seventy-two hours before the wood flooring is installed, if the concrete slab is at least sixty days old. If it is not, the radiant system should be on for thirty to sixty days before the floor is put down. It is suggested that a thermostat be placed outside the house in addition to the interior one so the system can anticipate the changes in weather and make gradual rather than abrupt changes in the heating. In selecting wood to use over radiant heating, consider the following parameters:

- Select a wood (such as cherry, walnut, mesquite or teak) that is known to be stable.
- Quarter-sawn and rift-sawn flooring are more dimensionally stable than plain sawn.
- Strip flooring is preferable to plank flooring; narrow boards expand and contract less than wide boards and have more seams to allow for movement.
- Engineered wood is very stable and a good choice for use with radiant heating.

12. Heat vents

Wood heat vents are available for those who would like them to match the look of the wood flooring. They are available in many species and sizes. They can often be purchased from a flooring supplier.

Advantages

- Wood has a natural beauty.
- It is versatile, going with most styles and designs. There are also many looks wood can have with various treatments available.
- It ages well and sometimes looks better with time.
- Wood is very durable and can last for the life of the house, if it is taken care of.
- It is available in many different formats—sheets, strips, boards, mosaic tiles, blocks and parquet.
- Wood is resilient; items dropped on wood will not necessarily break.

- It is quiet.
- It is cooler on the feet than carpet, warmer than stone or hard tiles.
- Wood comes in a variety of species.

Disadvantages
- Wood requires maintenance; finishes need to be renewed from time to time.
- Some wood can be damaged by narrow furniture legs and spike heels.
- The humidity will damage the floor in poorly ventilated bathrooms with showers.
- Most wood floors require professional installation (other than ready-made wood floors that the amateur may install).

resources

For further information about wood flooring, check with the National Wood Flooring Association at www.woodfloors.org or call 800-422-4556 in the United States; in Canada, call 800-848-8824. The Wood Flooring Manufacturers Association can be reached at www.nofma.org or visit The Canadian Wood Council at www.cwc.ca. Another excellent source of information is www.woodfloorsonline.com.

Laminate

Originally manufactured in Sweden in the late 1970s, laminate floors have improved greatly over the last several decades. At one time they mostly replicated wood grains but are now available in a variety of imitation stone, brick, ceramic tile and other looks as well. Early on, laminate floors had a very hollow sound when they were walked on and they chipped and delaminated. Today well-made laminate floor products no longer have a hollow sound due to advances in the core materials and methods of bonding and are stronger to resist chips, dents, stains and burns. Most laminate floors today come with a minimum of fifteen-year to lifetime warranties.

Laminates are made up of four layers:
- A surface layer is melamine (several layers of thin sheets of fibrous material) impregnated with aluminum oxide.
- A decorative paper or design layer can have any type of design or photograph. The surface and design layers are bonded or pressed to a substrate.
- Substrate is the core material (**MDF** or **HDF**), giving the laminate rigidity.
- Backing paper (included in many laminates but not in others) is beneath the substrate; it balances the board and acts as a moisture barrier.

Some manufacturers differentiate between high-pressure laminates (HPLs) and direct-pressure laminates (DPLs). HPLs have an extra layer of Kraft paper impregnated with resin and are compressed between the core and the design layer. Both types of laminates perform well for residential applications.

If a laminate floor is installed over concrete slab, a moisture barrier is required to prevent moisture from migrating up into the laminate. Some foam underlayment includes a moisture barrier built in; with others it must be added as an extra step in the installation. Some companies offer a layer of insulation attached to the underneath part of the laminate floor, which helps to reduce sound. Underlayment (any roll or sheet product used between the laminate floor and the subfloor) absorbs the sounds of footsteps, evens out subfloor imperfections, makes the flooring more resilient and protects the laminate from subfloor moisture. Most laminate floors are floating (they are not attached to the subfloor) and come with tongue-and-groove configurations or a variety of locking mechanisms. Tongue-and-groove flooring must be glued together. Some locking mechanisms should not be glued and for some it is optional. Not all locking mechanisms are the same. It is a good idea to try out the locking mechanism to make sure it is a tight fit. Expansion areas, which are concealed with wall base trim, are left around the perimeter of

In this kitchen two colors of laminate have been beautifully paired in a checkerboard pattern.

the floor for expansion and contraction of the laminate material.

Edges of the laminates are protected against moisture in a variety of ways. Companies treat the raw edges of the laminate plank or tile by wax-impregnating them or with other sealants to protect them against moisture; some companies do not treat them at all, making them more vulnerable to moisture. Laminate can be installed over existing flooring materials as long as they are smooth. Laminate most commonly comes in planks but are also available in large square tiles, rectangular blocks and accent pieces. Some laminates are available with pre-applied glue backing for easy installation. There are different quality laminate floors; higher quality ones are more likely to reduce the sound of footsteps, prevent water infiltration and resist denting, staining and scratching. They will also cost more and have longer warranties.

Some laminate companies now offer a permanent surface treatment to prevent the growth of bacteria and fungi. Some companies offer this treatment only on some of their laminates. Check to see if this is an option on the selected material.

Wilsonart Flooring

Some laminate flooring manufacturers:

Alloc	877-362-5562	www.alloc.com
Armstrong World Industries, Inc.	888-276-7876	www.armstrongfloors.com
BHK of America	800-663-4176	www.bhkofamerica.com
Formica Corporation	800-367-6422	www.formica.com
Kronotex USA, Inc.	866-892-4633	www.kronotexusa.com
Mannington Mills	800-443-5667	www.mannington.com
Mohawk Laminate Flooring	800-266-4295	www.mohawk-flooring.com
Pergo Flooring	800-337-3746	www.pergo.com
Shaw Industries, Inc.	800-441-7429	www.shawfloors.com
Tarkett	800-367-8275	www.tarkett.com
Wilsonart International	800-433-3222	www.wilsonart.com
Witex USA, Inc.	800-948-3987	www.witexusa.com

Various designs can be combined to give more unique looks; however, laminate floors should be from the same manufacturer and checked to be sure they will be the same thickness and specifications. Two-color squares can be used to create a checkerboard effect and modular faux stone tiles can be used with wood planks around the perimeter to break up the space.

resources

Check for products that have the seal of approval by the North American Laminate Flooring Association (NALFA) at www.nalfa.com, which requires products to comply with stringent requirements for certification.

Advantages

- Laminate floors are very durable, resistant to stains and dents and will not fade.
- Chemicals and UV rays will not affect laminate floors.
- They are easy to maintain.
- They are easy to install.
- Laminate floors come with fifteen-year to life-time warranties.
- Laminate floors are made from recycled materials, making them environmentally friendly.
- They can be installed over floors with minor imperfections, since the foam underlayment is somewhat forgiving.
- The padding absorbs sound.
- They come in a wide range of colors and designs.
- They do not require harsh chemicals for cleaning.
- They are comfortable underfoot.
- Some floors can be lifted and moved to other locations. This is only true for laminates that are not glued.
- They have an allergy-free surface that does not harbor dust or mites.
- Damaged panels can be replaced.
- Many homeowners are able to install laminate themselves.
- Laminate floors can be installed over radiant heating (if special installation procedures are followed).
- Early laminates tended to delaminate and chip.

Disadvantages

- They do not always look like the material they are imitating.
- Laminates still have a sound when walked on, even with the padding.
- Laminate floors cannot be used in moist areas such as near a swimming pool, steam room and so on. Water that is quickly wiped up will not cause problems.

- They have been vastly improved in the last twenty years.
- Laminates cannot be refinished.

resources

For further information about laminates, check with the North American Laminate Flooring Association at www.nalfa.com.

Some suppliers of linoleum:

Armstrong World Industries	717-397-0611	www.armstrong.com
Domco Tarkett, Inc. (C)	450-293-3173	www.domco.com
Forbo Linoleum	866-627-6653	www.themarmoleumstore.com

(C) = Canadian

Forbo

Resilient Flooring

There are many new and durable resilient floorings available today. Many of the varieties closely replicate the look of other materials, such as stone and slate, at a less expensive cost. These materials have been improved in quality and expanded in variety over the last several years. Colors and patterns can be combined to add interest to the floor. There is a wide range of costs within this category, with rubber relatively inexpensive and leather being quite expensive. For most varieties there are many colors, patterns and textures available. Some of the materials are more durable than others; linoleum may last many years while vinyl may have a shorter life. Resilient floorings tend to be soft, warm, lightweight and comfortable underfoot. Most resilient floorings are easy to maintain. Because they may be damaged by extreme heat and sun, they should be protected with window treatments. Be sure to check with the manufacturer about the cleaning requirements and products they recommend. Resilient flooring may be installed over concrete or plywood subfloor or existing flooring, as long as it is flat (such as wood or linoleum).

Opposite Page: A diamond-patterned linoleum floor created by using two different colors of tiles.

Linoleum

A resilient flooring, linoleum was first introduced in the United States by Armstrong in 1910, although a rubber manufacturer, Frederick Walton, patented linoleum in England in 1863. It was exceedingly popular in the early 1900s but fell out of favor in the United States in the 1960s. It has recently become popular again for the home environment because it is environmentally friendly and made of all-natural materials—linseed oil, powdered wood, and/or cork dust, ground limestone, tree rosin, drying agents and pigments attached to a backing of jute fiber. Linoleum is made from renewable raw materials and is recyclable. It is durable and has a high resistance to burn marks. The colors go all through the material, so nicks and scratches will not be as obvious as some other materials. Linoleum is available in a wide variety of colors, patterns and designs with borders and insets available to give the floor a more interesting look. It is available in tiles and sheets.

Advantages
- Linoleum is natural and ecologically friendly.
- It is healthy flooring for the home; it is antistatic,

Some of the resources for vinyl flooring:

Amtico	212-545-1127	www.amtico.com
Armstrong	800-233-3823	www.armstrong.com
Congoleum Corporation	800-934-3567	www.congoleum.com
Colmar Industries, Inc.	281-591-7200	www.colmar.com
Mannington Mills, Inc.	800-443-5667	www.mannington.com
Metroflorusa	866-687-6357	www.metroflorusa.com
Nafco	800-248-5574	www.nafco.com
Roppe Corporation	800-537-9527	www.roppe.com
Tarkett, Inc.	800-827-5388	www.nafco.com
Winton/Earthwerks Tile		www.earthwerks.net

Tarkett, Inc.

A vinyl redbrick pattern provides a rustic look to this kitchen.

either a foam or vinyl core backing, a design layer and a protective surface, or it can be vinyl granules fused on a vinyl or felt backing. It is inexpensive (price varying by the amount of PVC) and comfortable to walk on. Vinyl is available in a wide variety of colors, patterns and textures in sheets up to 12 feet wide and tiles that are generally 12-inch squares. Many of the vinyl tiles are peel-and-stick for easy installation. Some vinyl floors, once installed, can emit chemical fumes for an extended period of time. If possible, ventilate the area where the tile is installed for several days before occupying that space.

Advantages

- It is very durable—resistant to dents, scratches, moisture and stains.
- It is available in a wide variety of colors, patterns, styles and textures. These can be mixed to add interest to the floor.
- Vinyl is comfortable to walk on.
- It is modestly priced.
- It is easy to maintain.
- Vinyl is easy and quick to install.
- It can be used with under-floor heating.
- Damaged tiles can be easily replaced.
- It can be installed over other floorings.

Disadvantages

- Some vinyl comes with a photographically applied pattern, which may not wear well. Most vinyl comes with the pattern inlaid, which will be more durable.
- Many varieties need a flat subfloor or they will show minor discrepancies and protruding nail heads.
- It is not environmentally friendly; it can release potentially hazardous chemicals into the atmosphere. If vinyl catches fire, the fumes are toxic.
- Vinyl consumes nonrenewable resources of petroleum and natural gas, and the product itself is not biodegradable.
- It can tear with harsh treatment.

not attracting dust and house mites, which can trigger asthma or allergic reactions, and anti-bacterial, not allowing germs to breed on it or multiply.

- It is warm underfoot and resilient, making it comfortable to walk on.
- Linoleum is quiet.
- It is reasonably nonslip, even when wet.
- It can be used with under-floor heating.
- Some varieties can be laid by the do-it-yourselfer while others require professional installation.
- It absorbs sound, so it reduces any room noise, and it is thermally insulating.
- Linoleum is easy to maintain.

Disadvantages

- It is more costly than vinyl.
- Tile colors may be limited.
- The sheet product should be laid by a professional distributor.
- It is not available at large hardware stores.

Vinyl

This is synthetic flooring that contains some proportion of polyvinyl chloride (PVC). It has

Some resources for rubber flooring:

Activa Rubber Flooring (C)	905-670-5757	www.rubberflooring.ca
BurkeMercer Flooring Products	800-447-8442	www.burkemercer.com
Johnsonite	800-899-8916	www.johnsonite.com
Pawling Corp.	800-431-3456	www.pawling.com

(C) = Canadian

Novelty Floorings

There are so many interesting floor options to meet every household need. Some of these floorings have been around for a long time, such as rubber, but have only recently become popular in residential applications. Materials such as cork have become more popular recently because of concern for the environment and because there are many more colors available than in the past.

Rubber

Rubber tile is available in a wide range of colors, patterns, finishes and sizes. There are coloring effects such as marbling, striation and flecking and a variety of finishes such as smooth, raised studding (circles, squares and so on) and ribbed. Rubber tile is usually available in tile form but also comes in wide rolls, stair tiles and runners. It is available in interlocking tiles that can be easily installed by the do-it-yourselfer and even moved later to another location. The variation in price depends on the thickness (from 2 millimeters to $^3/_8$ of an inch) of the material. Tiles can be laid in one color or in several contrasting colors. Flooring is available in recycled rubber and virgin rubber, with the latter being more stable, less likely to shrink and more expensive. Most rubber today is made of Styrene Butadiene Rubber (SBR). Some of the recycled rubber may have natural rubber, which has latex; this can cause an allergic reaction in some people. If you are highly allergic and are considering purchasing a rubber floor, ask about the flooring contents. Rubber floors

The cork installed in this room has the look of natural flooring but with consistent thermal capability, absorption of sound and added flexibility.

are particularly well suited for in-house gyms, playrooms, bathrooms and kitchens.

Advantages
- Rubber is a good insulator and the surface is warm.
- It is durable and water/burn resistant.
- It has a natural resiliency and is comfortable underfoot.
- Rubber is sound absorbent.

American Cork Products, LLC

Some resources for cork flooring:

American Cork Products, LLC	888-955-2675	www.amcork.com
BHK of America	800-663-4176	www.bhkofamerica.com
Globus Cork	718-742-7264	www.corkfloor.com
Jelinek Cork	800-959-0995	www.corkandfloor.com
Natural Cork, LLC	800-404-2675	www.naturalcork.com
Torlys, Inc. (C)	800-461-2573	www.torlys.com
We Cork	800-666-2675	www.wecork.com
Wicanders	410-553-6062	www.amorimna.com

(C) = Canadian

- Many rubber floorings are easy to install.
- It has a raised or an etched surface and is nonslip.
- Some rubber surfaces can be lifted and re-laid in another location.
- Rubber is easy to maintain with just a damp mop.
- It is generally moderately priced.
- Some rubber flooring self-heals from scratches and abrasions.
- Some rubber floorings, particularly those that interlock, can be installed by do-it-yourselfers.
- Some rubber flooring is made from recycled tires and is good for the environment.

Disadvantages
- It is susceptible to grease and oil stains.
- Rubber tends to have an industrial look (which may not be a disadvantage in some homes).
- It may show imperfections in the subfloor.
- Rubber emits some volatile organic compounds (VOCs) that are toxic. Airing-out time is therefore required.

Cork
Cork is a natural material that comes from the outer bark of cork oak trees in the Mediterranean. The trees can be harvested every nine to fourteen years without harming the tree. The cork is ground up and coated with a non-toxic resin binder. A single color can be used or mixed with other colors to create a patterned look. Cork comes sealed or unsealed, and the thicker the tile, the more shock and acoustic absorbency will be present. When purchasing cork be sure to select flooring grade, not the cork intended for walls. Cork is sold sealed or unsealed, but it should be sealed (if necessary, on-site) to protect it from getting soiled and to make it water resistant. It is available in a wide variety of colors and patterns, in tiles, sheets and tongue-and-groove strip flooring. It can be installed over existing wood, ceramic or concrete floors. The tiles are glued down; the planks are floating.

Advantages
- It is durable and grease and oil resistant; it is easy to maintain.
- Cork is resilient, so it is very comfortable underfoot.
- It has a natural appearance.
- It is nonslip, even when it is wet.
- It provides acoustic and thermal insulation. It can also be used as an underlayment to absorb sound.
- Cork is resistant to moisture, mold and mildew.
- It is resistant to termites and many other insects.
- It is easy to install; some tiles can be glued

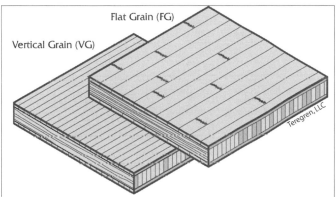

Vertical Grain (VG)

Flat Grain (FG)

Teregren, LLC

Bamboo can be installed with the grain flat or vertical.

There are many species of bamboo; the one that is most often used for flooring is the moso *(phyllostachys pubescens)* species, which is not a food source or habitat for panda bears in China. The culm, or stalk, of the bamboo plant grows to heights of 80 feet and diameters of up to 6 inches. The bamboo, which grows to maturity in 3 to 6 years, depending upon the region where it's grown, is harvested and split into strips to extract the premium part of the stalk. It is flattened into 1-inch strips, then laminated with an adhesive under high pressure to produce planks for flooring. The strips are typically treated with hydrogen peroxide and a natural borate solution to eliminate pests and mildew, then kiln dried to remove moisture.

Most bamboo manufacturers offer two grains and two colors. The vertical grain is composed of 1-inch strips laminated together face-to-face on

down; others are peel and stick.

- It is modestly priced unless it is custom made.
- Cork is natural and ecologically friendly.
- It is hypoallergenic and does not absorb odors.

Disadvantages

- It can dent and tear.
- Cork tiles cannot be used over radiant heat because the tiles will lift; it can be used over floating cork flooring.
- It requires refinishing with polyurethane every eight years.
- Delivery time may be delayed.

Bamboo

A fairly new flooring alternative to the hardwood category, bamboo is a rapidly renewable resource whose stalks are harvested every three to six years, depending upon the region in China or Indonesia where the particular species is grown. Bamboo has been used as a structural building material in Asian cultures since the dawn of civilization. Today the grass is growing in popularity as an attractive alternative to traditional hardwoods due to its aesthetic appeal, durability and environmental sustainability.

Bamboo flooring installed.

Teregren, LLC

Some suppliers of bamboo flooring:

Bamboo Flooring Hawaii, LLC	877-502-2626	www.bambooflooringhawaii.com
Bamboohardwoods	800-783-0557	www.bamboohardwoods.com
Bamtex	888-964-6832	www.bamtex.com
California Bamboo Flooring Co.	888-548-7548	www.californiabamboo.com
D & M Bamboo Flooring Co.	630-582-1600	www.dmbamboo.com
EcoTimber	888-801-0855	www.ecotimber.com
Smith & Fong Plyboo	866-835-9859	www.plyboo.com
Teragren, LLC (formerly TimberGrass, LLC)	800-929-6333	www.teragren.com

Coconut palm installed.

edge, while the flat, or horizontal, grain is composed of the same strips laminated together face-up, either two- or three-ply, which shows off the nodes of the bamboo stalk.

The natural color is the true bamboo color itself and the caramelized (some companies use the term "carbonized") color is derived from a process of pressure heating the fiber. The longer the fiber is heated, the darker the sugar compounds in the fiber become. The flooring is usually available either unfinished or prefinished. The finishes vary from manufacturer to manufacturer. Some may use aluminum oxide-based finish, while others may use a finish such as acrylic polyurethane. It is always supplied with tongue-and-groove configurations that can be nailed, stapled or glued down. It is best to check with the manufacturer for specific installation instructions for each product.

Look for bamboo that is uniform in color and thickness with no voids between the laminated strips. If anyone in the house has allergies, check with the supplier to make sure that the finishing products used are acceptable.

Advantages
• The vertical laminate style is harder than oak and maple; the horizontal (or wide-grain) style

Plyboo

Blackstone Leather, Inc.; photo by Henni Raaymakers

Leather floor tiles installed in a residence in the Netherlands.

almost has the hardness of red oak.
- Some manufacturers use either no formaldehyde or a low formaldehyde in the adhesive.
- Bamboo is dimensionally stable, which means less expansion and contraction due to climate.
- It is a rapidly renewable resource, harvested over and over from the same plant, unlike hardwoods that take forty or more years to mature.
- It has a natural appearance.
- Some companies offer warranties on the structure and finish up to a lifetime.

Some suppliers of leather flooring:

Ann Sacks	800-278-8453	www.annsacks.com
Blackstock Leather, Inc.	800-663-6657	www.blackstockleather.com
Edelman Leather	800-886-8339	www.edelmanleather.com

- It can be used with radiant heating systems. Check with the manufacturer.

Disadvantages
- Some companies do not use a low formaldehyde adhesive to laminate the strips together.
- Some companies do not use a water-based 100-percent solid, solvent-free finish.
- Some companies buy from more than one factory in China, which can mean mismatched milling and finishes.
- As suggested with hardwoods, avoid the use of bamboo in wet areas, such as bathrooms.
- It is available in few colors but may be stained like hardwoods
- Quality from manufacturer to manufacturer varies widely; check company background, references, warranties and distribution channels.

Coconut Palm
Coconut palm is plantation raised in Indonesia and, like bamboo, is a renewable resource. It grows around 60 feet in fifteen years; it would take an oak forty years to grow that tall. Like bamboo, it is also not considered a timber product but a stalk that is more closely associated with bamboo than trees. Coconut palm is raised for the palm oil that its fruit produces. After about eighty years a palm tree becomes sterile, no longer producing fruit, and it is these nonproducing palms that are used for flooring and plywood manufacture.

Manufacturing these products is a very slow process and only the outer portion of the palm is used because it is the densest and hardest part of the ring. A formaldehyde-free adhesive is used in the manufacture of the palm products. Palm is currently available in one color only, the natural color of the palm. The hue varies from a red/orange to a dark mahogany, and the density of the striation (a pattern that seems to move across the floor) can vary as well. Palm flooring comes in three-ply planks, ¾ x 3 x 72 inches, which are 100 percent coconut palm. This floor is harder than both red oak and hard maple.

Advantages

- Coconut palm is very hard and durable.
- It has a natural appearance.
- It is environmentally friendly.
- No formaldehyde is used in the manufacture.

Disadvantages

- It is not recommended for use in highly moist areas such as bathrooms.

resources

For further information about coconut palm, contact Smith & Fong Plyboo at www.dura-palm.com or call 866-835-9859.

Leather

Leather that is used for flooring is specially tanned and dyed for resilience, needing only a buffing with wax for maintenance. It should have a waxed finish to assist in moisture resistance, but spills wiped up immediately will prevent staining. Tiles are available in many colors, sizes and shapes with finishes that range from smooth to antique textured. Leather should not be used in heavy moisture areas such as bathrooms and kitchens, heavily trafficked areas such as entranceways and in areas of direct sunlight. It can be expected to last fifteen to twenty-five years.

Advantages

- It is warm to the touch.
- It has a beautiful look.
- Leather is resilient and comfortable on feet.
- It is sound absorbent.
- Leather is durable and improves with age, developing a patina.
- It is aromatic and has a comfortable tactility.

Disadvantages

- It is expensive; comparable in price to natural stone or the best quality ceramic tile.

Brushed metal flooring planks with a star accent tile.

Carina Works

Some suppliers of metal flooring:

Alumafloor	630-628-0226	www.aluminumfloor.com
Ann Sacks	800-278-8453	www.annsacks.com
Carina Works, Inc.	800-504-5095	www.carinaworks.com

- Waxing is required annually and buffing is recommended, depending on usage.

Metal

Metal flooring has been used in industrial settings for a long time. In the last several years, however, it has become fashionable as a material for residential applications as well. Metal flooring can include metal tiles, such as stainless steel, aluminum, copper, bronze, and metallic composite materials (that look like steel, bronze and other metals), and metal grating, metal panels or sheets. Many new and interesting tiles are available with several designs and color washes. Metal tiles are excellent as accent tiles with other materials such as stone, wood or ceramic or can be used on their own. They are usually made from recycled metal and are considered environmentally friendly. Metal is generally textured with raised or etched patterns that provide a nonslip surface. It can be sealed and is easily maintained.

Advantages

- Metal is generally recycled and is therefore considered environmentally friendly.
- It is easy to maintain.
- Metal adds a special modern look to the home.

Disadvantages

- It is cold and noisy to walk on.
- Some varieties of metal will rust.

Carpeting and Rugs

There are so many options available in carpet today, in natural fibers and synthetics, earth tones and bright colors, flat weaves and high piles. Many carpets can be bound to use as rugs, and there are carpets that can be picked up and re-laid elsewhere. So many choices are available in price, grade, composition, performance, color, pattern and texture; it is important to evaluate your needs and preferences before making a selection.

Carpeting is a very popular floor covering for its soft feel and warm appearance. Most carpets come with some degree of protective finish, but spills should be soaked up quickly to prevent stains. Carpet should be vacuumed regularly to remove dust mites that can trigger allergic reactions and asthma. Cat and dog fleas are attracted to carpet and may be difficult to eradicate. Check with a carpeting specialist to find out which carpets are best suited for your personal situations. Carpeting can be used in most rooms in the house, but it should be avoided in bathrooms where it will get repeated soaking.

Some of the conditions to consider when selecting carpet:

- Will the room be occupied by children? The carpet then needs to be very durable and stain resistant.
- Will there be a lot of sunlight exposure? Choose carpeting that is not as likely to fade—100 percent solution-dyed fibers.
- Will the room get a great deal of traffic? Again, a durable carpet is necessary.
- Will the room be occupied by someone with allergies? Select a carpet that will be less lightly to harbor dust and other allergens. Since carpet does trap dust, keep it out of the breathing zone until vacuumed. The Carpet and Rug Institute recommends vacuuming at least twice a week if people in the home have allergies.
- Will the carpet be changed in the near future? Often with children's rooms, flooring is changed with children's growing needs and styles. An inexpensive, durable carpet should be considered, or a modular carpet, which can be easily replaced.
- How much of the budget will be spent on the carpet? This may depend on how long you plan to live at that location and the amount of wear the carpet will have. When selecting carpet be aware of all possible costs, including cushion, installation, removal of old carpet and hauling and delivery of the new carpet. Get all agreements in writing.
- What style of house will be selected? The style should have a major impact on the carpeting

selected. There are many colors, designs and textures to go with every possible style. If possible, it is best to work with an interior designer in selecting those that best work with the style of the house and the furnishings. Budget will be another major concern; there are carpets available in a wide span of prices. The following are some of the factors to help you further understand carpet construction and make an educated decision when purchasing carpet.

Pile—Pile describes the basic way that the threads of the carpet are constructed to give the carpet its texture and pattern.

- Cut pile—This is one of the most popular types of carpet construction. The loops are cut, creating individual tufts. The durability of the cut-pile carpet will depend on the fiber, the density of the tufts and the amount of twists of the yarn. There are several varieties of cut piles, varied by the amount of twist in the yarn.
- Plush/velvet pile—The carpet is cut smoothly across and there is no twist to the yarn. This is generally one of the most formal types of carpet. This type of pile tends to show the most footprints.
- Saxony pile—The carpet is cut smoothly across but there is some twist to the yarn, making the yarn ends more visible. This is a less formal look and footprints are minimized. Textured saxony has some twist and some texture.
- Level-loop pile—The loops are uncut and are all the same height. This pile is more durable, informal and good used in high-traffic areas. The berber styles have this type of pile.
- Multilevel-loop pile—Like the level-loop pile, this one also has uncut loops but of varying heights. It creates a pattern effect and has an informal look.
- Cut-and-loop pile—This is a combination of cut and looped yarns. It can create several sculptured effects.

Texture—This is similar to saxony in that the yarns are twisted and it is informal and minimizes

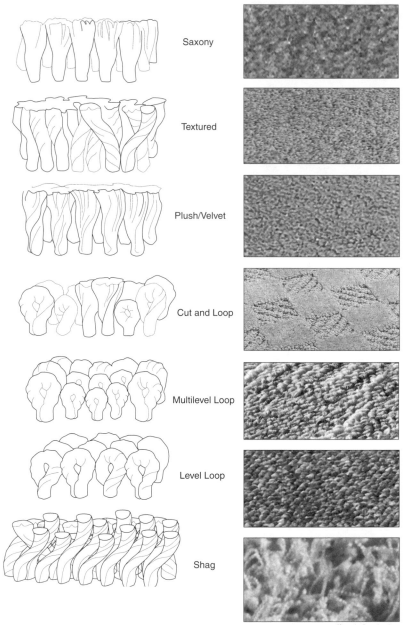

Saxony

Textured

Plush/Velvet

Cut and Loop

Multilevel Loop

Level Loop

Shag

Shaw Industries, Inc.

Rug Pile Types

footprints, but the top of the carpet is less smooth and textured.

Frieze (not shown)—The yarns are very twisted in this pile and have a curly, textured surface. This is a less formal look and minimizes footprints and vacuum marks.

Shag—A cut-pile carpet with an extra-long pile height. The yarns will tend to flop. This type of carpet was popular years ago but has become more popular recently. Today there are different yarns mixed together to give the carpet added interest.

The fibers—The fiber is the basic ingredient of the carpet that, along with the type of construction and density, will determine the durability of the carpet. The following are some of the most common fibers used:

- Wool is a very warm, natural, soft fiber that doesn't dent or flatten easily and is springy underfoot. It tends to be antistatic, comes in many colors, is luxurious to the touch but is expensive. Synthetic components are sometimes added to wool carpet to add strength and also to bring down the price. Wool carpet will fade if it has long exposures to sunlight, and several types of insects (such as moths) find the wool protein appealing.
- Nylon is the most popular fiber used in carpet in the United States because it is strong, durable, resists soils and stains, is available in vivid colors and is resilient; it resists crushing. It is easy to clean and is a good carpet for high-traffic areas. Depending on the quality, it can be expensive or very inexpensive. Nylon is likely to fade if there is prolonged exposure to sunlight.
- Polyester is a less expensive synthetic fiber, but it is soft (when used in thick, cut-pile textures), durable, easy to clean and resistant to water-soluble stains. It is not springy and is often used to make shag-pile carpet. It is likely to fade with prolonged exposure to sunlight.
- Olefin (polypropylene) is very strong and durable. It is also resistant to stains, moisture,

mildew and static. It is colorfast because the color is added during fiber production. It is generally a less expensive synthetic fiber used in many blends because it is durable and stain resistant. Many berbers are made of olefin. It flattens easily and is not suitable for deep-pile carpets. Olefin is treated to resist fading from the sun. Some olefin carpets are inexpensive; others can be very expensive.

- Blends are abundant in the market. There are wool/nylon, acrylic/olefin and nylon/olefin blends available. These are generally combined to offer the best characteristics of each fiber to create a better one.

Natural flooring materials—There are a group of several materials that are now becoming more popular because they are economical, natural looking and healthier than some of the available synthetics. Many of these carpets come with a latex backing. If you or someone in your family is sensitive to latex, look into getting a carpet with a different backing or find out if the latex is natural or synthetic. These carpets are generally very durable but most absorb moisture readily. They should only be used in dry areas of the house. These floorings must be vacuumed regularly and spills should be blotted up immediately until most of the liquid is removed.

- Seagrass is the smoothest of the fibers and is comfortable underfoot. It is durable, inexpensive, antistatic, does not stain and doesn't attract dirt. Any particles accumulating in the weave will eventually grind away at the fiber and reduce its life. Seagrass is not often dyed, so it is usually available in natural colors that range from a greenish tan to khaki olive, sometimes enhanced by colored strings in black, green, red or blue. It sometimes retains its grassy scent for a while after it has been woven but will eventually lose this aroma. Seagrass is not available in wall-to-wall carpet but can be found as area rugs.
- Sisal is usually creamy white to pale yellow in color but can have a reddish cast. It is often

combined with other fibers, especially coir and wool. Sisal is very durable, naturally sound absorbing and insulating, antistatic and more comfortable on the feet than some of the other fibers. It can be dyed to a variety of colors and is available in many patterns and weaves. It must be treated for stain resistance. Sisal is more expensive than coir or seagrass.

- Jute is slightly less expensive than the best sisal but far less durable. It is soft enough for use in the bedroom, is resistant to mold and mildew and will withstand abrasion but will deteriorate when exposed to moisture and sunlight consistently. Its natural color ranges from light tan to brown, but it can be bleached and dyed as well. Jute requires stain protection and is available in several weaves and tones. The fibers can be made into a fine yarn or a heavy cord. Jute is also used to add strength to other fibers such as wool carpet.

- Paper used for rugs comes from coniferous softwoods (fir, spruce, hemlock, balsam and pines), which produce stronger paper than the hardwoods. Pulp is blended with resin and (sometimes) dyed into paper, which is cut into strips, treated with a wax emulsion and then twisted by a machine to a particular number of twists per inch. The resulting cord is tightly woven and is used for carpets and area rugs. It is not recommended for very large rooms since it is difficult to seam. The wax adds to the fiber's water resistance, but like the other natural fiber materials, it should only be used in dry areas of the house.

- Coir is naturally coarse and therefore not very comfortable to the feet. It is a sturdy, durable material that is highly rot resistant, antistatic and naturally sound insulating. It is more moisture resistant than the other fibers, but water will cause discoloration of the carpet. The natural color of coir ranges from tan to golden brown to reddish brown, but it can be bleached and dyed to any color. Coir can be used for both carpets and rugs.

- Rush is a heavy, robust flooring. It is too smooth and slippery for stairs. Rush needs regular sprinkling of water to maintain its condition and makes good flooring for damp areas.

Maintenance—In order to keep carpeting looking as good as possible, it should be professionally cleaned every twelve to eighteen months the way the manufacturer specifies, in order not void out the warranty. It should also be vacuumed on a regular basis, at least twice a week in high-traffic areas. Accidental spills should be blotted rather than wiped to remove the liquid. Many of today's carpets are treated for stain resistance, but the stains must still be removed quickly to avoid their becoming permanent.

Air quality testing—About 90 percent of the carpet manufacturers participate in a program of testing the carpet at independent laboratories for indoor air quality. All carpets that have passed the test for chemical emissions will have the Carpet & Rug Institute name and telephone number (800-882-8846). If there is anyone in the home that has allergies, you should check to see that the carpet has passed these emissions tests.

Construction—There are several methods of constructing carpet:

- Most of the carpet today is tufted. It is the insertion of tufts of yarn through a carpet-backing fabric or primary backing, creating a pile surface of cut and/or loop ends. The backing is then coated with an adhesive (synthetic latex) to keep it in place, and a secondary backing may be added for increased strength, sometimes incorporating a foam-rubber underlay.

- Woven carpet is produced on a weaving loom in which the lengthwise yarns and widthwise yarns are interlaced to form the fabric, including the face and the backing. This is a very durable but expensive method.

- Needle-punched carpet is made by bonding pile fibers (usually synthetic) to the backing with adhesive, or needle punching them into the backing and sticking the pile fibers with adhesive. It is a non-woven carpet that is not likely to unravel.

Carpet cushions (padding, underlay)—
This is any material placed under the carpet to give it softness and adequate support. Ideally the cushion should be thin and firm to support the carpet backing and protect the fibers from foot traffic. If the cushion is too soft, the back of the carpet may flex too much, causing the carpet backing and fibers to break down. Cushion will also make the floor warmer, quieter and help compensate for some unevenness in the subfloor.

Carpet cushion manufacturers also participate in a program of testing the cushion at independent laboratories for indoor air quality. All cushions that have passed the test for chemical emissions will have the Carpet & Rug Institute name and telephone number (800-882-8846) on a label, which is usually green. If there is anyone in the home that has allergies, you should check to see that the cushion, as well as the carpet, has passed these emissions tests.

Some cushions are attached to the carpet, while others come separately. Most carpeting requires cushion, except for modular carpets. The type and thickness of the cushion used will depend on the type of carpet and the amount of traffic the carpet will endure. It should, however, not exceed $7/16$ inch for a cut-pile carpet and $3/8$ inch for berber carpet. Quality is determined by the denseness and thickness rather than by the material. There are many types of cushion. Each variety of cushion comes in grades that vary by weight (also called density), thickness and the amount of force it takes to compress it. The grade should be selected according to the type of room it will be used in and the expected traffic the carpet will get. The carpeting specialist should recommend the best cushion for your situation. There are three basic types of cushion:

Polyurethane foam—There are three types of foam cushion:

- Prime polyurethane foam is a soft cushion made by combining two liquid ingredients to form a large mass of foam, which is sliced into sheets for cushion.

- Bonded polyurethane foam is a recycled product made by combining chopped and shredded pieces of foam in different sizes and colors into a solid sheet. Waste is used for the cushion and the product.
- Froth polyurethane foam is a thin, dense foam produced by applying liquid ingredients either directly to the back of the carpet or to a non-woven material, creating a separate cushion.

Rubber—Rubber can be varied to produce different levels of density and firmness. The weight in ounces per square yard is the usual measurement for rubber cushion. There are two types of rubber cushion:

- A molded synthetic material, waffled rubber is heat cured to form a waffle pattern. It is a soft, resilient cushion commonly used for residential applications.
- Flat sponge rubber is a firm, dense cushion with a flat surface. It is commonly used for commercial flooring and with loop-type carpet, including berber.

Fiber—Felted fiber has natural or synthetic fibers (virgin or recycled) that can be interlocked into a sheet of felt used for cushion.

- Natural fiber carpet is the oldest type of carpet cushion; it is made with natural fibers of felt, animal hair and jute.
- Synthetic fibers are generally dense cushions with a firm feel. They come in many weights and are classified by the conditions under which they will hold up—light, medium or heavy traffic.

Felted fiber cushions or underlays are best with quality woven carpets. Foam or rubber underlays tend to be used under tufted rather than woven carpet; the best have a firm texture that does not crumble.

Radiant heating—Radiant heating can be used with carpeting, but a lower pile carpet should be used. It is not necessary to use a cushion with radiant heat, but if one is used, it should not exceed $3/8$ inch in thickness. In some situations, no cushion may be recommended.

When purchasing carpet for an area where radiant heat is installed, be sure to inform the carpet specialist so they can help select the most appropriate carpet and cusion.

resources

For further information about carpet cushion, contact the Carpet Cushion Council at www.carpetcushion.org or call 203-637-1312.

Terms Used by the Industry

There are several terms indigenous to the carpet industry that can sometimes be confusing:

Broadloom—This is a term used to denote carpet that is produced in widths wider than 6 feet. It is usually 12 feet wide but can be 13 $\frac{1}{2}$ and 15 feet wide as well.

Berber—It is a loop carpet that is tufted with thick yarn. It can also describe a multilevel loop-style carpet.

Performance rating—Some manufacturers participate in a rating program and put the rating on the label; other companies do not participate. Information on the performance rating, if used by the manufacturer, is usually given on the label with a number from one to five—one being the least amount of traffic and five being the heaviest traffic. If you have a high-traffic area, you would want to purchase a carpet in the four or five rating. For light traffic, ratings one through three will work out. Some manufacturers don't use the rating but describe the traffic on their label. Descriptions may differ among manufacturers.

Modular Tiles

Originally used commercially, modular tiles are available as a flooring system. The tiles have a low nap and are generally square. They can be purchased in many combinations of designs, textures and colors. They have self-adhesive dots on the bottom for easy installation and can be lifted to put in another room or another residence. The tiles can be put over any flat surface (concrete,

Interface Flor

vinyl and so on) and can be used as carpeting or as a rug. Some are made from recycled materials, making them ecologically friendly. In the home they are used in areas where there is a lot of wear and tear and where carpet may need to be replaced easily. Modular tiles are easy to install and replace. Systems like these are excellent for temporary flooring or areas such as children's rooms where change is imminent.

Modular carpet can be easily installed in a variety of colors and patterns to create unique designs.

resources

For more information about modular carpet, check with the following: Interfaceflor at www.interfaceflor.com or call 866-281-3567, Milliken Carpet & Rug at www.milliken-carpet.com or call 800-241-8666, or Bretlin, Inc., at www.bretlin.com or call 800-273-8546.

Advantages

- Carpeting is warm and comfortable.
- It eases foot and leg fatigue.
- It absorbs sound, reducing noise, and it insulates the sound between floors.
- In colder climates, it retains warm air longer than other flooring materials.
- It can minimize slipping, and it cushions falls.
- It is available in many colors, styles, textures and materials.

Disadvantages

- It requires professional installation.
- Carpeting is easily stained if it is not wiped up quickly. With today's stain protection on synthetic carpet, food and beverage stains clean up very easily, provided they aren't left for long periods of time before cleanup.
- Some carpets may be hazardous on stairs, particularly coir, because heels can get caught in them.
- It is impractical for damp areas.

Area Rugs

Area rugs provide warmth, comfort and sound protection while also defining a particular space and adding color to the room. Rugs counteract the disadvantage of cold, hard floors (such as stone or tiles) by adding warmth both aesthetically to the room and physically to bare feet. An added advantage is the portability of rugs; they can be taken along when moving to a new location. Rugs vary in construction, material, color, pattern and design. All rugs placed on the floor should be laid over a nonslip mat to prevent acci-dents. There is an endless variety of rugs to choose from in endless colors, designs and styles in every price range. Select a rug that goes with the style of the house, is proportionately the right size, will be durable enough for the area of the home it will be used in, fits into your budget and is practical in terms of cleanability for the area in which it is needed. Rugs can be woven, tufted, handgun tufted or pieced from tufted broadloom carpet. The most commonly used fibers are nylon, olefin and wool. Rugs are available pre-made in a variety of carpeting materials, or they can be custom made. Work with an interior designer to select the rug that works best with the style of the house and the interior decor.

resources

For further information about carpets and rugs and to locate carpet manufacturers, visit The Carpet and Rug Institute at www.carpet-rug.com or call 800-882-8846 extension 2114 (for free publications).

There are certainly many options to consider before selecting the carpet and rugs you want for your home. Your needs, budget, practical considerations and design preferences will guide you. Take time to look around and check out the many available products before making a choice.

Lighting

Lighting has become so second nature to us that we rarely think about it. We throw a switch or press a button and there is light. We take lighting for granted, until there is a black-out and we don't have any—we then begin to appreciate how important lighting is to our everyday lives.

There are two purposes for lighting in the home—functional and decorative. Lighting helps us to easily perform specific tasks adequately and move around the house safely without bumping into things. It also sets a mood, highlights beautiful paintings and objects in the house and is, in some cases, decorative.

One of the biggest complaints people have about their homes is inadequate lighting systems that don't function properly or that they don't know how to operate. Lighting is therefore not a place to economize when designing or building a house. Finding an experienced, knowledgeable professional is essential. It is best to have a floor plan of the rooms with furniture placement and a good idea of what tasks will be performed in each room. If the room will be multifunctional, the various uses must be considered. If a room will be used for entertaining as well as home-work, for example, several layers of lighting will be needed for the different functions.

Lighting specialists wear many hats. Some lighting dealers are very talented at creating lighting plans. There are lighting designers who don't sell lighting fixtures but just work on lighting plans and interior designers who have the expertise to design lighting. Some architects are qualified to make an excellent lighting plan; others are not. If you are working with an interior designer and/or architect, ask them if they feel comfortable designing the lighting or if they advise consulting with a specialist. Lighting is a special art and staying up-to-date on all the available options is difficult. If the initial lighting plan is not adequate, it will cost the homeowner a great deal more to add lights after the plan has already been bid. If there is any question about the qualifications of your designer or architect, consider consulting with a lighting specialist.

Things to consider when planning the lighting:
- What areas need to be lit?
- What tasks will be performed in those areas?
- What is the size of the room and height of the ceiling?
- What types of fixtures should be used to light those areas (taking into account the style of the house and the furnishings)?
- What colors and textures will be on wall surfaces? Dark colors absorb more light, so more lighting is required than for light-colored surfaces.

Matte surfaces or fabric-covered walls diffuse more light, while glossy finishes bounce the light to other surfaces. Less light is required for glossy-surfaced walls. Wall surfaces should be taken into account when planning the lighting.

- How often are you prepared to change light-bulbs? Are there areas in the house where it will be inconvenient to change bulbs, such as on high ceilings?
- What type of mood should be created in the room? Sometimes the lighting must be flexible for multifunctional rooms.
- What types of controls will be used?
- What are personal design preferences and needs?
- Will the chosen lighting be energy efficient?
- How about safety? Hot bulbs can burn little fingers and adults as well.
- Glare, hot spots and shadows should be kept to a minimum.

Components of Lighting

Lighting has two important components—color and temperature. Both of these have an influence on the type of lighting produced. Different types of bulbs will give off a different amount of heat, which can be a problem in both controlling the interior temperature of the house and limiting people's exposure to dangerously hot bulbs. The color emitted by the bulb is also important because it will set a mood in the house, will show the furnishings in a particular way, and in some cases, may make tasks more difficult to complete. **Color Rendering Index (CRI)** is the measure of the ability of a light source to show colors accurately, most resembling natural sunlight. A measurement of 100 indicates the accurate indication of color, and as the numbers go down, so does the accuracy of the color rendition. Incandescent lights, for example, usually render colors well and have high CRIs. The color temperature (the measure of the color appearance of a light source relative to sunlight or daylight) of

bulbs may vary tremendously from very warm reds to very icy whites. When selecting lighting take into consideration the color and temperature of the light sources. Various bulbs emphasize a particular part of the spectrum relating to Kelvin temperature. With fluorescent bulbs, particular colors can be emphasized by varying the phosphors. With incandescent lights, the coatings can be altered, but this will only alter the color slightly. Fluorescents can more specifically adapt to desired colors.

Types of Lighting

A well-lit room will have a layering of the following types of lighting with a variety of fixtures.

Ambient or general—The general illumination needed to have a comfortable level of brightness for walking around the house safely. The light is spread throughout the area rather than being focused on a particular area. It is generally indirect lighting coming from ceiling- or wall-mounted fixtures, chandeliers, recessed or track lights or built-in lighting in coves, soffits and cornices.

Task—This is the illumination needed to perform a variety of tasks, such as reading, cooking, sewing, homework and so on. Recessed and track lighting, pendant lighting and portable lamps are often used to direct light where it is needed without casting shadows or directly shining the light in eyes. Sufficient light is needed to avoid eyestrain.

Accent—This light is often used to highlight architectural features, show off a piece of artwork or focus attention on a particular surface. The light should be directed on the object or feature being accented. The accented item should have three times as much light as the general lighting around it. Accent lighting is provided by track or recessed lights or wall-mounted fixtures.

Decorative—This can be an interesting pendant, a chandelier, wall sconces and so on.

Terminology

Many of us rely on lighting professionals because understanding the dynamics of light is very confusing. For anyone not paying attention through high school science class, understanding lighting will be a big mystery. There are many terms used by the lighting industry that many of us hear from time to time but still may be ambiguous. The following terms are used by lighting professionals and in lighting brochures:

Lamp—The lighting industry uses this word to refer to any electric light source, including lightbulbs. The term "lamp" is commonly used by the rest of us to refer to a portable fixture, but in the lighting industry, these fixtures are called "portables."

Portable—This is any lighting device that sits on tables or the floor, commonly called "lamps" by nonlighting professionals.

Lumen—The amount of light that a bulb produces. The output of incandescent and most fluorescent bulbs is printed on the bulbs' packaging. There is a wide variation between the output possibilities of bulbs, from 100 lumens in a small chandelier bulb to 3,000 lumens in a fluorescent tube.

Wattage (W)—The amount of electricity consumed by a bulb. This rating is marked on all lightbulbs.

Foot-candle—The amount of light reaching a subject. One foot-candle equals one lumen per square foot of illuminance or light level.

Lumens per watt (LPW)—This is the effectiveness of a light source as it converts power into light. The range is from about 5 LPW to about 90 LPW. Comparisons of efficiency can be measured most realistically if two of the same types of bulb are compared with size.

Average-rated life (in hours)—This is the time that half of the bulbs in a sample test group failed and half were still operating. This figure varies with the type of bulb. There are

certain conditions that can shorten a bulb's life: vibration, extreme temperatures, a faulty fixture or wiring. The average-rated life of most incandescent lightbulbs is 750 to 3,000 hours; fluorescent bulbs are 10,000 to 20,000 hours. Bulbs are continuously being developed, resulting in longer lifespans.

Kelvin temperature (K)—The Kelvin scale is named after the British mathematician and physicist William Thomson Kelvin, who proposed it in 1848. In 1990 the National Energy Policy Act was passed by the United States to better describe the colors of fluorescent lightbulbs, and the Kelvin rating was adopted; 3,000 K for a yellow-orange color, 4,100 K for an almost-white color and 5,000 K for almost blue. This new initiative helps consumers to have a better idea of the color of the bulbs they are purchasing and their relationship to high-noon daylight.

Line voltage—This is the voltage typically used in the United States—110 to 120 volts. Most incandescent bulbs operate on this circuit.

Low-voltage—This type of circuit requires a transformer to reduce the electrical voltage to meet the correct level of the lamp. The transformer can be integrated into the fixture or can be a separate unit. Low-voltage lamps and fixtures can be smaller in size than line voltage ones.

Lighting Technologies

Many of us think that all lightbulbs are basically the same and all of them work similarly. All lighting is not produced in the same manner, however, and there are many different types of bulbs, or lamps, as they are referred to in the lighting industry. There are several lighting technologies, with new ones continuing to emerge. Incandescent lighting was one of the first technologies, perfected by Thomas Edison in 1879. Although it was a remarkable discovery, there have been other lighting technologies that have developed over the last several years that have advanced other technologies (home computers, televisions, etc.) and offer more energy efficiency.

Incandescent

These bulbs are the most common types of residential lighting. Light is produced when a thin **tungsten filament** wire is heated by the electricity flowing through it inside a glass bulb filled with inert gas (usually argon). The filament heats and then glows, or incandesces. At the temperature the **filament** heats to, a yellow-white light is emitted, approximating natural sunlight. Most of the energy used is actually turned into heat, with only a small amount used to make light. Incandescent bulbs are usually designed for a 120-volt current but are available in low-voltage versions as well. The pear-shaped A-bulb is the most common incandescent bulb, but there are also other available shapes and sizes in a variety of colors. Long-life bulbs usually have thicker filaments and run at lower temperatures than average bulbs, so it takes longer for them to melt and break. There are several types of incandescent lamps:

Nonreflectorized—These incandescent bulbs emit light in all directions for wide distribution. They are available frosted (etched to diffuse the light), clear (create a bright but harsh light), three-way (two filaments create three levels of brightness) and long life (they have a thicker filament that doesn't burn out as quickly but also gives off less light).

- General (A)—This is the most common pear-shaped incandescent bulb. Three-way bulbs and silver-bowl bulbs (SB), which have a silver cap to cut glare and produce indirect light (used in pendants), are also pear shaped. They come in clear, frosted and colored and range in wattage from 15 to 250.
- Globe (G)—These are ball-shaped incandescent

bulbs that come in white or clear glass.

- Tubular (T)—These are tubular-shaped incandescent bulbs that are available in clear and frosted glass. They are used in some portable lamps, as under-counter lights and picture lights. They may come with three different types of bases—large or small screw bases or

1 A19 incandescent
2 Globe incandescent
3 Tubular incandescent

Photos of bulbs 1–17 courtesy of Satco

Bulb
Inert Gas
Support Wires
Tungsten Filament

Glass Mount

Incandescent Lightbulb

Screw Thread Contact

Electrical Foot Contact

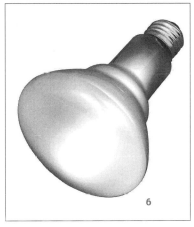

4 Decorative flame
5 3-way (incandescent)
6 BR 30 reflector
(incandescent)
7 Par 30 reflector
(halogen)

twin-pin bases known as "bayonet." Some are similar looking to fluorescent tubes but last a shorter time and are expensive.

- Decorative (D)—These incandescent bulbs come in flame shape, torpedo shape and some other shapes in frosted and clear glass. They are available in medium and small screw bases and twin-pin bases.
- Three-way—With two filaments that allow for three different light levels, these incandescent bulbs are typically 50 to 100 to 150 watts and 30 to 70 to 100 watts.

Reflectorized—These bulbs direct the light where it is needed. They are funnel-shaped bulbs with a reflective white or silver coating inside the bulb that directs light forward.

- Reflector (R)—They are larger than many other lights and are not as energy efficient as halogen lights will be. They emit a smooth field of light with a soft edge. They are commonly used in downlights. (There are halogen bulbs that are the same shape and size and can replace these reflectors but are also brighter, whiter and longer lasting.)
- Parabolic aluminized reflectors (PARs)—They have a specifically designed reflector that is highly efficient in pushing light into space. The most common size is PAR 38. They are

manufactured in narrow flood, spot and narrow spot versions, which means the spread of the light beam is controlled by the reflector.

Advantages
- Incandescent bulbs operate efficiently in a wide range of ambient temperatures.
- They are an inexpensive and compact light source.
- They have excellent color-rendering properties (CRI 95+).
- They fit a large variety of fixture types.
- They are easily dimmed.
- They do not require a ballast.
- They have screw-in bases that are commonly used.

Disadvantages
- They don't last as long as fluorescent bulbs.
- Incandescent lightbulbs are very hot during operation.
- Filaments are sensitive to vibrations and jarring.
- Incandescent lightbulbs emit 90 percent heat and only 10 percent light, wasting energy and making the bulbs very hot. To decrease the heat, use lower-wattage bulbs or use compact fluorescent bulbs.

- As incandescent bulbs age, the tungsten attaches itself to the inside of the bulb and causes the bulb to darken or blacken.
- Although the light is good for the growth of plants, the heat from the bulbs can burn the leaves of plants. There are special bulbs designed for this purpose.

Halogen—This is a form of incandescent light that includes a tungsten filament. It is like a regular incandescent light, but the bulb is filled with pressurized halogen gas. The filament in a halogen bulb is constantly being reinforced as the filament evaporates and the halogen gas causes the evaporated particles to redeposit themselves on the filament. This process is called the "halogen regeneration cycle," and it requires the bulb to maintain a high temperature. (This same process does not occur with standard incandescent bulbs; the filament just continues to break down over time.) Because halogen bulbs must operate at higher temperatures, the glass is made from quartz, which is stronger than the blown glass used in standard incandescent bulbs and can withstand high temperatures. Halogen bulbs produce a whiter crisp light and have a longer life than regular incandescent bulbs. They also are more efficient, providing more light, or lumens, per watt than regular incandescent bulbs. They are not as efficient as fluorescent lights, however. They are small and work well in low-voltage applications as well as in line-voltage fixtures. Some multi-mirror reflectors (MRs) and PAR bulbs are now available frosted, which produces a smooth, even beam, reducing the shadows, striations and hot spots associated with some traditional reflectors.

Line (120 volts) voltage—Lights with line voltage provide good beam control. They are available in spot and flood beams. They are used in track, recessed, for outdoor spots and floodlights.

- Parabolic reflectors—These are reflectorized bulbs used for beam control. They are used in track, recessed, outdoor spots and floodlights. They are larger than the MRs and provide more coverage. They are manufactured in narrow flood and spot versions. The spot produces a hot spot in the center of the beam and a hard edge. There are alternative bulbs with frosting (acid-etched lenses) that eliminate glare, hot spots and shadows.
- Tubular—Double-ended and single-ended bulbs (mini-cans)—These lights come with a variety of bases and are used in sconces, torchères and so on.

Low (12 volts) voltage—Lights with low voltage require a transformer to step down the voltage. They provide excellent beam control.

- Multi-mirror reflectors (MRs)—These are available as tiny bulbs (MR-16, MR-11, MR-8) that are used for downlighting, low-voltage tracks, pendants and cables. They are much smaller than PAR lamps. They are more energy efficient and they have lower heat, excellent color and very good beam control. The MRs are manufactured in wide flood, flood, narrow flood, spot, narrow spot and very narrow spot bulbs.

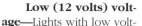

8 Par 20 reflector (halogen)
9 118 mm halogen

- PAR-36—These bulbs are slightly smaller than those used for line-voltage systems (PAR-38) and give coverage as very narrow spot, narrow spot and wide flood bulbs. They also come as halogen lamps.
- Tubular—These bulbs are miniature lights used

Opposite Page:
10 MR 16 halogen
11 Par 36 (back)
12 Par 36 (front)
13 Bi pin halogen

10

11

12

in pendants, desk lamps and some track systems.

Advantages

• The halogen gas helps to produce a brighter and whiter light than other types of bulbs.
• Halogens can last twice as long as other incandescent bulbs and use only half the energy to produce the same light output.
• They are excellent at directing light where it is needed.
• They come in a variety of bulb shapes.

Disadvantages

• They tend to be expensive.
• Halogen bulbs are sensitive to the oils on our hands and must be handled carefully. They should be handled with gloves or a clean, dry cloth.
• They burn particularly hot.
• Continuous dimming of halogen bulbs will cause the bulbs to blacken on the inside and reduce the light output. The bulb can later be somewhat restored by running it non-dimmed every so often.

Xenon—This is another form of incandescent bulb that contains xenon gas. These are often used in low-voltage fixtures and lighting systems; they are used for under-counter and

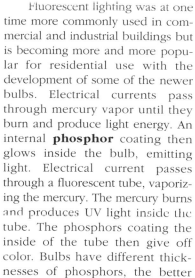

13

cove lighting. Many of the advantages and disadvantages are similar to other incandescent lamps.

Advantages

• They have a longer life than other incandescents.
• They are very small and fit well in recessed display and under-cabinet fixtures.
• They burn cooler than halogens.

Disadvantages

• They tend to be expensive.
• The light is not as white as in halogens.

Fluorescent

Fluorescent lighting was at one time more commonly used in commercial and industrial buildings but is becoming more and more popular for residential use with the development of some of the newer bulbs. Electrical currents pass through mercury vapor until they burn and produce light energy. An internal **phosphor** coating then glows inside the bulb, emitting light. Electrical current passes through a fluorescent tube, vaporizing the mercury. The mercury burns and produces UV light inside the tube. The phosphors coating the inside of the tube then give off color. Bulbs have different thicknesses of phosphors, the better bulbs having a thicker layer. Phosphors are also available in a variety of colors, which can alter the color of the light emitted.

Fluorescent lightbulbs require a ballast, which is an electrical device that supplies the proper starting power to a bulb and regulates its operation. Ballasts are used for fluorescent and High Intensity Devices (HIDs). The older versions are magnetic ballasts, which often cause the bulbs to flicker. The newer electronic ballasts eliminate flickering.

Fluorescent lightbulbs use less electricity than incandescent lightbulbs, with comparable lumen ratings, and they last up to twenty times longer. They are available in many types of bulbs, including recessed downlights, sconces, ceiling fixtures and track lighting. Fluorescent lightbulbs are now available with screw-in bases that can replace incandescents in standard lamp sockets. Whereas fluorescent lights were generally very cold white in color, today there are many bulbs available with warm light that render colors well, resembling incandescent light as well as daylight with a high CRI. They come in a wide spectrum of colors.

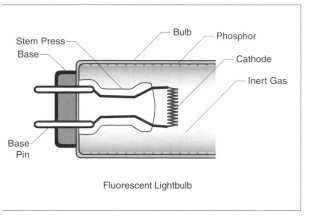

Fluorescent Lightbulb

Labels: Stem Press, Base, Bulb, Phosphor, Cathode, Inert Gas, Base Pin

Traditionally, fluorescent lights have always been tubular but are now available in a variety of compact fluorescents (CFLs), which are bent to minimize their bulky size, making them more adaptable for expanding residential applications. They operate at a cool temperature, making them practical for hard-to-vent locations, and they last a long time, making them an excellent choice for hard-to-reach locations. They are difficult to dim, requiring a special dimmable fixture ballast and a matching fluorescent dimmer. There are dimmable compact fluorescent lamps available today that work with standard dimmers. Whereas all fluorescents at one time only came in white, today there are a spectrum of colors ranging from very warm to very cool. They come in several configurations:

Tubes—These are the most traditional fluorescent design; they come in four sizes and in four diameters—T-2, T-5, T-8 and T-12. The number indicates the size in eighths; a T-8 is 1 inch in diameter. They come in several lengths, from 12 inches to 6 feet. There are several pin configurations: single, double and recessed. They must match the tube's ballast and be either preheat or rapid-start.

Circular tubes—These are circular fluorescents and fit into ceiling fixtures and pendants. They all used to be made with pin connections but are now available for screw-in sockets.

Compact fluorescents (CFLs)—The development of CFLs vastly expanded the possibilities for fluorescent lighting. They can be used in place of A-bulbs, with screw-in bases and have built-in ballasts. They fit into many more fixtures than traditional fluorescent bulbs and produce many more lumens (light) per watt than incandescent lightbulbs. They use 75 to 80 percent less energy than incandescent lightbulbs and last longer. Many CFLs have received the Energy Star approval for energy efficiency. They have a difficult time functioning at temperatures below 32 degrees; with colder temperatures, bulbs may not function at their full brightness. They should also not be used with electric timers, which have a small amount of electricity running through even when the lamp is off, causing the bulb to continually try to turn on. All CFLs have a long life of 10,000 hours; some have a slightly longer life. Compact fluorescents are available in spirals, in the shape of A-bulbs and globes.

14 T5 bulb (fluorescent)
15 Circline bulb (fluorescent)

14

15

16 13-watt minispiral (CFL)

- Three-way dimmable bulbs—A three-way CFL has been developed that has the Energy Star certification. It uses much less wattage than three-way incandescent bulbs, lasts far longer and can be dimmed with incandescent dimming controls. (These bulbs are available from several companies; some of them may not have the Energy Star certification.)
- Bug lights—CFLs are available that reduce the attraction of mosquitoes, moths and other insects.

Advantages

- Fluorescence is an even, shadowless light, spreading out in all directions.
- There are now some fluorescent lightbulbs that have a high Color Rendering Index (CRI), which determines color accuracy. Check by manufacturer to find out if they have bulbs that are close to natural sunlight.
- They are energy efficient, using about 60 percent less energy and lasting longer than incandescent bulbs. Some fluorescent bulbs can last up to 20,000 hours, compared to about 1,000 hours for incandescent bulbs.

Disadvantages

- Fluorescent lights perform poorly in abnormally hot or cold environments; they are not practical for outdoor use.
- They require a ballast.
- They can be noisy. This is usually caused by a loose or malfunctioning ballast.
- Many low-cost fluorescent lightbulbs have poor color rendition, giving off a cold green light. Look for bulbs that specify rare-earth phosphors and have a CRI of above 70.
- In order for a fluorescent light to be dimmed, it must be on a special fluorescent dimmer.
- Fluorescent lights contain mercury and in large quantities can be considered hazardous waste. Check on the best way to dispose of them.

High-Intensity Discharge (HID)

A light is produced when an electric current stimulates chemical compounds inside the bulb. These bulbs have a longer life and provide more light, or lumens, per watt than any of the other types of light sources. They are used for the home, for outdoor security and for landscape lighting, such as sodium lamps, mercury lamps and metal halide lamps. They are more commonly used for commercial and industrial applications.

Advantages

- Bulbs have a long life.
- They provide a great deal of light per watt, making them energy efficient.
- Ambient temperatures do not affect HID light output.
- HID light is a compact light source.

Disadvantages

- Until recently, HID bulbs gave poor color rendering, which has improved.
- They require a ballast.
- Older models hummed and flickered.

Neon

Neon was first discovered in 1898 and is the best known inert gas. An electric current is passed through a small amount of neon in a glass vacuum tube, and it glows bright orange-red. In 1915 the first patent was issued for a neon sign, and in 1925 blue tubes containing argon and mercury first appeared in England. Later a green light was produced by enclosing a blue tube in yellow glass. In 1933 fluorescent power coating of neon and mercury discharge tubes produced a whole new range of colors.

Advantages

• Neon lights can last for a long time.
• They are available in a large range of colors.
• They can be bent into many shapes and make excellent decorative lights.
• They are energy efficient.

Disadvantages

• Neon lights do not give off a great deal of light for task lighting.
• They are expensive.
• They require a transformer to operate. Some of the older transformers created a continuous buzz.

17

Light-Emitting Diodes (LEDs)

This is a new and expanding technology. Bulbs are small, long lasting (eleven years or longer), very bright and efficient. Currently they are used for such items as illuminating the numbers on digital clocks and transmitting information on remote controls; however, their uses are expanding. They are becoming less expensive and available in warmer colors than previously. LEDs are most often used for commercial and retail applications. There is some use of LEDs for the home, with possibly many more in the future. There are several types of LEDs on the market today:

Night spots—These are LED bulbs on a bendable arm, designed for reading in bed and wall mounted. These fixtures are adjustable and deliver pinpoint illumination. Four .5-watt bulbs offer 25,000 hours of lamp life.

resources

For more information on this product, check with Lightology at www.lightology.com.

Floods—This unit can be used for color washing walls or floodlighting specific areas of the room or exterior. They are available in a range of colors and can be programmed to change between all colors of the spectrum. The units are available with several quantities of very bright LEDs that must be linked to a 12-volt power source.

resources

For more information about floodlighting, check the web site of Lightology at www.lightology.com and Color Kinetics at www.colorkinetics.com.

Under-cabinet strips—A strip of five lights is spread out on an 18-inch cord. This fixture can be used under cabinets, in bookcases or in curio cabinets and will last up to seven years.

resources

For more information about under-cabinet strips, check the Web site of Gelcore at www.gelcore.com.

Plug-in accent lights—Plug-in lights are available that cast a beam of light and can change color. They plug into standard North American wall sockets and have controls to vary the color and intensity of the light.

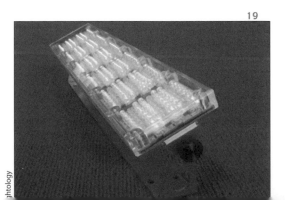

19

18

Lightology

17 Metal halide
18 Night spot LED flexible light—it puts out good light, uses only half the wattage and lasts as long as thirty-three regular bulbs.
19 LED color flood—it has a limitless sweep of changing colors, all with bright light, low heat and efficient power usage.

resources

For more information about plug-in accent lighting, visit Color Kinetics at www.colorkinetics.com.

Advantages

- LEDs can last for a great deal of time.
- They are durable since there is no filament to break or burn out.
- Their small size works well in tight applications.
- LEDs are safe because they use very low voltage.
- They are energy efficient.
- They produce a very bright light.

Disadvantages

- They are expensive.
- They are currently limited in residential applications.

Fiber Optics

Currently fiber optics are more decorative than utilitarian in the home. They are being used around the exterior of the house, around pools and under steps; they are not being used to light up an area. The purpose of fiber optics is to conduct light from a light source to one or more remote locations. The electrical connection and the heat associated with the bulbs are kept away from the illuminated area. Thin fiber-optic cables are connected to a projector box with one bulb. The light from that bulb (which can be halogen, metal halide, xenon metal halide or sulfur lamps) is then carried to various areas around the house where light is desired. The maximum recommended distance is 20 to 30 feet, with about a 50 percent loss in luminosity at the farthest distance. This is a safe system because there is no electricity directly connected to each fixture. Only one bulb must be replaced when it burns out, which is generally in a convenient location to get to. Light fixtures can include flood, spot, bollard, path, step and walk.

They are easy to install and safe around pools. The greater the number of cable strands used in the cable, the brighter the lighting will be. They can be used indoors and outdoors, and most illuminators are approved for both. There are, however, some models only approved for indoors. This is a very safe type of lighting in hazardous locations because fiber-optic strands do not conduct electricity and there is no electrical fire hazard at the location of the fixtures.

Advantages

- Fiber optics do not create a fire hazard.
- The electrical source is at a remote location.
- It is simple to replace just one bulb. This is particularly advantageous when the illuminated area is one that could be difficult to access.
- The mood and color of the lights can all be changed with the replacement of one bulb.
- Fiber optics do not conduct infrared (IR) radiation, which can degrade paint, wood and so on. They also do not conduct heat.
- Areas that are not easily illuminated can be illuminated with fiber optics, such as around pools.

Disadvantages

- They cannot light up an area.
- Light can be lost in the spaces between the optic fibers and in bends in the light guides or the cables.
- They are expensive.

Specialty Bulbs

Energy-saving lightbulbs—These bulbs will conserve energy and many are approved by Energy Star. For more information about these bulbs, check the section on compact fluorescent lamps on page 218.

Micro-electronic energy-efficient CFLs—A new patent was recently received on this tiny compact fluorescent lamp (CFL) with a built-in ballast (as all CFLs have), and it is available in eight designs, including spots, half-spots and globes. It is available in white, green, yellow, red and blue. Approval is currently pending with the Energy Star and Underwriters Laboratories listings for wet locations.

resources

For further information about micro-electric energy-efficient CFLs, check the Westinghouse Web site at www.westinghouselighting.com.

Lights for growing plants—Lamps are recommended that emit energy between 300 and 500 **nanometers** (the cooler side of the spectrum) for photosynthesis and other plant photo-responses. There are bulbs available that closely approximate outdoor light. For additional information, refer to a garden center or gardening text.

Eye-Saver—These bulbs have a chrome top that directs 40 percent more surface illumination at the optimum angle than conventional bulbs. This light source is said to reduce optical injuries related to eyestrain by helping people to see more easily.

resources

For further information about Eye-Saver, contact Westinghouse at www.westinghouselighting.com. Other companies may have similar types of bulbs sold under different trade names.

Three-way halogen reading light—It is a three-way lightbulb with two halogen capsules. These are more stable, last longer and are whiter and brighter with more lumens per watt than the typical incandescent three-way bulb. A lower-wattage bulb can be used since it will provide more light while also preserving energy.

resources

For further information about the three-way halogen reading light, visit Satco's Web site at www.satco.com.

Environmentally friendly bulbs—Bulbs are available with 70 percent less mercury than standard fluorescent lamps. This releases less mercury into the environment when they are discarded. They are also energy efficient and have a long life. Several manufacturers produce this type of bulb and many will be adding additional fluorescent bulbs to meet these environmental standards in the future.

Bug lights—Compact fluorescent bulbs are available that reduce the attraction of mosquitoes, moths and other insects to the light.

Safety glass bulbs—They are available in both incandescent and fluorescent bulbs. The incandescent bulbs have a Teflon outer coating to help keep the glass intact, and the fluorescent bulbs are wrapped in a thick shield of polycarbonate plastic to help contain glass fragments. These were developed to protect people, particularly children, from broken glass.

resources

For further information on how lightbulbs work, check the Web site www.howstuffworks.com.

Types of Fixtures

Light fixtures are sometimes called "luminaires." They contain the light source, a ballast (if the lamp is fluorescent or HID), components to protect and diffuse or distribute the light and a connection to a power source.

Some resources for safety glass bulbs:

General Electric	www.gelighting.com
Sylvania	www.sylvania.com
Philips	www.lighting.philips.com

Decorative Lighting

This comes in a variety of styles, finishes, materials and sizes of bulbs. There are several types:

Pendants—These can be suspended with a rod, chain or cord. They use a glass or metal shade to direct the light downward.

Chandeliers—These were first used to hold several candles in a more formal atmosphere, over a dinner table or in the center hall. Today they usually have several arms that hold a variety of different types of bulbs.

Wall fixtures, or brackets—These are available in several formats that either have an exposed bulb or a glass or translucent diffuser; an uplight bracket, which directs light upward, shines on the ceiling, and a downlight bracket can be stationary or movable for task lighting.

- Sconces were once used to hold candles and have light coming out of the top or bottom of the fixture, with or without a diffuser.
- An urn, or uplight bracket, directs light to the ceiling.

Ceiling fixtures—These are sometimes mounted flush with the ceiling, or they can also hang down several inches, known as semi-flush. These fixtures are available in a large variety of styles, shapes, colors and sizes. The lamps, or bulbs, are usually enclosed with either a plastic or glass diffuser. Smaller ceiling lights can be used in closets and pantries, and larger ones can be used for general lighting in the kitchen or bathroom area, for example. Most ceiling fixtures are enclosed by glass or plastic diffusers that must be removed to change bulbs. They can have incandescent or compact fluorescent bulbs.

Portables—These are convenient to install or change locations and can be taken along when moving to another location. They can be used for task or decorative lighting.

- Table lamps come in numerous styles in all different sizes and types of design. Some are sold with a shade; others must be purchased separately. Lamps, such as drafting lamps, can look high-tech. They are available with incandescent and fluorescent bulbs.
- Floor lamps often can be adjusted for height and the direction of the shade. Pharmacy lamps are an example of floor lamps. They are good for task lighting.
- Torchères direct the light upward, bouncing light off the ceiling. They are available in incandescent, halogen and fluorescent models.
- Uplight lamps can go on the floor and can highlight plants or wash a wall
- Plug-in night lights help people to move around the house at night.

Ceiling fans and light combinations—These cool the house in the summer (with a wind-chill effect) and move the warm air, which rises, to circulate around the room, warming the house in the winter. Ceiling fans can be a great source for energy-efficient climate control by lowering air-conditioning costs and heating bills, while also providing additional light (on many models). There is a large variety of styles, sizes and colors of bulbs. Below is a list to review before buying a ceiling fan.

- Installation—Some fans are very simple to install; others are more difficult.
- Size of the room—Blade sizes vary to maximize efficiency for the size of the room. Most ceiling fan companies have sizing recommendations in their literature and on their Web sites.
- Height of the ceiling—Fans should be 7 to 8 feet from the floor for maximum efficiency. Fans are available that are flush to the ceiling for needed clearance; extension downrods are available for high ceilings.
- Controls—Fans are available with pull chains, wall controls and remote controls.
- Blades—Wider blades at a good pitch will move the air more effectively.
- Motor—Motors vary with different models. The motor must have sufficient wattage to move the air without overstressing it.
- Noise—Poor engineering will cause the fan to be noisy, with inexpensive ball bearings, a lack of proper dampening between motor parts and extra-thin sheet-metal motor and mounting system parts.

223

Lighting Fixtures

Chandelier

Portable Lamp

Torchère

Pendant

Track Lighting

Ceiling Fixture

Under-cabinet Fixture

Wall Lighting
Uplight

Wall Wash   Accent   Downlight

Recessed Lighting

- Wobble—Many factors can contribute to wobble in ceiling fans. Find out about the quality of the fan you are considering and any information the company offers on this problem.
- Finishes—Check to see what finishes are available. See if the finish is even, resistant to tarnish, scratch and rust and has a protective finish.
- Style—Fans are available in a large variety of styles and colors to coordinate with other furnishings in the house.
- Location—Damp areas in the house and on the exterior require fans that are specifically designed and UL-listed for damp locations.
- Warranty—Find out what type of warranty is offered by the manufacturer.
- Bulbs—Ceiling fans require lights that are vibration resistant.
- Light—Ceiling fans are available with a variety of different types and styles of light. Lamps used in ceiling fans should be vibration resistant.
- Energy efficiency—Look for fans that have the Energy Star rating, indicating energy efficiency.

Strip lights—These are ropes with little incandescent or halogen bulbs spaced along the length of the rope.

They can be decorative but can also illuminate soffits and other niches. They are available rigid and flexible and can be joined with additional units to make a larger rope.

Architectural Lighting

This refers to track lighting and those fixtures built into the architecture of the house.

Recessed downlights—These are fixtures that are installed flush to the ceiling and can go straight down or be directed, as in eyeball lights, or diffused. They can be floodlights, which cast a wide light; a spotlight, which throws a concentrated light; or an ordinary bulb, which provides diffuse, all-over lighting. There are many types of recessed lights that are specifically designed for a variety of applications, such as pinhole fixtures to direct the light narrowly and gimbal rings to angle the light within the fixture.

Uplights—Usually in the form of cans on the floor or lights in cabinets, they highlight plants, sculptures and so on to add drama to a room.

Track lights—They offer a great deal of flexibility, since once the track is installed, the type of lights can be changed, moved and redirected, and/or lights can be added to change the mood or needs in the room. Tracks come in a variety of lengths, from 2 feet to 12 feet, in many finishes and several styles. Several companies offer these lights as kits, which includes the track and bulbs, and with low-voltage lights, a transformer as well. Tracks are available as traditional tracks or as flexible or monorail lighting systems.

- Traditional systems—These are available in line- and low-voltage systems. There are many types of fixtures available for these systems, and they are tried and true.
- Flexible or monorail systems—These are newer and more contemporary looking. The tracks are narrower (less than half the width of the traditional track) and have more flexible design options. They can be hand-bent to curve in a variety of ways to adhere to the design of the room. They are low-voltage fixtures and are more costly than the traditional tracks.
- 120-volt flexible system—New to the market is a flexible system that operates at 120 volts. This system does not require a transformer and provides bright lighting with the possibilities of a hand-bendable track. The homeowner can bend the track to its desired shape without the help of an electrician, although a qualified electrician should install the system.

For further information about ceiling fans, contact some of these fan manufacturers:

Emerson	www.emersonfans.com
Minka Aire	www.minkagroup.net
The Modern Fan Co.	www.modernfan.com
Hunter	www.hunterfan.com
Westinghouse	www.westinghouseceilingfans.com

Ceiling fans are now available in a large variety of styles and sizes to fit any home.

Minka

Minka

This system is currently available only from Tech Lighting.

Cable systems—Very high-tech looking, these are low-voltage wires stretched across a room. A variety of small fixtures are suspended across two wires. Several bulbs are available for these systems.

Some companies for track lighting:

Bruck Lighting Systems	www.brucklightingsystems.com
Juno Lighting	www.junolighting.com
Tech Lighting	www.techlighting.com
Translite Sonoma	www.translite.com
WAC Lighting	www.waclighting.com

Translite Sonoma

Cove lights—These are linear lights concealed under a horizontal or vertical trim or on the top of cabinets. Lights can be behind a cornice, a valence or under a cabinet. Fluorescent light strips are commonly used for these purposes. Low-voltage lights can also be used for a soft-lighting effect and rope lights can be used for areas that are very narrow.

Lighting Effects

Many different effects can be achieved with a variety of bulbs and fixtures. There should be multiple effects in each room so that the room is not one dimensional. Lighting should be functional and aesthetically pleasing. Subtle focal points add interest to a room by emphasizing architectural details, sculptures and so on. The following are some of the effects you may want to achieve:

Bounced light or indirect light—This is an effect created when light hits a wall or object and then bounces back to illuminate an object. It creates a softer light than downlighting.

Some resources for cable systems:

Bruck Lighting Systems	www.brucklightingsystems.com
Tech Lighting	www.techlighting.com
Translite Sonoma	www.translite.com

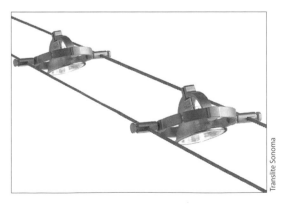

Translite Sonoma

Left: Flexible tracks can be shaped into a variety of configurations or used in a straight line.

Right: A cable lighting system.

Opposite Page: A hand-bendable monorail system with heads and pendants.

Tech Lighting, photo by Les Boschke, lighting designer: Gregory Kay

Wall washing—A wash of light is created when a wide beam of light is directed at a wall a few feet away.

Wall grazing—With this technique the light source close to the wall grazes the wall from a sharp angle, emphasizing the texture (stone, brick, nubby fabric and so on) and creating highlights and shadows on the surface.

Backlighting—Items are lit from behind to emphasize a particular item. This is particularly effective when the item is glass and the light shines through and often creates a glow.

Uplighting—An object is lit from below. Additional light is often used from above.

Downlighting—Light is directed down from the ceiling, a hanging fixture or a track to illuminate a particular item with a beam of light or a large area with floods of diffused light, to give the room a dramatic effect.

Effects to Be Avoided

Glare—Light from a bare bulb can be very harsh on eyes. Glare can be direct or bounced off an object or wall. A variety of different types of fixtures with louvers and diffusers,

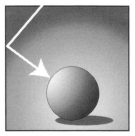

Bounced Light or Indirect Light

Uplighting

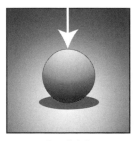

Downlighting

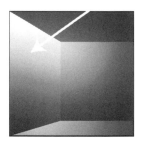

Wall Washing

Backlighting

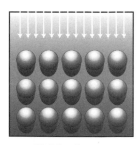

Wall Grazing

Lighting Effects

for example, can limit the glare. There are also bulbs that have silver bottoms, which lessen glare. Angle of incidence equals the angle of glare. Light will bounce back at the same but opposite angle.

Shadows—They can create interest if there is an object, such as a sculpture or a tree, that can create an interesting shadow on a wall. Being in the shadow, however, should be avoided.

Striations—Lines of light on walls and furniture should be avoided.

Hot spots—A central beam of light that is directed to a small concentrated location rather than dispersed.

Lighting Controls

Dimming an incandescent lightbulb reduces the energy consumption and extends the life of the bulb. Controls can be simple or high-tech, depending on need, budget, size of the house and personal preferences. There are several advantages to using lighting controls in a house:

• Save energy by shutting lights off when they are not being used and dimming lights to use less energy.

• Add flexibility to the lighting in the home. Note that with fluorescent bulbs, lighting controls interrupt the system and can shorten the life of a bulb, making it function less efficiently. Lighting systems allow the homeowner to alter the intensity of the light for particular needs.

• They can create a mood, or scene, in a room.

Types of Controls

Switches—These simply turn lights on and off but usually cannot dim the lights.

Dimmers—Dimmers are a simple way of limiting light levels, extending the life of (incandescent) bulbs and reducing energy consumption. There are three types of dimmers: simple, present and digital.

• Simple dimmers—The control is either turned or moved to turn the light on and make it brighter as the control is moved; when the minimum light is reached, the light is turned off. These dimmers can only control lights from one location (single pole) in the room. These can be rotary knobs, slider or toggle controls.

• Preset dimmers—These have separate controls for intensity and for switching the light on and off. The intensity can be preset, which can later be adjusted. Preset dimmers can also be rotary knobs, slider and toggle, which all work slightly differently. Preset dimmers can be used with three-way switches so the light can be controlled from two locations.

• Digital dimmers—They are equipped with a microchip processor that remembers two preset levels of light. They can be wired to provide three-way switching from two locations.

Central control or integrated dimming systems—Lights are grouped together on keypads to control several lights from one location. Preset lighting scenes can be created for various rooms in the house to create a mood, or lighting can be turned on for task or general lighting as well. Panels on the wall or remote control devices operate the various lights and scenes in a room or house. There are several types of lighting systems, including line-carrier systems, low-voltage

systems, line carrier/low-voltage combination systems and radio-frequency systems.

Occupant sensors—There are sensors that use either ultrasonic sound waves or infrared radiation technology to detect movement and turn the lights on or off at a designated period of time after the area is unoccupied. Photocell sensor devices are sensitive to daylight and will turn the lights on and off as needed in response to the amount of outside light. Motion sensor devices are often used on the exterior of the house for security.

Some resources for lighting systems:

Leviton Mfg Co, Inc	800-824-3005	www.leviton.com
Lightolier	800-526-2731	www.lightolier.com
Litetouch	888-548-3824	www.litetouch.com
Lutron	800-523-9466	www.lutron.com
Vantage	877-520-3984	www.vantageinc.com

Timers—Timers can be set to turn lights on and off at particular times when needed. Other timers can be set for a particular amount of time, such as the heat lamps often seen in bathrooms.

Outdoor Lighting

Lighting is needed on the exterior of a house for safety, accent and ambience. There are three types of lights that can be used—line voltage, low voltage or fiber optic.

Line voltage—This has a look of permanence with the wires buried in cables. Light can be projected a great distance for securing the exterior area. When line voltage is used, other appliances, such as patio heaters, can be plugged into the prepared receptacles.

Low voltage—This type of lighting is safer because it operates to 12 volts. It is generally more energy efficient and easier to install. Cables do not have to be buried but can be covered with mulch or foliage. No grounding hookups are required, and fixtures can be connected directly to the cable.

- Low-voltage simulated-brick-edging kits—The bricks can be used to line an exterior path. Bricks have the wiring built into them and they snap together, non-lit bricks alternating with lit ones. The amount of lit bricks and the intensity of the lights can be controlled to give the desired intensity.

Fiber optic—These are easy to install and energy efficient. Thin fiber-optic cables are connected to a projector box with one bulb. The light from that bulb is then carried to various areas around the exterior where light is desired. This is a safe system because there is no electricity directly connected to each fixture. Only one bulb must be replaced when it burns out, which is generally in a convenient location to get to. Light fixtures can include flood, spot, bollard, path, step and walk. They are also safe around pools.

Some Lighting Considerations

- The standards on lights and fixtures vary in different countries. Only use lights purchased from the same country as the fixture.
- The voltage marked on the bulb should correspond to the circuit voltage on the electric line or outlet.
- It is important that the voltage marked on the bulb corresponds to the circuit voltage light fixture.
- All electricity should be turned off before working with wires.
- A professional electrician should install all wiring in the home.

Energy Efficiency

There is a major emphasis today on constructing homes to be energy efficient. This not only preserves our environment from pollution by cutting down on the burning of fossil fuels but also saves on electrical costs. Since lighting uses a large percentage of the electricity in the home (as much as one-third), conserving energy in this area can substantially reduce energy costs. There are some basic rules to follow to save on electricity:

- Turn off or dim lights when they are not needed.
- Design the lighting to have the brightest lights where they are needed to accomplish various tasks.
- Use lighter colors on walls and ceilings to reflect light; they require less energy. Darker colors absorb as much as four times more light, requiring more energy.
- Use energy-efficient light sources. Fluorescent lights generate more light per watt than incandescent light sources. Today there are many fluorescent lights that duplicate the look of incandescent sources, using much less electricity and lasting up to three times as long.
- Make sure the selected fixtures direct light where it is needed, not create glare or trap light and waste it.
- Dust bulbs to increase their ambient light.
- Have exterior lights on a timer or on sensors so they can be turned off and on automatically.
- Use dimmers whenever possible.
- Use three-way bulbs so lighting levels can be kept low when brighter light is not needed.

resources

Lighting resources: American Lighting Association at www.americanlightingassoc.com or 800-274-4484 or Rensselaer Polytechnic Institute's National Lighting Product Information Program at www.lrc.rpi.edu.

Interior Doors

Unlike patio and entrance doors, interior doors don't have to address issues of energy efficiency and security. They have to look good, provide privacy, reduce noise and aesthetically fit into the locations they are needed. Recently interior door options have expanded with the introduction of larger-size doors and more design options.

The type of door used in any particular location will depend on budget, aesthetics, the amount of available space, extra light needed in the room and the amount of privacy needed.

Types of Doors

Swinging doors—These are the most popular type of interior door. They can be solid wood or veneer with one or more lights, mirrors or louvers. They can also have some type of art glass.

Sliding, or bypass, doors—They are usually used for closets but occasionally are used between rooms. There are generally two doors that move along double tracks and pass each other. Often used for closets, these doors can also be used in areas where swing doors are inconvenient or unfit.

Bifold doors—They consist of two or more panels hinged at the side and hinged together. One panel pivots near the doorjamb and the other glides in an overhead track. They always open outward, unlike those in phone booths that open inward. They are most often used on closets that are too wide for a swinging door and/or where there is little space for a swinging door.

Pocket doors—These doors slide into a space in an adjacent wall. They are most often used when there isn't enough space for a swinging door. An opened pocket door can also create an illusion of a bigger room when it is between two rooms.

Saloon, or café, doors—They are swinging doors that are hinged on either side of the door, opening and swinging in or out on hinges that close automatically after someone goes through (gravity-pivot hinges). These are excellent in areas where you might have your hands full, since you can just push yourself through. They do not offer a great deal of privacy, but can hide dirty dishes, for example, in the kitchen. They are excellent between the kitchen and dining room and also to separate the toilet and/or bidet in a bathroom. They can sometimes be purchased but are often custom made.

Considerations

Prehung or separate—Prehung doors are preassembled and come with jambs, header and

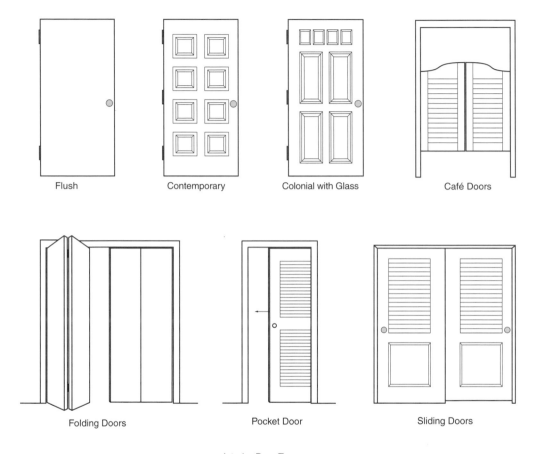

Flush Contemporary Colonial with Glass Café Doors

Folding Doors Pocket Door Sliding Doors

Interior Door Types

threshold, and mortised and attached hinges. A separate door is the door itself without any frame or preparation for hanging or fitting with hinges or doorknobs.

Primed or raw—Doors can be purchased with several coats of primer or raw. Primed doors require only a topcoat of paint.

Materials—Interior doors are constructed with either a solid wood or hollow core sandwiched between two surface veneers. Some of them are **paint grade** (knotty pine or poplar),

and some are often left with just a stain (red oak, maple, cherry, mahogany, birch, hickory or alder). Other surfacing materials may include wood grain, plastic or wood composition board.

Design

There is a variety of styles, sizes and configurations available. Door designs are selected to work with the architectural style of the house, personal preferences and budget.

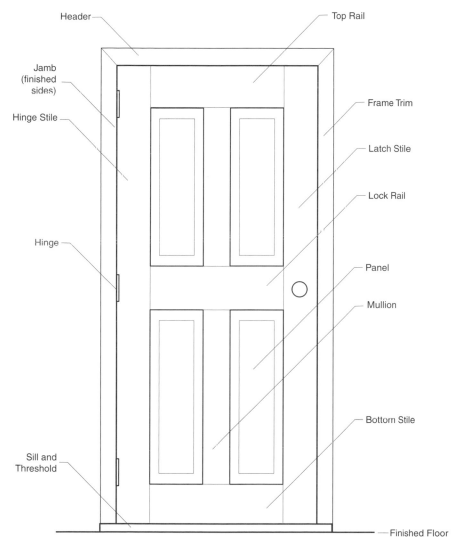

Header
Jamb (finished sides)
Hinge Stile
Hinge
Sill and Threshold
Top Rail
Frame Trim
Latch Stile
Lock Rail
Panel
Mullion
Bottom Stile
Finished Floor

Anatomy of an Interior Door

Flush or panel/sash doors— These are the two most common types of doors. Flush are smooth, flat and simple doors. The internal construction of the door is not visible, such as the core material, stiles, rails and blocking for the doorknobs. Panel, or sash, doors have stiles, rails and sometimes cross rails (intermediate rails) visible with recessed or raised areas; a panel may be replaced by one or more glass lights, louvers or mirrors.

• Glass lights—Doors are available with a variety of interior panes of glass (or lites) in numerous configurations. There can be one panel or several.

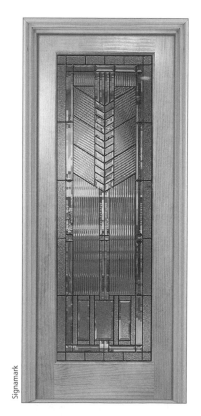

Signamark

Novelty glass is also available with stained glass, frosted glass, etched designs and so on. All glass in doors is made of tempered safety glass.

- Louvers—Doors can have half louvers or full louvers to allow the passage of air and feeling of openness. Part or all of the panels may be replaced by louvers, which may be movable or stable. Louver doors have a plantation or Caribbean look.
- Recessed and raised—They come with a variety of recessed and raised configurations.
- Mirrors—Vanity mirrors are available and used on closets or between rooms.

Batten door—Another type of door is the batten door, which has horizontal or diagonal cross-braces. Solid lumber is joined together vertically with horizontal or diagonal cross-braces. These doors tend to be heavy and are prone to warp unless they are finished well.

Solid- and hollow-core—Both of these types of construction have face panels on the exterior made of wood veneer, composition materials, hardwood, plywood, high-pressure laminates or a combination of materials. The structural inner core of a solid-core door is solid and can be made of mineral-based material (fire-rated), particleboard, wood blocks or composition materials. Hollow-core doors have strips or other units of material with intervening hollow cells.

Thickness—Standard widths for doors are 1 3/8 inches or 1 3/4 inches, but they are available in wider widths as well.

Sizes—Doors come in standard sizes: heights of 6 feet 8 inches, with smaller and larger sizes; and widths of 2 feet, 2 feet 4 inches, 2 feet 6 inches, 2 feet 8 inches or 3 feet. Custom doors can be made in any size but are limited by the amount of weight the hinges can hold. Doors will have a tendency to warp if they get too large.

Configuration—There are numerous combinations of doors with sidelights and transom options to go with every style and location in the house.

Shapes—Arched and other shaped doors are available on some product lines and can also be custom made.

Hardware—Interior doors either have passage locks, which are handles without locks, or privacy locks, which are for personal spaces, have a locking button on the inside and can be opened with a key, screwdriver or other household item in an emergency.

Hardware is available in a variety of styles, finishes and colors. When selecting hardware, you must take into consideration the use of the door and its weight. A heavily used door may require a ball-bearing hinge. Certain doors may have security features that may be incorporated into the hinges and/or the lockset. Door handles or knobs should match the other hardware in the house or the particular room that they are going into. In some cases you may want to have one type of metal on one side and another on the other. It is a good idea to make a chart of where each handle will go so you can make sure each item will go where it is planned. Other

Signamark

L. E. Johnson Products, Inc.

Special hardware was used to open the doors of this closet and create an office space.

hardware items include door closers, gaskets for soundproofing, strike plates, door mutes and bumpers. Hinges come in a variety of sizes and swing patterns, such as mortise hinges (plates linked by means of a pin) that are full, half, half-surface or full surface and have center pivots or offset pivots or are invisible and decorative types.

There are some specialty items available in hardware that can be used with doors to create more usable space. One particularly practical item is full-access hardware, which allows you to move bifold doors 180 degrees, so they lay flat against the wall and out of the way. With this, a closet or small area can be converted to an office or bar area without doors in the way.

resources

For further information about full-access hardware, check with L. E. Johnson Hardware at www.johnsonhardware.com or call 800-837-5664.

Questions to Consider

- What is the thickness of the door?
- What is the width of the stile?
- What is the backset or the distance from the door edge to the center of the door hole?
- Is it a left- or right-hand door? This should be determined from the outside of the door from the hallway into the space. Left-hand means the door hinge is on the left and the door swings into the space; left-hand reverse has the door on the left, but it swings into the hallway. The situation is similar for right-hand and right-hand reverse doors. This is important when the locking of the door is handed (left or right), as with levered door handles. What side of the door has a locking function is also important.

resources

For further information about interior doors, contact the Window & Door Manufacturers Association at 800-223-2301 or www.nwwda.org.

Some of the companies that manufacture interior doors:

International Door & Latch	541-686-5647	www.internationaldoor.com
Jeld-Wen		www.jeld-wen.com
Karona Doors	800-829-9233	www.karonadoor.com
Masonite International Corp. (C)	813-877-2726	www.masonite.com
Morgan Corp.		www.morgancorp.com
New-Tech Doors	800-622-0688	www.newtechdoors.com
Pinecrest	612-871-7071	www.pinecrestinc.com
Signamark	800-803-8182	www.signamark.com
Simpson	800-952-4057	www.simpsondoor.com
Trustile Doors, Inc.	888-286-3931	www.trustile.com
Upstate Door Co.	800-570-8283	www.upstatedoor.com
Woodharbor Doors & Cabinetry, Inc.	641-423-0444	www.woodharbor.com

(C) = Canadian

Eldorado Stone/Rio Grand River Rock, photo by John Bare & Assoc.

Fireplaces and (Heating) Stoves

Fireplaces continue to be a center of any room today, not only for their emanating warmth but also for the sense of tranquility they elicit. Once a necessity for keeping warm, they are still used to keep down heating costs and provide design and aesthetic appeal. Fireplaces add value to the house when it is being sold and are often a focal point in a room. As people extend their houses, incorporating the outside areas for entertainment and relaxation, fireplaces also become more popular for warmth and aesthetics outside as well.

Manufactured stone veneer creates a beautiful look in this rustic room.

Considerations

- Is there a convenient location for a fireplace in a particular room and is venting possible? Are there any structural limitations?
- What are the local building energy conservation or environmental codes that may limit the type of fireplace you can install? Before purchasing or building a fireplace, insert or stove, be sure that the product meets local codes and that you have obtained a building or equipment permit.
- What type of aesthetic look would you like to achieve?
- Are you going to use the fireplace for supplementary heat or aesthetics only? How energy efficient should the fireplace be if it is used for heating? Will the fireplace use outside air or heated room air?
- How important is the scent and sound of a wood-burning fireplace?
- How much time are you willing to spend tending to the fireplace and maintaining it?
- Do you have a place to store wood if a wood-burning system is selected?
- How accessible are other types of fuel, such as wood pellets, natural gas and so on?
- Does anyone in the house have a breathing disorder, and is interior air quality a major concern?
- Does your home have adequate ventilation?

Negative air pressure results when more air is leaving the house than is coming in. Air is forced out of the house with kitchen and bathroom attic fans and clothes dryers faster than air can infiltrate the living space. Houses can also act as chimneys; this is called the "stack effect." Air is heated and escapes the upper levels of the home, causing negative pressure zones in the lower sections of the home. Fireplaces can also use inside air to contribute to negative air pressure in the house. This will cause air to be sucked in at uncontrolled points, including the furnace or fireplace, bringing toxic combustion gases into the house. Make sure that your home is planned for adequate ventilation.

- How realistic should the fire look?
- How long will the fire be burning?
- How difficult is the installation of a particular fireplace?
- Do you prefer constant heat output or can the output vary?
- How much have you budgeted for the fireplace?
- How many views are desired on the fireplace? Can it be seen from one, two, three and even four ways?
- Is your fireplace energy efficient? Some fireplace designs are more efficient than others.
- Many fireplaces are inherently energy inefficient, since there is always the potential for conditioned air to go up the flue when fired or not fired. An added burden can be put on the heating system when air is lost through the flue or vent because the damper is secured open, as in vented gas fireplaces and with gas logs.

Note: All heating appliances and venting systems must be installed according to the manufacturers' installation instructions and local building codes.

Venting

Fireplaces, stoves and inserts are either vented or unvented, depending on the use intended and local code requirements. Venting can be in the form of a natural draft system (typical of many traditional fireplaces that are vented through the roof with a chimney) or direct vent systems (which go out the wall or roof to the exterior of the house). Vent-free units have no venting and are not permitted in most municipalities. Before deciding to include a fireplace or heating stove in any room, decide what type of venting will be possible in that area of the house. This will help to determine the type of unit and type of fuel you will be able to use. Today, the building and energy codes usually require fireplaces to have outside air intake venting for combustion in addition to a separate exhaust vent or flue.

Vented Direct Vent

This is the most efficient and inexpensive method of using a gas fireplace or heating stove. Air is drawn into the firebox for combustion, and the exhaust air is vented out either through concentric pipes or through separate intake and exhaust vents. The firebox is sealed, and no household air is used for combustion. Because air for combustion comes from the outside, it is not interfering with the heated interior air. Air is drawn from the outdoors for combustion, and the exhaust is vented to the exterior, eliminating the need for a conventional chimney system. A coaxial pipe system, which is a small pipe within a large pipe, is most often used. Outside air is drawn in through the outer pipe, and exhaust air is vented out through the inner pipe. These pipes can go vertically through the roof or horizontally through an exterior wall. The distance from the wall will depend on the size of the unit, the size of the room, the type of fuel used and so on. Glass panels are used in direct vent units to keep the combustion system sealed from the home, maintaining high efficiency and indoor air quality. Before purchasing a unit that will use a direct vent system, be sure that the dealer is qualified to advise you on the options that will work in your home. Direct vent systems are very efficient for helping to heat the house. Systems that are sealed off with a glass door from the interior of a house eliminate many indoor air quality problems. Direct power-vented fireplaces are the only type installed in the American Lung Association's Health Houses (see pages 309 and 311).

Advantages
- Direct vent systems can be installed anywhere in the house, including under a window or in a room divider.
- The installation is less expensive.
- There's no need for a chimney.
- They don't interfere with indoor air quality.

Disadvantages

- Flames are in a sealed combustion fireplace with no access to the flames.
- Wood cannot be burned in this type of fireplace.

Gas B Vent

This method is commonly used. A pipe runs from the appliance upward to the outdoors, expelling the products of combustion. Air can be drawn in from the room or from the outside. There is a potential for backdraft of combustion gases if there is too much negative air pressure in the house. Make sure the flue is designed in such a manner that the wind pressure does not blow downward.

Advantages

- Gas B vents are easy to operate.

Disadvantages

- They are less efficient than direct vent units.
- They may use heated interior air for combustion.
- Heated interior air is continuously lost through the vent.
- There is a potential for backdraft from negative air pressure in the house.
- Venting can be in the form of a vent or chimney that will carry the products of combustion outside the home. If the vent is not properly installed or is blocked or leaking, harmful pollutants can be released into the home.

Heat Recovery Ventilation

This new patented technology vents the fireplace through a heat recovery ventilator (HRV). This is an apparatus that exchanges the fresh outside air with the stale interior air, while transferring the heat. (For further information about HRVs, check the "Mechanicals" chapter on page 288). The HRV is integrated into a system of ductwork to power vent the products of combustion associated with the fireplace as well as carbon dioxide buildup, VOCs, house odors and excess

moisture out of the house. In warmer climates, such as Arizona, this system can eliminate the need for a furnace, according to a manufacturer.

Advantages

- A glass front is not required to prevent heat loss.
- Fireplaces can be vented horizontally or vertically, allowing for a flexible floor plan design.
- This system prevents about 65 percent of the heat loss normally existing through a fireplace's exterior flue vent.
- The house is ventilated at a rate of eight whole-house fresh-air changes every twenty-four hours, increasing indoor air quality. This helps control moisture levels and reduce the chances of mold and mildew buildup in the home.
- The heat from the fireplace is distributed throughout the house rather than overheating the room where it is situated.

This gas fireplace offers the simplicity of pure flame. A line burner recessed under the floor of the firebox allows the fire to come straight up into the fire chamber without logs or other effects.

Acantha Fireplaces, Ltd, European Home

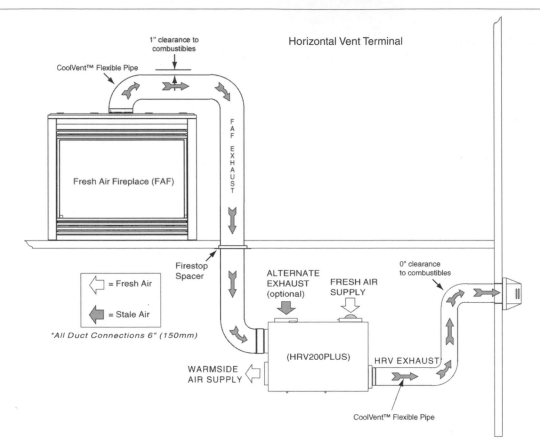

1" clearance to combustibles

CoolVent™ Flexible Pipe

Horizontal Vent Terminal

F A F   E X H A U S T

Fresh Air Fireplace (FAF)

Firestop Spacer

= Fresh Air

= Stale Air

*All Duct Connections 6" (150mm)

ALTERNATE EXHAUST (optional)

FRESH AIR SUPPLY

0" clearance to combustibles

(HRV200PLUS)

HRV EXHAUST

WARMSIDE AIR SUPPLY

CoolVent™ Flexible Pipe

This fresh-air fireplace transfers the heat energy contained in the exhaust air to an aluminum core. The exhaust air and combustion by-products are then power vented outside the house. Simultaneously, fresh outdoor air is power vented into the aluminum core, gaining the heat energy on its way to the home's ductwork.

Disadvantages

- This type of system requires a duct system.
- This system is simpler to install in a new house than to retrofit in an existing one.
- This system is more expensive than other gas fireplace configurations.

resources

For further information on HRVs, contact Heatilator Home Products at www.freshairfireplace.com or call 877-427-8368 (for gas fireplaces) or Condar Company at www.fireplacehrv.com or call 828-894-8383 (for wood fireplaces).

Natural Draft Vent (Vented through the Roof)

Products of combustion are vented to the outside of the house. The vents can be either decorative or heating units. Natural draft systems are required for wood-burning fireplaces and stoves. Wood can only be vented through a chimney in the roof.

Advantages

- Wood can be burned in this type of fireplace as long as it is classified as such.
- In the case of a masonry fireplace, the masonry

Unvented or Vent-Free (Room Vented)

This describes a heat-producing device that draws combustion air from inside the house and is designed to burn efficiently, eliminating the need for venting of exhaust gases. There are, however, hazards associated with ventless stoves or fireplaces, which are not actually ventless but are being vented into the room where the combustion is taking place. The EPA advises that some combustion appliances, including older fireplaces, can produce pollutants that can damage health or be fatal. The types of pollutants are dependent on the type of appliance—how it is installed, maintained and the type of fuel it uses. Some of the common toxins and pollutants produced are carbon monoxide (incomplete oxidation of carbon), nitrogen dioxide, sulfur dioxide and unburned hydrocarbons. Combustion also produces water vapor (natural gas and propane are compounds of hydrogen and carbon, which, when burned, combine with oxygen to produce water, carbon dioxide and carbon monoxide), which can produce high humidity and wet surfaces in the home, encouraging the growth of dust mites, molds and bacteria. Pollutants can cause a range of symptoms, from headaches and breathing difficulties to death. The effects of these pollutants can occur over a long period of time or immediately after exposure. (For further information about these biological pollutants, check the chapter, "Health and Safety," on page 318.)

Since 1980 unvented gas units have been equipped with **oxygen depletion sensors (ODS)**, which are safety-pilot systems. They automatically shut off the gas supply if the oxygen level in the room falls to 18 percent. Some municipalities will not permit these units to be used in the home. Some dealers may recommend using unvented gas units, but you should be aware of the potential dangers and limitations of this type of system and the local code requirements. Most building codes across the country now do not permit venting of fireplaces and heating stoves into the residence. Only electric fireplaces do not require venting.

Eldorado Stone

Kivas are often found in Southwestern-style homes.

is a thermal mass and radiates the residual heat held in the mass of the masonry out after the fire has subsided.

- If wood is burned, there is a pleasant scent and crackling.

Disadvantages

- There is a higher cost to building this structure: a foundation is required, as well as masonry for the hearth, a damper mechanism and a chimney.
- More maintenance is required for a wood-burning fireplace.

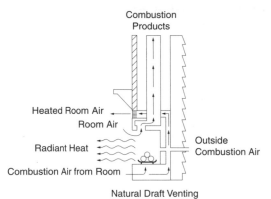

Combustion Products

Heated Room Air

Room Air

Radiant Heat

Combustion Air from Room

Outside Combustion Air

Natural Draft Venting
Wood or Gas

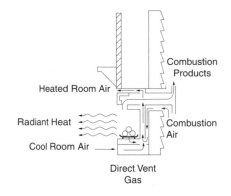

Combustion Products

Heated Room Air

Radiant Heat

Cool Room Air

Combustion Air

Direct Vent
Gas

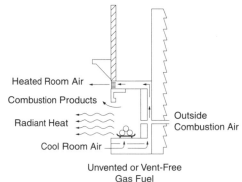

Heated Room Air

Combustion Products

Radiant Heat

Cool Room Air

Outside Combustion Air

Unvented or Vent-Free
Gas Fuel

Manufactured Fireplace Systems

Advantages

- Electric stoves, which can be unvented, require no gas line installation, chimney or vent system.
- Installation is simple.
- They are portable.

Disadvantages

- Any fireplace other than an electric one is dangerous if it is not vented and is prohibited by most codes.

resources

For further information about combustion appliances and indoor air pollution, check with the U.S. Environmental Protection Agency: www.epa.gov/iaq/pubs/combust.html.

Fuel

Wood—This is the most traditional type of fireplace. Used in earlier times almost exclusively for cooking and warmth, wood-burning fireplaces have been used for hundreds of years. The crackling sound and aroma are the side benefits of having a wood fireplace, but they can also give off warmth that can be an adjunct to a heating system, if designed that way, cutting back on heating bills or serving as the primary source of heat. Other fuels can be used with a choice of venting systems; wood must be burned in a fireplace with a natural draft chimney. The EPA has mandated that all wood-burning stoves and inserts sold after July 1, 1992 must emit no more than 4.1 grams of particulate matter per hour for catalytic-equipped units and no more than 7.5 grams per hour for **noncatalytic**-equipped units.

Catalytic-equipped units—Wood stoves and fireplace inserts have ceramic honeycombed chambers coated with a metal catalyst, usually platinum or palladium, that work to burn the smoke. This burns away gases and particulates normally emitted into the air—these are called "**catalytic** combustors."

Noncatalytic-equipped units—In these units combustion occurs in the firebox.

A note on wood-burning stoves: All EPA-certified wood stoves and inserts sold in the United States have a permanent EPA label on the back. The newer wood-burning stoves and inserts are technologically more advanced and create optimum conditions to burn the smoke, which is essentially unburned fuel. Smoke emissions can also be limited by using seasoned firewood (about 20 percent moisture content) or manufactured logs. Hardwoods such as oak, hickory and elm produce a longer-lasting fire and can reduce the buildup of **creosote.** Wood can be burned in freestanding stoves, manufactured fireplaces, fireplace inserts or in masonry fireplaces.

Advantages

- The crackling sound of a roaring fire is very appealing.
- The scent is also very soothing.
- A real fire has an aesthetic beauty.
- It can give off great warmth and reduce heating bills.
- Wood is a renewable resource.
- Wood can be an inexpensive resource for those who have to purchase it or for those who cut their own.

Disadvantages

- An area away from the house is needed for storing wood.
- Wood must be carried into the house.
- The fire must be tended from time to time to keep it going. (This may be an advantage for some and a disadvantage for others.)
- A chimney system is required.
- There is an inconsistent heat output.
- Firewood is not available in some areas.
- The chimney must be cleaned of creosote each year.

resources

For additional information about wood fireplaces, contact the Brick Industry Association at www.gobrick.com.

Gas—This encompasses a large portion of the fireplaces today. They are easy, safe and efficient and can burn either natural gas or propane (LP). Gas can be vented with either a direct or natural draft vent system and does not produce the higher temperature, hot gases and impurities that a wood-burning one does. An existing fireplace may be able to be converted to gas by adding a gas line and gas logs. Gas stoves, fireplaces or inserts, all of which can be used with gas, can be controlled with the flip of a switch, a thermostat or a remote control device. To make them appear as authentic as possible, a variety of log sets are available. They are made of durable fiber-ceramic, concrete or other heat-resistant substances and are made in forms modeled from real cordwood. Log sets can be purchased in species indigenous to the area for authenticity. Gas burners can either provide aesthetics or heat, depending on the vent system, which can be either natural draft or direct vent. Gas can be burned in freestanding stoves, fireplace inserts or high-efficiency fireplaces.

Most gas stoves and fireplaces have a pilot light that thermoelectrically generates the power to turn the gas off and on with a switch. Electricity is not needed, so the stove or fireplace can operate even in a blackout. Some state codes (California, for example) do not allow pilot lights in stoves and fireplaces because they burn all the time, unnecessarily wasting energy. In such areas, wood or gas logs must be used if you want to have a fireplace. Another alternative is the intermittent pilot ignition system that does not run all the time; it is only on when the fireplace is in use. This option is available on several gas fireplace systems. A battery backup system is also available on these systems, which would normally require electricity to light the pilot light during electrical blackouts. This is a patented system called Intellifire available from Hearth and Home Technologies.

resources

For further information on Intellifire, check www.heatnglo.com or call 888-427-3973.

Another important issue is that of the damper, which closes off the air from the fireplace to the vent. If the damper is open, warmed household air escapes through the vent. If the damper is closed, there is a chance of an accidental explosion from unburned gas if, for some reason, the gas is on. Building codes and manufacturers' installation instructions require that dampers be permanently opened when gas is used, again allowing heated air to escape.

The advantages and disadvantages of gas are listed below. Only a licensed plumber or HVAC technician should run a gas line to the unit.

Advantages

- Gas fireplaces are cleaner burning than wood.
- They're easier to handle; just flip a switch.
- They can be installed in more areas of the home.
- **Zero-clearance** construction is possible, which requires the smallest clearance from the wood framing or any combustible material.
- Heat output and flame height can be controlled.
- Gas fireplaces can be used as supplementary heating, reducing heating costs.
- They emit a consistent heat.

Disadvantages

- They lack the aroma and sound of a wood fireplace.
- There is no fire to tend, if that is desired.

Gas Logs

Gas logs are both decorative and heat producing and are made to imitate many different tree species. There are two types of logs: yellow-flame logs, which require venting, and blue-flame logs, which are made to burn hotter and cleaner and sometimes can be unvented. Yellow-flame logs are more realistic and attractive and will give off about the same amount of heat as a real wood fire, but they will generate soot and carbon, which is deposited in the chimney. Blue-flame logs are not as attractive; they burn hotter, and if they are unvented they cannot be used for long periods of time, to protect the indoor air quality.

Advantages

- Gas logs are inexpensive.
- They are easy to retrofit into existing fireplaces.
- They can be used in an existing masonry fireplace.
- The logs burn clean and there are no ashes to clean.
- They only require maintenance once a year.

Disadvantages

- They are less efficient in the use of fuel than other gas fireplaces.
- They are more expensive to operate than gas fireplaces or insets.

Propane

In some areas where gas

A stainless steel freestanding fire stove.

Krog & Iverson

lines are not available, propane gas can be used to fuel stoves. It costs more than natural gas and requires a storage tank. Check with the dealer before purchasing any unit, to be sure propane gas can be used with that unit.

Advantages
- Propane is cleaner than wood.
- It ignites easily and quickly.
- It will burn longer and more consistently than cordwood.

Disadvantages
- Propane gas fireplaces lack the aroma and sound of a wood fireplace.

Wood Wax Fire Logs

These are made from recycled sawdust mixed with wax and are available in many grocery stores. They are used in wood-burning fireplaces.

Advantages
- They are cleaner than wood, leaving little ash.
- They ignite easily and quickly.
- They burn more consistently than cordwood.

Disadvantages
- They lack the aroma and sound of a wood fireplace.
- They can only burn one at a time.
- There is limited heat output.

Pellets

They are made from compressed sawdust that would otherwise be discarded and are typically available in forty-pound bags. They burn much the same as cordwood but emit less smoke and soot. They can be used in freestanding stoves and fireplace inserts. The pellets are mechanically fed from a hopper to the fire at a rate determined by an interior thermostat. They can be used in a direct or a natural draft vent system in a freestanding stove or fireplace insert.

Advantages
- Pellets are cleaner than wood, emitting less smoke and ash.
- Pellets are a renewable product.
- They can burn for a long period of time (up to twenty-four hours).
- They do not have to be tended; the pellets are fed automatically according to the room thermostat setting.
- Pellets are easy to store.
- Some pellet stoves are self-igniting.

Disadvantages
- Appliances that burn pellets are generally more expensive than those that burn wood.
- They require electricity to feed the pellets from the hopper.
- Pellet appliances require a lot of maintenance and service.
- Pellets are difficult to find in some areas.

Coal

Some stoves can burn coal and wood and are called "dual-fuel" stoves. Coal is clean burning and produces no visible smoke or creosote but does leave a light ash deposit in the vent system. Coal can be burned in a freestanding stove or fireplace insert designed for coal use.

Advantages
- Coal is cleaner burning than wood.
- It creates no visible smoke or creosote.
- Coal can burn for up to forty-eight hours.
- It provides an even and controllable heat.
- Coal can be automatically loaded.

Disadvantages
- Coal lacks the aroma and sound of a wood fireplace.
- Coal is more difficult to start.
- Ashes must be removed daily.
- If the stove runs for extended periods of time,

the sulfur compounds, which are the by-product of coal, will deteriorate the interior metal surfaces.
- Anthracite coal may not be available in all areas; check to be sure it can be obtained before purchasing a coal-burning stove.

Oil

Oil provides heat at about the same cost as natural gas. It can only be burned in a freestanding stove.

Advantages
- It is cleaner than wood.
- It does not have to be tended to.
- It creates an even, long-lasting heat.

Disadvantages
- It lacks the aroma and sound of a wood fireplace.

Electric

These fireplaces do not require a gas line installation, chimney or vent system. They require a simple installation, are completely portable and have built-in heaters. Heat-resistant log sets are used to give the fire an authentic appearance, and they can be used with or without the heater, depending on the need for heat.

Advantages
- Electric fireplaces are cleaner than wood burning ones.
- They do not have to be tended to—just flip a switch to put it on; remote controls can also be used.
- They have built-in thermostats.
- They can be installed in an existing fireplace.
- They are simple to install and can be installed almost anywhere.
- They do not require venting.

- An electric stove can be moved to another room or house.
- The flames work independently from the heater, so the appearance of flames can be used on a warm day without the element of heat.
- They only need cleaning once a year.

Disadvantages
- They do not usually look authentic.
- They will not work during a blackout unless they have a backup battery.
- They have low heat output.

Gel Fuel

This is a solid fuel that comes in a can, which fits into a decorative log. It is a good choice in an area where a vent system would be difficult. The logs can burn for about two to three hours on a can of fuel.

Advantages
- Gel fuel does not need a vent system.

Disadvantages
- The logs lack the aroma and sound of a wood fireplace.
- The can of fuel must be changed every two or three hours.
- The logs cannot heat a room.

Fireplace Options

Masonry Fireplaces

They can be expensive to purchase and install and also require a solid foundation, but they can be kept fired all day long. Masonry fireplaces and masonry heaters can last a lifetime, unlike factory-built fireplaces, which have a life expectancy of approximately fifteen to twenty years.

Masonry fireplaces require a foundation. Some units can soak up enough heat after being ignited for two hours to radiate heat for up to eight hours. Units built with glass doors for closed combustion can emit more heat. Open combustion units offer the ambience of wood crackling and the wonderful scent of wood burning, but they will not be efficient for providing heat. Firebox designs such as Rumford and Bellfire can greatly increase heat output and reduce emissions. Building and energy codes may require a direct outside air vent supply into the firebox.

Masonry heaters can be site-built or prefabricated. The heat of the fire is absorbed by the high mass of masonry and then released slowly over time, up to eighteen hours. The heaters are generally fired intermittently because the heat is absorbed and will radiate for hours, more so than for a fireplace. They can be expensive to purchase and install and also require a solid foundation, but they can be kept fired all day long. They burn wood very efficiently and can function as a primary heating source. Some prefabricated models are made of ceramics or soapstone.

resources

For further information about masonry heaters, check with the Masonry Heater Association of North America at www.mha-net.org.

A few of the companies that produce masonry heaters:

Biofire, Inc.	801-486-0266	www.biofireinc.com
Temp Cast Masonry Heaters (C)	800-561-8594	www.tempcast.com
Tulikivi	800-843-3473	www.tulikivi.com
Vermont Soapstone Company	802-747-7744	www.vermontwoodstove.com

(C) = Canadian

Prefabricated or Manufactured Fireplaces

These units look much like site-built fireplaces but are composed mostly of metal. They include a firebox, a chimney system, damper and **chimney cap.** Most are lightweight, requiring no special support. Air is most often drawn from the outside, which makes them more energy efficient since warmed interior air is not being used for combustion. They can be retrofitted into existing homes or built into new homes. They must be installed according to the manufacturers' installation instructions. These are generally less expensive to purchase and to install than traditional masonry fireplaces. They are available in a variety of standard sizes and vary in their appearance and options. Units are available which are open on one, two (see-through), three (peninsula) and four (oasis) sides. Mantels and facing materials can vary to work with the style of the house. Various models of these fireplaces can be used to burn wood, natural gas or propane; electric models are also available. Many of these units come with twenty-plus-year limited warranties. Some units come with a faux stone facing that eliminates the black metal rim usually visible in manufactured fireplaces. Factory-built fireplaces must pass testing standards established by Underwriters Laboratories.

Wood-burning fireplaces can be closed-combustion systems, meaning they are used with closed glass doors, burn efficiently and generate a great deal of heat, if equipped with heat-absorbing ventilators. Open-combustion systems are the more traditional systems that do not use closed doors and have a great deal of ambience but not a great deal of heat. Closed-combustion units should be EPA-certified as clean burning.

Some manufacturers of prefabricated fireplaces:

Avalon	www.avalonstoves.com
Brillant	www.europeanhome.com
Dimplex North America (C)	www.dimplex.com
Fireplace Xtrordinair	www.fireplacextrordinair.com
Heatilator	www.heatilator.com
Heat-N-Glo	www.heatnglo.com
La Flame Industries, Inc.	www.laflame.com
Lennox Hearth Products	www.lennoxhearthproducts.com
Pacific Energy Fireplace Products Ltd. (C)	www.pacificenergy.net
Quadra-Fire	www.quadrafire.com
Regency (C)	www.regency-fire.com
RSF Energy (C)	www.icc-rsf.com
Town & Country Fireplaces (C)	www.townandcountryfireplaces.net
Wilkening Fireplace Co.	www.wilkeningfireplace.com

(C) = Canadian

Freestanding Stoves

Heating stoves can be purchased in many different sizes and styles to fit into almost any decor. They can easily be retrofitted into an existing home, utilizing a masonry fireplace, factory-built chimney, or for appropriate models, a direct vent system, and they can sometimes be moved to a different room or another location. They can be very efficient in heating a particular room and sometimes an entire zone in the house. They are made of steel, stone or cast iron with porcelain enamel and high-temperature paint finishes, and they sometimes have ceramic insets in the front of the unit for viewing the fire. Soapstone is often used as part of freestanding stoves and for the masonry around a fireplace. This is because soapstone has the ability to retain heat and emit it slowly over a long period of time after the fire has stopped burning. Room should be left all around the stove, per the installation instructions, so there is space for the unit to safely radiate heat.

Many different types and models designed for specific fuels and applications are available. Stoves can burn wood, gas, coal, wood pellets or oil. Pellets can be stored in a hopper and mechanically fed into the stove. A backup battery is needed to fuel the stove in case of a power outage. The dimensions of a room must be considered when selecting a stove so more heat is not produced than is needed and an excess of oxygen is not depleted. Before purchasing a stove, check with the building office for code restrictions and for convenience in loading the fuel and removing the ash.

Some of the companies that make freestanding stoves:

American Energy Systems	www.magnumfireplace.com
Avalon	www.avalonstoves.com
Country Flame	www.countryflame.com
Dimplex North America (C)	www.dimplex.com
Energy King	www.energyking.com
Hearthstone	www.hearthstonestoves.com
Heat-N-Glo	www.heatnglo.com
Jotul North America	www.jotulflame.com
Krog Iverson & Co.	www.warmfurniture.com
Lennox Hearth Products	www.lennoxhearthproducts.com
Lopi	www.lopistoves.com
Morso Stoves	www.morsousa.com
Osburn (C)	www.osburn-mfg.com
Pacific Energy Fireplace Products Ltd. (C)	www.pacificenergy.net
Quadra-Fire	www.quadrafire.com
Rais & Wittus, Inc.	www.raiswittus.com
Regency (C)	www.regencyqualitytime.com
Thelin Co., Inc.	www.thelinco.com
Woodstock Soapstone Co.	www.woodstove.com

(C) = Canadian

Fireplace Inserts

These are heating units that retrofit into an existing masonry or factory-built fireplace and burn wood, natural gas, propane or wood pellets. They should be listed for installation into that specific fireplace. They are boxes made of cast iron or heavy gauge steel with insulated self-cleaning glass doors. They must meet EPA guidelines for combustion efficiency and pollution control. They can transform a nonefficient fireplace into a heat producing unit. There are vent-free inserts, which do not require chimneys or flues; vented inserts, which utilize the existing chimney (though a flue liner or other modification may be necessary); and direct vent units, which can be used with gas. Many inserts now include the option of an electric blower, which pulls cooler air from the room, circulates it around the body of the insert and then blows the warmed air back into the room to circulate the heat. Fireplace inserts are heavy (600 to 1,000 pounds) and should be installed by fireplace professionals to assure a safe and efficient working unit. All inserts are closed-combustion systems and some require a direct air supply vent.

Some resources for fireplace inserts:

Avalon	www.avalonstoves.com
Country Flame	www.countryflame.com
Energy King	www.energyking.com
Heatilator	www.heatilator.com
Heat-N-Glo	www.heatnglo.com
Krog Iverson & Co.	www.warmfurniture.com
Lennox Hearth Products	www.lennoxhearthproducts.com
Osburn (C)	www.osburn-mfg.com
Pacific Energy Fireplace Products Ltd. (C)	www.pacificenergy.net
Quadra-Fire	www.quadrafire.com
Regency (C)	www.regency-fire.com
Wilkening Fireplace Co.	www.wilkeningfireplace.com

(C) = Canadian

Many are efficient in heating a room or an entire zone of a house. Fireplace inserts come in a variety of sizes, styles and finishes and vary depending on the fuel types they are designed to use.

Outdoor Fireplaces

There is a growing trend toward using the outside of a home for entertaining and relaxing. As patios and decks become more elaborate, so do the furnishings and cooking apparatus and conveniences. Outdoor fireplaces have become more popular in the last several years with the growth of many new options. There are fireplaces that look like sculpture, campfires and ancient Aztec pots. Some are similar to traditional interior fireplaces and some can also be used as grills. Units can be found to fit most needs, budgets and design requirements. There are several types of outdoor fireplaces:

Masonry fireplaces—These are built much like interior masonry fireplaces. Care must be taken to use a sealer (rated as water permeable) to waterproof the exterior surfaces.

Prefabricated fireplaces—Exterior fireplaces are available in a large variety of sizes, shapes and materials. Some of them are designed like sculpture, and some are more utilitarian in appearance.

Chimineas—They are pots that can be made like the traditional chimineas out of kiln-dried clay or the more modern cast iron in a variety of sizes and shapes. They are used for many purposes; one is for burning wood in an outside setting. They have an opening at the base for adding fuel, an air intake and a stack for smoke. Some areas of the country will not allow their use, such as Denver, Colorado.

Campfires or fire pits—These are fireplaces that use either gas or propane and are self-contained cartridges, which can be flush with the deck or built into a pedestal. One of the units found also has a fountain that recirculates water from the base of the unit.

Some resources for outdoor fireplaces:

Avalon	www.avalonstoves
Heatilator	www.heatilator.com
Heat-N-Glo	www.heatnglo.com
Rais & Wittus	www.raiswittus.com

Heat-N-Glo

Virtual Fireplaces

Still a very new concept, these fireplaces do not require venting, maintenance, fuel or expensive installations. They emulate the look and sound of a roaring fireplace with none of the effort that goes into maintaining one. They feature studio-corrected high-resolution digital images of real wood-burning fires. Inset units usually fit into a conventional fireplace cavity. Monitors can be purchased from local electronics dealers or through the Virtual Products company; however, all monitors purchased other than from the virtual fireplace dealer must be approved by the company in order to assure that the digital fireplace-processing system will work up to their standards. These products are warranted for two years.

resources

For further information about virtual fireplaces, contact Virtual Products at www.virtual-products.com.

Specialty Fireplaces

Kivas—They are in the shape of a beehive and often found in Southwestern homes. Generally rounded with shallow-angled walls, they are efficient at radiating heat outward.

Indoor/outdoor fireplaces—There are some unique fireplace units that can be used on exterior walls and viewed from the inside and the outside. The outside face acts as a vent, and the units are weatherproofed to withstand the elements.

Kitchen hearths—Raised hearths work particularly well in a kitchen, bringing the fire to a viewing level for diners. Some people like to

Heatilator

Far Left: This gas patio campfire offers a convenient and simple alternative to building a wood fire.

Left: This kiva-style fireplace can be used with many styles of architecture.

A see-through gas indoor/outdoor fireplace that emulates the need for a traditional venting system.

The virtual fireplace is a wonderful way of having the look of a fireplace without the heat and venting.

use their fireplaces for cooking, as people did hundreds of years ago. Masonry fireplaces can be fitted with a grill, a bread oven and a hook to support cooking pots for soups and stews.

Corner fireplaces—They take up little floor or wall space and work well in small rooms or rooms with little wall space, broken up with many doors and windows.

Inglenooks—They date back to the twelfth century, when fireplaces were used to warm the home. The hearth was large, so large logs could be burned. Benches were put around the fireplace so the family could sit around and keep warm. Today, inglenooks are sometimes built with benches around the fireplace, which are ornamental and functional.

Controls

The following are convenient ways of controlling the temperature and/or the size of the flame. Neither of these systems can be used with a wood-burning fireplace.

Thermostatically controlled—The unit senses the temperature at that location and controls the amount of fire given off by the fireplace or stove.

Remote control—The unit can be turned on and off with a wired or wireless remote.

Chimneys

There are many codes determining the construction of chimneys, required diameters, chimney heights, clearance between the exterior of the chimney and all combustible materials and so on. Flues, for masonry chimneys for fireplaces, are sized according to the height of the chimney and the size of the room opening to assure proper drafting of the fire. If you are remodeling, make sure your chimney meets the current codes, and if you are building a new chimney, make sure you and your builder are aware of the building codes regarding fireplaces.

Accessories for Fireplaces

Mantels—Ornamental facings surrounding the fireplace or just a shelf above a fireplace.

Andirons (or firedogs)—These are paired metal supports with four short legs used to keep the firewood off the hearth floor so the air can circulate beneath the wood for an efficient fire. The vertical parts prevent the wood from rolling into the room. Andirons are available in a variety of sizes and designs, both new and antique.

Grates—They work in a similar way to andirons to support firewood. They are more functional than andirons, which are more decorative. They also have four short legs to raise the wood so air can circulate beneath the wood. They are available in a variety of sizes and are generally made of steel or iron. Replacement grates for factory-built fireplaces should be made by the fireplace manufacturer.

Screens—Screens are used to prevent hot embers and sparks from flying out of the fireplace.

Folding screens—These are hinged panels placed in front of the fireplace.

Standing screens—These are ornamental units placed in front of the fireplace opening.

Curtain screens—These are installed on the fireplace opening and are closed with a pull chain. These are the most commonly used screens.

Glass doors—They close off the opening of the firebox so heat from the central heating system does not escape up the chimney when the fireplace is not being used. They also prevent sparks and embers from falling out of the fireplace.

Tools—There are a variety of tools that can be purchased as sets or individually. They sometimes come with stands, or they can be hung from hooks on the exterior of the fireplace.

Bellows—A tool for speeding up starting a wood fire; bellows feed air to the flames as it is forced out of an expandable bladder.

Brush and shovel—These are used to clean out ashes from the hearth floor.

Poker—Everyone's favorite tool, it can be used to rearrange and move the wood while it is burning.

Tongs—They are also used for rearranging the firewood and with a scissor action can lift and replace falling logs.

Long, heavy leather gloves—For handling hot material.

Covered ash can—Used for safe transport and disposition of ashes.

Safety Tips

- Make certain that the fireplace or the stove for heating has been built or installed with the required permit issued from a local building official.
- Clean the fireplace and have it inspected annually by a Chimney Safety Institute of America–certified chimney sweep.

resources

To locate a CSIA-certified National Chimney Sweep Guild member, check www.ncsg.org and do a search of your state.

- Follow the manufacturer's installation, maintenance and operating instructions.
- Use seasoned wood with a moisture content of approximately 20 percent because it burns cleaner than **green wood.** Dry wood is up to 25 percent more efficient, produces less creosote deposits and smokes less. Do not burn paper or other materials that can float up the chimney and cause a roof fire.
- Always use a fireplace screen to prevent sparks and flying embers from entering the room.
- Never leave a fire unattended.
- Store wood that is not being used outside and away from the house to prevent bringing bugs that may be in the wood into the house.

- Clean the area around the fireplace. Anything too close to the fireplace can cause a fire. Keep rugs away from the immediate area unless they are flame-resistant hearth rugs.
- Place logs in the rear of the fireplace, on a grate.
- Have a fire extinguisher on hand.
- Always have properly located smoke detectors and carbon monoxide detectors with fresh batteries in your home.

resources

For additional information about fireplaces or to locate a chimney sweep in your area, check the Web site of the Chimney Safety Institute of America at www.csia.org or call 800-536-0118. Also contact the Hearth, Patio & Barbecue Association at www.hpba.org for further information and resources.

Stairs and Elevators

Besides the obvious use of stairs to access upper and lower floors, stairs and elevators can add style and convenience to a home. A fine example of the drama of a beautiful staircase is the scene of Scarlet O'Hara descending the steps at Tara in *Gone With the Wind* and, for those who can possibly remember, Shirley Temple tap dancing down the stairs in *The Little Colonel* with Bo Jangles. The staircase can be a prominent architectural feature in the house or it can be totally functional and hidden away. As an important design feature, it should be consistent with the overall style of the house. Depending on the space, there are numerous options to select from in terms of style, materials and handrails. Selections should be made based on the design of the house and the personal needs of the residents.

An option gaining increased popularity is the installation of elevators in homes. Although homeowners may not need the elevator for current everyday use, they may want to include one for an elderly parent who may come to visit, a sudden accident that makes steps difficult or for help with heavy objects that may be moved periodically between floors. Elevators are a practical consideration if you plan to live in a house for a long time; no one knows what future needs may be.

A beautiful angled pine stairway.

Stairs

Considerations

Stairways can be beautiful and functional. The choices in materials and styles are numerous. Staircases can be built out of tree trunks, metal, poured concrete or more traditional wood options. When the house is in the design stage, there are many considerations to be examined:

- Staircases can be custom made or stock. There is a special skill in building a staircase. Either the builder can do it, or the staircase can be purchased from a stair manufacturer. Many spiral staircases, for example, are custom made in a shop and assembled on-site.
- Some staircases, such as straight, will take up more space than a spiral, for example. With the architect, decide the prominence the staircase will have in the house.
- Select the area of the house where you would like the staircases to be—out front or in the rear of the house.
- Decide how much money you are willing to allocate to this part of the project.
- Consider which type of staircase you prefer: straight, U- or L-shaped, scissor, winder or spiral.
- There are several codes—the International Residential Code (IRC), which in many states replaces Building Officials Code Administration

(BOCA), Uniform Building Code (UBC) and Council of American Building Officials (CABO) Code that dictate many of the dimensions of a staircase, the size between balusters, the maximum rise of each step, the minimum and maximum width of the treads, how high the handrail must be and so on. The requirements for stairs for emergency egress are more stringent than for convenience stairs. Codes also require a smoke detector at the top of the stairwell. Check to see if there are any special code requirements for your municipality.

- Stairs can be made of wood, metal, stone or concrete.
- Railings can be stock or customized in many materials but must meet code regulations. The style and materials should relate to the overall style of the house.
- Consider additional ways to make the staircase functional. Can the area under the stairs be used for storage? Is there room on the landing for a desk or comfortable chair?
- Lighting of stairs is a code requirement. Consider whether the staircase will require special lighting. Lights are sometimes installed in the wall adjacent to the steps for safety.

Parts of the Staircase

Stringers—The slanting board on a staircase that treads and risers are let into. Some staircases have open stringers; others are closed.

Tread—The part of the step one steps on.

Riser—The vertical section of each step from the surface of one tread to the surface of the next. The "total rise" is the height of the entire staircase.

Handrail—The rail that runs up the staircase.

Landing—The platform that separates two sets of stairs.

Newel post—The vertical post at the end of the handrail.

Balusters—The vertical posts that hold up the handrail.

Balustrade—The complete railing, including the balusters, newel posts and handrail.

Skirt board—The diagonal trim on the wall adjacent to the steps. Skirt boards are sometimes called "stringboards."

Nosing—The rounded front section of the tread that extends beyond the riser.

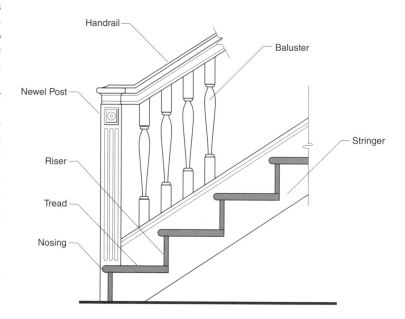

Code Requirements

Code requirements are stringent regarding staircases. According to the 2000 International Residential Code of the International Building Code (IBC), the following items are required:

- Treads must be a minimum of 10 inches.
- Rises must be a maximum of 7 $\frac{3}{4}$ inches.
- There must be 6 feet 8 inches of minimum headroom (except spiral staircases, which require 6 feet 6 inches).
- The minimum width of the stairs must be 36 inches.
- The landing space at the top and bottom must be a minimum of 3 x 3 feet.

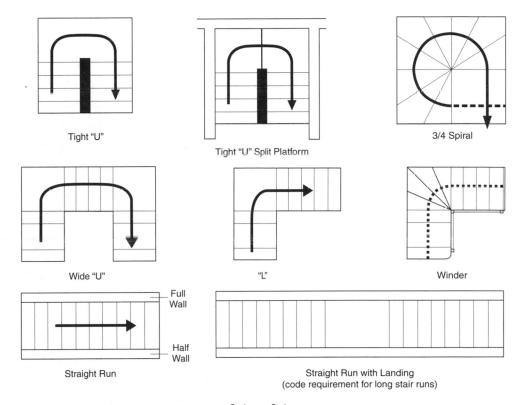

Tight "U"

Tight "U" Split Platform

3/4 Spiral

Wide "U"

"L"

Winder

Straight Run

Full Wall

Half Wall

Straight Run with Landing
(code requirement for long stair runs)

Staircase Styles

- Balusters must not exceed a maximum of 4 inches apart.

Configurations

Straight—This is the simplest type of staircase. It can have one or more landings if the stairs are steep and can have several formats: closed, open or half-wall.

- Closed—The stairs are attached to two parallel walls. Handrails are generally used on one side of the stairs.
- Open—One or both sides of the steps can be open and must be finished with a railing or **balustrade** on the open side.
- Half-wall—The top edge of one or both barriers

can be trimmed with a wood cap that serves as a handrail.

U- and L-shaped—Both of these configurations can be open or closed and use barrier or railing treatments.

Winder—Triangular steps are used instead of a landing when there is a lack of space. These steps can be dangerous and may not be permitted by some municipalities' codes.

Spiral—Spiral staircases are also used when there is a lack of available space. Small spiral staircases can be more difficult to use and should not be the main access unless it is necessary.

Elevators

Safe elevators were first sold by Elisha Graves Otis in 1853 in Yonkers, New York. Although elevators had been around for many years, Otis addressed the need for increased safety with his invention. By 1854 he sold three of his elevators for $300 each. The technology has vastly improved and the cost has gone up since then, but the concept opened many new technologies, particularly the construction of

Concord Elevator Co.

John McLean, Architect

skyscrapers. In the late 1800s Otis sold residential elevators to the rich and famous, such as the Vanderbilts and Julia Ward Howe (a champion for women's rights). Elevators have recently become increasingly popular with their use in the home. The elevator has made it possible for those with special needs to live in multi-storied homes and has also made life easier for anyone carrying heavy bundles, firewood and furniture between several floors. It can also facilitate a home office. In some cases having an elevator may be a neces-

Home elevators are available with a variety of design options.

Left: This stainless steel high-mirror finish spiral staircase is elegant and structurally solid.

sity, but for others it can be a great luxury. Elevators can be installed for current needs and possible future requirements, as well as adding to the future market value of the house.

Considerations

Cost—The cost of elevators varies, depending on whether they will go in a new construction or be retrofitted in an existing home. They can also vary by the size and finish of the car or cab, speed, drive system, number of stops and so on.

How many floors it will service—Some elevators will go to two floors; others will go to as many as six floors.

Capacity in weight—Elevators can carry from 450 to 1,500 pounds.

Speed—Elevators can move from 20 to 40 feet per minute.

Codes—American safety codes were established by the American Society of Mechanical Engineers (ASME A17.1); Canadian codes (CAN/CSA B44) were established by the Canadian Standards Association (CSA). In 2000 the codes were revised and harmonized so the American and Canadian elevator codes are identical. Each state, however, has the option of adapting the current code, a past code or defining their own codes. Elevators require a building permit prior to installation.

Stops—Residential elevators may make two stops or up to six stops, depending on the manufacturer. Most elevators also have a maximum lift height. Some elevators will go to a height maximum of 16 feet and others will go as high as 50 feet.

Car size—Cars are available in a variety of sizes that vary by manufacturer. Some of the common ones are 36 x 48 inches, 36 x 60 inches, 40 x 54 inches and 42 x 60 inches. Some companies offer custom-size cars.

Warranty—Most companies offer a one-year warranty on materials and workmanship.

Service contract—Ask whether the company offers a service contract to maintain the elevator.

Car or cab configuration—Cars may have front, rear or side openings. Some offer only one door; others offer entrances and exits on opposite sides or at a 90-degree angle from each other. Not all companies offer all configurations.

Drive system—There are basically four types of residential systems.

Four Types of Residential Systems

1. Winding drum—This is one of the most commonly used systems for residential elevators. There is a drum with a set of cables that are attached to the car. As the drum winds the cable in one direction, it lifts the car, and in the other direction, it lowers the car. If the backup battery will be used for lowering the car in case of a power outage, substantial power will be needed for carrying the weight of the car in order to lower it.

Advantages
- This system has been around for a long time and is tried and true.
- The cost for this system will be lower than for the hydraulic system.
- The cost of the battery, as a backup system, will bring the price almost equal.
- There is also no need for a separate room to house the machine.

Disadvantages
- Many winding drum systems have the motor in the shaft, which can be noisy.
- Room is required above, below or to the side of the elevator to house the motor and backup battery.
- They are more difficult to repair because the motor is in the shaft, or hoistway.
- A large motor is required to carry the full weight of the car.

2. Traction—Traction elevators, until recently, have been associated with multifloor buildings. The residential traction elevator has the motor mounted to the top of one of the guide rails. With the motor in the shaft, no additional space must be given for the hoist motor. If the installation is with a typical traction elevator, a separate hoisting motor room needs to be created and thereby increases the cost of the installation. There is an electric motor with a pulley. Over the pulley, a cable or a chain balances the car at one end, and at the other end is a counterweight. The car travels up and down along two steel tracks.

Advantages

- This system is easy and quick to install and in many states does not require the motor to be housed in a separate room.
- It requires a smaller motor than the winding drum system and is relatively efficient.

Disadvantages

- It is difficult to repair because the motor is housed in the hoistway.
- If a typical elevator is installed, an overhead space is required to house the workings, and because of this location, they can be noisy, if proper acoustical measures are not followed.
- Because space is required above the upper floor, it is difficult to retrofit this system in an existing house.

3. Hydraulic—Hydraulic systems have become one of the most popular options for residential applications in the last twenty years; they are typically used in structures with two to five floors. Hydraulic elevators move the car by pumping oil in and out of a steel cylinder, raising or lowering the elevator car. There are several types of hydraulic systems. The cable hydraulic is the prevalent technology; the car is pulled up and down from above. Residential elevators typically do not require the cylinder to be buried below the shaft. The cylinder can be mounted on the

side of the shaft, and it telescopes upward to lift the car with cables. For hydraulic systems, the motor (a pump) is only required for the up direction; gravity is utilized for the down direction. A smaller battery is required because gravity is essentially utilized during a power outage in lowering the car.

Advantages

- The motor does not have to be adjoining the car.
- It can be put in any temperature-controlled area away from the main living space (located 30 to 40 feet away), such as in a basement. (The temperature control is required to prevent the oil in the machine from getting too cold and thick or too hot and thin to operate properly.)
- Hydraulic systems tend to be quieter because the motor is submerged in oil, which muffles the sound. Not all motors are submerged in oil, but this is something to ask for when purchasing this type of system.
- Hydraulic systems offer a smoother ride with gentler starts and stops. They only require a small battery for lowering the car and for emergency lighting.

Disadvantages

- Hydraulic systems are more expensive than drum-style units; however, the requirement of drum units for a large battery makes both systems almost equal.
- A separate machine room is required for the hydraulic pump and the battery. Some states specify a specific-size room for this equipment.

4. Pneumatic—This is a very new patented system. The self-supporting tube and car are made of transparent polycarbonate, aluminum and steel. There are vacuum pumps or turbines that create pneumatic pressure and pull the car to the next floor. The safety features include locking devices at the upper and lower limits and a safe breaking device located on the roof of the car.

One of the newest types of elevators available is this Pneumatic vacuum elevator.

Perimeter seals on the doors are self-sealing due to the action of the atmospheric pressure. The car comes in three sections: top, bottom and middle. The height of the elevator can be adjusted by using all three parts or the top and bottom parts only. It can be used with up to three floors.

Note: All of the information on this system was obtained from the manufacturer and so any data mentioned here is just their contention. Further investigation must be done when this product is more readily available.

Advantages

- Installation takes two to three hours and requires no supporting structure.
- There is no excavation or engine room required. It can be retrofitted into an existing house by cutting out a hole that is 3 feet in diameter. It can also be disassembled and transported to another home.
- The system does not use energy on its descent and therefore does not require a backup battery for that operation. In a power outage, the car will automatically stop on the next lowest floor.
- The starting and stopping of this system is very smooth.

Disadvantages

- This is a brand-new technology, and there is no data on this as of yet.

resources

For further information about elevators, check with Pneumatic Vacuum Elevators, LLC, at www.vacuumelevators.com.

Shaft or Freestanding

Most elevators are contained within a shaft. Some elevators are available in freestanding configurations; the car can be seen going up and down. Another possible configuration is the through-the-floor access. This type of system can only be used with a two-floor configuration. The

Pneumatic Vacuum Elevators, LLC

floor comes up with the car. This type of car is always made of Plexiglas and is at least partially see-through. These can be used with hydraulic or cable drum systems, depending on the manufacturer. There is a pressure switch required with this system, which prevents the car from running if someone is standing on the trap door or underneath the elevator.

Car Doors

Elevators have car gates on the interior that can be manual or automatic accordion gates, bi-fold, or sliding, doors. These gates or doors come in a variety of colors and finishes. Elevators also have exterior doors that close the hoistway. Most hoistway doors have manual swing doors, but some have automatic center-opening sliding doors.

Inclinator Company of America

Hoistway doors must have an interlock, an electro-mechanical device, wired into the elevator's control, which prevents the door from opening unless the elevator is at the landing. Swinging doors can match the other doors in the house; automatic doors will have a more traditional elevator appearance.

Hall call and car operating panels (COP)—They are available in a variety of finishes. The COP should include a position indicator, emergency stop/alarm switch and emergency lighting.

Interior handrails—Handrails come in polished or brushed metal, stainless steel, bronze, brass, laminate or a variety of wood species.

Light fixtures—A variety of fixtures are available from the very simple to the elaborate. Most companies offer several options.

Interior finish—Elevators are available in laminate, wood veneer, hardwood, partial or full glass and stainless steel interiors.

Flooring—Some companies offer a variety of flooring materials, while others ship them without, so they can be customized.

Installation—The homeowner/contractor will be responsible for installation of 120- and 240-volt circuits (for the hoist motor and interior lighting), a telephone line and the elevator shaft using the elevator shop drawings. The elevator equipment must be installed by a licensed elevator contractor in some states (such as Massachusetts) or can be installed by an unlicensed contractor in other states (such as New Hampshire). Find out what the local requirements are before purchasing an elevator. Canada has no licensing requirement for residential elevator installations.

Inspections—Some states require elevator inspections every few years; others have no inspection requirements.

Safety measures—Safety features must comply with ASME A17.1.

• Elevators are equipped with a battery-controlled backup in case of a power failure; code only requires the battery to provide four hours of lighting and power to the emergency alarm. Code does not require the battery to lower the elevator to the next-lowest floor level, although most people opt for this safety feature anyway.

• Door locks (interlock) will prevent the elevator from working when any of the mechanical or electrical doors are open. It will also prevent the hoistway doors from opening when the elevator cab is not there.

• Emergency lighting and alarm; telephone is optional, although most people do put this in.

• All residential elevators have fail-safe systems that will prevent the car from functioning in a hazardous way.

• Handrails inside the car to grab on to are optional, although most people install them for safety and comfort.

• Code requires that there be a 5-inch harmonized code maximum space (on newer codes that have not been adopted by all states) between the cab and outer doors of the elevator so children will not get stuck between the doors. Special

With this free-standing elevator, the car can be seen going up and down.

Some of the companies that make outer doors for elevators:

Concord	800-661-5112	www.concordelevator.com
EZ Entry	716-434-3440	www.liftavator.com
Niargara Belco	888-465-9999	www.niagarabelco.com
Whirlteq (C)	800-298-1480	www.whirlteq.com

(C) = Canadian

power-operated doors are available either sliding or swinging open, but sliding doors are rare on residential applications. Power-swinging doors are shipped preassembled for easy installation. Check with the elevator manufacturer to find out if this type of door is available from them, or contact one of the manufacturers listed below to purchase doors that are compliant with most codes; there are municipalities, such as New York City, that require particular code designations. Most municipalities in the United States require the elevator door to be fire rated, but this is not a requirement in Canada. In addition, some areas in the United States require vision panels in the outer door; there is no such requirement in Canada for this either. If you are considering installing an elevator in your home, check with the local building office to find out about local code requirements.

resources

For additional companies, check the Web site of *Elevator World Magazine* at www.elevator-world.com.

Extras

There are many possible options available for residential elevators:

- Custom car sizing
- Custom wood interiors
- Specialty lights
- Recessed telephone cabinet
- Decorative wall panels
- External modem for remote diagnostics
- Clear panels on accordion car gates
- Skylights
- Earthquake Emergency Return (EER)— Equipped with a seismic sensor, the elevator will stop at the nearest floor below and the doors will open
- Interior mirrors
- Exhaust fan
- Automatic door operators for the car and hall

resources

For additional information about elevator safety, contact the Elevator Escalator Safety Foundation (EESF) at www.eesf.org.

Some of the companies that manufacture residential elevators:

Access Industries	800-925-3100	www.dreamelevator.com
CEMCOlift (Otis)	800-962-3626	www.cemcolift.com
Concord Elevators (C)	800-661-5112	www.concordelevator.com
Elevator Concepts	716-434-3440	www.elevatorconcepts
Inclinator	800-343-9007	www.inclinator.com
Lift-avator	716-434-1300	www.liftavator.com
Matot (C)	800-369-1070	www.matot.com
Niagara Belco Ltd. (C)	888-465-9999	www.niagarabelco.com
Pneumatic Vacuum Elevators	305-235-6707	www.vacuumelevators.com
Savaria Corp. (C)	800-931-5655	www.savaria.com
Schumacher Elevator Co.	800-779-5438	www.schumacherelevator.com
The National Wheel-O-Vator Co., Inc.	800-551-9095	www.wheelovator.com
Universal Elevator	800-547-0747	www.universalelevator.com
Waupaca Elevator Co., Inc.	800-238-8739	www.waupacaelevator.com

(C) = Canadian

Aaron Batkin

Mechanical Systems

Probably the least interesting part of the house is the mechanicals. Most people don't want to know too much about them; they just want them to work. When any part of the system breaks down, it is particularly upsetting because many of the comforts we have grown to expect are temporarily gone. This chapter is included so you will have an idea of what mechanicals go into a house and, if you are building a new house, what the options include.

Considerations

- What are the weather conditions for most of the year—is it hot and humid or cool and dry?
- What is the cost and availability of various fuels or energy sources locally? Fuel costs vary greatly from area to area.
- What is the cost of the appliance needed to convert the fuel to heat?
- What is the cost of maintaining the system?
- What is the warranty? Find out the length of time the equipment is covered and what components are listed under the warranty. Some companies also offer extended warranties. Find out from your dealer what labor costs are included in the warranty; this is generally not covered by the manufacturer. Find out if the warranty is offered from the manufacturer or the dealer.

- What type of heating/cooling emitters (delivery devices) do you want in the rooms—baseboard, floor registers, ceiling diffusers, wall registers, under-floor radiant tubing, etc.?
- Are there allergy or asthma problems that must be considered when planning a system? Ventilation and filtration systems can be used to help create a healthy environment by reducing airborne contaminants.
- How large will the system be? Evaluate the square footage of the house and any extensions you might add in the future. It is important to size the system for the appropriate amount of space. An oversized cooling system will cool down quickly (satisfying the thermostat) but not allow the moisture to be removed from the indoor air; this is referred to as short-cycling. An undersized air-conditioning system will not adequately cool the home on the hottest days. It is similar with heating systems; an oversized heating system will not be able to filter the air properly before the end of the cycle. It will also have frequent cycling or short-cycling, as the air heats up quickly, adding unnecessary wear and tear on the furnace. An undersized system will not adequately warm the house on the coldest days. A trained professional HVAC dealer will be able to help evaluate your home requirements. (Make sure the dealer you are using has certified technicians that have the knowledge to

properly install and service your system.) Make sure the contractor's personnel does a heat loss/heat gain calculation using the industry standard Air Conditioning Contractors of America (ACCA Manual J document). It is a simple form that shows a calculation of what you need. It is an important record in case questions arise at a later date. If you are building a new house, consult with one or several HVAC dealers in order to make decisions about mechanicals. Make sure the dealer is licensed (if there is a licensing program in your area) and is affiliated with one of the nationally known manufacturers. Ask for references and check on as many as possible. Get a written proposal that you can compare with other bids, and get a written agreement with the dealer you select.

- How energy efficient are the units you are considering? If a furnace is selected, note that furnaces that are 90 percent efficient or greater qualify for the EPA's Energy Star program and are identified with the Energy Star logo.

The following are some of the ratings that can be used to evaluate the efficiency of your system:

Energy Efficiency Ratio (EER)—This is a rating used for air conditioners and heat pumps that indicates their cooling/heating efficiency. The EER and Seasonal Energy Efficiency Ratio (SEER) are used by many utilities as criteria for rebate program qualifications.

Seasonal Energy Efficiency Ratio (SEER)—This is a seasonal rating used for air conditioners and heat pumps that indicates their cooling/heating efficiency. The higher the number, the better the efficiency, and the more costly the unit. The minimum standard established by the government for homes built after 1992 is 10 SEER. High-efficiency units have a SEER of at least 12; the maximum is about 17.

Heating Seasonal Performance Factor (HSPF)—This is a heating efficiency rating for heat pumps. In general, the higher the HSPF rating, the less electricity the unit will use to heat the house. High-efficiency units are usually 7.5 or higher. The maximum HSPF rating is 10. The minimum standard established by the government for homes built after 1992 is 6.8. In general, the higher the efficiency, the higher the cost for the unit, but the lower the utility bill.

Annual Fuel Utilization Efficiency (AFUE)—This is a rating system for indicating how efficiently the furnace and boiler convert fuel (gas or oil) into heat. The number is given in a percentage that tells how much of the fuel is converted to heat and how much is wasted. In 1992 the government established a minimum AFUE rating for furnaces in new houses at 78 percent. Mid-efficiency furnaces (noncondensing or induced-draft furnaces) offer efficiencies from 78 to about 80 percent. High-efficiency furnaces (condensing or sealed combustion furnaces) offer AFUE ratings from 80 to about 96 percent. Energy Star qualifies furnaces with an AFUE rating of 90 percent or greater. Old furnaces can be replaced with high-efficiency ones to reduce energy bills. Depending on the climate, the higher-efficiency furnace cost may be paid back quickly with the savings in fuel bills. AFUE ratings are also used on boilers. In 1992 the government established an 80 percent minimum AFUE for hot water boilers and 75 percent for steam boilers. Energy Star qualifies boilers with an AFUE rating of 85 percent or greater. The efficiency of these units is due to electric ignition, eliminating the pilot light (for gas), which is burning all the time. These are new combustion technologies that extract more heat from the fuel and sealed combustion that uses outside air to fuel the burner.

- What is the noise level on the outdoor units? Noise levels of outdoor units (the condensing units of the air-conditioning system and heat pumps) can vary. Try to keep them away from below bedroom windows. Creative use of fencing and/or shrubbery can also be used to help reduce noise.
- What type of thermostat will you use? There are several types available today. Electronic thermostats have a microprocessor inside that compares the thermometer reading of a room's temperature to the desired temperature

selected. It gives start and stop commands to the heating and cooling system to bring the temperature to a comfortable level. Programmable (smart) thermostats are programmed with the desired temperatures at particular times of the day. The thermostat will then continue to direct the system according to the program. This allows you to save on energy by setting back the energy when you will not be at home or when you are sleeping. The settings can also be altered to save energy when you are on vacation. Some units have daylight-savings keys and temperature overrides to change the temperature on a particular day if you are home when you would normally be away. Look for units that have backup batteries so settings are saved if there is a power outage, and look for units that are simple to operate (or offer consumer support). Check for Energy Star compliant thermostats when selecting a unit.

Some of the companies that produce programmable thermostats:

Aprilaire	www.aprilaire.com
Carrier Corp.	www.carrier.com
Invensys	www.about-i-series.com
Honeywell	www.honeywellthermostat.com
Hunter Fan Company	www.hunterfan.com
Lux Products Corp	www.luxproducts.com
White-Rogers	www.white-rogers.com

resources

You can locate an HVAC/R-certified technician from North American Technician Excellence (NATE) by going to their Web site at www.natex.org, clicking on the consumer patch and then clicking on the consumer contractor connection.

- Will you have one zone or several zones in the house? A multi-zoning system allows you to put the heating and cooling in the areas of the house where and when they are needed. This also reduces energy costs by limiting the amount of heat and cool air sent to areas of the house where it is not needed—spare bedrooms, unfinished basements and so on. Some systems include zone sensors located throughout the house to give temperature information back to the panel, which opens and closes dampers in the cooling and heating ductwork to control the temperature in every part of the house. This type of system also accommodates the needs of all the occupants by allowing everyone in the house to control the temperature in their own areas. The bedrooms can be heated or cooled according to individual needs. With some systems, such as radiant heat, each room can have its own individually controlled temperature setting.
- What type of fuel will you use? Fuels are selected by availability, cost per Btu, combustion efficiency and convenience.

Fuels

Natural Gas

Natural gas is the most commonly used fuel because it is readily available and adaptable to a forced-air system or hot water system, a simple method of heating and cooling the house.

Advantages

- Gas is a clean fuel.
- Gas systems are easily integrated with other mechanicals, such as air-conditioning.
- Natural gas is usually the least expensive heating fuel.
- Rates do not change often.
- Natural gas mechanicals do not require expensive routine maintenance.

Disadvantages

- Gas is not always available and is not a renewable resource.
- A chimney is required.

Liquid (Propane) Gas

Liquefied petroleum gas (LPG) or bottled gas is prohibited or restricted in some areas. It is also generally twice as expensive as natural gas.

Advantages

- Usually easy to obtain, even in remote locations.
- Liquid gas is a clean fuel.

Disadvantages

- A large storage tank is required, either underground or above ground.
- Fuel must be stored up and usage should be watched closely. If the fuel runs out, you are without heat.
- Strict safety, environmental and fireproofing restrictions are required.

Oil

Oil is often used in areas where gas is not available. It can be a good alternative.

Advantages

- Oil is a relatively clean form of fuel.
- Fuel is stored on your property.

Disadvantages

- The storage container may be costly to install. (Note: There is a government program called the Leaking Underground Storage Tank program that evaluates and removes risks caused by releases from petroleum tanks. If you have an underground tank that leaks, your liabilities and penalties are enormous. Selling a house with an underground storage tank will also be difficult.)
- Strict safety, environmental and fireproofing restrictions are required.
- Money can be tied up in fuel since it must be stored; oil can give off dirty emissions if the furnace/boiler isn't working properly. Yearly cleaning and maintenance is required; fuel must be stored up. If the fuel runs out, you are without heat.
- Oil is not a renewable resource.
- Unless one has a service contract, the price of oil can change with each delivery.

resources

For further information about the Leaking Underground Storage Tank program, check with the U.S. Environmental Protection Office at www.epa-gov/swerust1/.

Electric

This type of fuel is popular because it is easy to use in the specified areas. Electricity is the most universally available energy source.

Advantages

- Electricity is a clean fuel that leaves no residue.
- It requires no chimney.
- Maintenance is inexpensive.
- Electrical heating and cooling equipment is highly energy efficient.

Disadvantages

- Electrical energy rates are dependent on the local utility company, but rates are generally higher than for the heat energy obtained from other fuels.
- Blackouts will leave your home with no heat (unless you have a backup generator).

Wood

It is rarely used for heating the home but often supplements another heating system. Wood must continuously be fed into the fireplace, making it extremely inconvenient.

Advantages

- Wood is a renewable resource.
- It can sometimes be used from your own property.

Disadvantages

- It is labor intensive, requiring stacking, feeding the fire and cleaning the ashes.
- There is a risk of a house fire.
- A chimney is required.
- Wood can bring insects, dirt, fungus and bacteria indoors.
- The combustion of wood can be dirty.
- Wood takes up a lot of storage space.

If a gas system is selected, carbon monoxide detectors should be used. If the detectors go off, the levels must be checked. For further information about carbon monoxide detectors, check the chapter on "Health and Safety" on page 308.

A simple split system for heating and cooling a home.

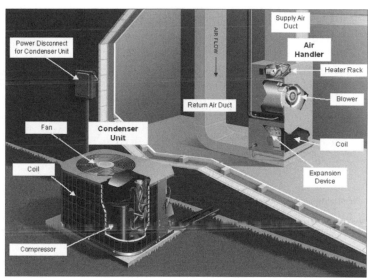

Unitary Products of York International

Packaged or Split System?

Packaged System

The heating and cooling systems are built into one outdoor (and sometimes indoor) unit. They are typically installed at ground level beside the house or on the roof. They are sometimes installed in the attic. They can use one fuel type or two different fuels for heating and cooling (for example, electric cooling and gas heating).

Split System

These are the most common configurations, requiring an outdoor unit (air conditioner or heat pump) and a unit inside the house (furnace or air handler). They are sometimes installed in the attic.

Heat pump—This is a system that can be reversed to either heat or cool a particular space. Heat pumps are more often used in moderate climates. They use the difference between outdoor air temperatures and indoor air temperatures to cool and heat the home. Geothermal heat pumps use the ground instead of the outside air to provide heating, air-conditioning and hot water.

Air handler—An air moving and/or mixing unit. Single speed, multiple speed or variable-speed fans push air over hot or cold coils, through dampers and ducts, to heat or cool a house. For the home, air handlers include a blower, a coil, an expansion device, a heater rack and a filter. In some models heaters are factory installed; in some they are sold as accessories. They are used as electric duct heaters in systems without a furnace.

resources

For a complete discussion comparing the efficiency and costs of the various fuels, check the Web site of the U.S. Department of Energy Office of Energy Efficiency and Renewable Energy at www.eere.energy.gov/consumer-info/refbriefs/cb5.html.

Types of Heating Systems

Forced Air

With this system, fuel (oil or gas) is burned or electrically heated (by a heat pump or heating coil) to create warm air that is forced by a fan through a system of ducts and blown through registers in various parts of the house. Cooled air is then most often drawn back in from the house through return ducts or mixed with air that can be drawn in from the outside, heated up again and then sent back through the house through supply ducts and registers. Before the air goes through the furnace to be heated, it goes through a filtration system to remove dirt and dust that may clog the furnace, allowing the furnace to work efficiently. An electrically powered blower is used to drive the air through the system. This is the most popular system used today because it is inexpensive, easy to install, the furnace can be located anywhere in the house and the ducts and blower that are used to heat the house can also be used for the central air-conditioning system, humidifier and other systems.

Registers are the outlets for the cool or heated air. Most rooms have at least one register; larger rooms may have two or more. There are several types of registers: floor, ceiling and wall registers. Many registers are made of metal, but wood registers are available to be used with wood flooring. In kitchens and bathrooms, registers are often in the toe kick, or baseboard, at the base of cabinets, both for aesthetics and to avoid getting moisture from mopping into the ducts. Returns (or return-air ducts) are grilles that the air goes through to be returned for reheating. Supply and return registers should be installed to provide a good mix of air for the room being heated and cooled. Registers should not be placed back to back in adjacent rooms so sound is not readily transmitted between the two rooms and privacy is not compromised. Supply air registers should be placed near the return air grille. When talking with the contractor, ask for information as to where locations will be.

A zoning system can be set up so areas of the house or individual rooms can be heated and cooled independently of the others. Each zone has its own separate thermostat that can be set regularly or programmed to go on and off at desired times. Dampers are installed in the ducts to direct the air to the sections of the house where needed. They are controlled by the thermostats and open and close depending on the heating needs in the various zones. Zones can be fixed with programmable thermostats according to need.

Some systems are available with a multi-speed or variable-capacity furnace or air handlers with two to four speeds. The speeds allow the units to run quieter with fewer on/off cycles as long as operational specification requirements are not compromised. Variable-capacity furnaces have "smart" motors that can monitor comfort conditions and automatically adjust the volume and speed of air.

Advantages

- The same ducts can be used for heating, cooling, humidification, dehumidification and filtration.
- Maintenance requirements are simply filter changes and annual service inspections.
- The airflow can be regulated to particular areas with zoning, utilizing multiple thermostats.
- Airflow can be regulated with fins or movable baffles inside the ducts or dampers that are part of the register and additional blowers.

Disadvantages

- A poorly maintained furnace can transport dirt and soot that can come through the registers.
- The air goes on and off depending on the heating call by the thermostat. It often overcompensates with air that is too hot or not hot enough when not properly designed, installed and maintained.
- Energy codes require the ducts to be insulated.

Some air is lost through the joints in the duct-work if not properly installed and sealed. Duct tape is not a good sealing system. If the duct-work is not insulated in unheated areas (such as garages and crawl spaces), the heat is lost, whereas if the ductwork is in heated areas, any heat lost from the ducts will at least be productive in heating the area.

- Warm air rises to the ceiling, sometimes leaving the flooring area chilly. Thus the locations of the registers and the return grilles are important.
- If interior doors are shut, rooms can be pressurized if they don't have return ducts. This can cause an imbalance in the heat and heat loss, and doors can shut from the air pressure.
- Blowers can sometimes be noisy.
- Hot-air furnaces can create a very dry heat called "scorched air."

Hydronic Heat

Although hot water, or hydronic heat, is not the most commonly used method of heating in the United States, it is commonly used in Europe. In this country, hot water systems are popular in areas of the country with longer periods of cold weather and in older homes. In Southern areas, with longer periods of heat and more dependence on air-conditioning, forced hot-air systems with ducts that can be used for heat and air-conditioning systems are more common.

Water is circulated in liquid form or steam; steam is not commonly used anymore. Hydronic heating is often not the first choice by builders because of the added cost of installation of vents for air-conditioning and pipes for heating. Water is heated in a boiler by gas, oil or electricity and then pumped through the house with a network of pipes to a baseboard radiation system (or hot water coils in the AC ducts) along the perimeter of the house or radiators. (Another option is in-floor radiant heating, which is discussed on page 207.) The pipes are attached to fins made of copper or aluminum. Radiators distribute the heat from the pipes. There are two types of radiators. Baseboard radiators are the more convenient radiator because they take up less room and are less intrusive. They heat the air in a room through natural convection or a circulatory motion of the warm air. Under-the-window radiators jut into the room and often get in the way of furnishings. They are used less frequently today than baseboard radiators. However, they heat through natural convection and thermal radiation, which means they heat the surfaces and occupants directly.

Another method of distributing heat is with the use of in-floor tubing. This type of heat is discussed later in this chapter.

Advantages

- Hydronic heat is a quiet, efficient and clean method of heating.
- It is adaptable to some of the solar heating systems.
- Hot water baseboards distribute heat efficiently.
- Baseboard radiators are easy to zone, so you can vary the heat level from one space to another and choose not to heat unused rooms.
- A cast-iron boiler for a baseboard system is likely to last longer than a furnace for a hot-air system.
- Boilers can be used for heating the domestic water and the heating system.
- Boilers can be used for heating spas or pools and melting snow on walkways and driveways.
- Dirt cannot be spread in pipes as it can be in ducts of hot-air systems.
- Pipes take up less space in the structure of the house than ducts.

Disadvantages

- There are no ducts to be used for cooling, humidification, dehumidification and filtration. The ducts have to be added, increasing the cost of the entire system. However, there is a chilled water system that is more involved than baseboard radiators: fan coil radiation systems with built-in condensate pans and their own blower motor for cooling.

- Pipes can develop a buildup of mineral deposits that reduce system efficiency when water is added to the system, because of possible leaks.
- Hot-water systems can sometimes be noisy when the heat is going on and off.
- Pipes are vulnerable to freezing if there is a power outage for an extended period of time or if the heat is turned off for several months, as in a vacation house. If a pipe breaks, it can create a flood on the floor. An antifreeze (propylene glycol), sometimes circulated in the pipes to protect them from freezing, can eventually break down and become corrosive. (This can be avoided by having a backup generator.)
- It is a slower system than a forced hot-air system; it takes more time for the water to heat up than air.
- It is more expensive to purchase and install than a forced-air system (which also provides air-conditioning).
- Radiators can be cumbersome.

Electrical Resistance Heat

Electrical heat can be distributed through baseboard heaters, through a system of radiant heating (discussed in the next section) or individual zonal heating units. Electricity is converted to heat when it moves through conductors or heating elements, which become hot and give off heat. The heat is then typically distributed via baseboard heaters, wall heaters, radiant heat and so on. Electrical heaters come in a wide range of sizes with different output ratings, so they can be used for general heating or for supplementary purposes. Each room has a thermostat that controls the electrical heating in that room.

Advantages

- Electrical resistance heat is simple and inexpensive to install.

- There is no furnace, boiler, chimney, plumbing or ductwork.
- It is a quiet system.
- The heat can easily be used only where it is required; each room can have its own control.
- It is a maintenance-free system.
- It is a clean system.
- Many systems come with warranties.

Disadvantages

- Heating elements can be dangerously hot if they are touched.
- Electrical rates can be very expensive.

Radiant Heat

This is becoming an increasingly popular method of heating because it is a natural zoning system; each room can be controlled and those rooms that are not often used do not waste heat. The largest selling feature, however, is the feeling of warmth on one's feet emanating from the flooring. Radiant heat is sometimes used to heat the whole house or to heat cold floors in selected areas such as a bathroom, kitchen or hallway, using another form of heating in the rest of the house. It radiates heat naturally upward and warms the room occupants evenly from toe to head. The two types of radiant heat that are commonly used in the home are electric radiant heat and hot water heat, or hydronic radiant heat.

- Electric radiant heat has electrical heating elements installed in or under the flooring. This can be a very expensive form of heating to operate, depending on utility costs (some areas of the country have very reasonable rates), if used for the main method of heating, unless the utility company offers "time-of-use rates." Money can be saved by charging the concrete floor at off-peak hours (approximately 9 p.m. to 6 a.m.) so the thermal mass of the concrete stores up the heat and radiates it during the peak hours without the need for additional electrical output. If radiant heat is used as a supplementary form of heating for one or two rooms, the economics may not be as much of an issue. In addition to the heating element configurations already mentioned, there is also a product available that is designed specifically for tile and natural stone floors. This product is in the form of mats, which come with a heating element already imbedded in the fabric. The mats are bonded (with thin-set tile adhesive) to the subfloor before the tiles are laid. An electrician must connect the mats to an independent circuit, and a thermostat is set up to program the temperature.

- Hot water heat, or hydronic radiant heat, is installed by imbedding special warm-water tubing in a pattern under the floor. Sometimes used with other heating systems, it is most compatible with a baseboard system and draws hot water from the same boiler as the baseboard. This is a more cost-effective type of radiant heating. The water for radiant heating is not as hot as for convection systems. Hot water from the furnace is tempered to the lower temperature and distributed throughout. The returning water must be reheated to a higher temperature before it enters the furnace/boiler to prevent the participation of harmful salts in the boiler or possible thermal shock.

The tubing for hot water, or hydronic radiant heat, can be placed with a wet or dry installation. In wet installations the tubing is embedded in a concrete slab, in a lightweight concrete slab on top of the substrate, or over a previously poured slab. Dry installations have become more popular because they respond faster and often require fewer modifications to conventional heating systems to install. The tubing may be suspended underneath the subfloor between the joists, or it may be installed between two layers of subfloor. There is a plywood subfloor material available that is manufactured with tubing grooves and aluminum heat diffuser plates already built into them, making installation in new constructions less expensive. Other systems are also available that make it easier to install a radiant system. There is a plastic mesh system with heating elements woven through that provides the spacing and is easily installed by stapling to the subfloor.

Advantages

- Radiant heat is a quiet system.
- Each room is controlled individually.
- Radiant heat is invisible, clean and efficient.
- The warmth emanates from the floor, where it is needed to warm feet, then radiates upward to warm the total person; forced-air systems tend to send air up toward the ceiling.
- Radiant heating systems deliver a constant, even temperature.
- When a radiant heating system is used with concrete substrate, the thermal mass of the concrete holds the heat and releases it slowly over time.
- Radiant systems don't create or circulate airborne dust, which is a plus for people with allergies.
- There is no furnace, boiler, plumbing or ductwork in electrical systems.

Disadvantages

- If the system breaks down, the flooring may have to be lifted.
- Radiant heat can overshoot or overheat unless it is balanced and controlled with a special thermostat designed for radiant heat.
- Air-conditioning must be a separate system.

resources

For further information about radiant heat or to locate dealers in the United States and Canada, check with the Radiant Panel Association at www.rpa-info.com.

Heat Pumps

Heat pumps do not burn fuel to make heat but use electricity to transfer (or pump) heat from one place to another. Like central air-conditioning systems, heat pumps have both interior and exterior parts that work together. In the winter, heat pumps transfer heat from the outside and move it to the inside; in the summer, heat pumps transfer heat from the inside to the outside. Heat pumps work as heaters in the winter and air conditioners in the summer. (There are also ground-source and water-source heat pumps that extract heat from the ground and bodies of water, instead of taking the heat from the air.) Heat pumps work best when the air does not go below 40 degrees Fahrenheit. In areas where below-freezing weather is common, supplementary heating is required. Air handlers are then used to circulate the conditioned air throughout the house. They are available with single or variable speed motors, which offer a variety of features including a high humidity control. Some heat pumps are matched with furnaces, with the heat pump outside and the furnace inside; other systems are in packaged units with all parts in one unit outside or through the wall installations. Heat pumps require a duct system, like forced-air systems, to carry the conditioned air throughout the house. Heat pumps require special ductwork differing from that used for other central air systems, so if you are renovating and there is a duct system in place, it may have to be modified to accommodate a heat pump system. Heat pumps are now required to have an HSPF of 6.8 and a SEER of at least 10. Some heat pumps have one-stage heating and cooling. Other units are available with two-stage cooling and three-stage heating, giving them a higher SEER rating. Having two stages allows the system to operate on a low speed most days, switching to another stage for additional comfort when needed.

Advantages

- With heat pumps, there is no furnace, boiler or plumbing, if air.
- It is a quiet system.
- This system is efficient and cost effective above 40 to 45 degrees.

Disadvantages

- Electricity can create a very dry heat.
- Resistant heat is expensive in most areas below 40 to 45 degrees.

Hydronic Air Systems

This is a system that sends hot water to one or more coils, and then a fan or blower forces the air over the coils and into one or more areas of the house. A heat-exchanger coil transfers the heat from the hot water to the air. Without fans or blowers, the heating system is a hydronic one, such as hot water convection radiator systems. This system allows the introduction of air-conditioning by using chilled water in lieu of the hot water. When air is blown over the coil, it is cooled and water condenses on the coil. That water then drips into the required condensate drip pan located under the coil. The condensate then drains to an appropriate connection. There are several versions of this type of system.

A heat exchanger and air blower in a distribution duct with a series of ducts delivers the heat to areas around the house. Many contractors will put together and install these systems. This is a quiet system because the heat is generated in the ducts. The retrofitting of a duct system into an existing house is reviewed on a site-specific basis. Some installations are easy and others are difficult or financially prohibitive.

In another type of system, the air is generated in a small fan-coil wall cabinet unit. Hot water is brought to a fan coil wall cabinet unit, which is like a radiator, except it has a fan or blower that forces the air through the heat coil or heat-exchanging coil and then exits the fan coil cabinet in the individual rooms. Hydro-air has a patented system like this. Each cabinet unit has a small blower (or fan) that pulls room air into the cabinet and blows the air over a heat/cooling coil; then the conditioned air is discharged into the room. This system eliminates the need for ducting and can be used for new construction or retrofitted in existing homes. Energy is moved through flexible plastic tubing (rather than ducts) to whichever rooms are to be heated or cooled. The small fan-coil cabinets thereby eliminate the ductwork needed for the former type system. The Hydro-air system is based on the original hydronic-air system that used fan-coil units; the units look like cabinet-style wall radiators. These units, usually located under the window, provide filtration (an intake to introduce fresh air) with a thermostatically controlled blower and fan-speed switching. These units run quietly.

Hot water can also be used to set up a hydronic heating system or it can be tempered for use in a radiant system in the floor and driveway. This system is designed to provide heating and cooling with the use of standard water heaters or boilers and standard outdoor condensers for chilled water or other refrigeration systems, provided condensation pans are installed and drained. The system, as well as others, can be used with any form of energy: solar, natural gas, electricity, oil, geothermal or essentially any fuel.

Advantages
- Hydronic air is a quiet system.
- Air is constantly filtered in the duct system because it is being circulated. The filtration is part of the blower section of the heat exchanger.
- It is potentially more resistant to mold or fungus growth, if it is maintained.
- It is easy to create zones with each having its own thermostat.
- It can be combined with a hydronic radiant floor system in the house and on the driveway.
- It does not require baseboard convection radiators.
- In most cases your furnace/boiler/hot water–maker can provide all the heating and hot water without a boiler.
- Walls and furniture are cleaner without dusty streaks on walls or drapes.
- It can be retrofitted in an old house.

- Heat is only delivered when required by the thermostat controlling the zone or space.

Disadvantages
- Not all installers are qualified to install.
- It requires a more complete zone-by-zone design analysis than a one-zone convection hot-water radiator system.
- Retrofitting a duct system can present more difficulties than Hydro-air.
- Access panels to the blower sections are needed in duct systems.
- The duct system requires return-air grilles so the air can recirculate for re-conditioning.
- The Hydro-air system is currently only available through wholesalers and sold as a packaged system.
- The Hydro-air fan-coil wall cabinet units may be noisy.
- The Hydro-air system does not provide for the filtration and humidification provided by the duct system.
- Not all local codes permit the use of plastic tubing. Many towns require copper tubing.

resources
For further information about Hydro-air, check www.popularhydronics.com or call 800-598-1019.

Solar
Solar energy has become increasingly popular over the last several years because of our concern for the environment and the preservation of our natural resources. Generally a solar system is used to augment a more conventional heating system because there are times when it may be difficult to collect enough heat. There are passive features that can be incorporated into the design of a house, such as the orientation of the house; the installation of south-facing windows in cold climate areas, which will warm the room; and the use of concrete with thermal mass, which can store up the heat and release it slowly. Large

overhangs can be used to block the sun in warm climates. More aggressive measures can be taken in the form of active solar heating. As discussed in the chapter on "Roofing" (see page 83), photovoltaic (PV) panels can be used to convert sunlight into electricity. Solar thermal technologies collect solar heat energy for direct heating of space and water and indirect production of electricity. Several methods can be used to capture the sunlight, to store it and then to distribute the energy where it is needed.

Advantages
- Solar energy is a renewable resource.
- It is clean.
- The fuel is free.

Disadvantages
- The system required for using solar energy may be expensive to set up.
- Solar energy cannot easily be stored up for a rainy day.
- Backup systems are required.

resources
For further information about solar energy, check the following Web sites: the U. S. Department of Energy (Energy Efficiency and Renewable Energy) at www.eere.energy.gov/power/consumer/hc_solar_spaceheating.html, the American Solar Energy Society (ASES) at www.ases.org and The Solar Energy Industries Association (SEIA) at www.seia.org. For renewable energy resources, check with Energy Resources at www.energy.sourceguides.com. The Web site of the Northeast Sustainable Energy Association at www.nesea.org offers many resources and links for those interested in green building and renewable energy. *Solar Today* is a bimonthly magazine that covers solar technologies, published by the American Solar Energy Society (ASES); the magazine can be ordered on www.solartoday.org. For additional information about solar heat, check the Web site of USA Solar at www.usasolar.net. For further information about heating systems, check with Heating Help.com at www.heatinghelp.com.

Air-Conditioning Systems

It hardly seems possible that just forty years ago air-conditioning was a novelty in the home. Today 80 percent of homeowners (according to the U.S. Census Bureau of 2000) have a form of air-conditioning. While in some areas of the country air-conditioning is rarely used, in others it is almost a necessity for most of the year. The federal government requires all new central air conditioners to have a minimum SEER rating of 10. Some systems have two compressors for two-stage cooling, to cool the house according to need.

resources
For a simple explanation of how air-conditioning works, check with How Stuff Works at www.home.howstuffworks.com/ac.htm.

Air-conditioning units with high efficiency ratings may be eligible for rebates in some municipalities. Check with your local utility company to find out about any available rebate programs.

Individual Air Conditioners
These can be installed in the walls or windows. Many older houses have this type of air-conditioning. When just a small area of the house needs cooling, this is a less expensive, though not as efficient, method. In mild climates, units should have an EER of at least 9.0; in hot climates they should have an EER over 10.

resources
For more information in determining the cooling capacity you require, check with the Association of Home Appliance Manufacturers at www.aham.org/cert/roomaircert.cfm.

Split Systems

How a ductless system works.

Split systems of air-conditioning are typically used in residential homes today. Part of the system is in the interior (evaporating coil) of the home and part is at the exterior (condensing unit). These two parts work together. They must be matched and when one part is faulty, they both should be replaced. The ducts that are used for a forced air heating system can be adapted for the air-conditioning. If another form of heat is used, then ducts will have to be installed for the air-conditioning. National minimum standards for central air conditioners, which will go into effect at the end of 2005, will require a SEER of 12 (units can, however, be purchased with SEER ratings up to 17). There are split systems designed for installation in individual rooms that require no ductwork. Most air-conditioning systems remove enough humidity from the air to be comfortable. For those people with allergies, dehumidifiers can be used to lower the humidity to a comfortable level of about 50 percent.

Some resources for air-conditioning systems:

Carrier	www.carrier.com
Mitsubishi Electric—Mr. Slim	www.mrslim.com
Panasonic	www.panasonic.ca
Sanyo	www.sanyo.com
Space Pak, Inc.	www.spacepak.com
Unico, Inc.	www.unicosystem.com
York	www.yorkupg.com

Packaged Units

There are also packaged units that include both parts of the air-conditioning system in one cabinet. These are placed either on the roof or on a concrete slab next to the house. Packaged systems often include electric heating coils or a natural gas furnace, eliminating the need for an indoor unit.

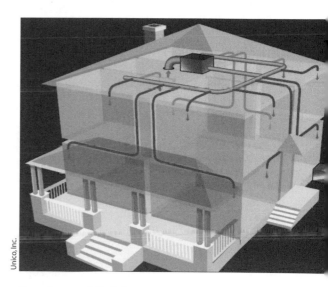

Unico, Inc.

Ductless or Mini-Duct

These are high-velocity air-conditioning systems that are a good choice for retrofitting air-conditioning in an older house. They can be used in a new construction as well. These systems have supply tubes or refrigerant lines that can be routed through ceilings, walls and floors much more easily than those used with typical ducts. They are split like traditional air-conditioning systems with outside components (condenser) and inside (evaporators) components but have inside units in all of the rooms for which the system will supply air-conditioning. A heat pump or hot water coil can be added to the system so it can function for heat as well.

resources

For further information about ductless air-conditioning and heating, contact the Air Conditioning and Refrigeration Institute at www.ari.org/consumer/ductless.

Evaporative Coolers or Swamp Coolers

These are other methods of cooling the air, which can only be used in hot and dry climates.

The air is pulled through a water-soaked pad by a blower, cooling the air and adding moisture. The air is then forced through ducts to ceiling-mounted registers. The cooling unit is mounted on top of the house and requires a water feed line connected to a water source. Evaporative coolers generally are used with a backup system for times when it is very hot (100 degrees or higher) and humid.

Whole-House Attic Fans

This type of fan is particularly efficient in areas with cool nights and hot days. In order to use a whole-house ventilation system, the house must have an attic and have adequate venting to exhaust the heat through the attic. Cool air in the evening is pulled in through open windows and screened doors, and warm air (along with the moisture) is exhausted through ceiling vents. Fans can be used alone or in conjunction with other forms of air-conditioning. Codes require that there be an access door to the attic fan in case of emergency. Adequate ventilation space is also necessary so all the air blown into the attic can escape. Fans can be wired to be operated manually or by a thermostat or humidistat. If the fans will be automatic, you must make sure to open windows and/or doors or the fan will not work properly. There are two types of whole-house fans available, direct drive (the fan blade assembly is fastened directly to the motor shaft) and belt-driven (a belt drive connects a pulley on the motor to a pulley on the fan blade) units. Belt-driven fans are the quietest because they have more blades, which means they have less work to do and can operate at a

slower speed. At the slower speed they are quieter. Whole-house fans use less electricity than air-conditioning, and the breezes created make the house feel cooler.

resources

Look for products that have been tested and certified by the Home Ventilating Institute (HVI) by checking their Web site at www.hvi.org.

Selecting an Air-Conditioning System

- Look for an Energy Star–qualified central air-conditioning unit. They have a higher SEER rating than standard models and are about 20 percent more efficient. They may be more costly units to purchase initially, but energy bills will be lower.
- Make sure the system is the correct size for the area of the house. It should not be larger than necessary. If it is, the system will cool the air quickly and not have time to efficiently remove the moisture from it. If the system is too small, the air will not be adequately cooled. Consider any additions that you may be anticipating, so the system you put in will still be adequate.
- Consider purchasing a cooling system with a two-speed or variable-speed motor which will allow the system to be operated at a lower or higher speed, depending on need. Operating the system at the lower speed will be more energy efficient than operating at the higher speed with the unit cycling on and off, and humidity will be removed more efficiently. In addition, the noise level will most likely be quieter at the lower speed.
- Keep outdoor compressors away from the sun so as not to overload the compressors' coils.
- Make sure there is a way to drain the condensed water.
- Check that the ducts are sealed, which will give the system better performance.
- Make sure ducts are properly sized to carry the proper airflow (heating and cooling) to the respective areas.

Some of the companies that sell attic fans:

Markel Products	www.tpicorp.com
Nutone	www.nutone.com
Superior Attic Fans	www.superioratticfans.com
Tamarach Technologies, Inc.	www.tamtech.com
Triangle Engineering	www.trianglefans.com

• The California HVAC Initiative High Efficiency Central Cooling and Heating Tier Specifications recommends a condensing unit and evaporation coil that meets Energy Star specifications. They offer a rebate for using specified equipment.

resources

Information on consumer energy is available at www.consumerenergycenter.org/rebate/index.php. Other states may have similar programs. Check with your local utility company to see if there are any rebate programs.

Ducts

Duct systems are made up of a network of tubes (air channels) in the walls, floors and ceilings that carry air from the furnace and central air-conditioning system to each of the rooms in the house. Many of the ducts today come with insulation already installed. It is also important that the ducts are well sealed to prevent air from seeping out of them. This is particularly important if the ducts will run through unconditioned areas (such as attics or garages) of the house where the heat and cool air will be lost, putting an added burden on the expense of heating and cooling the house. The number of elbows should be kept at a minimum and mechanical fasteners and sealants used at all joints. There are two materials gener-

ally used for the ducts. Both of these are usually fabricated in a shop and then brought to a house for installation.

• Fiberglass is quieter, sometimes assembled with staples and sealed with approved tape (UL 181 is the only accepted tape) or mastic (a caulking material) and fiberglass tape. Fiberglass is not as rugged as galvanized sheet metal.
• Galvanized sheet metal tends to be noisy, which can be reduced by lining duct interiors with insulating material that also deadens sound. This is usually required by code, especially for air-conditioning, preventing the loss of heat or in the case of cooling, condensation on the duct. Usually the only areas to be lined are those that will potentially cause the most noise (corners, the first 6 to 10 feet of return duct from the return air grille toward the furnace and so on). Metal ducts are assembled with stronger fasteners, including rivets.

Condensation Pump

These are small units that are rarely mentioned but are necessary in air-conditioning systems for removing the moisture by the condensate pan under the cooling coil. The pump is needed when the moisture cannot drain off by the force of gravity but must be pumped up and away to a drain. After several years they wear down and can produce a noise as the water is backed up. If they are not replaced they will automatically shut off, and if the moisture is not directed out of the house, a moisture pump could produce a flood. When your heating unit is periodically checked, have the condensation pump checked as well.

Backup Generators

If you have ever lived in an area where the power has gone off for several hours or several days at a time, you will understand the importance of having a backup generator. Many areas

Some of the suppliers of heating and cooling systems:

Carrier Corp.	www.carrier.com
Lennox Industries, Inc.	www.lennox.com
Mitsubishi Electric	www.mrslim.com
Rheem	www.rheemac.com
Trane	www.trane.com
Unico, Inc.	www.unicosystems.com
York	www.yorkupg.com

of the country have frequent power outages. The use of candles can be very dangerous with children in the house or people who are not steady on their feet and might have difficulty finding their footing in the dark. For those who work at home, a lack of power can mean several days of downtime. An excellent solution is the use of a backup generator, either portable or installed. Backup generators are simpler and less costly to install if the house has been prewired for them. Retrofitting a generator is possible; however, it will be a more difficult installation and more costly.

Considerations

- How much power will be required? Units are available in power output ranges from 800 watts to 1,500 kilowatts (a kilowatt is a thousand watts) or more. An electrician should be consulted to evaluate your household needs. You should consider how many items you will want powered by the backup unit—lights, refrigerator, heating units and so on. The more items included, the larger the unit will have to be.
- Will it be permanently installed or portable? Portable generators can be purchased at hardware stores and are fairly easy to use. An extension cord may be required and fuel to keep the generator going. Permanent automatic generators should be purchased from professional dealers experienced in installing generators. Power requirements must be assessed to determine the size of the system needed.
- How many items in the house will be powered by the generator? The essentials should be powered, such as the furnace, lights, security system, well and sump pump, refrigerator/freezer, air-conditioning and other items like computers and televisions.
- What fuel will be used to power the generator? It is best if the fuel source is one already being used in the house, such as natural or propane gas. If one of those is not being used, then the other options are gasoline, battery or diesel fuel. Gasoline will be very expensive and diesel fuel will get gummy in the generator if it is not used often. Gasoline generators are the least expensive to purchase but also run the loudest and wear out faster than diesel, propane or natural gas generators. Battery-operated units have the most limited running time.
- Will the unit be started automatically with a transfer switch or manually? Automatic units will go on within seconds of lost electricity on their own, even if you are not at home. Manual units must be turned on, which can be difficult in the dark and/or in stormy weather.
- How quiet should the unit be? Some of the newer models are substantially quieter than the older ones.

Parts of an Automatic Backup Generator

- A secondary panel with essential loads circuit
- Power cable and control wire
- Natural gas lines or propane tank—If the house already has natural gas lines, the generator can be connected to that system. If there is no natural gas available, a propane tank can be installed, which will have to be refilled periodically.
- Automatic transfer switch—The power switch automatically turns on the generator within seconds of the power outage. When the power is restored, the transfer switch turns off the generator, allowing the house to use the electrical source.
- Generator—These are available in a variety of sizes from 8.5 to 100 kilowatts. The size of the generator is determined by the size of the home and what components the homeowner wishes to have backed up. The lights, heat and sump pump (essential loads) or other things such as air-conditioning, computers and security system (whole load) can be backed up.

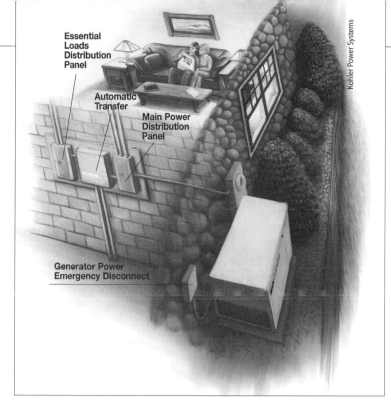
Essential Loads Distribution Panel

Automatic Transfer

Main Power Distribution Panel

Generator Power Emergency Disconnect

Kohler Power Systems

Some of the suppliers of backup generators:

Baldor Electric Co.	www.baldor.com
Coleman	www.colemanpowermate.com
Generac Power Systems, Inc.	http://www.generac.com
Kohler	www.kohler.com

A backup generator.

Accessories

- Mounting pad—Generally a cement pad is poured and the generator is placed on this. Some companies offer the generator with built-in mounting pads, eliminating the need to pour a cement slab, saving time and expense.
- Battery charger—Keeps the battery charged when it's not being used all the time. Generators can be set up to go on weekly or monthly, but a battery charger eliminates the need.

Be sure that whatever unit you purchase, you receive and read over the owner's manual so you are aware of the operating and maintaining procedures recommended for that generator.

Humidifiers

The more humid the air is, the warmer it feels. Adding humidity to dry air in the winter means less heat is needed because the house will feel warmer at a lower temperature. Dry air causes dry skin, cracked woodwork and static electricity and can contribute to sore throats and colds in the winter.

Particularly in the winter, humidifiers are needed to maintain an indoor humidity level of at least 30 percent; the optimal comfort range is 40 to 55 percent (as recommended by the EPA). Dry air in the house during the winter is principally the result of too much outside cold air getting into the heated space. The usual sources for this unwanted outside air are the many moving joints and seams of the doors and windows. A space will feel drafty because the cold outside air, when heated, becomes drier. Weather-stripping is the best measure to help stabilize humidity and save on energy costs; a humidifier is good for very cold, dry days.

It should be noted that an excess of humidity will encourage the growth of biological organisms that can cause allergic reactions, particularly for those with respiratory problems. Careful attention should be paid to achieving a healthy balance of humidity. This can be aided with the use of a hygrometer, which tells what the current relative humidity is and helps keep track of it.

Reasons It Is Important to Have Humidifiers

- People need a minimum humidity to help their bodies' immune systems defend against pollutants and irritants.
- Respiratory ailments (asthma, bronchitis, sinusitis) and dehydration of body fluids can be caused or aggravated by low humidity.
- Humid air feels warmer, requiring lower temperatures and reducing heating bills.
- Dry air can damage wood furniture, flooring and woodwork.
- Dry air creates static electricity.

Humidifiers are easy to install in homes with forced air and air-conditioning ductwork already in place. They are connected to the water supply, so moisture is available whenever it is needed. They are necessary with any type of heating system. In houses with hot-water heating systems or other types of systems, freestanding individual units can be used in those areas of the house. Whereas too little humidity will cause damage to furniture and may cause health issues, too much humidity will encourage the growth of mildew and mold.

There are several types of humidifiers, from the simple ones purchased in an electronics store to the more sophisticated models that are connected to the forced hot-air system.

Considerations

- Will the humidifier be connected to the heating/cooling unit (central) or be portable? Portable units encased in a cabinet for floor use are called "console humidifiers."
- How large is the area needing humidification (or how large is the entire house)? There are small units that can humidify a small room and whole-house units that can humidify an entire house. (A console model, centrally located, with doors open, will help throughout the house if kept filled with water. Humid air will go toward dry air.)
- How much maintenance are you prepared to do?
- Do you want a unit with a humidistat to control the amount of moisture circulated and to automatically shut off when the humidity has reached a comfortable level?
- Will you be adding rooms that may increase your need for humidification?
- What will the capacity of the unit be? (They hold from 2 gallons up to 12 gallons.)
- What is the warranty on the unit?

Types of Humidifiers

Portable Humidifiers

Humidifiers add moisture to the air and are sometimes combined with air cleaners to clean the air as well as humidify it. Some of these use high-efficiency particulate arrestance (HEPA) filters and others use UV light to kill germs and clean the air; some units use both methods. Some units that are humidifier and purifier combinations allow you to shut off the humidifier function when it is not needed while the purifier continues to work. There are several types of humidifiers available.

Vaporizer—This uses boiling water to humidify the air by dispensing it as steam. Keep in mind that the hot water and steam can cause burns and allergic reactions. Vaporizers do not, however, disperse substantial amounts of minerals, as some other systems do.

Warm mist—Water is heated to the boiling point and mixed with cooled air before being expelled as steam. There is still a risk of burns from the boiling water.

Impeller—A cool mist is produced by means of a high-speed rotating disk. These units spray out microorganisms and minerals (as white dust) into the air, since there is no filtering mechanism. A possible solution for this is to use distilled water, which contains a lower mineral content, and a filtration system, if available.

Ultrasonic or cool mist—This creates a cool mist with high-frequency vibrations. Ultrasonic humidifiers discharge minerals (as white dust) and microorganisms from the water tank into indoor air, which can cause an inflammation of the lungs. A possible solution is to use distilled water, which contains a lower mineral content, and a filtration system, if available.

Evaporative—This transmits moisture into the air using a fan to blow air through a moistened absorbent material such as a wick, belt or filter, releasing the water vapor into the room. It is not expected to disperse substantial amounts of minerals. (It has not been tested by the EPA for mineral dispersal.)

To alleviate potential problems, be sure to follow all manufacturers' recommendations, and for portable units, take care to empty the tank daily, clean it as directed, keep it out of the reach of small children and do not allow areas around the humidifier to become damp. If the unit contains a filter, it should be changed twice a season, when it begins to have a musty smell, or when directed by the manufacturer.

Advantages
- Portable humidifiers are easy to locate.
- They are simple to operate.
- They are portable.
- Some humidifiers have a night light built in.
- They do not require professional installation.
- Many have automatic shut-off valves to protect the motor from burning out when it runs out of water.
- They tend to be inexpensive.
- They prevent the particles in the air from being stirred up; the humidity keeps much of it on the floor.
- Some humidifiers have a medicine cup accessory for optional blending of respiratory medications with the moisture.
- Some units have two or three speeds to adjust as needed.

Some of the companies that manufacture portable humidifiers:

Bemis	www.bemis-store.com
Hamilton Beach True Air	www.trueair.com
Hunter	www.hunterfan.com
Kenmore	www.sears.com
Slant-Fin	www.slantfin.com
Venta-Airwasher	www.venta-airwasher.com.

Disadvantages
- They require regular maintenance.
- Some of them are noisy.
- They can only humidify a small area.
- Some humidifiers may dispense pollutants and minerals into the air.
- Replacement filters may not be readily available.
- In areas where there is hard water, the sponge or wick, in some units, must be replaced periodically or sediments will clog the filter.

Some of the suppliers of humidifiers:

Aprilaire	www.aprilaire.com
Carrier Corp.	www.carrier.com
Desert Spring Air	www.dspingair.com
Kenmore	www.sears.com
Lennox	www.lennox.com
Venta-Airwasher	www.venta-airwasher.com

Whole-House or Central Humidifiers

They are usually installed on a forced-air system. There are two types of systems used—steam or vapor/evaporative, both of which are also used in the portable units. There are varied mechanisms that take the air that is heated, pick up moisture and turn it into vapor, then fan the water vapor through ducts throughout the house. A humidistat is generally included to control the amount of moisture in the air. Most humidifiers feature an adjustable humidistat so you can control the exact amount of moisture in the air. The proper amount of moisture depends on the outdoor temperature and other factors. Most units are connected to the central water tank so there is a constant supply. The owner's manual has recommendations for the best settings for the conditions required in your house.

Advantages

- Whole-house humidifiers require minimal maintenance. Since they are attached to the water supply, they don't have to be refilled; they fill automatically.

Disadvantages

- They must be inspected and cleaned periodically and shut off for the summer.
- Water can be blown into the duct system, wasting the water and also possibly contributing to mold and mildew in the ducts.

Dehumidifiers

Dehumidifiers run on electricity and are used to take moisture out of the air in areas of high humidity where the moisture can lead to health problems (particularly for those with allergies), to discourage the growth of mold and mildew and for the comfort of everyone in the house. In most homes where there is central air-conditioning, that system alleviates enough of the moisture so as not to be a problem. However, some air-conditioning systems may not have the capacity to remove enough moisture and an additional dehumidifier may be necessary. High relative humidity may be problematic for those with allergies, and dehumidifiers can be used to lower the humidity about 15 percent to a more comfortable 50 percent. (The growth of mold, mildew and bacteria are accelerated in environments with a relative humidity over 55 percent, where there may also be dust and dirt present.) In homes without central air-conditioning, moisture can be a problem without some form of dehumidification. In certain areas of the house, such as basements, which are cooler than the other parts of the house although the specific humidity is the same, the relative humidity is higher because the cooler air is capable of holding less moisture, and the room can feel very damp or wet. Particularly during the hot and damp parts of the year, basements may then require a dehumidifier. They can be placed

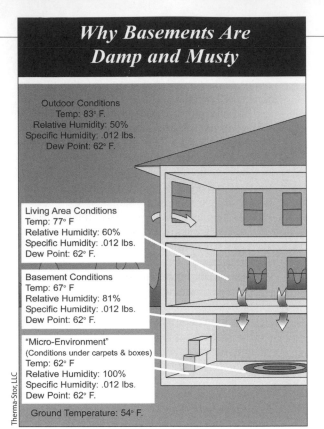

Why Basements Are Damp and Musty

Outdoor Conditions
Temp: 83° F.
Relative Humidity: 50%
Specific Humidity: .012 lbs.
Dew Point: 62° F.

Living Area Conditions
Temp: 77° F
Relative Humidity: 60%
Specific Humidity: .012 lbs.
Dew Point: 62° F.

Basement Conditions
Temp: 67° F
Relative Humidity: 81%
Specific Humidity: .012 lbs.
Dew Point: 62° F.

"Micro-Environment"
(Conditions under carpets & boxes)
Temp: 62° F
Relative Humidity: 100%
Specific Humidity: .012 lbs.
Dew Point: 62° F.

Ground Temperature: 54° F.

Therma-Stor, LLC

in specific areas where they are needed or can be used for the entire house, if necessary. There are several items to consider when purchasing a dehumidifier:

- How large is the space to be dehumidified? Units should be selected on the size of the area to be covered. Units can cover areas as small as 400 square feet up to 2,500 square feet. Although not always considered, the cubic footage of the room should be a consideration along with the square footage. If a ceiling is 10 feet instead of 8 feet, for example, approximately 20 percent more space will need to be dehumidified in that area. Before purchasing a dehumidifier, evaluate the width, length and height of the room.
- What is the water removal capacity? Units have the capacity to extract 25 to 106 pints per day of water.

- How portable are dehumidifiers? There are units that are wheel mounted with hand grips for easy moving. Ducts can be used with other units with the forced-air system. Some units have optional duct kits available.
- What are the operating temperatures? Units operate at various temperatures from 44 to 105 degrees. The units that operate at higher temperatures are able to remove more moisture than those that operate at lower temperatures.
- What about an adjustable humidistat? Some units come with a humidistat to control the amount of moisture removed from the air and will cycle the unit off and on to maintain a selected level of humidity.
- What kind of air filter will be used? Some units include air filters to remove particles from the air and prevent bacterial buildup. Some can be used with HEPA filters, while others cannot. Some filters can be washed and are reusable; others must be used and discarded.
- Are they noisy? Some units have foam insulation to keep the operation quieter. Others have optional muffler kits.
- What fan speed is best? Double fan speeds allow for quieter operation at a lower speed, which would be necessary in the bedroom, for example, and at higher speeds in the basement where noise may not be a factor.
- When will the unit turn off? The unit will automatically shut off when the tank is full or if there is an obstruction blocking the continuous drainage system. Some will have indicator lights showing when the tank is full. Other tanks are transparent so that you can tell how full they are.
- How about the automatic anti-frost sensors? The unit will shut off if it detects frost buildup.
- How will the unit drain? Units have different methods of discharging the water. Some units require manual emptying of a removable bucket, some use a gravity drain hose or a condensate pump (with some units they are optional; others are built-in) for continuous dis-

A few of the companies that manufacture dehumidifiers:

Comfort-Aire	www.comfort-aire.com
De'Longhi	www.delonghiusa.com
Ebac Industrial Products, Inc.	www.ebacusa.com
Fedders	www.fedders.com
Therma-Stor Products (Santa Fe)	www.thermastor.com
Whirlpool	www.whirlpool.com
W. C. Wood	www.wcwood.com

charge, and some are available with both options. See if they come with a duct kit for drainage.
- Where will air discharge be? Some units have air going in and coming out from the same side, out of both sides or out of the top, allowing the unit to be placed against a wall.
- Are dehumidifiers energy efficient? Those units that have the Energy Star rating from the EPA are more energy efficient.
- What about warranty? Check to see what warranty comes with the unit. Most units have a one-year warranty, but some go up to five years.

Ventilation

Because current construction techniques make houses so airtight, air exchange is limited and polluted air can be trapped inside. Modern construction methods geared at energy efficiency have created the problem of limited air exchange. Houses can have unhealthy gases from construction materials, the earth below and from the exhaled carbon dioxide from the people in the house. All houses need ventilation to exchange the inside air, which has moisture, odors and contaminants (such as formaldehyde, VOCs, and radon) with the outside air. The accumulation of contaminants can cause health problems in houses that are poorly ventilated. Unpleasant odors can linger in the house as well. Another problem in modern homes is negative air pressure. This happens when the pressure in the house is less than the pressure outside. This can be caused when fans are used in bathrooms, clothes dryers, attics and over ovens, drawing air out of the house. In order to equalize the pressure, combustion air and vent gases can be pulled in from a furnace or fireplace, bringing toxic gases into the living area. Having an adequate ventilation system can prevent this problem.

Natural ventilation—Years ago people left doors and windows open, which brought in a continuous flow of fresh air. Because of air-conditioning and heating, and our desire for privacy, this is no longer a popular method of ventilating in many parts of the country. Many houses today are airtight because of more efficient windows and doors that do not allow for air infiltration. Other methods of ventilation are then required.

Spot ventilation—Exhaust fans, most commonly used in kitchens and bathrooms, remove pollutants at the source. Even if a whole-house ventilation system is used, localized fans are needed to remove pollutants when and where they are required.

Whole-house ventilation—There are several types of systems to remove stale air from the house and bring in fresh air. The following section includes some methods for ventilating the whole house.

Air Exchangers or Air-to-Air Exchangers

Air exchangers expel the old air with its excess moisture, mold spores, gases (carbon dioxide and radon), airborne particles and VOCs (odors from cooking and pets), and they bring fresh outside air into the house. It is important to maintain a healthy humidity level and to create an environment where the house is allowed to breathe. Opening a window or door would alleviate the problem, but it would also cause the loss of heated and cooled air. An air exchanger brings in fresh air, removes stale air and transfers the heat or cooling to the fresh air drawn in, minimizing wasted energy. It does not mix the airstreams, and it maintains the energy efficiency of the heating and cooling system. The heat energy is transferred to the incoming cold air with up to 80 percent of the energy exchanged. Some units have built-in humidistats that automatically increase the air exchange when humidity rises. This helps prevent condensation on windows and potential buildup of mold and mildew on walls from an excess of moisture. Units generally have drains to remove the moisture accumulated during the energy exchange. Condensate pumps may also be installed to eject the drain water away. Units can be controlled with on-off switches or humidistats can be used to turn the machine on. Operation should be continuous so the low volume of fresh air brought in and expelled will create a healthier environment. Air exchangers come with five- to ten-year warranties. There are two types of air exchangers available.

Heat-recovery ventilators (HRVs)—These are usually used in cooler climates (with a longer heating season than cooling season); they exhaust stale air from the home and bring in fresh air from the outside. In the winter the heat in the outgoing air is transferred to the incoming, and in the summer the air-conditioned air cools the warmer incoming air. Filters may be included to minimize the entry of pollen, dust and insects. HRVs are designed to work all year long, and some models include defrosters for use in extremely cold climates. Units are available with independent ductwork or can be incorporated in existing forced-air heating and cooling systems. Filters should be changed periodically, and the appliance manual should be referred to when a filter change is needed. Many people recommend HRVs in the North because often with new construction many homes have too much moisture because the building products used need time to dry out. An HRV will have a better dehumidifying effect than an ERV during these months after the home is built. However, once the home dries out there is typically a need to preserve moisture during the winter and repel moisture during the summer (reduced humidity brought into the home lightens the air-conditioning load).

Energy-recovery ventilators (ERV)—They are designed for use in either warm or cooler climates and have the added benefit of moisture transfer. This can be beneficial in any climate because it will help control indoor relative humidity. In the heating season, an ERV will help to preserve essential moisture in the home while keeping it below excessive levels, and during the cooling season it minimizes the added moisture that the incoming airsteam may contain.

Some ventilators have three modes:

Recirculation mode—Recycles indoor air continuously and exchanges air only when humidity exceeds the desired level.

Continuous mode—The unit replaces indoor air with fresh outdoor air twenty-four hours a day.

Intermittent mode—The unit turns on only when humidity levels exceed the desired level. This is the most economical mode.

resources

For further information about heat and energy recovery ventilators, as well as other ventilating products, contact the Home Ventilating Institute (HVI) at www.hvi.org or call 847-394-0150.

Ventilation Control Systems

These systems provide fresh air to the home and cycle the air throughout the house for more even distribution. The HVAC equipment is used to draw outdoor air into the home through a fresh-air duct and uses the house ducts to distribute the air. A control monitors the run time of the equipment and opens a damper in the fresh-air duct to meet the desired amount of fresh air. If the HVAC equipment has been idle for a period of time or has not run long enough, the control (of the ventilation control system) will turn on the blower to assure the desired amount of ventilation to the home.

In addition, some systems regulate dampers to limit ventilation in extreme humidity and temperature situations. Aprilaire's patented system "knows" when the air handler is running, so combined with the temperature/humidity sensor, it

Some of the companies that offer air-exchanger systems:

American Aldes Ventilation Corp.	www.americanaldes.com
Aprilaire	www.aprilaire.com
Carrier Corp.	www.residential.carrier.com
Fantech, Inc.	www.fantech.net
Grantair (C)	www.nilan.com
Heatilator	www.airventilators.com
Nutech Brands, Inc. (C)	www.lifebreath.com
Venmar Ventilation, Inc.	www.venmar-ventilation.com
York	www.yorkupg.com

(C) = Canadian

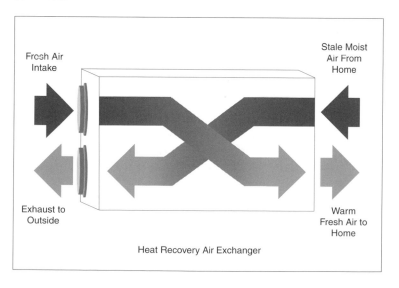

Fresh Air Intake

Stale Moist Air From Home

Exhaust to Outside

Warm Fresh Air to Home

Heat Recovery Air Exchanger

Some suppliers of ventilation control systems:

Aprilaire	888-257-8801	www.aprilaire.com
Lipidex Corp	781-834-1600	www.aircycler.com
Tamarack Technologies, Inc.	800-222-5932	www.tamtech.com

will bring in the right kind of air (in terms of humidity and temperature) as well as the right amount. This allows you to manage the quality of air, moderating the extremes of temperature and humidity allowed by other approaches.

Systems are controlled with a control pad and can be set to ventilate for a certain amount of time (from zero to sixty minutes) in any given period (ranging from one to twenty-four hours), varying by unit. Some units come with a lithium battery to save the settings in case of a power outage. The damper leading to the outside will open up (according to instructions given on the control pad), allowing air to come inside. The controller is wired to the air handler. The air handler draws the air in and disburses it through the house through the ductwork system. Unlike the air-exchange system, the ventilation-control system will not warm or cool the air coming indoors. It will, however, bring in fresh air and equalize the air pressure in the house. Ventilation-control systems are substantially less expensive than air-exchange systems; however, there are additional fuel costs associated with them because the air coming in is not cooled or heated.

resources

For further information about ventilation-control systems, log on to Toolbase Services of the NAHB Research Center at www.toolbase.org. For additional information about ventilation in the home, check with the Energy Efficiency and Renewable Energy Clearinghouse (EREC) at www.eren.doe.gov or call 800-363-3732 or the U.S. Department of Energy Oak Ridge National Laboratory at www.ornl.gov/btc or call 865-574-5206.

Air Cleaners or Purifiers

Air cleaners or purifiers are used to remove a variety of contaminants in the air, including odors, pollen, allergens and dust. They can be used most easily as an accessory added to the air-handling unit, as a method of purifying the airstream of the forced-air and central air-conditioning systems. The air handler comes with a one-inch filter that is changed according to the manufacturers' recommendation. This filter traps less than 20 percent of the particulates in the air. With air cleaners, those filters are eliminated because they discard so little of the particulates and also because they add unnecessary resistance to the system. When a house is equipped with other than forced-air systems, individual air cleaners can be used in rooms where they are needed. Air cleaners not only clean the majority of the microscopic airborne pollutants that we breathe but also allow for efficient operation of the heating or cooling system by keeping exchangers and blowers clean. They are excellent for those with allergies and asthma.

Considerations

Portable verses connection to the heat/cooling system—Portable units are only able to clean the air in the room in which they are placed. Air cleaners attached to the air handler are able to clean the air in the entire house.

Type of filtration—There are several types of systems used with air cleaners. There are mechanical, electronic and combinations of both. If you select mechanical units with filters, find out how difficult it is to remove the filter—some will just slide out; others require a screw driver and a bit more work.

- HEPA-filtered units—These are 99.97 percent effective in trapping particulates from the airstream. Because they are so restrictive, they generally are equipped with fans to force the air through. This type of system is usually used for people with severe medical conditions; they may be considered overkill for most other people. These filtered systems are considered "depth loading" systems because particulates are getting trapped in the pleats of the filter.

- HEPA-type air-cleaning systems—These use pleated-filter media that trap most of the particulates, although not as much as required by HEPA filters. They will collect particulates which are .35 microns, smaller than the 10 microns visible to the human eye. Because these filters have folds, their surfaces are increased, expanding the amount of time they can be used without replacing them. The filter should be changed according to the manufacturer's recommendations.

- Electrostatic systems—These have pleated-filter media but also have an ionizing grid that charges the particulate and is collected by the grounded filter, which draws the particulate to it. With this type of system, changing the filter is the only maintenance required. The most efficient electronic air cleaners will trap particulates down to virus-size, .01 microns.

- Electronically charged units—These do not have filters. They have metal plates which are electrically charged, attracting the particulates and trapping them. This type of system is called "surface loading" because the particulate is trapped on the surface of the plate rather than in the depths of the filter. Maintenance is more rigorous with this type of system since the plate must be cleaned or vacuumed every few months. Some units also make a popping or snapping sound. When selecting a unit, ask about any anticipated noise associated with it.

- UV light—Some electronic air cleaners also wash the air with UV light to help kill airborne microorganisms.

Air changes per hour—These vary by unit.

Some of the manufacturers of air purifiers:

Allerair (C)	www.allerair.net
Amaircare (C)	www.amaircare.com
Aprilaire	www.aprilaire.com
Austin Air Systems, Ltd.	www.austinair.com
Blueair, Inc.	www.blueair.com
Carrier Corporation	www.carrier.com
Clean Water Revival (CWR)	www.cwrenviro.com
De'Longhi	www.delonghiusa.com
Fantech, Inc.	www.fantech.net
IQ Air	www.iq-air.biz
Lennox Industries, Inc.	www.lennox.com
Slant-fin	www.slantfin.com
Trane	www.trane.com

(C) = Canadian

The warranty—Units come with one- to five-year warranties.

Energy efficiency—Those that meet HEPA standards trap 95 percent or more particles.

Considerations for Portable Units

- How large are portable units? It depends on the size of the area the unit will cover. Units vary in their capacity.
- How loud is the unit?
- How often are filters changed?
- How are these units transported? They have casters to move them around.
- What speeds are available? Some have several speeds.
- How convenient are portable units? Remote control is available with some units.

resources

For more information on air cleaners, check the U.S. Environmental Protection Agency's article "Indoor Air Quality" at www.epa.gov/iaq/is-imprv.html.

Water Heaters

Hot water tanks are the most popular method of having hot water in the home. Tanks range in capacity from 20 to 120 gallons, and in some large homes two tanks are used. Hot water is released from the top of the tank and cold water enters from the bottom to replace it. The water is constantly in the tank and periodically reheated, thus wasting some energy (called "standby heat loss"). Tanks are now available with less standby heat loss and are therefore less expensive to operate. EnergyGuide labels are affixed to every tank, indicating the energy efficiency ratings. The National Alliance Energy Conservation Act (NAECA) has established minimum energy factors for water-heating equipment used in residential applications.

Considerations

Type of fuel to be used—Tanks are available to run on gas, propane, electricity or solar energy.

Solar water heating—Solar water heating is becoming increasingly popular, with a variety of systems available. Although the initial investment is higher for solar water heaters, the fuel is free, with a substantial energy savings, and the systems are environmentally friendly. Often a backup system is needed to supplement the solar energy, in which case fossil fuel or electricity is used. Sunlight is absorbed within a solar collector or a storage tank. The collector most often used in residential structures is a flat-plate collector, which is an insulated box containing a dark absorber plate under one or more transparent or translucent covers. A heat-transfer fluid or the potable water flows through tubes attached to the absorber and picks up its heat. The heated water is then stored in a tank.

resources

For more information about solar water heating, contact the U.S. Department of Energy (Energy Efficiency and Renewable Energy) at www.eere.energy.gov/erec/factsheets/solr-watr.html and the American Solar Energy Society (ASES) at www.ases.org. For renewable energy resources, check the Web site of Energy Resources at www.energy.sourceguides.com. Also check for companies in your area under "solar energy" in the telephone directory and inquire at the Solar Energy Industries Association (SEIA) at www.seia.org whether they are a member of one of their chapters. Another resource for companies is Solaraccess at www.solaraccess.com.

The capacity of the tank—Each tank is required to have an EnergyGuide label which lists the first-hour rating (FHR). This rating tells how much hot water the heater will deliver during a busy hour. Consider what your needs will be in peak hours, perhaps in the morning, when the entire family will be showering. Gas water heaters have higher FHR ratings than electric water heaters of the same storage capacity. They typically come in 30-, 40-, and 50-gallon sizes and larger in new construction.

The energy efficiency of the tank—The Energy Factor (EF) is the best indicator of a heater's energy efficiency. It is determined by how efficiently the heater uses fuel (gas or electric) and retains heat during standby. There are many levels of energy efficiency within each category of water heater; a natural gas unit should have an EF of at least 0.6, and an electric unit should have an EF of at least 0.91. This is based on the recovery efficiency, which is how quickly the fuel transfers heat to the water, or the percentage of heat that is lost during standby times compared to the heat content of the water. Energy-efficient units use less natural gas or electricity to heat and store water mostly because of the greater amount of insulation put around the tanks. They should have at least 1.5 inches (3.8 centimeters) of foam insulation.

When purchasing a water heater compare not only the EF ratings but also the water storage capacity, making sure the units use the same fuel. Some utility companies offer a rebate for purchasing an energy-efficient water tank. Check with your local utility company to see if they make any such offers or check on their Web site to see if they list qualifying units.

The venting of the tank—Since most tanks are retrofitted into an existing house, most water heaters are standard vent systems. If, however, you are building a new house or have the option to relocate the water heater, you might consider one of the other ducting types.

- Standard vent—Most houses have a chimney, and the exhaust from the heater goes into the chimney. In this unit internal air from the house is used for combustion. One of the problems with this type of system is that already-warmed or -cooled air is used for the unit. This takes away from the energy efficiency of the unit.
- Direct vent—These units have a concentric pipe (one inside the other) system venting horizontally or vertically that draws air in for combustion and vents noxious air to the outside. Like a standard venting system, this type of unit must be close to the wall.
- Power vent—There is a fan at the top of the heater that expels the products of combustion out through a vent in the wall or the roof. Depending on the manufacturer, units can be vented up to about 80 feet from the heater.

With this type of system there is flexibility in placing the water heater, but it uses internal air for combustion. If there is a power outage, this type of water heater will not operate.

- Power-direct vent—These units can be farther from the wall and do not require a chimney. The exhaust is expelled by the fan, which can be at a distance from the unit, and external air is used for combustion. The fan can be noisy, but with the flexibility of placement, the vent can be located away from the unit to obscure the noise. This unit will also not function in a blackout. Therefore, any of the power-venting methods should be installed in a fail-safe manner so the heater continues to work safely, although not as efficiently. Note: New houses by code must provide outside air for combustion.

Cost of the tank—Always a consideration is the cost of the tank and its upkeep.

Special features—Tanks typically begin to leak from the corrosive action of lime buildup inside the tank. Some tanks are designed with self-cleaning features to help prevent minerals from attaching to the tank walls.

The warranty offered—Tanks today with longer warranties cost more up-front and generally cost less to operate. Warranties generally range from six- to twelve-years extended.

Indirect Storage Tank

With a boiler, an indirect storage tank is commonly used, which stores heated water from the boiler. The boiler is the heating mechanism and no additional heater is required. These tanks are most often used with oil boilers but sometimes with gas boilers as well. Tanks will hold from 30 to 120 gallons of water. As the water is used, it is immediately replaced. This is a more energy-efficient method of heating domestic water.

Some of the companies that manufacture water heaters:

AO Smith	www.hotwater.com
American Water Heater Co.	www.americanwaterheater.com
Bradford-White Corp.	www.bradfordwhite.com
Kenmore	www.sears.com
Lochinvar Corp.	www.lochinavar.com
Rheem	www.rheem.com

Tankless Water Heaters and Point-of-Use

Tankless water heaters and point-of-use are two other ways of getting hot water for use in the house. These are both ways of conserving energy and reducing water-heating costs. Some areas offer incentives to homeowners and/or builders for installing these systems. Check with the local utility to see if these are available in your area.

- The tankless water heater is a unit that hangs on a wall and turns on when a hot-water faucet is opened. It heats the water as it passes through a heating chamber and then goes to the pipe on the way to the faucet. When hot water is not being used, the heating elements turn themselves off. There is no storage of water in this unit; the energy that is consumed is only for the hot water that is used. The heaters can function at a variety of temperatures, which can be selected by the user. They come in a variety of sizes and vary in their capacities. Some can supply one major hot water outlet (bathtub, shower, washing machine) at a time and some can supply two. They are available in natural gas, liquid propane or electrical models. They must be professionally installed so they can be connected to the gas lines (and also adequately vented) or electrical circuitry needed for electrical models. Tankless water heaters cost more than typical 40-gallon water-heater tanks, but they generally have longer warranties (ten to fifteen years) and save money in the long run in energy bills.

- Point-of-use water heaters are installed at the point of use for a sink or two sinks or more, depending on the model selected. They will supply an endless stream of water for the units indicated. These avoid the wait and running of water while the water heats up. These units are all electric and should also be professionally installed. They generally have a three- to six-year warranty.

resources

For further information about these types of water heaters, check the Web site of two of the distributors of tankless and point-of-use hot water heaters: Controlled Energy Corporation, at www.controlledenergy.com or call 800-503-5028 and Envirotech Systems Worldwide, Inc., at www.tankless.com or call 800-251-6612. Another company to check with is Rinnai Corporation at www.foreverhotwater.com or call 866-746-6241. There are many other distributors of tankless water heaters and point-of-use heaters that can be found on the Internet or in the phone book.

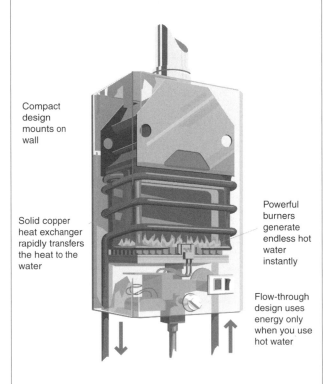

Compact design mounts on wall

Solid copper heat exchanger rapidly transfers the heat to the water

Powerful burners generate endless hot water instantly

Flow-through design uses energy only when you use hot water

Controlled Energy Corp.

A tankless gas water heater.

Information can also be found at the U.S. Department of Energy (Energy Efficiency and Renewable Energy) at www.eere.energy.gov/ buildings/components/waterheating/demand.cfm.

Energy Efficiency

Purchase heating and cooling systems that are energy efficient. Some heating and cooling products qualify for Energy Star labels, meaning they are recognized as energy efficient by the EPA. These units are sometimes more expensive, but they are more energy efficient than other similar products. The long-term energy savings may make up for the added expense of the product in a short time. The California Public Utility Commission offers rebates to California residents who install products that meet specified efficiency levels that may be similar or higher than Energy Star requirements. Other states may have similar programs.

Two other companies to check with are Rinnai Corporation at www.foreverhotwater.com or call 866-746-6241 and Takagi Industrial Company USA, Inc., at www.takagi.com or 888-882-5244.

resources

For more information about the California Energy Efficiency Rebate and Demand Reduction Program, check http://www.consumerenergy-center.org/rebate/index.php.

- Close blinds, shades and curtains in the summer, where the sun may be heating up the room.
- Leave blinds, shades and curtains open in the fall to take advantage of the sunlight to add warmth to the house.
- Close off rooms that are not being used so heat and cool air are not escaping to those areas.
- Use exhaust fans to pull hot air outside the house.
- Use ceiling fans to move the air and make the room cooler in summer and push the warm air (which rises) down to the living area.
- Make sure there are no obstructions by the outside air-conditioning units, which would impede exhaust of warm air.
- Set air conditioners to low when no one is at home.
- Change filters regularly on air and heating units.

Chadworth's 1.800 COLUMNS, designed by Kaki Hockersmith

Trim

Most of the other chapters in this book deal with necessary items needed to complete the house. Trim is a bit different; it is not generally used out of necessity but for enhancement of the design. Trim varies by style, period, budget and individual taste. Sometimes it is chosen for a functional need—to hide a joint where two materials meet, such as where flooring and walls meet, or to protect walls from scratches and dents, as in the case of chair rails. It can be used to define a particular space, by dividing a wall or ceiling, or to set a mood. My own house has beams and wood trim to add warmth to a great room that started out very cold and sterile. Most of the time, trim is a decorative element, chosen because it is consistent with a particular style and period. Trim can add to the beauty of the house and increase its monetary value. In some homes, trim may be used extensively and in others just minimally.

When you are starting to work on the design of your house, take pictures of any trim you see that you like. Often trim can be duplicated by a local mill or craftsman. If possible, plan for trim in the initial stages of designing the house, so it can be easily incorporated into the construction budget and scheduling. It is best to discuss trim preferences with the architect and/or interior designer working on the house so that the trim is an intrinsic part of the plan and well suited for the design. Often it is left up to the builder, and the owners do not get the quality or design they prefer. Whoever is selecting the trim should be well trained in this aspect of design since there are so many options now available.

Columns and molding enhance this beautiful setting.

Common Types

Molding

Molding comes in a variety of shapes and sizes and may be plain or decorative. There are S-shaped moldings called "ogee," and there are round (closet pole), half-round (used for edge-banding shelving, covering joints and as decorative surface trim) and quarter-round (used to trim inside and outside corners and as cleats for light shelving) moldings. Cove molding has a concave profile and is usually used where two members meet at a right angle; it has a rounded inside corner. There are numerous profiles available. Some of the more popular decorative molding styles include the following:

Egg and dart—Trim composed of alternating ovals and arrowheads, or darts. From the classical Greek meaning, the oval egg shape is said to represent life, and the dart represents death. This trim can be very large for crown molding or very small for decorative accent molding and can be used in many types of applications.

Dentil—A series of small square blocks uniformly spaced and projecting like teeth. They are available in a wide variety of shapes and sizes. The blocks and cuts can vary in size and shape: the cuts can be along one or two axes; the molding may be profiled, square or rectangular. They can be difficult to paint in the cut areas.

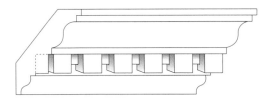

Rope—Trim that resembles a twisted rope. The most popular is a half-round trim with three strand configurations that looks like hemp rope. This is also available in $1/4$ and $3/4$ rounds in many different rope styles in crown molding and chair rails.

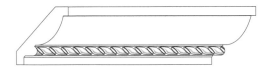

Acanthus leaf—A leaf motif coming from the *Acanthus spinosus* plant, it was first introduced as ornamentation in ancient Greek architecture. It has been changed and refined in different periods and cultures; it is now represented in a wide variety of designs and sizes.

Sometimes several moldings are used together for a more elaborate or grander look. Molding is usually identified by where it is used on the wall, although some are used in more than one location, such as baseboard molding that can also be used at the bottom of a wall and as trim around the door.

Crown molding (cornice, ceiling or crown-and-bed molding)—Covers the intersection of the wall and ceiling. It can also be used at the top edge of cabinetry that does not reach the ceiling.

Baseboard molding—Covers the intersection of the floor and the wall. It sometimes covers gaps between the floor and the wall and also protects the bottom of the wall from wet mops and vacuum cleaners.

Arch molding—This is a preformed half-round arch that surrounds half-round windows or pediments (the topmost member of a formal entryway).

Picture molding—This is installed high on a wall and can be used to hang artwork.

Cove molding—This is molding with a concave profile and is used primarily where two members meet at a right angle; it creates a rounded inside corner.

Corner molding—This is used to trim interior and exterior corners.

Cornice molding—Prominent horizontal projecting molding that is located where the ceiling or roof and wall meet. Several moldings are often combined to create a grander cornice.

Radius molding—Similar to arch molding, it goes over oval fixtures such as windows, mirrors and so on. It goes on items with definite beginnings and endings, 360 degrees around. It makes the item look more complete and brings attention to it.

Trim

Base shoes—These are quarter-round trims that fit between the floor and the baseboard, covering possible gaps between the two.

Base caps—Used at the top of plain, flat baseboard molding as trim and to hide gaps between the baseboard and the wall.

Chair rails—These are generally installed about one third of the way up from the floor and are used to protect the wall from backs of chairs or to separate two different materials on the wall, such as wainscoting and wallpaper or two different paint colors. Chair rails can also serve as an ornamental cap for wainscoting or paneling.

Casings—These form a frame around windows and doors, hiding the junction between the jamb and adjacent wall. These moldings can be mitered together or butted together for a more informal look. They can be made of an individual molding or a series of moldings.

Handrails—These are installed on one or both sides of stairs and can be very simple or elaborate.

Corbels—A massive horizontal bracket or block projecting from the face of a wall that supports a cornice, beam, shelf, balcony, mantel or arch.

Brackets—Similar to corbels but are typically narrower in width.

Wainscoting—This is paneling, tongue-and-groove planks or other material used on the lower portion of a wall between the baseboard and the chair rail. It is used for decorative purposes. Some wainscoting is solid wood and some is a **veneer** over engineered wood or wheatboard core (recycled wheat straw). Veneer over solid wood or plywood is also available. The engineered wood is more stable than natural wood, less susceptible to expansion and contraction, and more environmentally friendly.

Post and beams—These are generally structural components used in timberframe or post-and-beam construction. Sometimes, however, timbers can be used for decorative purposes and are nonstructural. There are also urethane foam timbers that can be made to simulate the look of timbers in any size and detail.

Right: Truss in expanded polystyrene (EPS).

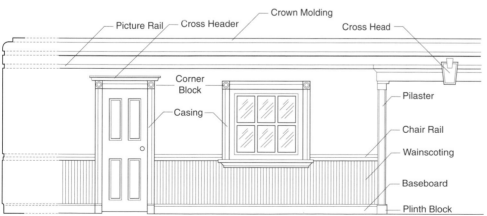

Wall of Trim

PCF Group

Columns—These are supporting or decorative pillars used in buildings. They are available plain or fluted and with a variety of capitals (the top part of an architectural column) and bases.

Pilasters—Vertical columns or piers, often ornamental, that slightly project from or are imbedded in the wall. They are decorative and can be rectangular or half round, often with a base (plinth block), shaft (middle section) and capital (top section). They are used as simulated columns in entryways and other door openings.

Mantel—The finish around a fireplace or a shelf above a fireplace.

Fireplace surround—A decorative element that surrounds the fireplace.

Niche—A wall recess traditionally used to display a sculpture or ornamental object.

Quoin—Units of stone or brick and sometimes, in wood, used on the exterior of houses to accentuate corners.

Rosette—A square block with a circular foliage or floral design, usually in relief, used as a decorative motif. They are sometimes used at the intersection of two pieces of door or window casing to eliminate mitering and are known as "head blocks."

Plinth blocks—Blocks used at the base of a casing or pilaster. They are usually taller and wider than the adjacent members.

Medallions—A tablet or panel in a wall or ceiling bearing a figure in relief, a portrait, or an ornament.

Finials—Ornaments found at the tops of spires or towers or any finishing or crowning addition.

Appliqués and onlays—Detailed ornamentation used to accent a wall or ceiling application.

Corner blocks—They are used with moldings for decoration or to avoid mitered cuts at the corners.

Keystone—The top member of an arch, often part of an entryway surround or window crosshead.

Crossheads—They are decorative elements that go on horizontally atop a window or door. They

Left: Fluted columns and pilasters with Roman Doric capitals create architectural interest and add balance to this open floor plan. When separating a large living area, columns provide definition but do not close off the space.

Above: A niche in expanded polystyrene (EPS).

Made from high-density polyurethane, these rosettes are lightweight and easy to install.

Appliqués and onlays enhance this window trim.

Medallions are often used with hanging fixtures for a more decorative look.

Several elements can be seen here: window crossheads, keystones, louver and shutters.

are larger at the top and then taper down at the bottom, almost like a triangle. They can sometimes look like little shelves.

Light coves—Molding that goes inside domes or around the bottom edge of vaults.

Dome—Interior and exterior hemispherical roof or ceiling.

Groin vaults—They are vaults formed by a right-angled intersection of two identical barrel vaults.

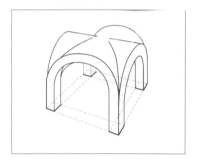

Shutters—A functional or nonfunctional cover for a door or window.

Louvers—They are used on the exterior of the house to allow air to ventilate the attic. Screen meshing is put behind the louvers to prevent insects and birds from coming through. Louvers are available in a variety of different shapes, including eyebrow, octagon, triangle, round and trapezoid. Some louvers are merely decorative and do not allow air movement.

Pediments—A decorative element above the crosshead of an entryway.

Friezes—These are usually installed between the cornice and

PCF Group

the entablature. Friezes are also used to add interest to a door system or fireplace.

Quantity

Trim should be used where it will enhance the room and not be overdone in any area—more is not always better. It is best to select trims that are most consistent with the architectural style and mood of the house. The trim should also be consistent throughout the house—if baseboard moldings are thick, then other moldings, such as door casings, should be proportionately thick. There are a myriad of books on every possible style to look through for ideas about the type of trim used for various periods and styles. Check in the library and bookstores before planning trim for your home.

Material

Wood

Wood has traditionally been used for trim, but there are now several other materials available that are easy to work with and look similar. Wood is available in a variety of species, both hard and soft, and can be purchased in solid wood, Medium Density Fiberboard (MDF) or plywood.

Solid wood—One of the most traditionally used trim materials. There is a variety of species available as trim, including poplar, white oak, walnut, mahogany, maple, beech, linden and cherry. The soft wood used is generally pine, available in finger joint, which means it has been dovetailed together. Wood is available in two grades—paint grade and stain grade, used for a natural look. If the wood will get a clear finish or be stained, it should be a good quality wood so defects are not showing.

Medium Density Fiberboard (MDF)—It is a molded product made from wood by-products. It looks like solid wood and is very strong. It is less expensive than solid wood and more stable. It can, however, swell and distort if exposed to excessive moisture.

Shutters in expanded polystyrene (EPS).

Chadsworth's 1.800 COLUMNS

Plain Tuscan columns add elegant architectural detail to the gallery of this home. The simple classic columns complement the groin-arched ceiling and Palladian windows.

Plywood—This is wood made of three or more layers of veneer joined with glue, with layers at right angles to one another. Plywood is more stable (less sensitive to fluctuations in humidity) and less expensive than solid wood. Edges must, however, be concealed with veneer tape or wood molding.

Plastics

High Density Polyurethane (HDP)—This is a polyurethane foam that has expanded in a mold, with confined expansion, creating a high-density product. It is used as a wood replacement and will not crack, split, rot or be attacked by birds and insects. It is used for interior as well as exterior applications. It will not absorb water and will resist the growth of fungus and mildew. If it is installed properly, according to manufacturer's instructions, joints will not show because the material will not move due to expansion and contraction, which is expected with wood. HDP is lightweight and easy to install. Some companies offer this material with a wood grain pattern and texture molded into it; it can then be stained. It is very rigid and cannot be bent. HDP is usually shipped primed, to be later painted on-site with latex paint. It is worked in the same way as wood and can be sanded, cut and nailed. It is maintenance-free. Like wood, HDP is combustible when exposed to open flames. A flame retardant can be added to the product for an additional cost.

Expanded Polystyrene (EPS) Foam—EPS foam is not a molded material but cut with a hot wire and computer generated according to a **CAD** design. The foam is coated with a variety of materials and can be made to look like wood, stone, precast concrete or gypsum. Various methods are used to put a finish coat on the foam, including spraying, troweling or applying the coating by machine. EPS is used for a large variety of interior and exterior trims. It is closed cell, which means it will not absorb water, is dimensionally stable, environmentally safe, resistant to rot and mildew and is recyclable. It is maintenance-free, light-weight, very durable and paintable. Depending on

Decorative window trim and crown moldings made of high-density polyurethane enhance the look of this room.

Chemcrest

the manufacturer, items can be selected from catalogs or can be custom made. Because the designs are CAD generated (and do not require a mold), producing individual items is not a difficult task.

Expanded Polyvinyl Chloride (ePVC)—This is an **extruded** wood replacement that can be sanded, sawn, nailed and painted like wood. It comes in sheets and is treated in the same way as wood, but it will not rot, and since it is a closed-cell material, it is impervious to moisture. It is about six times more expensive than wood, but it requires very little maintenance. It is difficult to get a smooth surface with ePVC, so it is best used for trim where a texture is acceptable. It can be used for interior or exterior applications.

PCF Group

Cellular PVC—This is also an extruded wood replacement that can be sanded, routed, nailed and painted like ePVC, but it can have a smooth surface or can have a wood grain surface. It does not absorb moisture, and it does not require maintenance. One product found (there are perhaps others) can be heated and bent to create radius curves (Azek trim boards). It comes in a white matte finish, but it can be painted. It can also be used for interior and exterior applications. Besides being available in lumber sizes, it can also be purchased as bead board in tongue and groove, which is excellent for moist areas, such as bathrooms or porches.

Polyvinyl Chloride (PVC)—This is a molded material that also looks very similar to wood, is water resistant and excellent for exterior trim. It comes in a limited number of designs; it has to be smooth and cannot have a raised pattern, such as a dentil molding. PVC is denser than ePVC, so it is very heavy and can be difficult

to handle. It also doesn't do well painted in dark colors. It is bought already extruded to be finished by the user. It is, however, an economical material and very durable.

Flexible molding (cast resin)—This is generally used in areas where curved molding is needed. It can follow the contours of the area easily. Often companies that supply flexible molding will offer other types of molding that will match, for areas that may not require the flexibility. Flexible molding can have a real wood appearance and can be tooled and stained in the same way as wood. It has almost the same composition as high-density polyurethane, but the foam remains soft and flexible. It is heavier and more expensive than high-density polyurethane and more difficult to install. It is adjustable on-site if measurements are slightly off. It is made from polyurethane but with different ingredients to make it elastic and less rigid. There are two types of flexible molding:

- Cast resin—Can be used indoors and outdoors. The back of the profile must be flat.
- Molded resin—Can be used indoors only because it will absorb water. The profiles are not limited the way the cast resins are.

Polymer over wood (wood dough or compo)—Polymer is mixed with fine sawdust to create a dough that is primarily a wood product. The dough is extruded in a bead onto a wood substrate, then run under a die wheel, which imparts a high-relief detail. It has the same density and porosity as wood and when painted is indistinguishable from wood.

Glass Fiber–Reinforced Composites

These are composites with fiberglass as the backbone ingredient. They are all molded materials and several types are offered that can be used for a variety of applications (columns, molding and so on), depending on whether they are specified for interior or exterior use.

Glass Fiber–Reinforced Gypsum (GFRG or GRG)—GRG is a composition of plaster and

A stone entry surround made of expanded polystyrene (EPS).

glass fibers. It is dense and heavy with the look and feel of stone or it can be painted to look like wood. It is class A fire resistant and more expensive and difficult to install than polyurethane. It can, however, be manufactured with a thinner profile and is lighter in weight than plaster but is still very strong. The gypsum (which is also an ingredient of drywall) will absorb moisture, so it can only be used for interior applications. It can be modified with a polymer to make it suitable for exterior use. GRG is the least expensive material in this category.

Glass fiber–reinforced polymer (plastic) (GFRP)—It is adaptable to complex shapes, is corrosion resistant, dimensionally stable, lightweight and strong. It can be made to look like painted wood, aged wood, stone, wicker or plaster. Anything that can be manufactured with plaster can be produced with GFRP. It can have a smooth finish or a textured surface with an integral color and texture. GFRP is very durable, impervious to moisture and typically lighter than plaster. This material is more durable than products such as HDP and EPS. It is stronger than GFRG and can be used for both interior and exterior applications. It is, however, the most expensive of the three glass fiber–reinforced composites, depending on the application. This material is commonly referred to as fiberglass, although all of the materials in this category include fiberglass in their compositions.

Glass fiber–reinforced concrete (GFRC)—GFRC is a combination of cement, fine aggregates and glass fibers and is typically used on exterior applications but can be used for interiors as well. It has the look and durability of precast concrete at one-third the weight. It is usually less expensive than GFRP and has a heavier, more stone-like feel. A large variety of finishes can be created with GFRC, such as travertine, coral and limestone. It is waterproof, impact resistant, durable and lightweight.

Plaster

This is used in place of stone, which was used in classical ancient constructions. Plaster is very fragile, heavy, difficult to work with and expensive, particularly if several profiles are used together. It may be difficult to find qualified installers. Plaster contains gypsum which absorbs moisture, so it can only be used for interior applications. Polyurethane is being used as a substitute because it is lighter, more durable and less costly. Plaster is used today for medallions, niches, quoins and other smaller items.

Joinery

Whichever style is used, the work should be done by a craftsman so the look will be continuous and even. Corners can be mitered, cut into each other on an angle or butted together. Mitered corners have a more formal look, while butted corners are more informal and typical of the Shaker period, for example.

Scarf joint—Joining boards by beveling (cutting on an angle) the ends to fit together and fastening them with bolts or the like.

Coped joint—Joint cut with a coping saw and used on baseboards, doors, window stops and other moldings. They are used instead of mitered inside molding joints because they do not open up when you nail them and changes in humidity will not cause them to open and close as noticeably.

Mitered joint—Joint made by cutting material ends at 45 degrees or at equal angles so they match exactly.

Butt joint—The surfaces of two materials are perfectly square.

Color

Color can be used to give a particular effect, such as using dark beams on the ceiling to make it appear lower. Certain colors are more consistent with a particular period or style. Colonial houses often have slate blue and brick red trim and Southwestern homes often have turquoise and peach colors, for example. It is worth the time to peruse books about a particular period or culture to get the look you want to achieve. When purchasing wood trim to be used with clear varnish or stain, stain-grade wood should be purchased. If the wood will be painted, paint-grade trim is fine.

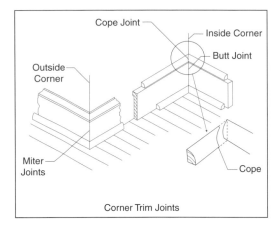

Corner Trim Joints

Clear finish—This allows the color of the wood to come through. Clear finishes are made with clear synthetic coatings or the original formulations for varnish, lacquer, linseed oil or shellac.

Stain—Wood sealer should be used on the trim before it is stained; this will make the stain go on evenly. A variety of stain colors can be used on wood to make it darker, redder and so on. Some woods change color over time with stain. Ask the dealer if they can show you what you might anticipate with a particular species. Soft woods tend to absorb stain faster and more unevenly. If a color is used that is close to the natural color, any inconsistencies will be less obvious. A finish coat should also be used; this can be varnish, polyurethane, shellac or oil (linseed or tung). Choose between glossy or matte finish, which will be less obvious.

Paint—Trim can be painted the same color as the wall, another shade of the wall color or a contrasting color. Paint can have a matte, semi-gloss or glossy finish and can be water-based (latex) or oil-based. Some companies offer specialized finishes that look like metal and marble, eliminating the need to complete these finishes on-site. Many different effects can be achieved with trim. Choices should be worked out as early as possible with the architect or interior designer.

Size

Trim should be used consistently in all areas. The trim should be sized in proportion to the size of the room; very large rooms or rooms with high ceilings will require larger molding profiles.

Stock Versus Custom Trim

Many trim styles are available in stock sizes, while many companies will custom make the trim to your own specifications.

Velcro-and-Adhesive System

Trim can be purchased that can be easily mounted without nails, but attached with Velcro. It is available pre-measured, pre-cut and factory finished, so it is easy to install (with no power tools) for the do-it-yourselfer. It is made of primed fiberboard or a substrate with maple, oak or cherry veneer. Panels, wainscoting and trim are available in a variety of sizes and stains.

resources

For further information about the Velcro-and-Adhesive system, contact New England Classic at www.newenglandclassic.com.

Some of the suppliers of molding and decorative trim:

American Millwork Corp.	574-295-4158	www.americanmillwork.com
Architectural Detail	435-753-0800	www.architecturaldetall.com
Architectural Innovations	800-845-2732	www.architecturalinnov.com
Architectural Molding & Foam Millwork (C)	877-337-2636	www.a-m-f-m.com
Azek Trim boards	413-787-1963	www.azek.com
Balmer Architectural Moldings (C)	416-491-6425	www.balmer.com
Bay Foam, Inc.	800-743-3626	www.bayfoam.com
Bendix Moldings, Inc.	800-526-0240	www.bendixmoldings.com
Burton Moldings (C)	888-323-8926	www.burtonmoldings.com
Century Architectural Specialties	877-262-1999	www.architecturalspecialties.com
Chadsworth's 1.800.Columns	800-486-2118	www.columns.com
Chemcrest Architectural Products (C)	800-665-6653	www.chemcrest.com
Classic Details	803-356-4545	www.classicdetails.com
Cumberland Woodcraft Co.	800-367-1884	www.cumberlandwoodcraft.com
Decorative Concepts	866-328-8033	www.decorativeconcepts.net
Enkeboll Designs	800-745-5507	www.enkeboll.com
Flex Molding, Inc	800-307-3357	www.flexmolding.com
Focal Point Architectural Products	800-662-5550	www.focalpointap.com
Fypon Molded Millwork	800-955-5748	www.fypon.com
HB&G	800-264-4424	www.hbgcolumns.com
Klise Manufacturing Co.	616-459-4283	www.klisemfg.com
Outwater Plastics Industries	800-631-8375	www.outwater.com
The PCF Group	888-511-3626	www.pcfoam.com
Saroyan Lumber Co., Inc	800-624-9309	www.saroyanlumber.com
Spectis Moulders, Inc. (C)	800-685-9981	www.spectis.com
Style Solutions	800-446-3040	www.stylesolutionsinc.com
Vintage Woodworks	903-356-2158	www.vintagewoodworks.com
White River Hardwoods-Woodworks, Inc.	800-558-0119	www.moldings.com
WindsorOne	888-229-7900	www.windsormill.com
Worthington Group, Ltd.	800-872-1608	www.worthingtononline.com
ZaGo Manufacturing Company, Inc.	973-643-6700	www.flexibletrims.com

(C) = Canadian

New England Classic

Panels can be fastened with mechanical methods or Velcro for the do-it-yourselfer.

Health and Safety

People are becoming more and more concerned about building a beautiful, safe, healthy, comfortable and energy-efficient home. There have been many extensive programs developed in the last several years to meet the challenge of a more concerned, better educated population. Two of the most excellent programs developed in the last several years are the Universal Design program pioneered by Ronald L. Mace at North Carolina State University and the Health House program of the American Lung Association. The following discussion will include just a small portion of the information offered by these valuable programs. Both have extensive Web sites with a great deal of information that is worthwhile reviewing in general and especially before building or remodeling a house.

It has been established over the last decade that the use of smoke alarm devices and fire sprinkler systems saves lives. The use of smoke alarms has increased over the last ten years, but the use of fire sprinkler systems has not become as mainstream as perhaps it should in residential housing. This chapter includes just a small amount of the information you should know about these systems and vehicles for finding additional data about these important safety measures.

Universal Design

At one time people adapted the home to accommodate the needs of their children, older adults and people with limited abilities who would be living in their home at the time. Today, the trend is toward designing the home with sensible design features that are good for everyone and can provide a supportive and comfortable home environment for a lifetime. This concept is called "universal design": environments and products that accommodate persons of all ages and abilities and are usable to the greatest extent possible.

People with grown children rarely think about making their house child safe, until in the not-so-distant future, grandchildren are coming to visit. When people move into a house and are in perfect health, they rarely consider that illness and accidents can change their life in an instant. Many of us build or remodel our homes to meet our current conditions, but, as we all know, those conditions can change quickly and then accommodations have to be made later.

At North Carolina State University, The Center for Universal Design was established to educate people about universal design, to conduct research in developing designs for all user needs and to support the building industry and product manufacturers in the development of universal design solutions.

The Center offers a great deal of information on universal design and products that create a well-designed home environment that benefit the household members and those visitors welcomed by a spacious and comfortable home. This concept will not only make the house more accommodating to the current owners but will accommodate anyone who may be interested in buying the house in the future.

Seven Principles of Universal Design
Principle one: Equitable Use
The design is useful and marketable to people with diverse abilities.
Principle two: Flexibility in Use
The design accommodates a wide range of individual preferences and abilities.
Principle three: Simple and Intuitive Use
Use of the design is easy to understand, regardless of the user's experience, knowledge, language skills or current concentration level.
Principle four: Perceptible Information
The design communicates necessary information effectively to the user, regardless of ambient conditions or the user's sensory abilities.
Principle five: Tolerance for Error
The design minimizes hazards and the adverse consequences of accidental or unintended actions.
Principle six: Low Physical Effort
The design can be used efficiently and comfortably and with a minimum of fatigue.
Principle seven: Size and Space for Approach and Use
Appropriate size and space is provided for approach, reach, manipulation and use, regardless of the user's body size, posture or mobility.*

* Copyright 1997 North Carolina State University, The Center for Universal Design. Compiled by advocates of universal design, listed in alphabetical order: Bettye Rose Connell, Mike Jones, Ron Mace, Jim Mueller, Abir Mullick, Elaine Ostroff, Jon Sanford, Ed Steinfeld, Molly Story and Gregg Vanderheiden.

The following are just a few of the kinds of accommodations that you may want to consider when you are building or remodeling your home.

Bathroom
- Grab bars should be installed in the tub, shower and even near the toilet. All people can benefit from having bars to help get into and out of the tub or shower. Some people may need special assistance.

Some suppliers of grab bars:

Ginger	800-842-4872	www.blazemaster.com
Hafele	800-423-3531	www.globesprinkler.com
Otto Bock	800-795-8846	www.ipexinc.com

Ginger

These grab bars are made of powder-coated steel, available in three colors and can support 330 pounds of weight.

- Mirrors should be installed behind the sink, right down to the backsplash. This will accommodate children as well as people who are seated.
- There should be easy-access controls for the shower and tub. Controls should be put in a location where they can be accessed without having to reach into the tub or shower. It will work better for people who have difficulty reaching in and it will help them not get soaked when the water is operating.
- Shower heads should be adjustable to accom-

modate all heights. This will also help to avoid getting hair, bandages and casts wet.

- Use anti-scald devices to prevent scalding from a surge of hot water.

Kitchen

- Lever-type water controls are easier to use to adjust water temperature and volume.
- Include counters of varying heights to accommodate the entire family. For food preparation, a baking area can be included, which is generally lower for rolling out dough and other baking tasks and can function double duty for children and seated people to work at as well.
- Pull-out shelves should be included in base cabinets. This makes it easier to reach items in the rear and makes it easier to maneuver large stored items.
- A pantry should have shelves that are low as well as high, so items are accessible to people of all heights.

The House in General

- A minimum of 32-inch clear door openings, which improves circulation and reduces damage to doorjambs when moving furniture, appliances and so on.
- Lever door handles are easier to use by everyone.
- Handrails, which are easy to grip, should be on both sides of the stairs.
- Use glow-in-the-dark light switches in those areas where it will be poorly lit at night.
- Try to have one level entrance into the house. This will accommodate not only baby strollers but will make the entrance less hazardous in wet and snowy conditions.
- Have a covered entry which will provide protection from the elements for yourself while opening the door, for delivery people and for children who might be waiting for a bus or carpool.
- Have adjustable closet rods. This will accommodate children using the closet and will also increase the storage space by allowing for double hanging of rods.

These are just a few of the many accommodations one can make for a safer home environment.

resources

For further information about universal design, visit www.design.ncsu.edu/cud, and check some of the books listed on page 353.

With a similar theory, James Pirkl (a retired professor at Syracuse University who coined the term "transgenerational design") teaches a design strategy that is also for all ages and abilities and to motivate consumers to search for solutions that do not discriminate against any group, including children, older adults and so on. He believes houses should be designed for all eventualities. A teenager with a sprained foot or a pregnant woman who may have difficulty bending—all are temporary conditions but make traditional design difficult to maneuver. He has built his own home with pull-out cabinets that make it simple to get in for small children, adults and people in wheelchairs. Like the people at the Universal Design Center, Pirkl believes in having grab bars in bathrooms and wide decks to more easily get into bathtubs and spas.

resources

For more information about transgenerational design, visit www.transgenerational.com.

American Lung Association Health House Program

According to the EPA, the air inside a home can be two to five times more polluted than the air outside the house. Because of this situation, which is particularly problematic to those with asthma, allergies and other diseases, a program was developed to combat this problem. The American Lung Association Health House program is a national effort to educate homeowners and set guidelines for builders to improve indoor air quality, construct homes with building materials that are environmentally friendly, produce houses that are low maintenance, energy efficient and durable, and create a comfortable home living environment.

The Health House program seeks to achieve this goal through the careful selection of building materials, advanced framing and insulation techniques, energy-efficient windows and appliances (which are sealed combustion appliances), high-efficiency air filtration and ventilation systems and moisture control. The initial cost of this type of house will be about 3 to 5 percent more costly than for a traditionally built house, but there should be a long-term savings in utility bills, in some cases, reduction in mortgage payments and a more healthy existence for all inhabitants, people and pets. Several major U.S. companies, notably Honeywell and 3M, are helping the nonprofit program spread the word about healthier homes through educational sponsorships and nationwide media campaigns.

First developed in 1993 by the Minnesota chapter of the American Lung Association, the Health House program has developed home construction standards that are among the most stringent in the country for building and maintaining a healthy home. Standards for this program were developed in consultation with experts in the building science, builder, engineering, environmental health, indoor air quality, medical and academic communities to establish a healthy and comfortable environment. A training program was developed for builders, and model houses were constructed to demonstrate the characteristics of a healthy home environment. Since the program began, over 120 Health House demonstration sites have been built in thirty states.

resources

Builder guidelines for Health House homes can be found at www.healthhouse.org.

American Lung Assoc. Health House

Some general construction rules to consider when building or remodeling a house in order to establish a healthy indoor environment:

1. Make sure the entire house is well ventilated, particularly the bathrooms and kitchen to avoid buildup of moisture.
2. Make sure the heating and cooling system is checked periodically and high-efficiency filters are used, minimum of MERV 10. Make sure that the system, if there is an existing one, will handle HEPA filters, which will restrict the flow.
3. All fireplaces, gas stoves and gas-burning appliances must be sealed combustion or power vented to the outside.
4. All potentially dangerous substances, such as gasoline or powerful solvents, should be properly stored or discarded after use.
5. If possible, the house should be designed to divert water away from the walls and windows. This can be achieved with large overhangs around the house.
6. The foundation should be designed for waterproofing, and the exterior drainage system should divert the water away from the house. The downspouts should be away from the house, and the irrigation system should also be away from the foundation of the house.

This home in Woodbury, Minnesota, was built following the American Lung Association Health House program guidelines.

7. Materials selected for the house should be free of dangerous contaminants, such as formaldehyde. If this is not possible, make sure the products (some floorings, paints and varnishes) are ventilated during and shortly after installation. If you walk into the house and can smell the product, then it is not totally ventilated and requires more time to be aired out.

8. Interior furnishing should be easy to clean and durable, such as wood and vinyl flooring.

9. Select windows and doors that will not allow air infiltration and will be energy efficient.

10. Be prudent about controlling moisture so it is maintained at about 35 to 50 percent relative humidity. Be sure to tend to leaks and the materials damaged by the leaks, which may grow mold.

11. Well water should be tested before the house is constructed and then periodically afterward. The EPA has set standards for municipal water systems; water must be tested on a regular basis, and local governments are required to publish the results once a year. You can request this information at any time.

The following are some of the topics the program recognizes as negatively affecting indoor air. Specific recommendations are listed after each. This is only meant to call attention to some of the potential problems. Check the noted Web sites for additional information.

Radon

Radon is an odorless, colorless gas produced by decay of naturally occurring uranium and radium in the ground. When radon is formed in the ground, it can enter a building through its foundation, regardless of how well sealed the foundation may be. Radon will further break down into particles that, when inhaled over long periods of time, can increase the potential of lung cancer. Although a significant health concern, there are reliable solutions that can also improve other indoor air-quality issues as well as improve the value of your home.

Recommendations

When a house is under construction, it is the best time to deal with radon. First check with the EPA map of radon zones at www.epa.gov/radon/zonemap.html to see if your home is in an area where a high incidence of radon concerns have been observed in homes. If it is, consider having a passive system installed during construction. This should be an inexpensive system of piping in which the radon is released from the ground. After the construction is complete, the house should be tested and if the reduction in radon is not satisfactory, then the system can be activated with the addition of a fan attached to the piping system. This treatment will not only reduce the concentration of radon in the soil, but it can also reduce the moisture, thereby reducing mold concerns as well. The EPA recommends all houses be tested for radon. If you are remodeling an existing house, it should be tested before the construction has begun. Testing should be done by a National Environmental Health Association (NEHA) tester or a state-certified radon tester. The test can be done by a homeowner if a radon measurement device used is certified by the state and the manufacturer's instructions are followed.

resources

Information on privately run programs can be found on the EPA Web site at www.epa.gov/radon/proficiency.html. (A book for do-it-yourselfers: *Protecting Your Home from Radon* by Doug Kladder and Dr. James F. Burkhart. For further information, call 800-513-8332 or visit www.colorodovintage.com.) If radon is found to exceed the federal guidelines of 4 pCi/L (picocuries per liter is the measurement used for concentrations of radon in water and air) after a carefully executed test, a certified mitigation contractor should be contacted to eradicate the gases. For more information about radon or to locate a certified mitigation contractor, contact the National Environmental Health Association (NEHA) at www.neha.org or call 800-269-4174, the National Radon Safety Board (NRSB) at www.nrsb.org or call the county or state radon office. Other sources of information: the EPA's consumer hotline, 800-SOS-RADON, American Association of Radon Scientists and Technologists (AARST) at www.aarst.org, The Radon Information Center at www.radon.com and the Western Regional Radon Training Center (WRRTC) at www.wrrtc.com.

Carbon Monoxide

Carbon monoxide is an invisible, odorless, toxic gas that is produced by the incomplete burning of fuels such as gas, oil, kerosene, wood or charcoal and can be released into the home by fuel-burning appliances that are not working properly or are used incorrectly. The automobile exhaust fumes from an attached garage can also produce carbon monoxide in the air. Low levels of exposure can cause headaches, nausea, dizziness, drowsiness, weakness and shortness of breath; high levels can cause death.

Recommendations

A monitor alarm meeting Canadian Standard CSA 6.19 should be installed in the house. Have a trained professional periodically check, clean and tune up the central heating system (furnaces, flues and chimneys) and fuel-burning appliances. Make sure the heating system and appliances are properly vented.

Asbestos

Asbestos is a mineral fiber that has been used for construction materials such as insulation, fire-retardant barriers and ashes and embers used in gas-fired fireplaces. Products made before the 1970s may contain asbestos; most products today will most likely not. If asbestos-containing materials are not damaged, the fibers will not become airborne and will not pose a health risk. Asbestos fibers must also be inhaled at high concentrations over an extended period of time. If the fibers are inhaled they can get lodged in the lungs and can cause cancer or other lung diseases over time. Symptoms are not usually apparent for several years after exposure began.

Recommendations

Before you purchase a house or remodel an existing one, it should be inspected for damaged or airborne asbestos fibers. (If you are purchasing or building a new house, there is no need to inspect for asbestos.) If asbestos material exists in the home and is in good condition, it should be left alone. If damaged asbestos exists in the home, it should be removed or encapsulated by state-licensed professionals (or can legally be removed by the homeowner if it is an owner-occupied, single-family home). Homeowners can contact the local health department for information on the proper handling and disposal of asbestos items.

resources

For further information about asbestos, check with the U.S. Environmental Protection Agency at www.epa.gov/asbestos or the Agency for Toxic Substances and Disease Registry (ATSDR) at www.atsdr.cdc.gov/toxfaqs.html.

Molds

Molds are simple, microscopic fungi that produce spores (tiny living cells) that can land on damp spots indoors and grow and digest whatever they are growing on to survive. Mold requires a food, such as wood or paper, and moisture to grow. If large amounts of spores are inhaled in the home environment, they can contribute to asthma, allergies, and other health problems.

Recommendations

All leaks should be repaired and all the materials damaged by the leak should be cleaned or repaired. Mold, caused by the leak, should be cleaned by washing with no more than a 10 percent bleach solution and allowed to dry completely. Materials that have been damaged by mold should be removed. If carpet is damaged by mold, it should be lifted and dried with a fan within the first forty-eight hours of its occurrence. If it is not dried in forty-eight hours, the carpet should be disposed of because spores will be impossible to remove. All other porous materials, such as dry wall, should also be disposed of if they are not dried within the first forty-eight hours of being soaked. Relative humidity in the home should be kept between 40 to 50 percent all year long. Local exhaust ventilation should be used in moisture-producing areas such as kitchens and bathrooms and the proper use of air-conditioning or dehumidifiers can also help control moisture in the home.

resources

For further information about molds and moisture control, contact the U.S. Environmental Protection Agency at www.epa.gov/iaq/molds. For guidelines in dealing with mold, check the New York City government Web site at www.ci.nyc.ny.us.

Dust Mites

Dust mites are tiny microscopic organisms that feed on skin flakes and can be found in various places in the house, including mattresses, pillows, carpeting and furniture. Dust mites thrive best in moist air and produce particles that can trigger asthma and allergic reactions.

Recommendations

Reduce the relative humidity in the house to 50 percent or below by using air-conditioning or dehumidifiers. Use a damp mop to remove dust. In bedrooms, if possible, use hard-surface floors such as linoleum, tile or wood rather than wall-to-wall carpeting. Use a vacuum cleaner with either a double-layered microfilter bag, a central vacuum system or a HEPA filter to trap allergens that pass through a vacuum's exhaust.

Cockroaches

Substances that produce allergic reactions are found in cockroach feces, saliva, eggs and shed cuticles. When these particles become airborne they trigger allergic reactions and asthmatic episodes.

Recommendations

The best way to discourage the presence of cockroaches is to eliminate food and crumbs from being left open in the kitchen and other areas of the house and by limiting water sources such as leaky faucets and drainpipes. If cockroaches do appear, pesticides should be carefully used according to manufacturers' instructions.

resources

For further information about pesticides and pest control, contact the National Pesticide Information Center at 800-858-7378 or at www.npic.orst.edu/index.html.

Basement Moisture

Moisture problems are common in basements, caused by ground water infiltration, pipe leaks, and humid air generated by interior moisture from bathrooms, cooking and unvented clothes dryers, which cause condensation on cool basement surfaces. The moisture encourages the growth of mold and mildew.

Recommendations

The source of the moisture must be identified and corrected. Exterior grading and proper drainage will help avoid the entrance of ground water, and proper and controlled ventilation in areas prone to moisture, such as kitchens and bathrooms, is essential. Clothes dryers should be vented to the outside.

Backdrafting

This occurs when there is combustion or smoke spillage from gas or oil furnaces, boilers, hot-water heaters, fireplaces (wood-burning and gas type) and gas ranges. When venting systems are poorly designed or not working properly, the fan may draw air from the house, causing normal chimney flow to be reversed—this is called "backdrafting." Backdrafting can include carbon monoxide (causing symptoms such as headaches, dizziness and maybe even death) and nitrogen oxides, which can damage the lungs, lower resistance to colds and cause respiratory illnesses.

Recommendations

Regular maintenance is necessary to check for heat-exchanger leakage, evidence of start-up spillage in appliances and condensation in chimneys. As mentioned earlier, carbon monoxide detectors should be installed in every house, and all vents should be checked to make sure they are operating efficiently.

Second-Hand Smoke

Studies have shown that second-hand smoke can be harmful, particularly to children, triggering asthma, sudden infant death syndrome (SIDS), bronchitis, pneumonia and ear infections. It may also cause lung cancer and contribute to heart disease.

Recommendations

The way to resolve this potential risk is the simplest of all: do not allow visitors or family members to smoke in the house.

Formaldehyde

Pressed woods, such as particleboard and fiberboard, used in such items as kitchen cabinets, are often made with urea formaldehyde resin, which offgases formaldehyde, especially when new. Formaldehyde can cause eye, nose and throat irritation and allergic reactions and may even cause cancer.

Recommendations

If possible, use pressed woods that contain phenol resins rather than urea resins. This resin is usually used in exterior-grade pressed-wood products. When selecting carpet and carpet padding, choose those with little or no formaldehyde. If items are brought into the house that contain this substance, be sure to increase the ventilation for several days.

resources

Information on the effects of formaldehyde: Agency for Toxic Substances and Disease Registry (ATSDR), www.atsdr.cdc.gov/toxfaqs.html.

Volatile Organic Compounds (VOCs)

Materials such as paints and coatings in the home may contain VOCs that offgas into the home. Common VOCs are benzene (paint supplies and stored fuels), toluene (paint thinners, fingernail polish, lacquers and adhesives), and formaldehyde (pressed-wood products).

Recommendations

Whenever products are used that emit VOCs, ventilation should be increased. These products should be purchased as needed and safely disposed of after use. Water should be tested periodically. If VOCs are found, treatment will be specific to the contaminants present.

Pesticides

Substances used to kill household pests can be very toxic for the inhabitants (people and their pets). These can cause irritation to eyes, nose and throat, fatigue, headaches, nausea, damage to the central nervous system and even cancer. Pesticides poison 110,000 people each year in the United States. This category includes disinfectants, fungicides, herbicides, insecticides, repellants and plant-growth regulators.

Recommendations

Be aware of what substances you and the pest control company are using; whenever possible use nonchemical methods. Be sure pesticides are used in the recommended quantities and with increased ventilation. Consider alternative, nonchemical methods of controlling pests (perhaps in addition to the chemical means) by such methods as using screens on doors and discarding overripe fruits to control fruit flies and fungus beetles.

resources

For further information about pesticides and alternative methods of controlling pests, visit the Health House Program at www.healthhouse.org/tipsheets/pesticides.asp, the University of Minnesota at www.extension.umn.edu/distribution/horticulture/DG6269.html and the California Environmental Protection Agency at www.cdpr.ca.gov/docs/factshts/factmenu.htm. For information about pesticides and pest control, contact the National Pesticide Information Center at 800-858-7378 or www. npic.orst.edu/ index.html.

Lead

People can be exposed to lead (a highly toxic metal) through water (from solder joints in old plumbing), deteriorating house paints, dust and so on. Some paint on existing walls may contain lead but not be dangerous unless it is disturbed, sanded or burned. Elevated blood-lead levels can be particularly dangerous in children, causing impaired mental and physical development.

Recommendations

Have the water analyzed for the existence of lead as well as other contaminants. When the water is tested for lead, make sure the water sample is taken first thing in the morning before the water is used for showering, cooking and so on. If you are removing paint that may contain lead, have it tested to be sure it is removed properly. Make sure that there is no lead paint in areas that children may chew on, such as windowsills.

resources

Information about the effects of lead: Agency for Toxic Substances and Disease Registry (ATSDR), www.atsdr.cdc.gov/ toxfaqs.html, the Health House Program at www.healthhouse.org/tipsheets/lead.asp, the Environmental Protection Agency at www.epa.gov/lead or the National Lead Information Center at 800-424-LEAD.

Furnace Filters

High-efficiency furnace filters used in forced-air heating/cooling systems can remove pollen, pet dander (tiny particles, as from skin or hair), spores, smoke, bacteria and other harmful contaminants. Look for the highest possible MERV rating (Minimum Efficiency Reporting Value)—a number from a test method designed by the American Society of Heating, Refrigeration and Air Conditioning Engineers to help people compare filters; a higher MERV rating generally indicates a better filter performance, which is usually listed on the packaging.

Breathing in large amounts of these particles

can cause respiratory irritations, allergic reactions, infectious diseases, decreased lung function and cancer. Filters should be changed in heating/air-conditioning units every two to three months; more frequent replacements may be necessary if there is someone in the house with asthma, allergies or other lung diseases. Changing the filters does not necessarily increase the efficiency of the filter, but if it isn't changed on a timely basis, it will restrict the airflow and the efficiency of the system. Heating/cooling units should also be inspected by a professional yearly. To download free reminder software that will notify you when it's time to change your air-cleaning filter, visit www.filtrete.com and click on "Reminder Service."

Healthy Cleaning Alternatives

Check to see that cleaning products used in the home are free of pesticides. Check labels to see if there is an EPA warning on the label, which will indicate that the product is classified as a pesticide. Items such as aerosol spray products (health, beauty and cleaning products), chlorine bleach, rug and upholstery cleaners and insect/rodent repellents may cause minimal risk if they are used according to the manufacturers' instructions for short periods of time; however, prolonged exposure can cause allergic reactions, respiratory irritations and, in severe cases, cancer. There are many alternative methods of cleaning without the use of harmful chemicals. For example, instead of using moth repellant, cedar chips can be used in cotton sachets.

resources

For more information about alternative cleaning options, check with the Health House Program at www.healthhouse.org/tipsheets/cleaning.asp.

Dehumidifiers

Humidity is the amount of moisture or water vapor in the air; the relative humidity in the house should be between 35 and 55 percent. Moisture enters the house through showering, drying clothes, washing dishes and so on. Excessive humidity can cause discomfort and an environment conducive to the growth of biological contaminants. Be careful in the use of humidifiers, which can grow mold. A hygrometer can be used to measure humidity levels in the home; this can be purchased at a local hardware store. The moisture can be controlled with the use of dehumidifiers.

resources

For further information about dehumidifiers and their care, visit the Health House Program at www.healthhouse.org/tipsheets/dehumidifier.asp.

For further information about this program and additional information about any of these pollutants, check the Web site of the Health House program at www.healthhouse.org or call 800-586-4872 or contact the American Lung Association at www.lungusa.org.

Smoke and Carbon Monoxide Detectors and Fire Sprinkler Systems

According to the U.S. Fire Administration, fire breaks out in one out of every ten American homes each year.* **The National Fire Protection Association (NFPA)** estimates that smoke alarms in the house reduce the probability of dying in a fire by 40 to 50 percent. One out of every five smoke detectors, however, is inoperable in the 94 percent of homes that have them. The reason most often reported for faulty fire detectors is missing, dead or disconnected batteries. Automatic fire sprinkler systems in homes reduce the chances of dying in a fire and reduce the

---

* This includes unreported fires, as well as reported ones; all the following statistics are only for reported fires.

average property loss by $1/2$ to $2/3$. In addition, wherever sprinklers have been properly designed and are functioning, there have never been more than three people killed in a fire and these have been people intimately involved with the ignition. These are important reasons for including these systems in new homes or renovation projects.

Smoke Alarms

Statistics from the NFPA supports the fact that smoke detectors save lives. Since the 1970s, when homeowners (and landlords) began installing smoke alarms in the home, the home-fire death rate has been reduced by half. One-half of home-fire deaths occur in 6 percent of homes without smoke alarms.

Smoke alarms can be part of a security system or purchased individually to be placed in particular areas of the house. The NFPA recommends a smoke alarm be placed on each level of the house and outside each bedroom, unless the doors are closed in bedrooms, then they should also be placed inside the rooms. Codes for new houses (NFPA 72, National Fire Alarm Code) require fire alarms in each bedroom. Batteries should be replaced every year (such as during fire protection week in October or on the home-owner's birthday) or when the alarm begins to chirp. Detectors should be tested periodically (according to the manufacturers' instructions) and should be replaced every ten years. (Unfortunately today, homes with nonfunctioning smoke alarms outnumber homes with no smoke alarms at all.) In houses with people with hearing impairments, alarms with a louder alarm or a strobe light should be installed. (Contact the NFPA's Center for High-Risk Outreach at 617-984-7826 for a list of manufacturers that distribute alarms for the hearing impaired.) Any alarms purchased should have a label from an independent testing lab, such as Underwriters Laboratory. Where it is feasible to install them, alarms hot wired to a home's electrical system are more advantageous than battery detectors as

they do not require annual battery replacement and therefore tend to be more reliable. They should be installed by a qualified electrician.

There are three types of smoke detectors available:

- Ionization detectors—Most of the available detectors are ionization detectors. They activate more quickly for fast-flaming fires.
- Photoelectric detectors—These function more quickly for slow, smoldering fires. They are often recommended for locations where ionization-type detectors frequently give false alarms, such as in areas adjoining kitchens or near bathrooms.
- Detectors with both types of sensors—They are better than either type alone, but they are more expensive.

Detectors can be powered by one of three sources:

- Batteries—Batteries must be tested periodically and replaced annually.
- Household current (AC)—These should be replaced with AC-powered alarms with battery backup to meet the current building codes.
- Household current with a backup battery—Building codes now require these be installed in all new homes.

Carbon Monoxide Alarms

Many building codes now require the use of carbon monoxide alarms in homes that use gas or oil heating or have a fireplace. Carbon monoxide and smoke alarms may be dual functioning and should be placed on each level of the house and by each sleeping area (according to the Consumer Products Safety Commission recommendation). Alarms are powered in the same ways as smoke detectors—with batteries, AC or AC with battery backup. Those with batteries, like smoke alarms, should have the batteries replaced yearly. The sensor in some carbon monoxide alarms must be replaced regularly, so this should be a consideration when selecting a carbon monoxide alarm. Any alarms purchased, however, should have a label from an independent testing lab, such as Underwriters Laboratory.

Automatic Fire Sprinkler Systems

According to sprinkler industry humor, the choice is "a puddle of water or a pile of ashes." It is clear that sprinkler systems save lives and reduce property loss. Several municipalities around the country have already adapted ordinances requiring residential automatic sprinkler systems. San Clemente and Corte Madera, California, were among the first to pass such ordinances; other communities have also followed. Napa, California; Scottsdale, Arizona; and Cobb County, Georgia, have not had a single residential fire fatality since they adopted ordinances requiring fire sprinkler systems. Other communities offer incentives, such as tax breaks, to those homeowners who have fire sprinkler systems installed. When moving into a new neighborhood, find out if there are any such requirements or incentives. There are some important facts to consider about sprinkler systems:

- The cost of these systems is estimated to be $1 to $1.50 per square foot for new construction. Retrofits will cost approximately 50 percent more.
- Sprinklers can be inconspicuously installed on the wall or ceiling and almost completely concealed by plates that can be matched to room colors.
- Residential sprinklers are fast response, which allows them to be able to respond five times faster than commercial sprinklers and are designed to require less water than commercial sprinklers; since the fire is much smaller when the sprinkler activates, much less water is therefore needed to put out the fire.
- Either a city water connection can be used or an additional storage tank and a pump can be utilized as a water supply.
- Proper design and installation are standardized nationally in a standard defined by the NFPA 13D (which is titled Installation of Sprinkler Systems in One- and Two-Family Dwellings and Manufactured Homes).
- Some sprinkler systems can be tied into the plumbing system in the home. Other systems are separate and apart from the plumbing system. Some municipalities, however, require the water used for sprinkler systems to be isolated from that used for domestic purposes. Backflow prevention devices are available for that purpose.
- Sprinklers can prevent fires from becoming intense and more destructive than they would if extra time lapsed until a fire engine arrived. The fire department randomly applies hose streams, each of which flows either 150 or 250 gallons per minute to the structure. The normal residential sprinkler flow rate is less than 20 gallons per minute per operating sprinkler. According to the Home Fire Sprinkler Coalition, 90 percent of all house fires are stopped by a single sprinkler.
- Some insurance companies offer discounts to homeowners with fire sprinkler systems installed. The Insurance Services Offices recommend a discount of 13 percent for a NFPA 13D system in the home and an additional 2 percent for the presence of smoke alarms.
- Sprinkler systems increase the resale value of the house.
- A few municipalities have policies charging homeowners fees for the initial connection of the water sprinkler system (connection fees) and for maintaining the availability of water (standby charge).

Myths About Automatic Fire Sprinklers

Some people believe all sprinkler heads will go off if there is a fire. Automatic fire sprinklers are individually heat-activated and tied into a network of pipes with water under pressure. Only the sprinkler heads in the vicinity of the fire will be activated.

It is believed that sprinkler systems will often go off accidentally. The chance of a sprinkler accidentally going off is one in sixteen million.

Some believe the sprinklers will cause more damage than the fire. According to the Scottsdale Report*, a fifteen-year study of sprinkler system effectiveness conducted in Arizona, 8 $\frac{1}{2}$ times less water was found to be used by a sprinkler system than by firefighters, reducing water damage to the home. Sprinklers operate in the immediate area of the fire and optimize the use of the limited water that they distribute.

Questions to Ask About Fire Sprinkler Systems

- Will the system be installed in accordance with NFPA 13D?
- What types of sprinklers and finishes are available?
- Does the company offer a warranty on piping? Fittings? All products used?
- Are all of the system components (pipe, fittings, hangers, sprinklers, valves and so on) UL (Underwriters Laboratories) and C-UL (Underwriters Laboratories of Canada) listed?
- Is the installing contractor reputable? Does the installer specialize in the design and installation of residential fire sprinkler systems?
- Does the system require local inspection and/or approval? Are all permits and fees included in the installed price?
- Is the system equipped with some type of alarm-initiating device that activates with water flow? Will a local alarm result in the event of a sprinkler activation? Can the alarm be monitored at an off-site location?

Some states have licensing programs for fire sprinkler contractors, while others do not. Before putting in a fire sprinkler system, check with the authority having jurisdiction in the community, such as the fire marshal or fire inspector and find out what the local certification requirements are.

* By Assistant Chief Jim Ford, Rural/Metro Fire Department, Scottsdale, Arizona.

Locating Fire Sprinkler Contractors

- Look in the phone book under "sprinklers—automatic fire."
- Check with the local or state fire marshal. In states with licensing requirements, contact the state licensing board for a current list of contractors.
- Contact fire sprinkler contractor associations (AFSA and NFSA Web sites are listed on page 322).
- Check the Internet for local contractors.

Fire sprinklers are individually heat-activated and tied into a system of piping. When the heat of a fire raises the sprinkler's temperature to a specific level, a liquid-filled glass bulb shatters or a fusible metal link melts, opening that single sprinkler, releasing water directly over the heat source. There are several sprinkler choices available. They don't all have to be the same type but should have the same operating characteristics; the more attractive heads can be used in the more visible areas and the less attractive (and less expensive) ones in the basement where they will not be as visible. Some sprinklers have higher activation temperatures and are designed to be in warmer places, such as in the kitchen by an oven or in the vicinity of a fireplace. The appropriate temperature ratings are addressed by the NFPA standards.

Sprinkler Head Options

Recessed pendent—The sprinkler protrudes down about an inch, with most of the sprinkler frame concealed.

Concealed pendent—All that is visible is a small plate; some can be factory painted to match most ceiling colors. The paint thickness on the plates affects the thermal response characteristics of the plate; therefore, painting of sprinklers MUST only be done at the factory by the manufacturer. If there is a fire, the plate falls off and the sprinkler is activated. There is also a small space between the plate and the ceiling that allows heat to access the sprinkler above the plate. The

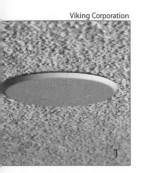

sprinkler remains thermally sensitive above the plate in its enclosure and must reach its operating temperature. There are two types of concealed pendants—a **flat plate** and a **domed plate.** The domed type is less expensive; the flat plate is a bit more attractive.

Flush pendent—The sprinkler is flush with the ceiling but generally incorporates a thermal element that protrudes below the ceiling. In general, these are not as aesthetically pleasing as the concealed sprinklers but are more attractive than standard sprinklers.

Horizontal sidewall—The sprinkler is mounted horizontally and protrudes from the wall.

Recessed horizontal sidewall—About an inch of the sprinkler frame and deflector are visible on the wall; most of the sidewall sprinkler is concealed.

When to Plan for a Sprinkler System

The system should be designed to the proper NFPA standards by a qualified sprinkler contractor, if possible, before the final plans are approved. Many fire sprinkler contractors have engineers on their staff who also design sprinkler systems. It is easiest to install the system when the home is under construction and the joists are exposed. Fire sprinkler systems can be retrofitted into existing homes but require professional planning and installation.

resources

For further information about sprinkler systems,

contact the Home Fire Sprinkler Coalition at www.homefiresprinkler.org, the American Fire Sprinkler Association (AFSA) at www.sprinklernet.org or the National Fire Sprinkler Association (NFSA) at www.nfsa.org.

Guidelines for Fire-Prone Areas

With the rash of wildfires in southern California, Florida and many western states, it seems prudent to consider the following items when building or remodeling a house in a dry, wooded area prone to fire.

Make sure there is adequate clearance between the house and the woods or high grasslands. Vegetation is the fuel for fire. The following should be kept a safe distance from the house: trees, dead tree stubs, long dry grasses, dead leaves and shrubs. Legal requirements for clearance around the house differ by municipality. Unfortunately these guidelines are rarely enforced. In areas prone to wildfires, they should be

Opposite Page:
1. Flat plate concealed pendant
2. Dome cover concealed pendant
3. Flush pendant
4. Recessed pendant
5. Recessed horizontal sidewall
6. Surface-mounted pendant
7. Surface-mounted horizontal sidewall

adhered to with additional space, if possible, for added safety. Stone walls and swimming pools should be located between foliage and your house, if possible.

Construct the house with materials that will be the least combustible. Roofs are particularly vulnerable in wild fires. Flying embers are one of the most dangerous threats. If they fly onto the roof and burn the roofing material, embers will enter the house and destroy it. Roofing materials to consider are some heavy gauge metal, slate, tile and fire-resistant asphalt shingles. Check with the manufacturer to find out about a roof's combustibility. The assembly and how they are put together with other materials will also be an issue to be considered with an architect or engineer.

Window frames are likely to burn if there is a wild fire. Choose a steel or aluminum material with silicon gaskets. Exterior metal shutters can be an excellent option to reduce the radiant heat coming through the windows and prevent embers from entering the house.

Framing and structural materials should be considered in these areas. Concrete is not a combustible material; wood is combustible and plastic is highly combustible. Consider one of the several concrete techniques, checking first for combustibility. For further information about concrete construction, see the chapter on "Construction Types."

Siding must be noncombustible as well. Consider one of the cementitious materials such as fiber-cement, masonry, stucco, brick or metal siding. For further information about siding materials, see the chapter on "Siding."

Water tanks may be a necessity, especially if water becomes unavailable or the pressure is low from town or city main lines because firefighters are using the water or electrical lines are down. A water tank should be installed on the roof or in close proximity to the house. Tanks can be made of galvanized steel, concrete, fiberglass or polyethylene. Rainwater can also be collected. A hose can then be used to put out any small fires that may occur around the house.

Sprinkler systems will only protect against any ember attack, which should be minor if the shell of the house is well protected. Entry and exit points should be available in two directions, if possible. One of those points should be located on the side of the property, away from the greatest potential hazard. Wood for the fireplace should be stored a safe distance from the house, not up against it. Fuel supplies should be stored in a shed located away from the house.

resources

In Australia they have trained people to prepare their homes for brush fires and to stay at home rather than evacuate. The Web site of the Victoria Country Fire Authority has some excellent publications available at www.cfa.vic.gov.au. For guidelines developed by The National Fire Protection Association (NFPA), check the document NFPA 1144, "Standard for Protection of Life and Property from Wildfire," 2002 edition, available to order on their Web site at www.nfpa.org (put in the search word "firewise") or visit www.firewise.com.

For further information about fire safety in general, check with the National Fire Protection Association (NFPA) at www.nfpa.org or call 800-344-3555 and the U.S. Fire Administration at www.usfa.fema.gov.

Some manufacturers of sprinkler systems:

BlazeMaster Fire Sprinkler Systems (C)	www.blazemaster.com
Globe Fire Sprinkler Corp.	www.globesprinkler.com
IPEX, Inc. (C)	www.ipexinc.com
Reliable Automatic Sprinkler Co., Inc	www.reliablesprinkler.com
Tyco Fire & Building Products	www.tyco-fire.com
Viking Corporation	www.vikingcorp.com
Victaulic Company of America	www.victaulic.com

(C) = Canadian

Workbook

Architectural Styles

_____

_____

_____

_____

_____

_____

_____

_____

_____

_____

_____

_____

_____

_____

_____

_____

_____

_____

_____

_____

_____

_____

_____

_____

Construction Systems

Type:

_____
_____
_____
_____
_____

Manufacturer:

_____
_____
_____

Contact:

_____
_____

Telephone Number:

_____

Address:

_____
_____
_____

Type:

_____
_____
_____
_____

Manufacturer:

_____
_____
_____

Contact:

_____
_____

Telephone Number:

_____

Address:

_____
_____
_____

Type:

_____
_____
_____

Manufacturer:

_____
_____

Contact:

_____
_____

Telephone Number:

_____

Address:

_____
_____
_____

Notes:

_____
_____
_____
_____
_____
_____

Roofing

_____
_____
_____
_____
_____
_____
_____
_____

Material:

_____
_____
_____
_____

Maintenance Procedures:

_____
_____
_____
_____

Cost:

_____
_____
_____
_____

Installation Details:

_____
_____
_____
_____
_____
_____

Material:

_____
_____
_____
_____

Maintenance Procedures:

_____
_____
_____
_____

Cost:

_____
_____
_____
_____

Installation Details:

_____
_____
_____
_____
_____

Notes:

_____
_____
_____
_____
_____
_____

Siding

Material:

_____

_____

_____

_____

_____

Maintenance Procedures:

_____

_____

_____

_____

Cost:

_____

_____

_____

_____

Installation Details:

_____

_____

_____

_____

_____

Material:

_____

_____

_____

_____

_____

Maintenance Procedures:

_____

_____

_____

_____

_____

_____

Cost:

_____

_____

_____

_____

Installation Details:

_____

_____

_____

_____

_____

_____

_____

Notes:

_____

_____

_____

_____

_____

_____

_____

_____

_____

_____

Windows

Frame Material:

_____
_____
_____
_____

Type of Glass:

_____
_____
_____
_____

Insulation:

_____
_____
_____
_____

Special Features:

_____
_____
_____
_____
_____
_____
_____

Manufacturer:

_____
_____
_____

Information:

_____
_____
_____
_____

Manufacturer:

_____
_____
_____

Information:

_____
_____
_____
_____

Manufacturer:

_____
_____
_____

Information:

_____
_____
_____

Manufacturer:

_____
_____
_____

Information:

_____
_____
_____

Notes:

_____
_____
_____
_____
_____
_____

Patio Doors

Material:

_____

_____

Type of Glass:

_____

Insulation:

_____

Special Features:

_____

_____

Manufacturer:

_____

Information:

_____

_____

Notes:

_____

_____

_____

_____

_____

_____

_____

_____

Exterior Doors

Material:

_____

_____

Type of Glass:

_____

Insulation:

_____

Special Features:

_____

_____

Manufacturer:

_____

Information:

_____

_____

Notes:

_____

_____

_____

_____

_____

_____

_____

_____

Interior Doors

Material:

_____

_____

Insulation:

_____

_____

Special Features:

_____

_____

Manufacturer:

_____

_____

Information:

_____

_____

Manufacturer:

_____

_____

Information:

_____

_____

Notes:

_____

_____

_____

_____

_____

_____

_____

_____

Garage Doors

Material:

_____

_____

Insulation:

_____

_____

Special Features:

_____

_____

Manufacturer:

_____

_____

Information:

_____

_____

Manufacturer:

_____

_____

Information:

_____

_____

Notes:

_____

_____

_____

_____

_____

_____

_____

_____

Flooring

Common Areas:

Kitchen:

Master Bedroom:

Bedroom:

Bedroom:

Bedroom:

Bathroom:

Bathroom:

Bathroom:

Powder Room:

Playroom:

Misc.:

Lighting

Common Areas:

Kitchen:

Master Bedroom:

Bedroom:

Bedroom:

Bedroom:

Bathroom:

Bathroom:

Bathroom:

Powder Room:

Playroom:

Misc.:

Flooring

Common Areas:

Kitchen:

Master Bedroom:

Bedroom:

Bedroom:

Bedroom:

Bathroom:

Bathroom:

Bathroom:

Powder Room:

Playroom:

Misc.:

Lighting

Common Areas:

Kitchen:

Master Bedroom:

Bedroom:

Bedroom:

Bedroom:

Bathroom:

Bathroom:

Bathroom:

Powder Room:

Playroom:

Misc.:

Fireplaces

Type of Fireplace:

_____
_____
_____
_____

Type of Fuel:

_____
_____

Supplier:

_____
_____
_____

Contact:

_____
_____

Telephone Number:

_____
_____

Type of Fireplace:

_____
_____
_____
_____

Type of Fuel:

_____
_____

Supplier:

_____
_____
_____

Contact:

_____
_____

Telephone Number:

_____
_____

Staircase

Configuration:

_____
_____
_____

Material:

_____
_____

Handrails:

_____
_____
_____

Baluster:

_____
_____
_____

Elevators

Size:

_____
_____
_____

Weight Capacity:

_____
_____
_____

Number of Floors:

_____
_____

Options:

_____
_____

Manufacturers:

_____
_____

HVAC

Type of System:

Heating

_____

_____

_____

Air-conditioning

_____

_____

_____

Ventilation

_____

_____

_____

Humidification

_____

_____

_____

Air Exchange

_____

_____

_____

Other Items:

_____

_____

_____

Manufacturer:

_____

Warranty:

_____

Contact:

_____

Telephone Number:

_____

Manufacturer:

_____

Warranty:

_____

Contact:

_____

Telephone Number:

_____

Manufacturer:

_____

Warranty:

_____

Contact:

_____

Telephone Number:

_____

Manufacturer:

_____

Warranty:

_____

Contact:

_____

Telephone Number:

_____

Manufacturer:

_____

Warranty:

_____

Contact:

_____

Telephone Number:

_____

Trim

Type:

_____

_____

Material:

_____

Manufacturer:

_____

Contact:

_____

Type:

_____

_____

Material:

_____

Manufacturer:

_____

Contact:

_____

Type:

_____

Material:

_____

Manufacturer:

_____

Contact:

_____

Fire Safety

Types of Systems:
Smoke Alarms

_____

_____

_____

_____

Carbon Monoxide Detectors

_____

_____

_____

Sprinkler Systems

_____

_____

_____

Components:

_____

_____

_____

Dealer:

_____

_____

Installer:

_____

_____

_____

CEA Survey Notes

_____
_____
_____
_____
_____
_____
_____
_____
_____
_____
_____
_____
_____
_____
_____
_____
_____
_____
_____
_____
_____
_____
_____
_____
_____
_____
_____

Contacts

Name:

_____

Company:

Telephone:

E-mail address:

Name:

_____

Company:

Telephone:

E-mail address:

Name:

_____

Company:

Telephone:

E-mail address:

Name:

_____

Company:

Telephone:

E-mail address:

_____

Notes

Graph Paper

List of Terms

air handler—An air moving and/or mixing unit. It is the blower or fan section of the central air-conditioning, furnace or heat pump system that moves heated or cooled air throughout a home's ductwork. Single- or variable-speed fans push air over hot or cold coils, then through dampers, ducts and registers to heat or cool a house.

allergen—A substance capable of causing an allergic reaction because of an individual's sensibility to that substance.

anodize—To subject a metal to electrolytic action in order to coat with a protective or decorative film, such as anodized aluminum.

Annual Fuel Utilization Efficiency (AFUE)—This is a rating system for indicating how efficiently the furnace and boiler convert fuel (gas or oil) into heat. The number is given in a percentage that tells how much of the fuel is converted to heat and how much is wasted.

Apron—(Carpentry) The horizontal trim board under a window stool. (Masonry) A transition, such as the one that slopes away from a garage door.

ASTM (American Society for Testing and Materials) International—Organized in 1898, ASTM International is one of the largest voluntary standards development organizations in the world. ASTM International is a not-for-profit organization that provides a forum for the development and publication of voluntary consensus standards for materials, products, systems and services.

architectural sheet metal roofing—A roof covering made up of sheets of metal in a traditional shop-fabricated pattern, such as standing seam, flat seam or batten seam.

atrium—(Historic) An interior courtyard that is usually open to the weather. (Comtemporary) A high space where surrounding rooms open to and a space that may have a glass roof or skylight or a ceiling.

awning window—A window hinged along the top edge.

backerod—A continuous material that is available in several shapes and sizes; it is used behind sealant materials such as silicone or urethane and the chinking in log construction.

backset—The horizontal distance from the edge of the door to the center line of the knob hole. Used when ordering locks for doors. Most prehung pre-bored doors use a 2-inch backset hole.

ballast—(Roofing) It is a heavy material which is installed over a roof membrane in order to prevent wind uplift or to protect the membrane from the harmful effects of the sun. (Lighting) It is also a device that starts a bulb or lamp and regulates its operation.

balustrade—A decorative railing system for stairs or a parapet, including a top rail, newel post and its balusters.

baluster—Vertical poles used to support a stair handrail or porch railing.

bat—A piece of brick with one end intact and the other end broken off.

batten—(Roofing) A strip of wood or metal put over a roof seam for decorative purposes and to conceal fasteners. (Carpentry) A wood strip used to cover the joints between wood boards.

batten seam—The seam used in a sheet metal roof, which encloses a wood batten.

bay—It is the area between two columns or pillars or within a bent as a section of a wall. It can also mean the floor area contained within the spacing of posts or columns.

bay window—A bumped-out window, usually with three glass panels, two of which are at an angle to the middle panel.

beam—A horizontal structural member in a building's frame that spans between supports.

bearing wall—A wall that helps support any loads in addition to its own weight.

bel—A logarithmic scale used to measure sound or loudness; 1 bel equals 10 decibels. The word derives from the name of Alexander Graham Bell.

bent—The vertical and horizontal structural network of timbers or steel that makes up one cross-sectional piece of the frame.

bevel siding—Sometimes called clapboard; boards are cut at an angle so the broad side faces are not parallel.

bitumen—A sticky mixture of hydrocarbons, such as asphalt or tar.

board and batten—a type of siding that is usually vertical, where wood strips (battens) cover the seams where the wider boards are joined.

book size—The height and width of a door before prefitting.

box or box bay window—A three-panel window system in which two glass panels are at right angles to the middle panel.

brick ties—These are veneer anchors which are attached to the backup wall and span across an air space in order to laterally stabilize the brick veneer. Also known as masonry ties.

Btu (British thermal unit)—It is a measure of the amount of heat required to raise the temperature of one pound of water by one degree Fahrenheit. Thus, it is used to measure the heat given off when fuel is burned, and for cooling, it is a measure of heat extracted from the home.

building code—Regulations and ordinances established by state and local governments stating the requirements for a building permit and minimum standards for design, construction and maintenance of a building.

built-up roofing (BUR)—Roofing applied to flat roofs with three to five layers of asphalt-saturated felt or roll roofing and bonded together with bitumen or pitch. It is designed to waterproof the structure and resist ponding water that remains after rainfall, until it evaporates.

butt joint—A joint created when two materials meet or almost meet at their edges. A joint where two logs are connected end-to-end in a log wall system or two pieces of wood are aligned in the same way for trim.

CAD (Computer-Aided Design)—It is a general term referring to computer programs that are used for drafting or drawing as an aid in design. CAD is used in the design of buildings.

catalytic-equipped—Wood stoves and fireplace inserts that have ceramic honeycomb chambers coated with a metal catalyst, usually platinum or palladium, that work to increase the rate of combustion. This burns away gases and particulates normally emitted into the air. In noncatalytic-equipped units combustion occurs in the firebox.

camber—A description of stone: crooked, arched, a slight convex curve of a surface. (Structural) The vertical upward curve of a beam.

capping—A method of applying one-tab shingles centered and applied longitudinally to the ridge or hip of a roof. Or the last course of roll roofing centered and applied longitudinally to the ridge.

cap sheet—A sheet, often granule-coated, which is used as the top-ply of some built-up or modified bitumen roof membranes.

casement window—A window that opens on the side like a door.

casing—Window trim. It is exposed molding or framing around a window or door to cover the space between the window frame or jamb and the wall.

CFM—Cubic feet per minute. It is the volume of air that can be moved in a one-minute interval.

chalking—A process by which paint finishes develop a loose powdery surface from weathering or UV light exposure. In some cases chalking causes premature disappearance of the paint film and discoloration. This can be reduced by selecting a paint that the manufacturer says is slow-chalking.

checking—The separation of wood fibers caused by tension of uneven drying.

chimney cap—Also called a rain hat, it is installed at least 12 inches above the chimney to prevent water from entering the chimney and causing deterioration to interior components.

chink—Used to fill in cracks or fissures. A material used in log cabins to fill in the cracks or joints between the logs.

cladding—With regard to windows, it is a protective sheath of aluminum or vinyl covering a window's exterior wood surfaces. The exterior protection or the finished exterior siding of a structure.

clapboard—Siding that uses tapered horizontal boards, thickest on their bottom edge, with each overlapping the one below.

clerestory—A window in the upper part of a lofty room that admits light to the center of a room.

ceramic granules—Fire-hardened material added to asphalt and fiberglass shingles to provide color and weather resistance.

coil—A roll of sheet metal.

collar tie—The horizontal connector between a pair of rafters used to reduce their sagging or spreading.

Color Rendering Index (CRI) —The measure of the ability of a light source to show colors accurately, most resembling natural sunlight. A measurement of 100 indicates the accurate indication of color and as the numbers go down, so does the accuracy of the color rendition.

condensation—The water developed during the process of water vapor changing to the liquid state.

control joint—The grooves placed in a concrete surface in order to control the natural shrinkage of concrete and maintain its appearance.

coping—(Masonry) The protective cap on the top of a masonry wall. Also refers to the ceramic rim around a swimming pool. (Carpentry) The top finishing piece of wood. For exterior wood protection, this sheds water away from the structure or materials below.

corbel—A massive bracket, shelf or block projecting from the face of a wall that supports a cornice, beam, shelf, balcony or arch. A type of arch created with successive corbels.

cornice—The exterior trim of a structure at the meeting of the roof and wall or the uppermost molding along the top of a wall.

corridor—A passageway into which compartments or rooms open.

coving—The angled sides of a firebox.

crenelation—The stonework at the top of a structure with open spaces that were used to protect castle walls. Also called a "battlement"; the raised portions are called "merlons" and the openings are called "crenels."

creosote—A very flammable by-product of burning resinous wood that can build up within the smoke pipe and chimney and then ignite, causing a chimney fire.

cresting—An ornamental roof ridge, usually of wood or metal.

cross windows—A pair of windows divided by a mullion and transom bar, seen on Châteauesque-type houses.

cup—A curl in the cross section of a board or timber caused by unequal shrinkage or expansion between one side of the board and the other.

cupola—A small polygonal-shaped structure set on the ridge of a roof used for ventilation and/or aesthetics.

curtain wall—It is the exterior wall of a structure, which is not load bearing and dependent on the frame of the building or structure for support.

damper—Found in ductwork, this is an adjustable flap or a series of vanes that open and close to control airflow. For zoning, they regulate airflow to certain rooms or zones.

dead load—This is the weight of the building, including roof, floors, walls and so on.

decking—The structural material used across beams or joists to create a floor or roof surface.

delamination—The separation of the plies in a roof system.

dentil molding—It is a type of crown molding with an even pattern of little squares and blank spaces.

dimensional stability—The ability of a material or assembly of materials to keep its original shape and size over time, with changes in climate (temperature and humidity).

dormer—A structure projecting from the slope of a roof and containing one or more windows that gives more headroom in the attic.

double-hung window—A window with two vertically sliding sashes, both of which can move up and down.

drainage—The removal of water.

downspout (leader)—A pipe for draining water from roof gutters.

drip edge—A metal strip placed along the edge of a roof to prevent water from crawling back under the roofing material.

eaves—The outside edges of the roof deck that over-hangs or terminates at the outside wall.

Energy Factor (EF)—The energy efficiency of the water heater determined by how efficiently the heater uses fuel (gas or electric) and retains heat during standby.

Energy Star—A program developed by the Environmental Protection Agency/Department of Energy to promote energy-efficient products. All qualifying products are identified by the Energy Star logo.

EPA (Environmental Protection Agency)—An agency of the United States government established during the Nixon Administration in 1970 to establish and enforce environmental protection standards, to conduct research on the adverse effects of pollution and on establishing methods of controlling causative conditions.

entablature—A decorative treatment, associated with classical architecture, that forms the part of the structure between the column capital and the roof or pediment, comprising the architrave, frieze and the cornice.

equilibrium moisture content (EMC)—The point at which the internal moisture content is in equilibrium or balance with its environment.

eyebrow windows—Low, inward-opening windows with a bottom-hinged sash; usually attic windows built into the top molding of the house.

eyelid dormer—A curved window in the roof.

extrusion (extruded)—Material pushed through a die and in the process shaped or formed.

facade—The face or elevation of a building, especially the front.

felt—Light-building paper used to temporarily waterproof a roof deck; an underlayment for the smooth application of shingles and roll roofing. Roofing felts are made of glass fibers (glass fiber felts), vegetable fibers (organic felts), or asbestos fibers (asbestos felts).

fascia—The flat finishing board applied to a wall immediately below the roofline.

field tile—The tile that is used overall on a wall.

filament—A fine thread-like object that produces light when heated.

firebox—The enclosure of the combustion chamber of a furnace or stove. The surrounding enclosure of the fire in a fireplace.

fire surround—Also called a "chimneypiece" or "mantelpiece." Shelf and side elements framing a fireplace.

fishmouthing—When a portion of the front edge of a shingle rises. This does not have an effect on the durability or life expectancy of the material.

fish scale shingles—A particular type of shingle design that has a rounded edge on one side and resembles the scales of a fish.

flagstone—Flat slabs of stone (usually slate or limestone) that often have irregular edges and are used outdoors for pool decks and patios and indoors for sunrooms.

flange—Metal or plastic trim or fitting used to water-proof the penetration in the roof deck of a pipe or other venting unit.

flashing—Water-resistant material used to protect, cover or deflect water from exterior joints where different materials meet at slopes or at level changes such as those occurring at chimneys, skylights, vents, windows and doors.

flat-seam roof—A sheet metal roofing seam that is formed flat against the surface of a roof.

floating—Referring to flooring; it is an installation method in which individual boards are glued only at their edges and end joints, without direct attachment to the subfloor.

flue—A vent or chimney used to exhaust the products of combustion.

fluoropolymer—A metal resin also known as PVFF used in paint to protect the color from fading on galvanized steel or aluminum. Trade names for this finish are Kynar 500 (a registered trademark of Atofina Chemical, Inc.) and Hylar 5000 (a registered trademark of Ausimont USA, Inc.)

fogón—A bell-shaped corner fireplace.

furring—Wood or metal strips used to build out a surface to provide a base for fastening other materials.

gable—The triangular end of a house formed by a pitched roof.

gable vents—A screened and louvered opening in a gable, which is used for ridding the attic of excess heat and to equalize the relative humidity in the attic to the outside relative humidity.

Galvalume—The patented trade name for the aluminum zinc alloy applied to sheet steel for resistance to corrosion.

galvanized steel—Steel coated with zinc for corrosion resistance.

gambrel roof—A ridged roof having two slopes on each side with the lower slope steeper than the upper one.

gauge—The measurement used for metal thickness.

girder—This is a major beam supporting other beams or joists.

girt—A major horizontal timber that connects posts at the exterior or perimeter of the structure or building.

glazing—The windowpane itself; materials such as glass, plastic (acrylic or polycarbonate) or other clear or translucent materials.

grate—An iron frame used to hold burning fuel in a fireplace.

green wood—Wood that has a high water content before it is kiln or aired dried.

gutter—Troughs along the roof eaves that channels rain and melted snow from the eaves to the downspouts.

half-timbering—Wall construction in which the spaces between the timber framework of the building are left exposed and are filled in with brick, stone or other material and often covered with white stucco. The frame is left exposed, as opposed to being covered by clapboard, as was common in New England.

hardwood—Wood of certain deciduous trees, such as oak, maple and ash.

HDF—High Density Fiberboard is fiberboard with a density greater than 50 pounds per cubic foot (or 800 kilograms per cubic meter).

hearth—The paved or tiled floor of a fireplace.

heat pump—A mechanical-compression cycle refrigeration system that can be reversed to either heat or cool an area.

header—(Masonry) Brick laid with the short end at the face of the wall. (Construction) A horizontal beam placed over an opening, such as a window or door.

HSPF (Heating Seasonal Performance Factor)—A measure of a heat pump's heating efficiency. The higher the HSPF rating, the less electricity the unit will use to heat the house and the more efficient the product.

HEPA—High-Efficiency Particulate Arrestance (filters) supply particle removal from the air. These filters are often used in homes occupied by people with severe respiratory symptoms.

HERS (Home Energy Rating System)—A rating system for evaluating the energy efficiency of a home. There are several organizations that have these systems, including the Energy Star program.

hip—The sloping ridge formed by the intersection of two adjacent roof planes.

hip or hipped roof—A roof that slopes to each outside wall of the building, thereby forming a hip.

honed—Sharpened or smooth.

hood—The canopy overhanging a fireplace to increase the draft.

hood molding—A large molding over a window; it is designed to direct water away from the wall.

hopper windows—An in-swinging window hinged at the bottom.

humidistat—A humidity-sensing control that cycles the humidifier on and off.

ice dam—A condition formed at the lower-roof edge by the thawing and refreezing of melted snow on the overhang. It can force water up and under shingles, causing leaks.

inglenooks—A nook by a large open fireplace, and a bench occupying this nook.

inverter—A device for converting direct current (DC) into alternating current (AC).

jalousie window—A window composed of overlapping narrow glass, metal or wooden louvers; it is operated with a crank for adjusting the louver angles.

jamb—A vertical element at the side of the window or door frame.

jig—A device used to hold work during manufacture or assembly.

joinery—The art of connecting wood or timbers using wood-working joints.

joint—The connection or gap between two materials.

joist—Repetitively spaced light metal or wood beams arranged parallel to each other in order to frame the floor or ceiling.

keyway—A joint between the footing and foundation wall.

knee brace—A small timber that is framed diagonally between a post and beam.

Kynar 500—The fluoropolymer coating that is added to paint to make metal more scratch resistant, resistant to degradation by UV light and, in general, more durable. It creates better color retention, better gloss retention and better resistance to chalking. See fluoropolymer.

lantern—A structure built on the top of a roof with open walls or walls with windows.

lap siding—Any siding that overlaps, such as clapboard.

lath—The base to which plaster is applied.

light (or lite)—A pane of glass within a window.

lintel—The horizontal beam placed over an opening to support the masonry above.

load—A force or weight that is acting on a structure, such as gravity or wind.

louver—Ventilating unit with slats, usually placed on gables.

louver door—A panel door with part or all of the panels replaced by louvers.

low-slope roof—Any roof with a pitch 2 $\frac{1}{2}$:12 pitch or less, which must be covered with a continuous membrane rather than with shingles. It is sometimes inaccurately referred to as a flat roof.

MDF—Medium-Density Fiberboard is made of wood particles bonded together and compressed into sheets. See HDF.

mansard roof—The bottom pitch is very steep at each outside wall of the building, and the top pitch is gentler, so it is not seen from the ground. A hipped roof with two pitches.

masking—The plastic covering on metal panels used to protect pieces during transit. This covering must be removed immediately after installation.

mastic—Roof coating used for bonding thermal insulation or waterproofing around vents and other roof obstacles.

masonry—Bricks, stones, concrete blocks, glass blocks or tiles bonded together by mortar.

melamine—It is the clear or decorative finished surface; a plastic-type resin that adds durability to plastic laminates or laminate flooring or planks.

membrane—A sheet material that is impervious to water or water vapor.

mortise—A groove or slot into which a tenon is inserted.

mortise-and-tenon joint—Any joint in which a tenon (projection) on one end of a timber is inserted into a mortise (groove or slot) in another.

mullion—A vertical dividing piece between windows.

muntin—Bars that hold the edges of individual pieces of glass within a window sash.

nanometer (nm)—It is one-billionth of a meter. Nanometers are used to measure wavelengths in the electromagnetic spectrum.

neoprene—Polychloroprene or Neochloroprene; a synthetic rubber.

net metering—A credit given by the utility company for excess electricity that is generated by the customer and not used in the home. This is available in some states.

NFPA—National Fire Protection Association.

NFRC—National Fenestration Rating Council.

NRCA—National Roofing Contractors Association.

nonbearing wall—A wall which is not carrying a load.

ODS (Oxygen Depletion Sensor)—A safety device activated by the gas flame monitoring sensor in case excessive levels of carbon monoxide are detected; it turns off the gas supply automatically. (Carbon monoxide is the product produced when there is insufficient oxygen present for complete combustion.)

Oil-can—A ripple or wavy effect on metal surfaces caused by the difference in expansion and contraction between the metal and the substrate or the perimeter framing.

Oriel window—A bay window on an upper floor.

OSB (oriented strand board)—A type of structural flakeboard composed of numerous layers, each consisting of strand-like wood flakes oriented at right angles to each other and bonded with phenolic resin glue.

paint grade—A description of a wood that yields a painted surface without the woody characteristics registering in the dry film surface of the paint.

palladian window—A tripartite window opening with a large arched central light and flanking rectangular side lights, originated in the sixteenth century by the Italian architect Andrea Palladio.

parapet—A low wall on the edge of a roof, bridge or terrace.

pediment—A low, triangular, gable-type decoration over a door or window.

pent roof—A sloping roof attached to the side of a building.

pergolas—An open structure made of wood and serving as a framework on which vines grow.

phosphor—Any substances that give off visible light when they are exposed to UV or other radiation. There is a coating of phosphor inside fluorescent lightbulbs or TV picture tubes.

photovoltaics (PV)—The science of turning light into electricity.

photovoltaic (PV) roofing—Roofing materials that can convert solar energy to electricity.

pilaster—A flat, rectangular column attached to the face of a building or wall, usually resembling a classical column with a capital and base.

pickling—Treatment which can be done on wood to make it look old. An acid solution applied to a metal to remove scale or oxide materials from its surface.

pitch—The angle of inclination that a sloping surface or roof makes with the horizon, measured in inches of rise per foot of run. In the case of ramps or driveways, it is calculated as a percentage: rise divided by the run.

pitting—Small pinholes caused by corrosion.

plate—The horizontal wood framing that ties the tops of the wall studs together and forms a bearing surface for the floor or ceiling joists or the roof rafters.

plumb—Perfectly vertical.

pocket door—A door that slides in and out of a wall pocket formed as a finished slot in the jamb.

porte cocheres—A covered entrance porch for people getting in or out of carriages or vehicles. This feature is not intended for parking and is not, therefore, a carport.

post—A vertical or upright timber. Structurally, it is a column.

pultrusion—A forming process for fiberglass plastic material where the material is pulled through a die; it is used for fiberglass window frames. See extrusion.

purlin—A beam spanning from roof truss to roof truss, usually located where the roof deck panel joints occur.

quatrefoil window—A round window that is composed of four equal lobes, like a clover leaf.

quoin—A rectangle of stone, wood or brick used in vertical series to decorate the corners of a building.

R-value—The resistance of a material to the passage of heat through its thickness. The higher the R-value, the more resistant the material is to heat loss.

radon—A radioactive gas formed by the decay of uranium isotope.

rafters—A structural framing member of a roof that runs up and down the slope of a pitched roof and is used for support.

rake—Edges of the roof deck running parallel to the slope.

red iron—A structural steel that is coated with a red oxide coating to resist rust.

relative humidity—The amount of moisture present in the air at a specific temperature in relation to the maximum amount the air can hold at that temperature.

ribbon windows—A row of adjacent windows; looks as if it could be one continuous window.

ridge—The horizontal junction of the two sloping-roof sections.

ridge pole—A horizontal timber at the peak of the roof to which the rafters are attached.

ridge vent—A construction element mounted along the ridge of a roof to aid in ventilating the attic space.

riven or split—Refers to stone that is treated so it is nonslip.

roll roofing—Asphalt-based roofing material laid horizontally over low-pitched roofs.

roofline louvers—Louvers placed in the roof for ventilation.

saddle notches—Notches created by milling a half-circle into the bottom of a log.

sash—A window frame surrounding glass. May be fixed or operable.

sawn—Sawed wood rather than hand split.

scarf—A joint for splicing two timbers end to end.

sealant—Any material used to close up cracks or joints, usually to protect against water entering the joint.

SEER (Seasonal Energy Efficiency Ratio)—A rating used for air conditioners and heat pumps indicating their cooling efficiency. The higher the SEER rating, the more efficient the product. The government's minimum SEER rating established for homes built after 1992 is 10.

shake—Hand-split, edge-grained wood shingle.

sheathing—Boards, plywood or particle wood

panels used to cover the wood framing of the roof and exterior walls and as a base for the siding.

shed dormer—A dormer with a shed roof.

shingle—Roofing made from asphalt, fiberglass, wood, aluminum, tile, slate, metal or other water-shedding material.

shop drawing review—An architectural review of an entire house (such as from a modular company) or a small part of a house (such as by a cabinet maker) to be sure that the drawings comply with the original design intent.

side light—A fixed, usually narrow glass window next to a door or window opening.

sill—Interior or exterior shelf below a window unit. Interior sill may be called a "stool."

sill timber—A horizontal timber that rests on the foundation of a house.

slope—The degree of incline of a roof plane, usually given in inches of rise per horizontal foot of the run.

soffit—The finished underside of a roof overhang; the section of ceiling that drops below the main ceiling or the finished underside of a kitchen cabinet, for example.

softwood—The wood primarily of a conifer or evergreen tree, such as pine, spruce or Douglas fir.

soldiers—Course of brick standing on its ends, such as over windows.

spalling—Flaking off of the surface of concrete.

specific humidity—The amount of moisture in the air, expressed as a decimal.

splines—Thin strips of rigid material used in butt joints and corners to connect and maintain alignment, such as two logs spliced in log construction.

square—A measurement of roofing materials—1 square is 100 square feet of roofing.

standing seam—A sheet metal roofing seam that projects at right angles to the plane of the roof.

steep roof—A roof pitched in the range of 3:12 to 6:12.

step flashing—A flashing method used where a vertical surface meets a sloping roof plane.

stiles—The vertical pieces of the framework of a door.

stretchers—Brick laid lengthwise along the wall.

strut—A short compression-resisting timber that is placed in a structure either diagonally or vertically.

substrate—The base material on top of which the roofing or waterproofing membrane is installed, such as the structural deck or rigid insulation.

tab—The material between the factory cutouts on asphalt or fiberglass shingles.

tenon—The projecting end of a timber that is inserted into a mortise.

terne—An alloy of lead and tin; used to coat sheets of carbon steel or stainless steel for use as metal roofing sheet.

thermal insulation—A material that greatly retards the passage of heat.

thermal mass—The inertia to heat change in a particular material. It is the ability of high-mass materials, such as thick masonry, to absorb and retain heat energy. This absorption can improve energy efficiency by modifying energy demands.

thermal resistance—The resistance of a material or assembly to the conduction of heat.

tile—A fired clay product that is thin in cross section as compared to a brick, either a thin, flat element (ceramic tile or quarry tile); a thin, curved element (roofing tile); or a hollow element with thin walls (flue tile, tile pipe, structural clay tile); also a thin, flat element of another material, such as an acoustical ceiling unit or a resilient floor unit.

tongue and groove—Strips of wood milled on the edges to fit together; one edge has a continuous groove and the opposite side edge has a continuous tongue that fits into the groove of the next piece of board or strip flooring.

transom bar—The horizontal divider separating a large lower window from a small window above it or separating a door from the window above it.

transom or transom window—a fixed or operable window or light above a door or window.

truss—A span or beam made from members arranged in triangles.

tumbled—A method of distressing brick to give it a unique and aged look.

tungsten—A metal that has the highest melting point of all elements.

turbine vents—Turbine vents use a series of specially shaped vanes to catch the wind and provide rotary motion; this motion pulls hot and humid air from the attic. Turbine vents provide a low-cost ventilation alternative in areas where wind speeds are at least 5 mph.

Tyvek—A brand name for a paper-like plastic material that is on very wide rolls and wraps around the exterior or outside walls of a house, providing a moisture and wind barrier. It is used in lieu of tar paper or construction felts.

underlayment—Asphalt-saturated felt beneath roofing to provide additional protection for the deck. Also used to describe the substrate or underfloor on which finished flooring material is installed.

Underwriters (UL) Classification—UL listing means that samples of a product or material have been tested and evaluated, and if they pass, the product or material is listed in various UL Product Directories.

U-value—The rate or coefficient at which heat is transmitted through the material or materials separating the inside from the outside. The lower the U-value of a window, the more heat the window is able to keep inside the house.

uplift—Wind load on a building that causes a reduced air pressure, thus a loading in an upward direction.

valley—The internal angle formed by the junction of two sloping roof sections. It has the opposite geometry of a hip.

vapor barrier (vapor retarder)—A metal foil, plastic or treated paper membrane placed on the warm side of the insulation to prevent water vapor from entering the insulation and condensing into liquid. Thus, in hot climates, with the use of air-conditioning, the vapor barrier is on the outside of the house. In cold-climatic areas, it is on the inside. The materials are rated in "perms," a measure of its permeability to water. Zero perm is the best; no water or water vapor passes through it.

veneer—Thin sheets of wood or stone.

ventilation—A system of intake and exhaust that creates a flow of air.

verge board (or bargeboard)—Decorative slanting boards on the gable end of a roof.

vibrated (regarding concrete)—An electric tool vibrates the wet concrete mix to get the air bubbles out of the concrete.

viga—A large pole beam used to support the roof of Southwestern adobe houses.

vitreous—The process of making clay product glass-like for the purposes of making it impervious to water.

Volatile Organic Compounds (VOCs)—Harmful carbon-based compounds that easily vaporize.

wainscoting—Matched boarding or panels covering the lower portion of a wall.

watertable—A projected brick section in the foundation that adds dimension and sheds water away or outward.

water vapor—Water in its gaseous phase.

weep hole—A small hole made in brick mortar joints to permit water to run out of masonry walls rather than accumulate and do damage.

weep screed—A strip of wood, metal or plaster that establishes the level to which concrete or plaster will be placed at the bottom of an exterior stucco wall, terminating the system above grade to allow moisture to seep out.

weld—A joint between two pieces of metal formed by fusing the pieces together, usually with the help of additional metal melted from a rod or electrode.

wythe—A measure used for each continuous vertical section or layer of masonry that is one unit in thickness.

zero clearance—This refers to fireplaces that are factory-built and are constructed so they can be safely placed close to combustible materials.

TechHome Rating System

Cars, computers and breakfast cereals have labels that make comparison shopping easier. But when shopping for a home, consumers are often left in the dark about what is behind the walls. An effort by The Consumer Electronics Association (CEA)* has addressed this issue by developing a rating system to help consumers, home builders and realtors assess the technological capabilities and systems of a home. The rating helps consumers determine whether a home can support a home office, high-speed Internet and other applications critical to today's home buyers. The TechHome Rating System (THRS) allows consumers to compare homes based on their respective technology ratings, much like consumers can now compare homes based on other standardized criteria such as the R-value of insulation. Adoption of the rating system, first launched in 2001, is spurred on by consumers looking to make the most informed home-buying decision.

The THRS consists of a single page form on which consumers list a home's technological features to arrive at a rating between one and ten, ten being the most technologically sophisticated. The Rating System allows consumers to evaluate and compare homes based on a set of standardized criteria. It divides the electronic systems in a home into five categories based on the primary function or benefit the system provides.

- The Home Entertainment category contains information on the home's television and audio distribution capabilities and measures its ability to support a multi-room audio or home theater system.
- The Communications section rates the telephone system.

* The Consumer Electronics Association (CEA) is the preeminent trade association promoting growth in the consumer technology industry through technology policy, events, research, promotion and the fostering of business and strategic relationships. CEA represents more than 1,500 corporate members involved in the design, development, manufacturing, distribution and integration of audio, video, mobile electronics, wireless and landline communications, information technology, home networking, multimedia and accessory products, as well as related services that are sold through consumer channels. Combined, CEA's members account for more than $90 billion in annual sales. CEA's resources are available online at www.CE.org, the definitive source for information about the consumer electronics industry. CEA also sponsors and manages the International CES—Defining Tomorrow's Technology. All profits from CES are reinvested into industry services, including technical training and education, industry promotion, engineering standards development, market research and legislative advocacy.

- The PC Networking and Internet Sharing section measures the availability of broad band (high-speed) Internet access and wiring that would support a computer network.
- The Home Security and Home Comfort and Convenience categories cover the other home systems, including alarm, energy management and lighting control.

A home with a structured wiring system (which consists of special-purpose jacks in most rooms that are separately connected by high-performance in-wall wires to a central distribution box or panel) qualifies a home for bonus points because this type of system can be easily adapted to provide any current and future technological services. To provide additional detail on a home's capabilities, space is provided on the form to indicate the number of rooms served by each category of service and to offer descriptions of the systems, although these factors are not considered when scoring the form.

resources

To determine the TechHome Rating of your home, visit www.CE.org/techhomerating to download a free copy of the TechHome Rating System worksheet.

Books

In general

New Old House: Designing with Reclaimed Materials by Edward Knapp, Gibbs Smith, Publisher, 2002.

Architectural Styles

American Homes: An Illustrated Encyclopedia of Domestic Architecture by Lester Walker, et al, First Black Dog & Leventhal Publishers, 2002.

American House Styles: A Concise Guide by John Milnes Baker, W.W. Norton & Company, 2002.

Great American Houses and Their Architectural Styles by Virginia McAlester, et al, Abbeville Press, Inc., 1994.

Identifying American Architecture: A Pictorial Guide to Styles and Terms, 1600–1945 by John G. Blumenson, et al, W.W. Norton & Company, 1990.

The Visual Dictionary of American Domestic Architecture by Rachel Carley, Henry Holt & Company, Inc., 1997.

What Style Is It? A guide to American Architecture by John C. Poppeliers, et al, John Wiley & Sons, 1995.

Construction types

Log

American Log Homes by Arthur Thiede, et al, Gibbs Smith, Publisher, 1986.

Hands-On Log Homes by Cindy Teipner, et al, Gibbs Smith, Publisher, 1998.

Cabin Fever by Rachel Carley, Gibbs Smith, Publisher, 1998.

Cabins and Camps by Ralph R. Kylloe, Gibbs Smith, Publisher, 2002.

Log Cabin with a Twist by Barbara T. Kaempfer, Collector Books, 1995.

Log Cabins by Janice Brewster, Friedman Michael Publishing Group, Inc. 1999.

Log Houses: Classics of the North by Peter Christopher, et al, Boston Mills Press, 2003.

Log Spirit by Linda White, Gibbs Smith, Publisher, 2000.

The Cabin: Inspiration for the Classic American Getaway by Dale Mulfinger, et al, Taunton Press, 2001.

The Log Home Book by Cindy Teipner-Thiede, et al, Gibbs Smith, Publisher, 1999.

The Log Home Plan Book by Cindy Thiede, Gibbs Smith, Publisher, 1999.

The Not So Log Cabin by Robbin Obomsawin, Gibbs Smith, Publisher, 2003.

The Owner-Built Log House: Living in Harmony with Your Environment by B. Allan Mackie, Firefly Books, 2001.

Small Log Homes by Robbin Obomsawin, Gibbs Smith, Publisher, 2001.

Timberframe

Timber Frame Joinery & Design Workbook by the Timber Framers Guild.

Timberframe: The Art and Craft of the Post-and-Beam Home by Tedd Benson, Taunton Press, 2002.

Timberframe Plan Book by Michael Morris, et al, Gibbs Smith, Publisher, 2000.

Concrete

Built to Last: A Showcase of Concrete Homes by Tina Skinner, Schiffer Publishing, Ltd., 2002.

The Portland Cement Association's Guide to Concrete Homebuilding Systems by Pieter A. Vanderwerf, et al, McGraw-Hill Professional, 1994.

Structural Insulated Panels

Building with Structural Insulated Panels by Michael Morley, Taunton Press, 2000.

Strawbale

The Beauty of Straw Bale Homes by Athena Steen, et al, Chelsea Green Publishing, 2000.

The New Strawbale Home by Catherine Wanek, Gibbs Smith, Publisher, 2003.

Health and Safety

Accessible Housing Design File by Barrier Free Environments, Inc., John Wiley & Sons, 1997.

Affordable and Universal Homes: A Plan Book by NCSU School of Design, 2000.

Beautiful Universal Design: A Visual Guide by Cynthia Leibrock, et al, John Wiley & Sons, 1999.

Building for a Lifetime by Margaret Wylde, et al, Taunton Press, 1994.

Design Details for Health by Cynthia Leibrock, John Wiley & Sons, 1999.

Prescriptions for a Healthy House by Paula Baker-Laporte, et al, New Society Publishing, 2001.

Products and Plans for Universal Homes by Home Planners, LLC, 2000.

The Healthy Home by Jackie Craven, Rockport Publishers, 2003.

The Healthy House by John Bower, The Healthy House Institute, 2000.

Universal Design Handbook by Wolfgang F. E. Peiser, McGraw-Hill Professional, 2001.

Universal Kitchen and Bathroom Planning by Mary Jo Peterson, McGraw-Hill, 1998.

Fireplaces

Fireplaces by Alexandra Edwards, Chronicle Books, 1992.

Floors

Floors: A Design Source Book by Elizabeth Wilhide, Stewart, Tabori & Chang, 1997.

Ortho's All About Floors and Flooring by Martin Miller, Ortho Books, 2002.

Sunset Ideas for Great Floors, by the Editors at Sunset Books, Sunset Books, 2002.

Lighting

Ortho's Indoor & Outdoor Lighting Solutions: Atmosphere, Function, Security, edited by Larry Johnston, et al, Meredith Books, 2003.

Sunset Ideas for Great Home Lighting by Scott Atkinson, et al, Sunset Books, 2003.

Stairs

Stairs by Alan Blanc, et al, 2nd edition, Architectural Press, 2001.

Trim

Decorating with Interior Trim by Lisa Stockwell Kessler, et al, Sunset Publishing, 2003.

Historic Millwork: A Guide to Restoring and Re-creating Doors, Windows, and Moldings of the Late Nineteenth Through Mid-Twentieth Centuries by Brent Hull, John Wiley & Sons, 2003.

Index

Page numbers in *italics* refer to illustrations or pictures.

U

Universal Design, 309–10
Uplighting, 227, *228*
Uplights, *224*, 225
Urethanes, 190

V

Vacation homes, 39
Ventilation: roofs, 82–83; wood shingles, 87; direct vent, 240–41, *244*; gas B vent, 241; heat recovery (HRV), 241–42, 288–89; natural draft, 242–43, *244*; unvented, 243–*44*; energy recovery (ERV), 289; control systems, 289–90
Vinyl: siding, 110–11, *112*; window frames, 137, flooring, 196

W

Wainscoting, *299*
Wall grazing, 227, *228*
Wall washing, 227, *228*
Warranties: basics, 9; roof, 81; garage doors, 163–64
Water heaters: considerations, 292–93; types, 293–95; energy efficient, 295
Wax, 190
Weather considerations, 10, 170
Wedge vent systems, 127
Weep screed, 116–17
Windows: considerations, 129–30; types, 131–36, *133*; glazing options, 135–36; novelty glass, 136; frames, 137–38; insulation and safety options, 139–41, 146–47; spacers, 141; divided light, 141; hardware, 141; options, 141–42; storm, 142–43; replacement, 143–44; new glazing technologies, 144–46; self-cleaning, 146; solar, 147

Wood: log construction, 48–59; dry types, 49; glue-laminate, 49–50; timberframe construction, 57–58; shingles and shakes, 85–87; siding, 105–10; window frames, 137; exterior doors, 154–55; garage doors, 163; flooring, 184–92; fireplace or stove fuel, 244–45, 270–71; trim, 302
Wood fasteners, 50–51

X

Xenon, 217

Z

Zinc: roof, 91–*92*; siding, 114